Voice in Motion

MATERIAL TEXTS

Series Editors

A complete list of books in the series is available from the publisher.

Voice in Motion

Staging Gender, Shaping Sound in
Early Modern England

Gina Bloom

PENN

University of Pennsylvania Press
Philadelphia

Copyright © 2007 University of Pennsylvania Press
All rights reserved
Printed in the United States of America on acid-free paper

10   9   8   7   6   5   4   3   2   1

Published by
University of Pennsylvania Press
Philadelphia, Pennsylvania 19104-4112

A Cataloging-in-Publication record is available from the Library of Congress

ISBN 978-0-8122-4006-1

For my parents and for Flagg

Contents

Introduction

From Excitable Speech to Voice in Motion

*[I]s the agency of language the same as the agency of the subject? Is there a
way to distinguish between the two?*
—*Judith Butler,* Excitable Speech[1]

Writing hundreds of years before poststructuralist theory,
French author François Rabelais provides an answer to Judith Butler's
queries concerning linguistic agency. In book 4 of Rabelais's *Gargantua and
Pantagruel*, Pantagruel and his fellow sea travelers are startled by disembodied voices they hear in the air. To assuage their fears—"not unnatural," since
they could "see no one, yet could hear voices"—the ship's captain explains
that the travelers are hearing the noises of a battle that took place the previous winter; the sea battlers' voices were literally frozen in time, transformed
into ice blocks that are now beginning to thaw. Pantagruel throws handfuls
of the unthawed words, "which looked like crystallized sweets of different
colours," onto the deck, and the men, after warming the words with their
hands in order to melt them, examine the materials. The narrator writes: "I
saw some very sharp words among them; bloody words which . . . sometimes return to the place from which they come—but with their throats cut;
some terrifying words, and others rather unpleasant to look at. When they
had all melted together, we heard: Hin, hin, hin, hin, his, tick, tock, crack,
brededin, brededac, frr, frrr, frrrr, bou, bou, . . . trrrrrr, on, on, on, on, on,
ououououon, Gog, Magog, and goodness knows what other barbarous
sounds."[2] Rabelais's retelling of Plutarch's story reflects on problems of
communication by representing the voice as matter, vocal sound material-
ized into the form of ice. The capacity of the voice to convey the terror experienced by a speaking subject (the sea battlers of a previous winter) to a

listening subject (Pantagruel and his companions) depends on the forces of time, distance, medium, and most particularly, climate. Rabelais implies that such mediations constitute at the same time as they compromise effective vocal transmission: it is only because the sea battlers' voices have assumed this frozen form that they can be carried to listeners distant from the site of the original utterance; yet the voices, however they were intended, emerge for listeners only as gibberish. Rabelais captures with fascination and horror the strange materiality of the voice: durable, substantial, and potent, yet at the same time transient, disembodied, and ephemeral. The voice's material form (ice that can melt) enables communication, but the instabilities of that form render the voice susceptible to a range of forces beyond speakers' control, undermining communicative agency.

As Judith H. Anderson has argued, Rabelais's story of frozen words, though written in France, encapsulates the materialist emphasis of linguistic theory in Tudor and Stuart England: for Rabelais and his English contemporaries, "human language has not simply intelligible substance but also material dimensions."[3] In the early modern period words were imagined to *be* things, rather than just to refer *to* things. And as Rabelais's story demonstrates, the effectiveness of language could be explained through narratives about this material form. Like most scholars who attend to the materiality of language in the early modern period, however, Anderson focuses the bulk of her analysis on the physicality of writing and printing.[4] *Voice in Motion* pushes such insights in a new direction by considering how early moderns conceived of the materiality of spoken articulations.

What does it mean to say that the voice is material? A range of early modern texts—including medical treatises, song books, pronunciation manuals, acoustic studies, religious sermons, and especially stage-plays—insist that the human voice possesses a number of attributes we might readily associate with material substances: specifically, the voice (1) has a temporal and spatial life; and (2) is constituted through a process of production, transmission, and reception. The medical and scientific writers I discuss in Chapter 2, for instance, describe voice as crafted air that gains momentum for movement from the speaker's lungs. Shaped into pronunciations by the tongue, teeth, and palate, shifted in tones by the gullet, windpipe, and vocal cords, vocal sound travels through the air to enter the air-filled chambers of the listener's ears. As we will see in Chapter 3, Protestant sermons describe the voices of God and the devil as seeds that have the potential to take root in listeners' hearts. And as in the sermons, in Shakespeare's late plays, listeners are represented as either tilled ground ready to be penetrated by voices or aural fortresses prepared to resist sounds. While early modern writers recognize the voice as ephemeral and often invisible, they represent vocal matter as taking on a variety of forms (breath, seed, and so on) that are alienable from the speaking subject. Whereas work by scholars like Anderson and Butler might prompt us to read such representations in terms of a history of language or theory of linguistic performativity, respectively, I examine what these representations mean for a history and theory of *vocal performance*. If the voice is produced by unstable bodies, transmitted through volatile air, and received by sometimes disobedient hearers, how can voice be trusted to convey an individual's thoughts to a listener? And in a cultural climate in which speech marks political and social power, who stands to lose and who to gain when speech assumes this unsteady material form?

My approach to these questions differs from that of others who have examined the issue of vocal performance. Practitioners of speech-act theory and conversation analysis describe how speakers establish and uphold social relationships and signal social and political authority (or lack thereof) through certain styles of speech and linguistic codes.[5] The command, for instance, announces and instantiates the power of a ruler, and the supplication, the deference of a servant. In a related vein, studies of early modern rhetoric examine the historical and cultural conditions of particular oratorical styles and methods. Wayne Rebhorn discusses, for example, how Renaissance orators persuade audiences by generating in themselves the passions they wish audiences to experience.[6] Rather than approach vocal authority and persuasive power as a function of oratorical techniques or styles of speaking, I consider how authority and power are imagined to inhere (or fail to inhere) in the material attributes of the voice, what Leslie C. Dunn and Nancy A. Jones describe as the "non-verbal meanings" of the "concrete physical" voice.[7] As Dunn and Jones note in their collection, *Embodied Voices: Representing Female Vocality in Western Culture*, the body—associated historically and devalued along with the feminine—has too frequently been ignored in analyses of voice. Roland Barthes's notion of the "grain of the voice" provides Dunn and Jones a way of theorizing "the very precise space (genre) of *the encounter between a language and a voice*," between verbal, culturally inscribed meaning and material, bodily inscribed meaning.[8]

To examine this encounter between language and voice, we need not confine ourselves to song or even to "embodied" voice, however. The play-texts written by Shakespeare and contemporary dramatists inscribe on their pages the voices of actors—voices that exist at the nexus of the verbal and the concrete.[9] Dramatists' figurations of voice complicate Barthes's definition of the concrete as "the body *in* the voice," for dramatists constantly remind their audiences that the body of the actor is only one of many physical sites that give shape and texture to the voice.[10] The air through which the voice moves and the active work of audience members in the theater space, for instance, determine how language and voice intersect in plays.[10] English authors, on and off the stage, echo Rabelais when they emphasize the detachment of the voice from the body, reminding us, for instance, that vocal communication depends in large part on the successful conveyance of breath beyond the speaker's body. *Voice in Motion* provides a material history of this detached voice, examining how early moderns represented the production, transmission, and reception of the voice. Early moderns insist that voice is not synonymous with, but rather a technology of, communication, one of many "language machines."[11]

Recent scholarship on the early modern period has investigated a variety of technologies of communication, but most studies have focused on manuscript and print culture, what Bruce R. Smith calls "brain-to-eye-to-brain communication."[12] There are sensible historical reasons for the tendency to privilege visual forms. In the sixteenth and seventeenth centuries, England underwent major transformations due to increasing literacy rates and the spread of printing technologies. Changing methods for producing, distributing, and reading books dramatically shaped a range of cultural practices, from the pursuit of pleasure to the interpretation of the Bible.[13] There are also sound theoretical reasons for scholars' emphasis on manuscript and print culture. Following Jacques Derrida, scholars point to early modern textual production as demonstrative of the instabilities of language, the *différance* between sign and signifier, and the tension between speech and subjectivity. Early modern technologies of writing, as Jonathan Goldberg and others have shown, disrupt problematic Western assumptions about transcendent presence.[14] These historical and theoretical concerns are not limited to writing and textuality, however. As Smith argues in his landmark study *The Acoustic World of Early Modern England: Attending to the O-Factor*, voice was not equated with self-presence for all early modern authors. In fact, authors emphasize a range of things that "make the voice strange," imbuing sound with the same deconstructive potential as writing.[15] Noting the persistence of the face-to-face encounter in early modern life, Smith argues persuasively for the importance of attending to aural artifacts and "brain-to-tongue-to-air-to-ear-to-brain" interactions.[16] My book responds to this call, targeting specifically the material conditions involved in the communication of voice in an effort to theorize the relation between voice and agency. I find that as early modern writers investigate the material dimensions of the voice—the way the voice performs in time and space—they betray concern that the motion of the voice cannot be choreographed. Skeptical of the process by which the voice is invested with agency, authors distinguish the agency of speech from the agency of the speaker, demonstrating the material means by which the former makes possible the latter.

Staging Gender, Shaping Sound

Through my emphasis on the materiality of voice, I aim to intervene in three key, and overlapping, areas of current scholarship on the early modern period, especially concerning its dramatic production: materialism, performance, and gender.

First, my emphasis on the ways voice is produced, transmitted, and received signals my alliance with the literary, theoretical, and historical investments of "materialist" scholarship, investments articulated elegantly in Jonathan Gil Harris and Natasha Korda's introduction to *Staged Properties in Early Modern English Drama*. Harris and Korda's collection draws attention to "histories of production, ownership, and exchange that constitute objects' trajectories through time and space," arguing that such attention is crucial because "[l]iterary criticism of early modern drama in general and of Shakespeare's plays in particular has belittled or ignored these histories . . . privileging the aesthetic over the economic, the textual over the theatrical, the ineffable over the material, the human over the mechanical, the subject over the object."[17] While I share the aims of "materialist" scholarship, my focus on voice challenges some of the problematic assumptions emerging in work on material objects. In particular, I question the tendency of many scholars to limit "matter" to visible and tangible realms. Voice, I am arguing, has a history of production, ownership, and exchange, a history that has been overlooked for many of the same reasons cited by Harris and Korda. Whereas literary critics have tended to conceive of voice as language, equating it solely with aesthetic and textual concerns, early moderns considered the spoken and heard voice, on and off the stage, to be a substance with economic, theatrical, and mechanical dimensions. Early modern scientific writings and numerous stage-plays consistently describe vocal sound as "made" of breath, for example. While there are obvious differences between, for instance, stage props and human voices, there are also important similarities. Like props, voices often are imagined as unmanageable, beyond the control of those who ostensibly operate and "own" them. The use of pubescent boy actors on England's public stage helped promote such perspectives, as boys going through puberty appear to lack control over the vocal sound they produce.

Additionally, a material study of voice helps critique the positivist ethos of recent turns toward "the material." Voice provides an ideal test case for recent debates about the ideological and historical aims of what has been called the "new materialism" in early modern studies. As Douglas Bruster, Harris, Korda, and others maintain, the turn to the "material" has often been accompanied by a post-Marxist fascination with commodities, a "critical fetishism."[18] Historical matter, as a consequence, often takes on the illusion of stability, as if the study of material objects will give modern scholars access to some realm of the real, some "graspable 'thing' that exists beyond, and untouched by, the textuality of history and ideology."[19] Voice dispels such illusions. Invisible yet substantial, ephemeral yet transferable, voice destabilizes any easy assumptions about the category of matter. Moreover, what enables the material voice to become a site of agency and tool of resistance to oppressive cultural forces is not its stability or instrumentality, but its volatility.[20] I argue that when early modern texts highlight the difficulties of producing, tracking, and controlling inherently unmanageable vocal matter, they (paradoxically) lay the groundwork for a model of vocal agency that benefits those whose expressive acts were curtailed or marginalized. In particular, I am interested in how early modern representations of the voice as unruly matter generate resistance to early modern hierarchies of gender—a point to which I will return.

My approach to voice addresses another problem for material culture studies and, more particularly, for work on what are often called the "material conditions" of the early modern theater—and this constitutes the second of my interventions, into performance. Our understanding of early modern drama has benefited immensely from a range of studies of the conditions in which plays were performed, from the professional theater's location in the liberties to the status of playwrights to the props present onstage.[21] Although the thoughtfulness of such work has done much to dissipate time-worn debates about the relative value of the page versus the stage, a binary of text versus performance continues to hold sway, especially where studies of Shakespearean language are concerned. In these studies speech often remains the province of "the text." Yet in an institution like the theater that depends in large part upon voices to communicate the images, characters, and themes of play-scripts, language and materiality, text and performance, are not competing systems in collision, but rather interdependent variables inevitably in collusion.[22] Part of my goal in this book is to examine the nature and implications of this collusion: how imagery of voice—such as air, seed, echo, and the like—arises out of as much as it informs the theatrical conditions of vocal performance.

Central to my method for exploring this collusion between text and performance is integration of the study of plays with nondramatic texts. Plays performed in the theater were only one subset of early modern cultural performances featuring sound, and a range of nondramatic texts from the period reflect and inscribe events involving vocal production, transmission, and reception.[23] These nondramatic texts, like plays, urge their readers to conjure live vocal performance as an analog, setting, or provocation for the making of meaning. For instance, the printed Protestant sermons on hearing that I discuss in Chapter 3 represent themselves as recording actual sermons that were once delivered to a live audience; indeed, the sermons almost always recall in their titles a particular date when and place where the sermon was spoken. The medical and scientific writings I discuss in Chapters 1 and 2 claim to capture former live investigations of their subject matter: Helkiah Crooke's anatomy book explicitly recalls prior acts of dissection as it describes in great detail the procedural methods for locating particular vocal organs; Bacon's writings on acoustics claim to report on auditory phenomena that the author or his colleagues have observed or demonstrated. Auditory phenomena serve a similar authorizing function in the commentary George Sandys offers on Ovid's "Echo and Narcissus" episode, which I discuss in Chapter 4. Sandys records how real auditory events—observed by him or others—explain the otherwise eerie phenomenon of the echoic voice in Ovid's poem. Finally, the treatises concerned with voice training that I discuss in Chapter 1 present themselves as applicable in practice: Richard Mulcaster's pedagogical writings prescribe particular exercises for his young students; music manuals, similarly, advise their readers to put into practice the methods outlined on the page. Whatever their relationship to "real" vocal or auditory events, these various nondramatic texts ask to be read in a performative dimension.

When these nondramatic texts are read alone and alongside the period's drama, they help present a more thorough understanding of early modern performance culture, of the plays of Shakespeare and his contemporaries, and of our own theoretical perspectives on the problem of vocal agency. My analysis of these various discursive constructions of vocal performance attempts to enliven and complicate imagery that can easily be overlooked or oversimplified when we read the plays in isolation. Knowing, for example, that early modern Protestant preachers ally deafness with spiritual fortitude reveals much concerning the imagery of closed ears that reappears frequently in Shakespeare's late plays; in turn, this dramatic imagery of closed ears sheds light on the practice of hearing that was so crucial to early modern theatergoing. As "text" and "performance" collude, they reveal, in this case, that communicative agency can inhere in the position of listening, not just in speaking. As should be evident, I am not suggesting that these nondramatic texts are the cultural or ideological "context" for drama or even that early moderns would have imagined these various texts in dialogue with drama. The dialogue I initiate between sermons and the late plays or between pedagogical treatises and children's company plays is one that I, as critic—and as critic armed with training in particular theoretical approaches—initiate. One of my contentions in this book is that creating such dialogues is, in fact, a productive part of doing performance history.[24] The point here is not to subject early modern texts to the critic's theoretical overlay, but rather to recognize the ways the texts themselves articulate theories of the relation between voice and agency. Listening to early modern views on questions that have preoccupied generations of modern critics does more than simply remind us to respect historical difference; because they are so self-conscious about vocal performance, these texts can also teach us a great deal about how voices (on and off the stage) are invested with power.

This brings me to the third of my critical interventions, into our understanding of the way gender difference and hierarchy are constructed in early modern drama and culture. When performed plays underscore the ephemerality of the voice, they put pressure on one of the foundational ways gender difference was established in early modern England. For early modern men, controlling voice—their own as well as those of subordinates (children, servants, and women)—often functioned as a signifier of manly identity. Whereas early modern women and children were discouraged and even barred from certain forms of vocal expression, men often were coached from an early age in the skill of oratory in an effort to prepare them to speak effectively. A similar dynamic is represented in many of the plays of the period. Loss of vocal control is often indexical of male characters' social and political disempowerment. For instance, when Piero, the articulate Duke of Venice in John Marston's *Antonio and Mellida*, discovers that his daughter has eloped with his enemy, he begins to stutter. In Shakespeare's *King John*, the political defeat of the Pope's persuasive legate Pandulph is signaled when Pandulph's voice is compared to a "weak wind" (5.2.87).[25]

Shakespeare's *Coriolanus* dramatizes just how much is at stake for male identity in the loss of control over voice. Roman law insists that the senators' choice of consul be ratified by the "people," and thus in order for Coriolanus to be granted the consulship, he must be "given" the voices of Rome's male citizens. The voice is figured as something that can be transferred from one man to another. Concomitantly, it can be withheld from systems of transaction: though there is little reason for the citizens to "deny him" their voices, as one citizen points out, "We may, sir, if we will" (2.3.3). The citizens' voices are, ostensibly, *theirs* to give. *Coriolanus* codes vocal mastery as a masculine prerogative that, when exercised successfully, instantiates male power and superiority. Indeed, ownership and, concurrently, exercise of voice enable the citizens to perform publicly their political power and social standing. It is not surprising, then, that the citizens are resentful when they realize that Coriolanus has cheated them out of their voices. Rather than offering his deeds in exchange for their vocal support, Coriolanus presents the transaction as already completed:

Your voices! For your voices I have fought,
Watched for your voices, for your voices bear
Of wounds two dozen odd; battles thrice six
I have seen and heard of for your voices, have
Done many things, some less, some more. Your voices!
Indeed I would be consul. (2.3.116–21)

Coriolanus's rhetoric of entitlement surreptitiously accepts the voices of Rome's citizens without the citizen-speakers even acknowledging that a transaction has occurred. The citizens, as a result, feel duped. "They have chose a consul that will from them take / Their liberties, make them of no more voice / Than dogs" (2.3.203–5). Echoing an ancient Aristotelian idea that the possession of voice delineates human from animal, the citizens imply that not only their manhood but their very humanity is compromised by this loss of control over voice.

Mastery of the voice may have been a conceptual ideal in *Coriolanus*'s Rome and in Shakespeare's England, but early moderns often represented this ideal as a practical impossibility. Insofar as vocal matter is alienable, mobile, and precarious, the male privilege to speak is accompanied frequently by anxiety. In *Love's Labour's Lost*, for instance, the powerful vows that establish male identity and community evaporate as quickly as they are spoken, threatening the ground upon which male identity is based. No sooner have Longaville and his fellow courtiers sworn (to the king and to one another) to devote themselves to years of study and celibacy than the men fall in love with the first women they see, breaking not only their vows but what are supposed to be powerful homosocial bonds. When Longaville announces that such vows are useless because words are "but breath, and breath a vapour is" (4.3.63), he intimates that what threatens male friendship and masculine honor in *Love's Labour's Lost* is not only men's encounters with women but the recognition that the durability of vocalized promises is a material impossibility. Vows, even if articulated with the greatest of fervor by the most sincere of male speakers, are still composed of ephemeral vapor; and the male community constituted by these vows is revealed to rest on unsteady ground. Male identity is, in many ways, aleatory, contingent upon forms of vocal utterance that are inherently unstable.

Early modern plays repeatedly stage the efforts of male characters to reassert control over the fugitive, unpredictable voice, substantiating Michael C. Schoenfeldt's argument in *Bodies and Selves in Early Modern England* that a "regime of self-discipline" was in many ways productive of early modern subjectivity, "a necessary step towards any prospect of liberation."[26] Focusing specifically on the disciplining of the body prescribed by humoral physiology, Schoenfeldt critiques earlier work on corporeality that claims the porous, "leaky" body to be solely a site of shame rather than empowerment.[27] I similarly find that controlling the body's "flows," specifically, the flow of voice, was thought to be sometimes enabling of early modern subjectivity. However, as my approach to embodiment and materiality accounts for gender differences in a way that Schoenfeldt's does not, I reach different conclusions about the regulative power that his book proposes. For one thing, I follow Gary Spear and others who have described self-restraint as a defining trait of early modern masculinity.[28] The value of restraint is not gender neutral. Where vocal control is concerned, a model of emancipatory disciplining is constructive particularly of *male* subjectivity. Indeed, early moderns assume men are more capable of and responsible for disciplining bodily flows. As Gail Kern Paster shows in *The Body Embarrassed: Drama and the Disciplines of Shame in Early Modern England*, medical authorities viewed women's bodies as inherently less manageable, the flow of blood and milk offering evidence of a fundamental lack of discipline.[29] The disorderly flow of voice from women's bodies served as an analogous symptom of the female body's extraordinarily porous boundaries.

The consequences of this gender difference are complicated, however. Certainly, as Paster persuasively argues, views of women's natural lack of bodily control helped justify early modern gender hierarchies. Where voice is concerned, many conduct-book writers argue that women need the strong guidance of husbands and fathers because they cannot control their own speech. Such prescriptive literature, in fact, instructs women in how to talk to others—husbands, servants, and so forth.[30] Yet this ideological pressure to regulate the flow of voice exists in tension with an understanding of the material voice's inherent unmanageability, consequently leaving early modern men in a particularly difficult position. For, unlike women, most men were *expected* to be capable of regulating voice, and, thus, were at greater risk of being perceived as weak and ineffectual when voice eluded their control. The inherently unmanageable nature of vocal matter becomes a greater problem for men than for women. I argue that early modern male subjects (on and off the stage) who try to assert mastery of the voice sometimes suffer a disadvantage in comparison to vocally marginalized subjects, like women and boys, from whom less vocal discipline is expected.

Moreover, I contend that female characters who embrace, instead of attempting to overcome, their unpredictable vocal flows are able to elude patriarchal regulation and exercise less obvious forms of vocal agency. Thus, *Othello* represents Desdemona as most persuasive about her innocence not when she forthrightly challenges Othello through impassioned speech but when she lies sleeping, seemingly unconscious that her "balmy breath," the substance early moderns associated with the production of voice, "dost almost persuade" Othello not to murder her (5.2.16–17). In other words, the ideological asymmetries that establish early modern gender hierarchies—promoting the perspective that women are less capable than men of controlling the voice—also provide the conditions for undoing or challenging those hierarchies.[31] For women, vocal agency may be constituted, not disrupted, by the voice's volatility. Indeed, early modern plays suggest that a woman's voice may be most effective not when it is owned and mastered by her, but when she relinquishes it to the environment beyond her body. Pursuing the implications of this idea to their limits, I argue that it is often as listeners, more than as speakers, that early modern women can most successfully disrupt and reshape their world.

A History and Theory of "Voice" as Agency

The model of vocal agency I have begun to describe differs significantly from models prevalent in the history of feminist thought. Scholars and activists frequently figure the voice as analogous with agency, suggesting that the capacity to speak out, to "own" one's voice, secures personal and political power. The value of women having "a voice of their own" has been central to a range of feminist movements and thinkers. A brief overview of key ideas in some of these movements is instructive. For so-called "liberal feminists," who are interested in ensuring women's cultural, political and economic equality, the goal of feminist practice is to ensure that women "have a say" in how an organization or institution is run.[32] One assumption behind the National Organization for Women's "Statement of Purpose" (1966) is that if women are present in a particular organization (especially if they hold a position of authority in that organization), they will "speak for" women and, as a consequence, improve the lives of women.[33] Relatedly, a goal of many women's groups is to encourage women to "speak out." Many of those called "cultural feminists"—who argue that the problem is not the exclusion but the devaluation of female attributes in cultural production—use the trope of voice to call attention to ways that women participate in a society differently from men. As Carol Gilligan famously put it, women speak "in a different voice" from that of men, and only when that voice is valued on its own terms can women truly participate in and transform a culture.[34] For some "cultural feminists," the specificity of the female voice is connected to the unique features of the female body, especially its maternal capacities. For certain French feminists, the term "voice" stands in for the trace of feminine corporeal difference—a difference that manifests itself in the ways women express themselves in speech and writing.[35] Theorists who take issue with white, Western feminism's tendency to "speak for" minorities similarly appeal to the trope of voice to argue that women can inhabit particular subjectivities as a consequence of their racial or ethnic identity.[36] As is evident in titles such as *Feminist Readings of Native American Literature: Coming to Voice* or *Hear Our Voice: Women in the British Rabbinate*, the term "voice" conveniently signifies scholars' interests in exploring the agency of groups traditionally ignored by academic, political, or cultural institutions.[37] In sum, whether "voice" refers to the specificity of the female body, to feminine expression, or to women's subjectivity, it functions as a shorthand metaphor for women's access to personal and political power.[38]

The overview I have provided is admittedly reductive and by no means inclusive of the nuances of feminist thought, but it helps to demonstrate the degree to which a range of feminist writings imply an undertheorized system of analogies between voice, body, subjectivity, and agency. Although this system of linkages often serves a strategic role, there are benefits to uncoupling these terms from one another, at the very least to understand better the circumstances that give rise to their equation. My efforts to untether these equivalences has been informed by, but also extends beyond, poststructuralist scholarship on performance and performativity. Theorists have tapped and crucially expanded upon two aspects of J. L. Austin's early work in speech-act theory. First, questioning Austin's insistence that "the utterer must be the performer," some theorists emphasize the instability of the performing agent.[39] Through approaches as diverse as psychoanalysis, Marxism, Foucauldian analysis, deconstruction, and discourse analysis, theorists complicate Austin's vision of the speaker as equivalent to the agent. Second, Austin's appeal to the context of speech has burgeoned into a field of inquiries into what Andrew Parker and Eve Kosofsky Sedgwick term the "thither side" of the speech-act, "the complex process . . . of uptake" by silent, implied, or actual auditors.[40] By advancing critical focus beyond the body of a speaker, theorists demonstrate how accountability for speech is dispersed and shared by a number of sources. Rather than locating the power of an utterance in the body of the performer-speaker, theorists prompt analysis of factors that affect the transfer of speech from speaker to listener. Perhaps the most successful application of theories of linguistic performativity to concerns about agency is Butler's *Excitable Speech*, which demonstrates the ways a theory of the performative is embedded in recent political discourse on hate speech, thereby extending into an explicitly political realm Butler's arguments about the agency of language. Butler submits that if the meaning of an utterance depends not on its site of origination in a particular speaker, but on its circulation, then it is possible for a hurtful invective (for example, "queer") to gain affirmative meanings. A term meant to injure particular individuals or a group can undergo a reversal of meaning and, instead, mobilize the injured party socially and politically. Butler thus shows how untethering speech from subjectivity enables a more expansive conception of agency.

Butler's insights provide a fruitful theoretical ground for my approach to vocal agency, but they are limited in their applicability. For although *Excitable Speech* grapples more closely than much of Butler's earlier work with the material conditions of linguistic performativity, it does not explain how the *practical* performance of language constitutes its condition of generative instability. These shortcomings are most evident in Butler's attempts to account for the role of the body as a site for the performance of speech.[41] Butler recognizes that the body of a speaker imbues an utterance with a different sort of "force" than is evident in writing, but her book does not theorize how the body generates this force.[42] Moreover, although Butler notes that the success of an utterance can be undermined during its transmission between speakers and listeners, she does not consider the physical aspects of this transmission, only its social and linguistic features. In short, Butler's theory of the "performativity" of language does not account for the material practice of vocal performance in the way, for example, that Derrida accounts for the material practice of writing.[43] My approach to early modern vocal communication essentially conjoins Butler's theory of the politics of expression with Derrida's emphasis on the materiality of the linguistic medium in order to ask what sorts of "obstacles" the physical voice encounters as it propagates meaning, and how recognizing these obstacles can prove productive for feminist approaches to agency. The answers to these questions are not the same in every historical period or in every culture. Thus, to construct a theory of vocal power that serves a feminist politics, we not only need to infuse Butler's abstract theory of linguistic performativity with a Derridian account of the material realities of vocal performance; we also need to historicize voice.

This kind of historicization of voice has significant benefits for feminist scholarship of early modern literature, especially drama, which has been invested particularly in understanding the relation between gender, agency, and vocal expression. Noting the frequency with which Shakespeare and his contemporaries dramatize the Pauline prescription for femininity—chastity, silence, and obedience—feminist critics have considered the extent to which a rhetoric of female silence structured and limited women's expressive lives in fiction and in reality. Some critics outline methods by which early modern patriarchal systems tried to prohibit women from expressing themselves through the imposition of ideological and physical constraints on women's bodies and the use of legal and social pressures to discourage women from participating in public life.[44] Other critics point to the many examples of women who circumvent restrictions on their voices and speak powerfully despite various cultural pressures to be silent.[45] Although this work has broadened our understanding of early modern literature and culture and the role of women in both, it is often limited by a narrow definition of the relation between voice and power. As Christina Luckyj observes, feminist critics have tended to accept as fact that in the early modern period "speech is a privileged site of authority" and "silence is a site of gendered oppression."[46] Luckyj and others problematize these assumptions by demonstrating the ways in which silence can be a powerful rhetorical posture. Work on silence expands the parameters of what constitutes female agency in the period, but while it deconstructs one side of the speech/silence binary, it often leaves intact the other side, reinforcing a narrow understanding of speech. In declaring silence a kind of eloquent speech, scholars leave unanswered the question of how and whether speech itself becomes powerful.

My efforts to widen the signification of speech have been influenced by prior studies of voice by such scholars as Lynn Enterline, Jonathan Goldberg, Elizabeth Harvey, and Carla Mazzio, all of whom complicate the relationship between gender, voice, and agency by examining the ways early modern texts figure the alienation of the voice from the speaking subject.[47] Yet for these scholars, tropes of voice ultimately are interesting because of what they reveal about early modern ideologies of language or textual production and transmission, not vocal performance. For example, Mazzio, noting the increasing textualization of early modern English culture, sees tropes of voice as signaling early modern anxieties about the relation between oral and written forms of articulation. Goldberg queries the authority of voice in an effort to demonstrate the ways a character's individuality and psychology are a function of textual inscription. For Enterline and Harvey, the trope of voice is a tool for poets anxious about the practice of their poetic craft. *Voice in Motion* argues that voice is not just a trope for poetic subjectivity or a vehicle for understanding writing and textual transmission; voice is also a specific material form, whose modes of production, transmission, and reception need to be historicized and theorized.

One of the few feminist critics who has considered vocal performance in such terms is Dympna Callaghan. In "The Castrator's Song: Female Impersonation on the Early Modern Stage," Callaghan argues for the crucial role of voice in producing a spectacle of gender difference on the stage. In the English professional theater, Callaghan points out, boys were not physically castrated like eunuchs on the Continent, which meant that boys' capacity to mimic the female voice in performance would have been compromised by the physical effects of puberty.[48] For Callaghan, this performance condition ultimately underscores both the occlusion of women from the professional theater and the theater's troubling recuperation of dominant gender ideologies; the transvestite stage fails to operate as the liberatory, subversive space that many feminist critics have imagined it to be. Yet this conclusion about the stage's ideological conservatism is based on a limited definition of how the voice works in theatrical space. Callaghan contends that "[u]nlike beards, codpieces, and so on, voice is not available as a stage property. Embodied rather than prosthetic, the voice accords presence."[49] My broader analysis of the conditions of voicing in the theater reveals that such assumptions do not hold true for many early modern authors, who often imagine the voice as eerily *dis*embodied. A boy actor with a squeaking pubescent voice may not be able to don an aural pitch the way he dons a codpiece, but early modern plays consistently underscore that this is proof of, not proof against, the prosthetic nature of voice: voice is not *em*bodied as much as it is temporarily attached, released, and exchanged *by* bodies. As a consequence of its mobility and spatial indeterminacy, the voice has the capacity for even greater flux than "the body" and can effect surprising forms of subversion to early modern gender ideologies. By exploring the potential for such subversion, I am by no means endorsing an uncritical celebration of Shakespeare and his contemporaries as protofeminist. Rather, I maintain that because of the volatility of live performance and the particular conventions of the Elizabethan and Jacobean stage, transgressive perspectives on vocal agency can emerge, regardless of whether playwrights consciously write such ideas into their scripts.[50]

Voice in Motion

Voice in Motion underscores its arguments about the relation between gender, agency, and vocal performance by mirroring through its organization the trajectory of vocal matter. The chapters follow the motion of the physical voice from the speaker's body, through the air, and to the listener's body, examining at each stage the way in which the voice's material form can compromise the directness and efficacy of speech. I argue that the farther from a speaker's body the voice is imagined to be located, the less the voice can be counted on to perform a speaker's will and the more voice undermines male investments in vocal control—producing instead unexpectedly robust models of female agency. It is the voice's distance from, rather than presence in, the body that constitutes the conditions of agency.

Chapter 1, "Squeaky Voices," examines texts in which the volatile voice is a function of the unmanageable body of its speaker. Analyzing a range of texts concerned with vocal training and performance, including most prominently a pedagogical treatise by Richard Mulcaster, I argue that early modern theories of humoral physiology influenced the period's views of vocal instability and its implications for gender identity. Focusing on the voice changes that accompany male puberty, I consider how humoral explanations for vocal instability shape the way masculinity is represented on stage, especially by boy actors. Through readings of a range of characters played by boy actors—including the male youths in Shakespeare's *Coriolanus* and Ben Jonson's *Cynthia's Revels* and especially the courtiers and noblemen of John Marston's *Antonio and Mellida*—I show how the squeaky, pubescent voices of boy actors challenge the early modern masculine ideal of vocal control, destabilizing early modern systems of gender differentiation.

Chapter 2, "Words Made of Breath," pursues the voice as it is imagined to leave the speaker's body and enter the air in the form of breath. According to a range of early modern cultural discourses—philosophical, medical, and scientific—the breath that produces and transports vocal sound is an ambiguous indicator of expressive agency, for insofar as it is composed of mere ephemeral air, breath easily disintegrates, undermining the successful transmission of words. The chapter investigates how concerns about breath's fragile materiality triangulate with anxieties about gender and power differences in several of Shakespeare's plays: *Richard III*, *Titus Andronicus*, *Othello*, and especially *King John*. Male characters in these plays secure their power over others both by claiming they can control the motion of the breath used to speak and also by representing others, especially women, as incapable of managing their voices. Yet breath's ephemeral, unpredictable material nature—which necessarily reveals itself in performance—undermines such confidence in vocal authority. At the same time, female and other ostensibly disempowered characters that embrace the volatility of their voices become capable of unexpected vocal agency. Thus, tongueless Lavinia in *Titus Andronicus* communicates her trauma through blood that is imagined to be pushed out of her mouth by her "honeyed breath." Noting that vocally marginalized characters like Lavinia were played by boy actors, who faced their own very real vocal challenges in the theater, I argue that the plays' thematizations of vocal agency arise from and reflect on the conditions of theatrical performance.

Chapter 3, "Fortress of the Ear," examines what happens to vocal communication when the voice reaches its most unpredictable destination, the listener. I read Shakespeare's *Pericles, Cymbeline, The Winter's Tale*, and *The Tempest* in light of Protestant sermons on hearing. The plays, like the sermons, represent receptive ears as crucial for salvation, while at the same time suggesting open ears are a liability if they are not defended properly from evil. In these late plays, hearing functions as a site of gender differentiation: aural obstruction is disruptive for men, but constructive for women, whose chastity is contingent on aural closure. However, as the line between harmful and beneficial aural closure becomes blurred, efforts to shore up female chastity—and female difference—paradoxically imbue female characters who shut their ears with a method of resisting authority; as a consequence, women emerge as *acoustic subjects*. This argument sheds light, for example, on *Tempest*'s Prospero and his concern about commanding the obedience of his aurally resistant daughter. The plays suggest, moreover, that resistance to sound constitutes the acoustic subjectivity not only of female characters like Miranda but of theater audiences, whose potential for blocked ears helps establish their role as active participants in the creation of theater.

Chapter 4, "Echoic Sound," brings the book's argument full circle through an examination of early modern representations of the mythic, female figure Echo, whose seemingly unintentional repetition of the voices of others demonstrates how the auditory agency identified in Chapter 3 can become the vocal agency elucidated in Chapter 2. At the center of the chapter is a close reading of George Sandys's English translation of and commentary on Ovid's Latin poem, "Echo and Narcissus." In Ovid's poem the power of the echoic voice stems from its ambiguous relation to the body of Echo. The echoic voice in Ovid resists being traced back to a particular site of origin, eluding classification as either human "voice" or mere sound. I argue that as Sandys's project of *Ovide moralisé* redefines Ovid's Echo so that she conforms to this binary, the text provides insight not only into early modern anxieties about the eerie vocal agency Echo represents but also into the representational strategies by which Sandys's early modern text addresses and alleviates such anxieties. Sandys's text, I suggest, has useful applications to our understanding of drama. For though Sandys's textual medium differs markedly from the live performance medium used by playwrights, Sandys shares with playwrights the challenge of working with the volatile, disembodied voice.

The differences between written text and live performance are the subject of the book's Epilogue, "Performing the Voice of Elizabeth." The Epilogue examines George Gascoigne's treatment of the Echo figure in his entertainments at Kenilworth Castle, which included a scene in which Echo appears before—and is made to speak for—Queen Elizabeth, a figure known for her own powerfully unpredictable voice. I argue that Gascoigne's written "record" of the live event, like Sandys's commentary on Ovid, forecloses the power of the volatile female voice: Gascoigne overscripts the voices of Echo and Elizabeth, stripping them of their capacity to speak their own desires. Gascoigne's representation of the female voices at Kenilworth is contested, however, in a competing written "record" of the events, *Laneham's Letter*, which depicts the Kenilworth Echo scene as more unstable than Gascoigne's account admits. Giving Elizabeth a surprise, starring role in the Echo scene, the *Letter* demonstrates the ways her voice eludes the control of Kenilworth's male courtiers, and it mocks them for underestimating the unpredictable nature of performance. As such, the *Letter* demonstrates my book's argument about the ways women in particular can take advantage of the volatility of the voice in performance.

Chapter 1

Squeaky Voices: Marston, Mulcaster, and the Boy Actor

Perhaps because of the burgeoning industry of Shakespeare films and the late twentieth-century fascination with everything Elizabethan, new students of early modern English drama often are surprisingly familiar with the conditions under which Shakespeare's plays were originally performed, even the very unmodern convention of using boys to play female parts. And though some consumers of Shakespeare still echo Stephen Orgel's query about why the English professional stage took boys for women, another intriguing question concerns process: not why but *how* was gender negotiated on an all-male stage? Whereas work by Orgel and other scholars has been most attentive to the visual aspects of early modern gender performance, I am interested in how the aural dimensions of the Elizabethan theater shaped its representations of gender.[1] The impact of sound on the performance of gender is at the heart of two recent popular interpretations of Shakespearean theater, John Madden's *Shakespeare in Love* and Michael Hoffman's *William Shakespeare's A Midsummer Night's Dream*.[2] In each of these Hollywood films, a major turning point of the plot involves a male actor realizing that his physiological state prevents him from mimicking a woman's voice effectively, a failure that threatens to undermine the success of the play. Although Madden's and Hoffman's films approach the Bard in distinct ways, they resolve this play-within-the-film vocal crisis in strikingly similar ways. In *Shakespeare in Love*, the cast of *Romeo and Juliet* is surprised to learn a few minutes before the curtain rises that the voice of the boy who will play Juliet has begun to change. The film maintains that this is cause enough to pull the actor from the part, even though the only possible substitute for him is a woman, whose presence on the stage thwarts royal decree.[3] Hoffman's *A Midsummer Night's Dream* imagines what would happen if a postpubescent male actor, with a fully cracked voice, were allowed to play the female role. When the deep-voiced Flute uses a falsetto vocal style to personate Thisbe in the play within the film, his audience breaks into laughter at his aesthetically unpleasant, squeaking sound. The solution here is not to bring in a real woman's voice, as in *Shakespeare in Love*, but to allow the grave voice to be used. Flute completes the play in his natural voice and the performance, like that of *Romeo and Juliet*, is portrayed as a smashing success. In Madden's and Hoffman's dramatizations of the boy-actor stage convention, the success of a play is contingent on the physiological state of the male body and its capacity to produce a satisfying aural experience for the audience. Both films suggest that it is better to risk legal censure or the audience's distraction than to allow an unstable, squeaking male voice onstage.

In their displacement of squeaking voices, these modern performances diverge from early modern theatrical practice. For in contrast to today's audiences, early modern theatergoers had ample opportunity to hear unstable male voices. Whether the frequent staging of squeaking voices in early modern plays points to a dramatic convention or offers evidence of a theatrical custom—that boy actors continued to perform while their voices were changing—there is much at stake in noting the role of these voices on the stage and in the culture at large.[4] Onstage or off, a squeaking voice announced a boy's transition into manhood at the same time that it indicated that the transition had yet to be completed. As it attested to a boy's liminal position in a gradual and uneven process of pubescent change, the squeaking voice exposed the fragile condition of young male bodies and, as a corollary, the aleatory nature of gender differentiation.

This chapter examines how early modern authors, on and off the stage, figure the unstable voice as a function of an unmanageable body, focusing on the implications of these views for the dramatization of male masculinity.[5] My approach to boy actors and the enactment of gender differs from that of prior scholars, most of whom have focused on the ramifications of boys playing the parts of women. I examine the implications of boys playing a range of male parts, including youth characters in plays by adult companies like the King's Men and male adult roles in plays by the children's companies that were popular in England in the first decade of the seventeenth century.[6] Even when not playing women, boy actors were sites for complex cultural negotiations about gender identity. For as boy actors were approaching or undergoing puberty, their voices were on the verge or in the process of breaking. I argue that these unstable voices would have been a source of uneasiness for early modern male actors and audiences, for vocal control was a signifier of masculinity. As I noted in the introduction, ideal men were expected to exhibit command over their own voices as well as the voices of others—such as wives, servants, and children. Thus, the successful theatrical performance of masculinity would have been undermined by the particular vocal properties of the actors responsible for representing manliness. Rather than displacing the unstable voice from the stage—as Madden and Hoffman do in their interpretations of early modern theater—early modern plays and the theaters that presented them appear to cultivate a space onstage for these voices. In so doing, the early modern professional theater exploited men's fears of losing control over not only the production of voice but the production of gender difference as well. Attending to the material practice of voice on the stage thus enables us to unpack the relation between vocal control and masculinity and to consider how early moderns coped theatrically with the volatility of the male performing body and concomitant anxieties about gender hierarchies.

Listening for Masculinity

To understand the role of the voice in cultural and dramatic performances of masculinity—that is, to listen for masculinity—we must recognize a historical difference between early modern and contemporary representations of the relation between gender and voice. Contemporary popular culture stereotypically depicts masculinity aurally through a bass voice. In Hoffman's *Midsummer Night's Dream*, for example, the hypermasculine Oberon (played by Rupert Everett) sports not only buff pectorals but a deep, sultry voice as well. Early modern texts also equate masculinity with a deep voice, but more is at stake in their understanding of this feature than aural aesthetics. According to early modern humoral theories, the quality of a man's voice, as it testifies to the physiological state of his body, also denotes the condition of the social, political, and cosmic world he inhabits. Order in these macrocosmic spheres—order that is vital to a smoothly functioning patriarchal system—is intertwined with the body's maintenance of a humoral equilibrium (balanced amounts of heat versus coldness, of wetness versus dryness).

Varying levels of body heat and moisture, explains Francis Bacon in

Sylva Sylvarum (1626), determine the deepness of the voice: "*Children, Women, Eunuchs* have more small and shrill *Voices,* than *Men.* The Reason is . . . from the Dilatation of the Organ; which (it is true) is . . . caused by Heat. But the Cause of *Changing* the *Voice,* at the yeares of Puberty, is more obscure. It seemeth to be, for that when much of the Moysture of the Body, which did before irrigate the Parts, is drawne down to the Spermaticall vessels; it leaveth the Body more hot than it was; whence commeth the Dilatation of the Pipes."[7] In other words, when the testicles become "Spermaticall vessels" or agents of generation—one defining feature of early modern masculinity, notes Rebecca Ann Bach—they draw moisture away from the rest of body, causing it to become hotter. That heat subsequently dilates the vocal pipes, causing the voice to sound deeper. Levinus Lemnius in *The Touchstone of Complexions* (1576) considers how the body's changing levels of heat have implications for vocal aesthetics and for character:

They therefore that have hoate bodyes, are also of nature variable, and chau[n]geable, ready, pro[m]pt, lively, lusty and applyable: of tongue, trowling, perfect, & perswasive: delyvering their words distinctly, plainlye and pleasauntlye, with a voyce thereto not squekinge and slender, but streynable, comely and audible. The thing that maketh the voyce bigge, is partlye the wydenes of the breast and vocall Artery, and partly the inwarde or internall heate, from whence proceedeth the earnest affections, vehemente motions, and fervent desyers of the mynde.[8]

The ideal voice being described in this passage, Bruce R. Smith points out, is a man's voice, for according to humoral theory, only men have enough heat to produce what the passage suggests are aesthetically desirable vocal features.[9] Women and children, having bodies that tend to be colder than men's, are endowed with smaller vocal instruments; rather than producing a voice "perfect, & perswasive . . . comely and audible," delivered "distinctly, plainlye and pleasauntlye," women and children produce unpleasant, "squekinge" or inaudible, "slender" voices.

Although a voice "soft" and "low" may be, as Shakespeare's King Lear claims, "an excellent thing *in a woman*" (*King Lear* 5.3.247, emphasis mine), the "squekinge" that characterizes the voices of women and children sets them, and anyone who sounds like them, apart, announcing the presence of an unmanageable body. Numerous early modern texts advance the notion that a squeaky voice is rooted in an uncontrollable body. For instance, Robert Herrick's epigram mourning the state of the theater after Ben Jonson's death laments that the stage became occupied with "men [who] did strut, and stride, and stare, not act. / Then temper flew from words; and men did squeake, / Looke red, and blow, and bluster, but not speake."[10] According to Herrick, the squeaking of an actor's voice signals his inability to contain the emotion behind his words—"temper flew from words." The uncontrollable squeak is not merely substandard vocal performance, Herrick maintains, but not speaking at all, a claim underscored by his end-rhyme contrasting men who "squeake" and men who "speake." Indeed a squeaking sound is associated in the early modern period (as it continues to be today) with animals and inanimate objects. Bacon writes that objects emitting a squeaking sound include "*Cart-Wheeles* . . . when they are not liquored" and "a Doore upon the Hinges."[11] The squeak is the sound made by animals, like "a pigge when he is sticked,"[12] and especially by rats.[13] Not coincidentally, it is also the sound that women are imagined to make when in the throes of excitement, especially of a sexual nature. In Thomas Heywood's *The Fair Maid of the West* (1631), Roughman boasts that he will win the affections of Bess: "Ile have her . . . I will put her to the squeake."[14] The lusty gentleman Master Thornay of James Shirley's *Changes: or, Love in a Maze* (1632) begs of Cupid's arrow that it will "strike" his beloved and "make her squeake."[15] And Maquerelle in John Marston's *The Malcontent* (1604) describes one gallant as "even one of the most busy-fingered lords. He will put the beauties to the squeak most hideously."[16] Squeaking is not just a signature of difference, but of inferiority—an aural symptom of the body's surrender to irrational, lower passions.

As Gail Kern Paster has importantly demonstrated in *The Body Embarrassed: Drama and the Disciplines of Shame in Early Modern England*, early modern humoral physiology expects women, who are understood as physiologically colder than men, to lack control over their passions and their naturally leakier bodies.[17] As a corollary, early modern men, who could not be "excused" in the same ways for physiological frailty, were expected to meet higher standards of bodily discipline. These differing expectations for men and women undoubtedly worked to reinforce a troubling hierarchical gender system and to propagate misogynist beliefs in women's ostensibly "natural" inferiority to men. But the expectations also inflicted on men greater cultural pressures to maintain bodily control. Indeed, the management of bodily "flows" that Michael C. Schoenfeldt argues to be essential to identity formation in this period is imagined to be especially critical for early modern men.[18] Insofar as a squeaky voice evinces an unruly body, it may be "natural"—ironically, as in the *Lear* example, even sometimes praised—in women but is a sign of deficiency in men.

This deficiency extends well beyond the particular male body concerned, for, as early modern writers frequently maintain, the body is a microcosm with concordances to macrocosmic spheres of family, nation, and God. Thus, a man unable to keep his voice from squeaking manifests a breakdown in patriarchal order. Male identity and, concurrently, male superiority are contingent on men maintaining control over the flow of their vocal sounds. A scene from John Marston's play *Antonio's Revenge* suggests as much. When Antonio, Pandulfo, and Alberto—the drama's three disempowered men—join together to wail against the injustices that have brought disorder to their social and political lives, Antonio asks a page if he will "sing a dirge." But Pandulfo discourages the singing: "No, no song; 'twill be vile out of tune" (4.2.88–89). Alberto thinks that Pandulfo is referring to the physiological state of the boy's voice—"Indeed he's hoarse; the poor boy's voice is cracked" (90)—but Pandulfo, lamenting his failure to obtain retribution for the murder of his son and his banishment from the dukedom, has a more profound thought in mind:

Why, coz, why should it not be hoarse and cracked,
When all the strings of nature's symphony
Are cracked and jar? Why should his voice keep tune,
When there's no music in the breast of man? (4.2.91–94)

The boy's hoarse voice is symptomatic of not only a physiological but also a social, political, and spiritual disturbance. The pubescent boy's inability to control the microcosm of his body is figured as homologous with Pandulfo, Antonio, and Alberto's failure to maintain macrocosmic order.

When Marston's play was originally performed by the Children of Paul's, a hoarse voice was not only a fictional concern for the pubescent boy represented in this scene; it may have been a real source of uneasiness for the pubescent actors playing the parts of Pandulfo, Antonio, and Alberto. Their fragile physiological condition threatened to disrupt their enactments of ideal male character. Since voice changes were considered in this period, as in our modern era, an inevitable experience of puberty, representations of and dramatic allusions to the cracked male voice served as reminders that the "homeostatic masculine body" was an impossible ideal.[19] If early modern patriarchal systems were, as scholars have argued, predicated on clear and fixed differentiation between the sexes, then the pubescent voice—unpredictably modulating between (female) squeakiness and (male) gravity—

not only upset binary gender systems but the logic and operation of early modern patriarchy itself.[20]

The social significance of the voice and the theatrical production of gender difference have been examined as separate issues in feminist scholarship, but the relations between the two have rarely been discussed. Moreover, prominent work on each of these topics has been focused, in the first case, primarily on women's bodies and, in the second case, on spectatorship and visual practice.[21] One key exception is Dympna Callaghan's essay on the transvestite stage, in which she examines how representations of men's failure to control the voice can be read as attempts to grapple with the fraught process of sexual differentiation. Callaghan notes the practice of castration in barber surgeon houses that were located near the theaters, and she calls attention to the difference between the castrati of the Continent, whose vocal states are virtually fixed by surgery, and the prepubescent boys of the English stage, whose voices, subject to maturation, have the propensity to crack at any time. For Callaghan, the quality of the stage performer's voice is ultimately symptomatic of the "presence or lack of male genital sexual equipment."[22] To be sure, male genitalia feature prominently in early modern assessments of the voice and its relation to gender. The production of voice and its relation to gender identity, however, were also thought to be influenced by and to have implications for less localized bodily processes. As I have already noted, early modern humoral physiology explains gender differences in voice as a function of the body's heat level, which affects the size of the windpipe. Although texts associate increasing heat with the development of sexual organ function (the production of sperm), the presence or absence of these sexual organs is not the sole determinant of gender difference. Often putting genitalia aside, early modern texts present the cracking, squeaking voice as indexical of a body in flux, always in transition. If the voice is a signifier of gender identity, then the squeaking, cracking voice that betrays the liminal state of the male body also disturbs the stable functioning of gender categories.[23]

To contextualize my reading of the place of voice in theatrical representations of masculinity, this chapter begins by surveying late sixteenth- and early seventeenth-century writings on vocal training and performance. I closely examine one text partly devoted to voice instruction for boys, Richard Mulcaster's *Positions Concerning the Training Up of Children* (1581).[24] Written by a pedagogue whose theories of voice find their basis in Galenic humoral theory, Mulcaster's treatise can be read in dialogue with contemporaneous medical texts that address the precariousness of young male voices in similar terms. Furthermore, as it is authored by a theater professional, Mulcaster's text helps define the nature of vocal crises that arise on the early modern stage. With such vocal training in mind, I then examine several early modern plays for their thematization of cracking and squeaking male voices. First, through an analysis of plays by adult companies that feature roguish youths—significantly termed "cracks" in colloquial early modern English—I investigate how boys, through their association with the cracking voice, underscore the vagaries of masculinity and the challenges of its performance by male actors. These challenges are thematized even more explicitly in plays in which boys are responsible for performing the parts of both youths and adult men, the subject of the final segment of the chapter. In an extended reading of John Marston's *Antonio and Mellida*, I argue that the play grapples with the fraught vocal dynamics of the professional stage, self-consciously enacting the challenges of taming unruly boys' voices.[25] In *Antonio and Mellida* the physiologically unstable voice of the male actor is a persistent subtext in a drama that defines masculinity as, in part, the ability to control one's voice. Listening for the tension between the narrative action and the realities of its dramatization in the theater, I examine the ideological implications of vocal instability for the play's representations of masculinity.

"Pathetical Rosin" and Mulcaster's Boys

When early modern writers reflect on the workings of the human vocal system, they often compare it to a musical instrument that can produce fine sounds when played properly. The analogy is especially pervasive in the period's drama. In Ben Jonson's *Poetaster*, the ineloquent tongue is described not as naturally and permanently dissonant but as "untuned."[26] In Marston's *Antonio's Revenge*, a cough provides a "most pathetical rosin" for the voice, much as rosin on a bow helps the viol's strings produce a clear sound (3.3.41–42). And in *Antonio and Mellida*, the companion play to *Antonio's Revenge*, a melancholic lover requests a song of a page, whom the lover compares to a musical instrument:

Let each note breathe the heart of passion,
The sad extracture of extremest grief.
Make me a strain; speak groaning like a bell

That tolls departing souls.
Breathe me a point that may enforce me weep. (4.1.132–36)

Though the commissioned singer may be like a bell, his human body and
the sound it produces differ from this inanimate instrument and its sounds
in significant ways. First, the material form of the young singer's music is
breath; it is the breathing of notes that will enable this body-instrument to
provoke weeping in the listener. Although instrumental music is capable of
influencing listeners' emotions, the sounds produced by the human body
are particularly potent insofar as human breath is, according to some early
modern writers, a transporter of the soul, something I'll discuss further in
Chapter 2.[27]

But breath can only have these effects if it departs successfully from the
body, carrying the harmonious voice with it. And such success, for many
early modern writers, could not be taken for granted. A second difference
writers note between vocal and instrumental sound is the material properties of the bodies that produce them. If one repeatedly strikes a bell made,
say, of bronze or tin with the same force, in exactly the same place, and using
the same baton, the bell will produce the same sound each time. The human
body, however, is not so predictable. If the vocal cords or larynx has developed even minor irritations, the voice can emerge hoarse or raspy. Indeed,
in making his musical request, the melancholic lover quoted above adds,
"Thou hast had a good voice, if this cold marsh / Wherein we lurk have not
corrupted it" (4.1.128–30). The lover has heard the page's fine voice but
knows that a "good voice" cannot be expected on every occasion. Because
early modern humoral theory understood the body to be in a state of con-
tinual flux between cold and hot, moist and dry, an excess of coldness, such
as that of the marsh, might allow a surplus of phlegm to accumulate on the
larynx, corrupting the movement of the breath that carries vocal sound and
preventing a "good voice" from emerging. This is not to say that an inanimate bell could not develop an "irritation"—it might fall from its tower and
fracture. But alterations to the human vocal organs were considered more
difficult to diagnose and more unpredictable in their development, given
the complicated physiology thought to underlie them.

Despite the fact that the voice was often figured in physiological terms
as unruly and resistant to training, or perhaps because of it, early modern
writers interested in vocal instruction overwhelmingly insisted on its need
to be disciplined.[28] Texts regarding oratory, for instance, emphasize the bod-

ily control essential to proper vocalization. Describing the way the voice's volume, "Loud or soft" can be adjusted, Charles Butler's *The English Grammar* (1633) points to "the natural and ordinari force of each voice: which is to bee strained, or slacked."²⁹ Robert Robinson's *The Art of Pronunciation* (1617) explains in detail how the physiological processes of vocal articulation are an exercise in discipline:

A sound is an accident effected by the opposition of these two contraries, namely motion and restraint: motion of the ayre out of the inward parts of the body, and restraint of it in its motion. . . . *Of the instrumentall causes of this motion.* They are the lungs and hollow parts of the body, wherein the ayre is contained, which being drawne together by the motion, or rather the will of the mind, doe thereby expell the ayre, and cause it to be mooved through divers passages, as the throat, mouth, and nostrils. *Of the instrumentall causes of the restraint of this motion.* They are the breast, throat, pallat, gums, tongue, lips and nostrils, stopping or hindering the free passage of the ayre in it's [*sic*] motion.³⁰

For sound to result, there must be a flow of air, of breath, from the lungs, through and out of the body cavity. But, Robinson's tract explains, the art of speech—of producing sounds that will be comprehensible within a system of signification—involves applying measured "restraint" on this flow of air. The loci of such constraint are the various bodily organs used in vocalization. Robinson's manual is devoted to teaching the reader how to shape the oral cavity—how to purse the lips, hold the teeth, and organize the tongue so as to achieve the desired vocal sound. Speech, in effect, is sound that has been disciplined by the body.

Discipline is also central to the way early modern music theorists describe skillful vocal practice. The preface to John Playford's *A Brief Introduction to the Skill of Musick* (1658) explains that grammar and music are taught "for the ordering their Voyce in Speech and Song; meerely to Speak and Sing are of Nature, and this double use of the Articulate voyce the Rudest Swains of all Nations do make. But to Speak well, and Sing well, are of Art, neither of which can be attained but by the Rules and Precepts of Art."³¹ Anyone can produce sounds using the voice, but ordered sound—the art of singing and speaking—can only be created by the restrained vocalizer. Though published in 1658, Playford's passage concerning the difficulty of "ordering" the voice shares much in common with the writings of voice pedagogues publishing earlier in the seventeenth century, during the heyday of the English professional theater. The preface to Charles Butler's *The Principles of Musick* (1636) discusses the need to build vocal skills because of the vagaries of singing—"the many Accidents of the Notes, the sudden changing, or rising and falling, of the voice."[32] According to musician John Dowland, who translated Guido d'Arezzo's introduction to singing in 1609, singers must carefully limit the degree to which their voices rise and fall. For instance, there is a "naturall compasse of mans voice, which going above this, is rather a squeaking; and going under, is rather a humming than a *Voyce*."[33] The ancients, Dowland explains, call this "disdiapason," and it is figured mathematically by a "quadruple proportion."[34] When vocal performers attempt to exceed their voice's "naturall compasse," the squeak or hum they produce violates the rules of "sence" as well as "reason."[35]

Although the aesthetics of sound—that which appeals to the senses—is commensurate with the body's "naturall" disposition, the body must, paradoxically, learn to cultivate such an ordered voice through training. Dowland explains, for instance, that the tendency of most vocal performers is to articulate with too much fervor, loosening constraints in order to produce a forceful voice. But Dowland cautions, "Let a Singer take heed, least he begin too loud braying like an Asse, or when he hath begun with an uneven height, disgrace the Song. . . . [I]t is not . . . the noyse of the lips, but the ardent desire of the Art, which like the lowdest voice doth pierce Gods eares."[36] Measured control over the voice, not unbridled expression, will be effective aesthetically and spiritually. Corroborating Schoenfeldt's argument about the emancipatory benefits of self-regulation, music theorists of the period present vocal discipline not as uncomfortable or restrictive, but pleasurable—a fulfillment of the voice's potential for order and spiritual harmony. Indeed, it is when singers liberate the voice without regard to the "rules" of vocalization that their voices hum and squeak dissonantly.

Similar claims about the restraint essential for effective and satisfying vocal performance appear in Mulcaster's *Positions*. In this treatise on children's education, Mulcaster lays out an extensive program for the conditioning of children's voices, a program he claims will benefit children's mental acuity in addition to their physiological well-being. Mulcaster's text is especially useful in the context of an account of vocal performance on the stage, for Mulcaster had an intimate connection with the theater industry. A preeminent educator in late sixteenth- and early seventeenth-century England, Mulcaster served as the master of the Merchant Taylors' school for twenty-five years (1561–85) and as the high master of St. Paul's School for a decade (1596–1608). In those capacities, he supervised the education of boys who would later contribute in important ways to the English theater: writer Thomas Lodge, dramatist Thomas Kyd, and actor and playwright Nathan Field. As the director of a boys' company, Mulcaster was also directly responsible for theatrical productions. In the latter half of the sixteenth century, when children's companies were receiving tremendous favor at court, Mulcaster's students from the Merchant Taylors' school performed for Queen Elizabeth on at least six occasions.[37] And some theater historians suggest that when Mulcaster changed jobs later in his career and took on leadership of St. Paul's School around the turn of the century (1596), he might have helped revive the Children of Paul's, a company that, after a hiatus from the records, returned to popular status during the first decade of the seventeenth century.[38] To his contemporaries, then, Mulcaster was known for his skill in coaching young boys in the classroom and for the stage.[39] His dual interests are evident in his first major publication, *Positions*. Although scholars have tended to use the treatise to discuss Mulcaster's ideas about school curricula, the text also deals with performance-related matters, helping to map out some of the central issues at stake in a history of the voice.[40] Specifically, *Positions* reminds us that the young male voices so important to early modern performance were understood in the period to be highly precarious and vulnerable to unpredictable alterations in character.

Mulcaster's theater experience seems to seep into the educational program he presents in *Positions*. Dancing, wrestling, walking, and running—all activities that, according to stage directions that appear in plays, would have had some place on the stage[41]—are among the nineteen exercises Mulcaster includes in his physical fitness program. Mulcaster is especially preoccupied with the fitness of children's voices, and he offers theories on and practical pointers for disciplining children's unruly vocal systems. Citing the practices promoted by ancient medical writers like Galen and early rhetoricians such as Quintillian,[42] Mulcaster's treatise urges supervised vocal exercise for all boys, and even for girls—though he much more carefully spells out the dangers of exercise where the "more weake" female body is concerned (176). One of the exercises he prescribes is modeled after an ancient oratory practice called vociferation. The exercise involves the orator slowly and carefully increasing the volume and pitch of the voice, playing with its range, and then softening and deepening it: They "first beg[a]n lowe, and moderatly, then went on to further strayning, of their speeche: sometimes drawing it out, with as stayed, and grave soundes, as was possible, sometimes bringing it backe, to the sharpest and shrillest, that they could, afterward not tarying long in that shrill sound, they retired backe again, slacking the straine of their voice, till they fell into that low, and moderate tenour, wherwith they first began" (58). Like pedagogues Robinson and Butler, Mulcaster explains voluntary shifts in the character of the voice as resulting from the vocalizer's restraint: "strayning, of their speeche," "slacking the straine of their voice."

This language of discipline has cognates in early modern physiology. Sixteenth- and seventeenth-century medical writers conceive of vocal characteristics—such as pitch and volume—as a function of the size of the vocal organs, which can be manipulated to some extent by "strayning" and "slacking." Nicholas Culpeper's translation of Johann Vesling's *Anatomy of the Body of Man* (1653) explains how organ size and vocal quality are related: "[T]he larger the *Larynx* is, the larger is the *Glottis*, and as that is larger, so the Voyce is stronger and graver: The lesser . . . and narrower the *Larynx* is, the weaker, and shriller is the Voyce."[43] Anatomist Helkiah Crooke points out in *Mikrokosmographia: A Description of the Body of Man* (1615) that the very structure of the vocal organs allows for their manipulation; the intersecting layers of gristle that make up the larynx, for instance, accommodate our "voluntary command" over constriction and expansion of the organ.[44] The movable vocal organs produce an array of sounds when they are pushed, pulled, slackened, and strained, much like the strings of a viol. Of course, manipulation has limits; to a significant degree, the body's age and sex determine the minimum and maximum size of its organs. According to most early modern anatomists, the vocal organs of Mulcaster's prepubescent boys would have looked like those of women, and they would have been disposed toward producing a similar high-pitched, softer sound. Mulcaster's loud speaking exercise requires the young pupil to alter voluntarily the size of the vocal instruments as much as possible in order to experiment with range.

In addition to instructing the pupil in pitch and projection, exercises improve the overall quality or timbre of the voice by ridding the vocal organs of superfluous debris. Following Galenic physiology, Mulcaster writes that a clear voice results when the "sundry superfluities" that "darkened, weakned, and thickned the naturall heat" are "dismissed [from the body]" (56). Culpeper elucidates the relation between "superfluities" and vocal sound in further physiological detail: if the membrane covering the windpipe is "rough with flegm, the voice is hoarse."[45] This physiological process is especially important to Mulcaster, for his young male pupils, according to humoral theory, are naturally moist, and thus especially prone to accumulating too many "sundry superfluities."[46] Vocal exercises, by stimulating the larynx, vocal cords, windpipe, and lungs, increase the natural heat in these areas, allowing the body to dislodge superfluous phlegm. That speakers tend to expectorate when they talk is evidence, Mulcaster claims, that these humors are being expelled (56).

Because vocal exercises help regulate the body's humoral system, they not only improve the sound of the voice but simultaneously help the body maintain general levels of fitness. Excess moisture that remains on the vocal organs breeds disease, in addition to compromising the clarity of the voice. Because loud speaking exercises "encreaseth, cleanseth, strengtheneth, and fineth the naturall heat" (55), they can treat multiple somatic problems: "pewkishnesse of stomacke . . . vomiting . . . hardnesse of digestion . . . faintnesse . . . naughty constitution . . . painfull fetching their breath" (56), to name only a few. Mulcaster cites other "indoor" exercises that, operating under the same humoral principles, have similar benefits—benefits that Mulcaster could observe for himself, since these "indoor" exercise were a regular feature of the plays his pupils staged. Loud singing, for instance, "sturreth the voice, spreadeth the instruments thereof, and craveth a cleare passage" (59). An excellent cure for digestive ailments and headaches is the exercise of loud reading (60–61), discussed separately from loud speaking. Soft reading, though it works much less efficiently than does loud reading on the same parts, has the benefit of being sanctioned for practice directly after the pupil eats; loud reading after meals can interfere with digestion, and thus should be avoided (61). Talking, or *sermo*, remedies drowsiness (62). Cold heads and chests can be warmed up by the exercise of laughing, and further salutary benefits result from holding one's breath and weeping (63–71).[47]

Mulcaster's modern editor, William Barker, remarks that these exercises likely strike today's readers as "unusual, even ridiculous."[48] But these methods for loosening the humors in the throat and windpipe are less peculiar when we consider their historical company. For instance, Ann Brumwick's manuscript collection of home remedies offers a much more curious cure "for dispersing any humour gathered to the Thorat [*sic*] or for any soarnes in the same."[49] This involves blending dog dung with various organic powders, stuffing the mixture into a tobacco pipe, and then blowing the pipe into the patient's throat two or three times a day. As the patient is instructed not to eat or drink for an hour after the treatment, it seems clear that the purpose is to provoke coughing, a stimulation of the lungs, throat, larynx, and windpipe, so as to achieve effects similar to the ones Mulcaster describes.

That recipe books are filled with treatments to dislodge excess humors from the vocal instruments suggests that vocal production generated anxiety for many early modern men and women and merited creative forms of attention. The kinds of patients who might use these cures are rarely mentioned, but it seems obvious that those who depended on healthy voices for their livelihoods would have been especially attentive to the functioning of their vocal organs. Though Mulcaster does not explicitly mention the benefits of vocal exercises for the voices of his performing children's troupe, such exercises certainly would have been useful for warming up boys' voices before a play or concert. In fact, the original function of these exercises, as they were developed by ancient rhetoricians, was to prepare the voice for oratory competition and performance. Given Mulcaster's interest in training his pupils to perform at court and before a paying public, he knew the importance of voice to the success of a dramatic production. As a director of children, he would have been especially sensitive to the exertions of playing on a young voice: less physically mature boys would likely have had to strain their voices in order to be heard in noisy theaters, an action that could have detrimental long-term effects on their vocal instruments.

It is impossible to know how or even if Mulcaster put into practice his vocal exercise program. Perhaps these exercises were only part of a utopian physical fitness program created by a pedagogue who never practiced on the stage what he preached on the page. How useful is Mulcaster's text, then, to the study of the early modern theatrical experience? I would suggest that it is highly useful, not necessarily to establish proof of particular stage practices—such as whether Mulcaster's boys actually trained with vociferation exercises—but in order to consider cultural attitudes toward vocal training and performance and to theorize the ideological implications of these attitudes. Before drawing out these implications, I would like to pause and consider what is at stake for theater history and performance studies in my proposed analysis of Mulcaster's text, remarks that pertain as well to my analysis of nondramatic works throughout this book.

Theater history scholarship, notes William Ingram, often has been characterized by positivist approaches to evidence: the use of archival documents to write conclusive, event-centered narratives about the past.[50] One long-standing debate about vocal practices in the theater, for instance, has concerned which kinds of speaking styles were used by children's companies. Scholars who argue that the style was declamatory have claimed as evidence records of a strong relationship between stage acting and oratorical training, citing rhetoric manuals that taught boy actors how to modulate their voices during stylized oratorical address. Those who maintain that boys' delivery style was more "natural" advance as proof passages in city comedies or other plays written in colloquial language.[51] Of course, no matter what we include as evidence or how we integrate it, we cannot know what early modern listeners heard in the theaters or how they reacted to what they heard.[52] Though Mulcaster's text is not an accurate reflection of "how it was" and cannot with any certainty increase our knowledge of specific theatrical customs, it does help us consider what is at stake in early modern representations of vocalization as a material practice. In using Mulcaster's text to theorize early modern attitudes toward vocal performance, I extend the insights Mark Franko and Annette Richards offer regarding historical performance studies: they urge the performance critic to "reconfigure the epistemological status of the past as a theoretical activity of the present (or of other, subsequent past times) that becomes actual in and as critical performances."[53] Mulcaster's writings, like many of the early modern nontheatrical writings I discuss in this book, provide not simply an historical "context" to facilitate the contemporary critic's reading of drama; they constitute "theoretical activity," elucidating for the modern critic how the pressures of bodily control heighten the stakes of a vocal performance. What Mulcaster's pedagogical treatise shares with Ann Brumwick's recipe book and Culpeper's and Crooke's anatomical tracts is a view of human vocal organs as fragile and vulnerable to malfunction, a crucial observation for any history of the stage.

The frailty of vocal instruments is most evident in Mulcaster's repeated warnings about the dangers of overstimulating the vocal organs; too much agitation "hurtes the voice" in addition to helping it. In fact, the more effective an exercise is in removing bodily humors that breed disease, the greater the risks that the exercise will create further problems, not only for the vocal instruments but for other areas of the body. For instance, the exercise of vociferation "filleth the head and makes it heavie"; it "causeth the temples [to] pante, the braines to beate, the eyes to swell, the eares to tingle" (57). The very processes that underlie the success of vocal exercises account for their dangers: the "chafing of the breath, and the breath instruments" in loud speaking "disperpleth [disperses], and scattereth corrupt humours, thorough out the whole bodie" (57).

These dangers become even more pronounced when vocal exercises are practiced by young boys, who at the age of puberty experience a major shift in body temperament. As indicated above, an increase in heat is responsible for the comparatively graver and louder voice that mature men possess, for the influx of heat causes the vocal organs to expand, indeed to crack. Arviragus in Shakespeare's *Cymbeline* observes that a voice that has "got the mannish crack" (4.2.237) can still be manipulated to produce a range of sounds, but these sounds cannot always be carefully controlled. Guiderius's response to his brother's bid to sing captures this sense of the pubescent voice as unmanageable. He tells his brother that he'd prefer to speak, not sing, his eulogy, for "notes of sorrow out of tune" (4.2.242) would disgrace Fidele's memory. It is not clear from Guiderius's remark whether the notes would be untuned because of his weeping or, since this comment directly follows his brother's, because his voice has "got the mannish crack." The ambiguity underscores that what is at stake in the youths' singing is the degree to which they can manage their voices. Once they achieve mature manhood, the scene implies, Guiderius and Arviragus would have the capacity for physiological *and* emotional control, both of which would be manifested not in a deep or loud but a stable, manageable voice.

This complete alteration in a boy's vocal sound does not happen overnight, however. Because puberty involves a gradual metamorphosis of the body, the pubescent boy's voice has an unpredictable pattern of change. A high pitch impossible to sing one morning may again be in reach that very afternoon. The precarious state of boys' bodies is the basis for countless stage jokes about the cracked and squeaking male voice. As Firk in Thomas Dekker's *Shoemaker's Holiday* sings a round of "*Hey down a-down derry*," he apologizes for the "squeaks" of his "organ-pipe," claiming it needs "liquoring."[54] And, of course, there is Hamlet's oft-discussed address to the itinerant playing company that visits the palace. Turning to the young boy brought to play the women's parts, Hamlet gently mocks: "What, my young lady and mistress. By'r Lady, your ladyship is nearer heaven than when I saw you last by the altitude of a chopine. Pray God your voice, like a piece of uncurrent gold, be not cracked within the ring" (2.2.408–11). The boy's growth in "altitude," or height and age, Hamlet hopes, has not been accompanied by a growth in his vocal organs, which might compromise his ability to play the part of the lady.

In its gloss of Hamlet's imagery, the *Riverside Shakespeare* compares the actor's voice to a cracked ring: "a coin with a crack extending far enough in from the edge to cross the circle surrounding the stamp of the sovereign's head was unacceptable in exchange (*uncurrent*)."[55] Hamlet hopes, in other words, that the boy's voice is not cracked and, like a ruined coin, unusable as currency. Smith appreciates the physiological emphasis of this line, arguing that "ring" also puns on the shape of the actor's windpipe, a round organ that cracks as it expands during puberty, changing the boy's vocal range.[56] At least one other play from the period, Thomas Dekker's *Honest Whore*, Part I (1604) substantiates Smith's reading of the image's physiological resonances. When Viola struggles to prevent her brother Fustigo from taking a ring from her finger, his response to her employs a similar pun on ring: "I ha sworne Ile ha't [have the ring], and I hope you wil not let my o[a]thes be cracktin the ring, wil you?"[57] Viola's resistance to Fustigo's theft may crack the ring on her finger, and, insofar as she prevents him from fulfilling the oaths he has voiced (to "ha't," [have it]) she may also cause a crack in the "ring" that produced his oaths, his windpipe.

With the physiological implications of the ring pun in mind, the *Riverside* gloss on *Hamlet* and boy actors' voices requires nuancing. Like a coin, the boy's voice becomes "uncurrent" only when its crack reaches a certain point—when it is "cracked within the ring." If the boy's voice is still in the early stages of changing, the boy may still be able to play the part of the lady; the partially matured voice, while it may portend an end to a boy's performance career, does not insist on its immediate demise. As the partially cracked coin has market value in spite of its degraded appearance, the boy's aesthetically unpleasant, squeaking voice may have purchase power in the theater. Hamlet's comments suggest that only when the voice is fully cracked will the theater consider it "uncurrent."

When Hamlet compares this cracked voice to "a piece of uncurrent gold," he nevertheless reminds us of the value the early modern theater placed on boys' voices. Whether boys were so precious because they could approximate women's vocal sound on the all-male stage or because they had often been trained as choristers and could sing beautifully, the voice was part of a boy's "currency" in the theater, and a fully broken voice altered a boy's worth in ways that we can never entirely know. Given the organizational and financial variables at issue, it must have been disconcerting that, in physiological terms, the rate of a boy's vocal growth was not easily predictable. Hamlet's speech suggests that a boy's height and age are not inherently linked to a particular stage in vocal development, and Mulcaster concurs when he writes that "ripenes in children, is not tyed to one time" (19). The precariousness of boys' voices likely made the jobs of directors like Mulcaster difficult indeed. Perhaps in rehearsals the boy playing Cleopatra had been able to use his uncracked or partially cracked voice to deliver in a shrill pitch the line "I shall see / Some squeaking Cleopatra boy my greatness" (*Antony and Cleopatra* 5.2.215–16). But within a day, that range could exceed the actor's bodily capabilities, perhaps damaging his fragile vocal organs, or at least provoking laughter from the audience at the tragic climax of the play. The director of an all-boy theater company was, in a very real sense, playing with creatures of time. Regardless of what the theater did with boys whose voices had cracked completely, we must account for the possibility that boys in vocal limbo were a presence onstage.

Cracks "not tyed to one time": Becoming Manly

The presence of cracking voices on the stage had the potential to be not only an aesthetic but also an ideological liability; for the cracked voice, as it evinces a body in transition, reveals the precarious, shifting nature of male identity. Early modern commentators consider adolescence and youth— terms that were sometimes conflated, sometimes distinct—the most unpredictable times in life, which is divided into a set of stages that separate birth and death.[58] Movement from one phase to the next was marked, and arguably even constituted, by certain cultural practices. For instance, once infants had been weaned (around age three), they were considered to have proceeded into childhood. Around age seven children's dress became sex specific, with male children "breeched," or made to wear doublets and hose, as they entered boyhood. Between boyhood and manhood, which usually coincided with marriage, was a phase of "youth" during which time male children were sent outside the home to begin working and/or receiving an education and training to prepare them to work.[59] As Smith points out in his insightful analysis of this process of male maturation, "youths between the ages of 10 and 23 occupied a precarious position in the social order."[60] They were no longer boys and thus expected to demonstrate independence, but they were not yet men and thus were still controlled by parents or parentlike masters (at school or, in the case of apprentices, on the job). Youths occupied a precarious position in the physiological order as well. Since a youth's progression to manliness, from the perspective of Galenic humoralism, was thought to involve a heating up of the body, this progression was considered a temporally inflected process over which emerging men had no control. Early modern youths, in effect, floated physiologically and socially in an unsteady limbo of youth, their maturation, as Mulcaster would say, "not tyed to one time."

The liminality of youth, with all its attendant anxieties, registers itself in compelling physical terms through the cracking of the pubescent male voice. As is implied by the definition of term "crack"—a partial fracture, not a full breakage[61]—a youth with a cracked voice treads the line between boyhood and manhood. His voice, wavering between childish and manly sound, evinces his status as partly both and completely neither category of male identity. In particular if part of what makes a man a man in early modern England is the controlled quality of his voice, then youths, whose vocal quality can change from day to day, even minute to minute, serve as material reminders of the impossible ideals of vocal control that adult men are pressured to meet. Squeaky-voiced youths underscore that male identity, as Judith Butler argues about gender identities more generally, is established through iterations and performances of normative gender codes.[62] Male youths reveal the extent to which manhood is not a given or an essence, but a state of becoming, and a precarious one at that.[63] In a patriarchal culture that relied upon clear differentiation of the sexes in order to maintain social and political hierarchies, pubescent boys thus become the repositories and the instigators of social and political anxieties. When early modern writers use the term "crack" to describe the voice changes that accompany puberty, they draw attention to the temporal contingencies of masculinity and underscore the challenges that boys as well as men face in performing manliness.

The ideological and the aesthetic converged in early modern English theaters. Because the commercial theater industry relied on pubescent boys for the production of plays, it continuously produced the conditions for ideological discomfort about male identity. How did the stage cope with the squeaking boys' voices that were a persistent feature of its industry? It would seem they coped by making the cracking voice a subject of dramatic investigation as well as humor, by staging again and again the unchoreographable, squeaking voice. In other words, many plays attempt to convert the liability of boy actors' voices into a resource. In the next section, we shall examine how children's acting companies—in which, as one might expect, there was an especially significant dramatic focus on the cracking, squeaking voice—exploited for theatrical effect boys' vocal vulnerability. But allusions to cracking voices appear in plays by adult companies as well, including especially the plays of Shakespeare, where youth—that liminal period of transition between boyhood and manhood—is the most frequently dramatized of the stages of men's lives.[64]

Notably, allusions—both direct and indirect—to cracked and squeaking voices appear in plays precisely at the moment when a play is commenting on a character's purchase on masculinity. For instance, Arviragus's assessment of his and his brother's voices as having "got the mannish crack" appears during a scene in which the young men struggle to find an appropriate masculine mode for grieving over the loss of Fidele. The brothers, occupying that phase of life between boyhood and manhood, gravitate toward contrasting views about the appropriate masculine response to Fidele's death. When Arviragus eulogizes Fidele through poetry, placing flowers upon the youth's grave in a speech that resonates with *Hamlet*'s Ophelia's, his brother interrupts him and derides the eulogy as effeminate and childish: "Prithee, have done, / And do not play in wench-like words with that / Which is so serious" (4.2.230–32). It is a time for action—"To th' grave!" (4.2.234)—not mere words. But the grieving Arviragus is less capable of distinguishing the effeminate child's "play" of grief from the man's "serious" work of burial and asks that his brother Guiderius (known to him as Polydore) join him in singing a dirge they once sung as boys over the grave of their mother, Euriphiles:

And let us, Polydore, though now our voices
Have got the mannish crack, sing him to th' ground
As once to our mother; use like note and words,
Save that "Euriphile" must be "Fidele." (4.2.236–39)

Not only does Arviragus persist in grieving through "wench-like words," but he also wishes to grieve with the same sounds—"like note and words"—that he and his brother used when grieving as children for their mother. Using the cracked voice as a symbol of the temporally protracted process of development, the play meditates on a larger tension between boyish "play" and "serious" or mature manliness. Whereas Arviragus blurs these states, singing through the serious work of the burial, his brother anxiously insists upon a clear differentiation between boy and man.

The cracked voice is such a potent symbol of the blurring of boyish and manly masculinity—and concomitant anxieties about that blurring—that some early modern plays refer to pubescent boys simply as "cracks." Defining "crack" as "a lively lad, a 'rogue' (playfully), a wag," the *Oxford English Dictionary* editors are unclear about the genesis of the term. Noting variations "crack-rope" and "crack-halter," they propose a connection to hanging: "cracks" are troublemakers who barely escaped the noose when the rope broke or "cracked."[65] I would suggest, however, that "crack" and its variants also draw on a connection between youthful wags and the uncontrollable voice. Although the *OED* supposition concerning hanging is credible given that "rope" and "halter" can refer to hanging implements, both terms were also used in the sixteenth and seventeenth centuries to refer to the utterances a youth might make. Rope could be "used in angry exclamations" or be "an allusive or derisive cry"; and halter can refer to "one who wavers"[66]—perhaps, in the case of "crack-halter," referring to one whose cracked voice wavers. The connection to uncontrollable, young male voices also helps make sense of the fact that "crack" is used only to refer to young men rather than any troublemakers. When read in light of the ideological significance of squeaky male voices, allusions in plays to boys as "cracks" can shed light on the ways in which plays are grappling with the precarious and performative process of gender-identity formation.

A brief example from Ben Jonson's *Cynthia's Revels* (1601) demonstrates the representational crisis afforded by metatheatrical references to boys as "cracks." Mercury and Cupid, roguish youths played by boy actors, enter in act 2 discussing how they will successfully inhabit the role of pages (the disguises they have chosen for their prank). Mercury emphasizes that the successful representation of a "crack" page involves mimicry, especially of his voice: "since we are turned cracks, let's study to be like cracks; practise their language and behaviours, and not with a dead imitation: act freely, carelessly, and capriciously, as if our veins ran with quicksilver, and not utter a phrase but what shall come forth steeped in the very brine of conceit, and sparkle like salt in fire."[67] For Mercury and Cupid to be convincing in their disguise as pages, their oral mimicry must be so seamless that it will not sound like a "dead imitation." Their utterances should seem naturally "capricious," like that of real pages. There is an interesting tautology in Mercury's assessment that since they have "turned cracks," they should now "study to be like cracks." On one level, Mercury—whose very name encapsulates the mercurial, shifting nature of childhood[68]—suggests that since they have now assumed the role of cracks, then they must learn to play that role effectively. But at the same time, the remark suggests that when boys have "turned cracks," their performances of identity, like those of the adult men they begin to approximate, become more self-conscious, more practiced and studied.

The *OED* credits Shakespeare with the first usage of "crack" as a waggish youth, but Thomas Heywood includes the term as early as 1588 in his play, *The Second Part of, If You Know Not Me, You Know No Bodie* (published 1606), when Apprentice 1 refers repeatedly to Apprentice 2 as "fellow Crack."[69] In Heywood's play, as in others of the period, the appellation "crack" signals a fellowship shared by male youths—a camaraderie usually cemented through roguish behavior, for which apprentices were renowned on and off the stage. Although apprentices' street fights and tavern brawls were a nuisance to many moralizing commentators, the dramatic representation of apprentices—in a range of plays from Dekker's *Shoemaker's Holiday* to Heywood's *If You Know Not Me*—suggests that such "harmless" youth violence was to some extent excused in the popular imagination, much as many in our modern day dismiss young men's "harmless" violence with the caveat that "boys will be boys."

It is precisely in this vein that Shallow in *2 Henry IV* remembers the young Falstaff as a "crack." Waxing nostalgic about his student days at the Inns of Court, when he was called "lusty Shallow," Shallow muses:

By the mass, I was called anything; and I would have done anything indeed, too, and roundly, too. There was I, and little John Doit of Staffordshire, and black George Barnes, and Francis Pickbone, and Will Squeal, a Cotswold man; you had not four such swinge-bucklers in all the Inns o' Court again. And I may say to you, we knew where the bona-robas were, and had the best of them all at commandment. Then was Jack Falstaff, now Sir John, a boy . . . I see him break Scoggin's head at the court gate when a was a crack, not thus high. And the very same day did I fight with one Samson Stockfish, a fruiterer, behind Gray's Inn. Jesu, Jesu, the mad days that I have spent! And to see how many of my old acquaintance are dead. (3.2.15–31)

I quote Shallow's speech at length because I want to attend to the context in which Shallow refers to young Falstaff as a "crack." Recalling his mates by name and celebrating their triumph as the greatest "swinge-bucklers" in the history of the Inns of Court, Shallow chuckles at the memory of seeing young Falstaff "break Scoggin's head." He intimates that Falstaff's boyish tussle mimicked the masculine brawls of Shallow and his fellow "swinge-bucklers" at the Inns of Court, a connection underscored by the recollection that on this "very same day," Shallow engaged in a scuffle of his own. Notably, Shallow calls young Falstaff a "crack" at the moment when he is recognizing, but also attempting to challenge, a similarity between men and boys, whose mimicry of manly masculinity, I would suggest, threatens to expose the latter as childish "play." Certainly Shallow seems oddly compelled to reiterate the success of his own violent brawl, as if to confirm to himself and his audience that the "crack" who could "break Scoggin's head" was not in the same league as the "swinge-bucklers" who ruled the school. That this rhapsody on boys playing like men is tinged with some anxiety for Shallow is evident in his concluding meditations on his current purchase on masculinity. Shallow admits he is no longer the rapscallion who raised a ruckus with his fellows, many of whom have died, and he laments not only his comrades'—and, inevitably, his own—passing from life, but the related passing of youthful male camaraderie. Shallow's aging body would have been understood in this period as going through a virtual reversal of puberty: according to Jacques's famous description of the ages of man's life, Shallow is currently at a phase when his "big, manly voice" is or soon will be "[t]urning again toward childish treble, pipes / And whistles in his sound" (*As You Like It* 2.7.160–62). With age the man's voice not only becomes smaller and higher in pitch ("childish treble"), but also exhibits shakiness and other aural impurities, like "whistles in his sound." As Arviragus and his brother battle with the temporality of masculinity through discussion about the proper manly expression of grief, Shallow struggles with the same issues by reflecting on the proper manly exercise of violence. In both scenes a youth's cracked voice—represented both directly and indirectly—operates as an aural signifier of an uncontrollable body and thus a point of focus for concerns about performing a masculinity that is temporally shifting and imprecise.

The reference to a boy as a "crack" serves a similar role in the beginning of *Coriolanus*, helping to set up the play's dramatization of Coriolanus's anxieties about performing his masculinity. As in Shallow's speech, the reference in *Coriolanus* to a boy as a "crack" appears at a moment in the play when adult male masculinity is being defined against boyish masculinity. Seminal feminist work on the play has interpreted 1.3 as offering crucial observations about Coriolanus's relationship with his mother, a central relationship for the play's overall reflections on masculinity.[70] Less prominently discussed but equally important to understanding the central conflicts of the play is the scene's invocation of Coriolanus's son Martius. When the scene opens, Volumnia is chastising Coriolanus's wife Virgilia for not being supportive enough of her husband's military engagements. Whereas Virgilia frets about Coriolanus's loss of blood, Volumnia famously champions her son's injuries, exclaiming that she derives great honor from her son's valor, whether he comes home alive or dead. In fact, Volumnia maintains, she has encouraged her son's pursuit of martial valor from the earliest age at which she could send him to war: "When yet he was but tenderbodied and the only son of my womb, when youth with comeliness plucked all gaze his way . . . [I] was pleased to let him seek danger where he was like to find fame. To a cruel war I sent him, from whence he returned, his brows bound with oak. I tell thee, daughter, I sprang not more in joy at first hearing he was a manchild than now in first seeing he had proved himself a man" (1.3.5–15). Volumnia relates how as soon as her son matured into "youth," she shipped him off to war to have him "prov'd . . . a man." Not given much time to dawdle in the limbo of the "man-child" phase of life, Coriolanus was encouraged to mature quickly into the man he continues to prove he is.

Whereas Volumnia forcefully moved her son out of the liminal "manchild" stage of "youth," her daughter-in-law Virgilia is less hasty with her progeny. In the second half of the scene, the women turn their attention away from Coriolanus's masculinity and toward that of his son, the young Martius, who, like little Jack Falstaff at the gates of the Inns of Court, has already begun to mimic the violent behavior that is an attribute of adult male masculinity. Young Martius already prefers to "see the swords and hear a drum than look upon his schoolmaster" (1.3.52–53). Valeria, a visiting friend, reports to Virgilia and Volumnia of her most recent vision of the young Martius chasing a butterfly, catching and releasing it "again, and over and over" (1.3.57–58). The culmination of the boy's innocent gaming, Valerie reports, was his capture and senseless destruction of the insect: "whether his fall enraged him, or how 'twas, he did so set his teeth and tear it! O, I warrant, how he mammocked it!" (59–61). Valeria, like Shallow, is amused by a boy's mimicry of adult violence: "O' my word, the father's son!" (54), she reflects. Like Volumnia, who celebrates young Martius's behavior as presaging his likelihood of following in his father's footsteps—"[o]ne on's father's moods" (62)—Valeria commends young Martius as a "noble child" (63). Martius's playful destruction of the butterfly is imagined as a parallel to his father's serious destruction of the Volscians—who will, Volumnia fantasizes, turn from their general "As children from a bear" (28) when they witness the mighty Coriolanus on the battlefield.

When Virgilia finally weighs in on this glorification of boyish violence, she offers a different perspective: young Martius's destruction of the butterfly denotes him not as "a noble child," but rather "A crack" (64). If "crack" is simply interpreted to mean rogue or rascal, as editors of the play have suggested, Virgilia could be viewed as joining in the women's approval of young male violence as proof of the tautology that boys who act like boys will grow up to be real men. But if "crack" is read as a reference to young Martius's pubescent male development, as I have been arguing, then Virgilia's remark that young Martius is not a boy but a *crack* reveals her apprehension about the broader significance of young Martius's precocious adult masculinity. Only moments earlier, Volumnia had contrasted her happy release of her "man-child" into battle with Virgilia's shameful failure to revel in her husband's military pursuits. The women's discussion of young Martius has implied that the boy has begun to show signs of becoming a "man-child," undoubtedly an issue of alarm for Virgilia, who is far less eager than Volumnia to have her son test his manly valor in war. Virgilia's characterization of her son as a "crack" indicates her resigned recognition that young Martius will, sooner than she hopes, follow his father's footsteps into battle. At the same time, unlike her mother-in-law, who encouraged her son to bypass youth, moving almost immediately from child to man, Virgilia holds onto the hope that her son's movement through youth, like the cracking of his voice, will take time.

Virgilia's reinterpretation of young Martius as a "crack" serves an even more disruptive purpose, however, in that it works (more quietly than her earlier debate with Volumnia) to devalue the adult male violence that Volumnia praises in young Martius's father. As young Falstaff's fighting threatens to expose the childishness of "swing-bucklers" who pick fights at the Inns of Court, the young Martius's game of killing insects on the playfield undermines the seriousness of Coriolanus's valiant work on the battlefield. When Volumnia and Valeria compare young Martius to his father, they emphasize the former as a "boy" and the latter as a man, thus attempting to distinguish carefully between young Martius's noble play and Coriolanus's real heroism. Yet Virgilia's reframing of young Martius as a "crack" situates him in the more liminal phase of youth, where the boundaries between boy and man are not so clear. If a comparison of father and son imparts a layer of seriousness to young Martius's boyish games—he is proving that he will follow his father's valiant example—it also may suggest that there is an element of play at the root of Coriolanus's manly behavior.

It is this element of play that Coriolanus stringently resists throughout the drama, to his detriment. One might argue, in fact, that Coriolanus's fail-

ure to accept his resemblance to his crack son, for whom masculinity is entirely "play," is what leads to the military hero's downfall. Like his mother—
who was so eager for him to overcome the liminal "boy-man" phase of life
that she sent him to war prematurely—Coriolanus has little tolerance for
the blurring of manly and boyish duties. He will not submit to the childish
rituals of the masses that require him to perform his masculinity in the mar-
ketplace—to show his wounds to the gaping plebian audience, playing the
warrior for the public.[71] Coriolanus views war as serious business and believes he can define his masculinity in relation to some abstract sense of military virtue. But the Romans of *Coriolanus* define manliness, it would seem,
on a continuity with boyishness, emphasizing the ways men, even great
men, must play certain roles. For the Romans, Coriolanus is not unlike his
butterfly-chasing son.

Coriolanus's struggle to articulate the difference of manhood—to differentiate it not only from womanish effeminacy, as other critics have
demonstrated, but also from boyish masculinity—is explored toward the
end of the drama in a fascinating revisitation of the butterfly image. When
Coriolanus is poised to invade Rome, Volumnia, Virgilia, Valeria, and young
Martius plead for him to desist from "tearing / His country's bowels out"
(5.3.103–4)—an image that resonates with young Martius's earlier demoli-
tion of the butterfly, which was "mammocked" when he "did . . . tear" it.
Coriolanus, who claims, "These eyes are not the same I wore in Rome"
(5.3.38), has changed drastically from the man he was when he left Rome, or
so he believes. The wise Menenius comes to believe this, too, reporting de-
jectedly that Coriolanus will have no mercy on the Rome he once loved and
served so valiantly. When asked by Sicinus, "Is't possible that so short a time
can alter the condition of a man?" (5.4.7), Menenius responds with a parable about the absoluteness of change in the natural world: "There is a differ-
ency between a grub and a butterfly, yet your butterfly was a grub. This
Martius is grown from man to dragon. He has wings, he's more than a
creeping thing . . . He is able to pierce a corslet with his eye, talks like a knell,
and his 'hmh!' is a battery. . . . There is no more mercy in him than there is
milk in a male tiger" (5.4.9–24). Although the butterfly was, in its infancy, a
grub, once it matures, it loses all connection to the thing it once was. It is
like the "male tiger" that, despite consuming the milk of its mother during
its infancy, loses any trace of that milk of mercy now that it is grown. As the
butterfly has nothing of "creeping thing" in it, so Coriolanus, who has become a "dragon" of war, has no more of the merciful "man" in him.

Yet Menenius is proven wrong in his assertion that the phases of growth through which a man moves are mutually exclusive and absolutely distinguished from each other. Indeed, Coriolanus turns out to have some milk of mercy in him yet, for, unbeknownst to Menenius, Coriolanus has bowed to his mother's wishes, turning his back on the army of men he leads and brokering a peace for Rome. Whatever this may mean for the tragic hero's fate, it points to a dominant preoccupation of this play with the indeterminacy of maturation. Just as every winged butterfly has the potential to return to its roots as a creeping grub, so every man who speaks with the masculine surety of a warrior— "talks like a knell, and his hum is battery"— may be beneath his polished manly exterior a mere "crack."

"Clear your Voice and Sing": *Antonio and Mellida*

The notion that a "crack"—with all the historical implications of the term— lurks behind every articulate, masculine man is, in Shakespeare's *Coriolanus*, a thematic device; but in early modern plays that were performed by all-male children's companies, this thematic device is a theatrical reality. In plays by these children's companies, real "cracks," male youths, were behind the performances of adult male roles. In companies in which "cracks" played the roles of both male youths and adult men, the blurring of adult and youth masculinities that we have seen in Shakespeare is particularly acute and the performative nature of masculinity especially accentuated. Dramatists writing for all-boy companies lose no time taking advantage of their rich—and potentially anxiety-provoking—theatrical circumstances. In the induction to Jonson's *Cynthia's Revels*, the boy actors present themselves preparing to stage a play and, most importantly for my purposes, preparing to enact the parts of both men and boys. The induction dramatizes the attempt of two boy actors to hijack the spotlight from the boy who is supposed to speak the prologue. The situation quickly degenerates when one of the boys, #3, tries to sabotage the play by revealing its entire plot to the audience while the other boys chase after him, wrestling in an attempt to silence him. Boy #3 agrees to surrender only if he is given the Prologue's cloak so that he can deliver one final "device": he assumes the role of the adult men in his audience, mocking the gallants' masculine habits:

Now, sir, suppose I am one of your gentle auditors, that am come in (having paid my money at the door, with much ado) and here I take my place, and sit down: I have my three sorts of tobacco in my pocket, my light by me, and thus I begin. By this light, I wonder that any man is so mad to come to see these rascally tits play here—They do act like so many wrens, or pismires—not the fifth part of a good face amongst them all—and then their music is abominable—able to stretch a man's ears worse than ten—pillories, and their ditties—most lamentable things, like the pitiful fellows that make them—poets. By this vapour, and 'twere not for tobacco—I think—the very stench of 'em would poison me, I should not dare to come in at their gates—a man were better visit fifteen jails—or a dozen or two of hospitals—than once adventure to come near them. How is't? Well? (ll. 100–114)

Representing his male auditors as, in effect, characters with particular gestures and lines, Boy #3 suggests that pursuits like smoking tobacco excessively and pompously complaining about boy actors' talent (especially vocal talent) are exaggerated performances, roles men of the audience play to prove manly character. Moreover, the boy's conclusion—"How is't? Well?"—as it denotes his desire for his audience's approval, simultaneously gestures toward his auditors' preoccupation with approval. Like him, they are compelled by a need to perform their masculine roles well—a feat made difficult by the plays' continuous focus on the performative nature of these roles, on the possibility that the answer to the question "How is't?" might *not* be "well."

In Jonson's induction, it is not just the boy playing a man's part that undermines the seamless portrayal of adult male masculinity but the juxtaposed presence of a boy playing the part of a roguish, precocious youth, the "crack" who plays *like* a man. Boy #2 occupies this position when he decides to take part in Boy #3's next device, involving a "more sober, or better gathered gallant" (116–17). Boy #2 joins in the skit, announcing that he will enact the part of a boy actor: "and I step forth like one of the children, and ask you; 'Would you have stool, sir?'" (125–26). Through his role (playing himself), Boy #2 proceeds to mock the gallant played by Boy #3 for not understanding the purpose of buying a stool, which is to "throne your self in state on the stage, as other gentlemen use" (131). Boy #2 uses the jest to tease the gallants of the audience even further, as their practice of sitting on the stage is revealed to be based on the same kinds of narcissism that drives their other excessive performances of masculinity—narcissism of gallants being a central concern of the entire play. And it is within the context of this skit about adult male masculinity being a foolish performance that the gallant played by Boy #3 refers to the youth played by Boy #2 as a "crack": first, when he accuses the boy of making him a stage prop—"Sir crack, I am none of your fresh pictures that use to beautify the decayed dead arras, in a public theatre" (139–41). The gallant character uses the term again when he responds with pity to the boy character's facetious complaint that the author of their play is not, like other authors, prone to hang about backstage, abusing the actors for "every venial trespass we commit" (151–52). "Nay, crack, be not disheartened" (154), the gallant character says sympathetically. As in the examples from Shakespeare, the appellation of "crack" is invoked at the moment when youth mimicry of adult male masculinity denaturalizes the latter, exposing its breaking points. In this case, however, the vulnerable nature of adult male masculinity is accentuated by the fact that manhood and boyhood are both represented physically onstage by pubescent, potentially squeaky-voiced boys. That is, the scene thematizes on a fictional level a breakdown of masculine control by presenting on the level of performance actors who are understood as struggling to manage their voices.

The thematization and performance of vocal failure come together perhaps most elegantly in John Marston's children's company play *Antonio and Mellida*. Many of Marston's plays ponder and showcase young male voices, but I take as exemplary *Antonio and Mellida*, a play that offers insight into the functioning of patriarchal systems and the manner in which gender identity and sexual difference were rendered intelligible in the theater and in English culture at large. Concerned with defining male identity—what it means to be a prince, courtier, father, son, indeed any man—*Antonio and Mellida* links failing patriarchal power structures of court and family with unstable male voices. This analogy weaves through the play not only thematically but performatively, for *Antonio and Mellida* frequently calls attention to the vulnerable vocality of boy actors.

That self-conscious attention to boys' voices should be so evident in Marston likely comes as little surprise to his critics. Scholarship on Marston since the 1930s has noted the playwright's immersion in and self-conscious exploitation of the theatrical medium.[72] Anticipating the dramatic antics of modern playwrights like Tom Stoppard, Marston exposes his audience to the backstage realities of playing.[73] One critic writes of Marston that "no writer of the period . . . reminds us so persistently that we are in a theatre watching a play,"[74] and, I would add, hearing one too. A playwright who insists that his "scenes [were] invented merely to be spoken" and that the "life of comedy rests much in the actor's voice," Marston reflects on the bodily processes that enable, and sometimes disable, actors' vocality.[75] *Antonio and Mellida* figures the vulnerability of male voices and indexes male effeminacy or a failure of masculine identity not only by the tropes that other scholars have noted—cowardice in battle, excessive love of women, and vanity—but also by an incapacity to control the voice.[76]

The character that most exemplifies stock traits of early modern masculinity in *Antonio and Mellida* is Piero, the duke of Venice. We are introduced to Piero early in act 1 as he emerges victorious from battle. The stage directions describe a lavish procession, files of admiring courtiers, and Piero decked out in armor. He proceeds to give a bombastic speech detailing his great feats in overcoming his enemy, Andrugio, the duke of Genoa. Most of all, he boasts that in defeating Andrugio, he has prevented the marriage of his daughter, Mellida, to Andrugio's son, Antonio. He has, in one single sweep, secured his patriarchal interests in both the public and private realms: he has ensured, through battle, that the young lovers have no way to legitimize their desires for one another, and, at the same time, he has won the adoration of his subjects. No sooner has he testified to his victory and announced his decree to pay twenty thousand double pistolets to "whosoever brings Andrugio's head, / Or young Antonio's" (1.1.69–70), than the audience is invited to consider the dangers of the masculine excess that Piero exhibits. Cautioning Piero about displaying too much pride, court satirist Felice also warns against the use of "public power" to bolster "private wrong" (1.1.85), drawing attention to potentially conflicting roles for the prince-father. Felice advises well, for, as the play unfolds, Piero's decision to continue using his power as duke to "prosecute [his] family's revenge" (1.1.88)—to keep Antonio away from Mellida—becomes problematic in terms not only of its ethical rectitude but its practical feasibility. Because he conflates his two patriarchal roles, prince and father, Piero heightens performance pressure in both realms: should he falter in his duties as a father, he will compromise his leadership of the state.

Indeed, this scenario almost comes to pass. In act 3, Piero discovers that Antonio, disguised as an Amazon woman, has infiltrated the court and intends to run away with Mellida. Piero's fury at the moment he learns of his daughter's planned defection manifests itself as a breakdown in vocal articulation. The swaggering soldier who earlier declared confidently, "My fate is firmer than mischance can shake" (1.1.41), now gives orders like a madman:

Run, keep the palace, post to the ports, go to my daughter's chamber. Whither now? Scud to the Jew's. Stay, run to the gates; stop the gondolets; let none pass the marsh. Do all at once. Antonio! His head, his head! [To Felice] Keep you the court.—The rest stand still, or run, or go, or shout, or search, or scud, or call, or hang, or d- d- do s- s- s- something. I know not wh- wh- wh- what I d- d- do, nor wh-wh- wh- where I am. (3.2.171–77)

Shouting out brief (mostly four- or five-syllable) orders to his men, Piero follows with a series of single-word imperatives, then falls into stuttering. The very performance of this passage is likely to quicken the breathing of the speaker, simulating or even provoking frenetic emotions. Piero's vocal confusion and distress reflect anxiety that his inadequacies as a father and, by association, as a ruler have been exposed to his court. But the duke quickly regains his composure and his vocal control, at least for the moment, pledging to drink a toast to Genoa "in Antonio's skull" (3.2.229). The comment is delivered with such venom that one witness declares, "Lord bless us! His breath is more fearful than a sergeant's / voice when he cries, 'I arrest'" (3.2.230–31). When Piero finds his renegade daughter, he publicly enacts his patriarchal authority, sending her back to the court and vowing to marry her off to a Milanese prince that very evening.

Piero's masculinity, displayed visually with armor and aurally through his (usually) controlled voice, is contrasted in the play with the effeminacy and frequent vocal failure of two Venetian courtiers, Castilio and Balurdo. Castilio and Balurdo manifest all the signs of early modern male effeminacy: they are cowards in battle, are enslaved by their passion for women, and exhibit excessive vanity. Whereas Piero is reputed to have bravely led his ships to victory over Genoa, Castilio and Balurdo cowardly hid their military rank to avoid being shot (2.1.29–30). Where Piero bravely dons his armor, Balurdo is reported to have wished for "an armour, / cannon-proof" (2.1.32–33). Castilio and Balurdo's cowardice on the battlefield is accompanied by incurable and effeminizing lovesickness at home.[77] As desperate but unsuccessful wooers of Piero's niece Rosaline, Balurdo and Castilio willingly give up their masculine self-respect in exchange for her affection.[78] In their efforts to attract Rosaline, the courtiers also exhibit vanity, a characteristic that, like cowardice and excessive passion, can turn men into women. Indeed, in a stunning enactment of the commonplace notion that men can turn into women if they behave like women, Marston transforms Balurdo into a mirror version of Rosaline. The stage directions in the middle of act 3 scene 2 instruct Balurdo to enter backward, with his page, Dildo, "following him, with a looking-glass in one hand and a candle in the other." Flavia, Rosaline's servant, follows, coming in backward holding the same props up to Rosaline. Standing in mirrored postures, the two pairs proceed to carry on separate, but intermingled, dialogues in which both servants similarly beautify and flatter their masters. Should the analogy between Rosaline, the vain woman, and Balurdo, the effeminate man, somehow be lost on audiences, Felice draws attention to the comparison: "Rare sport, rare sport! A female fool and a female flatterer" (3.2.158). Either part of Felice's description, "female fool" or "female flatterer," could apply to the "fool" and "flatterer" of each pair: if Rosaline and Balurdo are female fools, then both Dildo and Flavia flatter a female. But where Rosaline merely exhibits the "foolishness" early modern audiences might expect from a woman—women are constantly accused of vanity in early modern drama—Balurdo's womanishness is constituted by his performance of womanly behavior, in this case, vanity.

In addition to demonstrating what other critics have described as trademarks of male effeminacy, Castilio and Balurdo are characterized by a failure to control their voices.[79] Balurdo's difficulty in articulating himself before the woman he desires is figured literally as an emasculating experience. When asked by Rosaline whether he would like to be her servant, he stumbles to respond, "O God! Forsooth, in very good earnest la, you would make me as a man should say . . . as a man should say . . ." (2.1.67–68), and he is unable to complete the thought. Balurdo's statement, beginning and ending with "as a man should say," is revelatory. A man who cannot say what "a man should say" is not, by the logic of this sentence, a man. Balurdo constantly reveals his unmanly rhetorical skills, often stumbling to find the right words for his thoughts and frequently using other people's words incorrectly.

What compromises the courtiers' success in wooing women is not just a weak command over language but an inability to master the physiological production of voice. This is most evident in Castilio's failure to keep his voice from squeaking. In act 3, Castilio describes his plan to serenade Rosaline: "I will warble to the delicious concave of my mistress' ear, and strike her thoughts with the pleasing touch of my voice" (3.2.33–34). Castilio assumes he can impress Rosaline by pressing his "pleasing" voice into her ear, an ear that, by nature of its concave shape, seems ready and willing. The only person affected by Castilio's voice, however, is the gentleman Felice, who is awakened by Castilio's "treble minikin squeaks" (3.2.31). The term "minikin" nicely captures the gist of the insult, for the term can refer to the catgut used for the treble string of a viol or lute as well as to a girl or woman.[80] In emphasizing that this "minkin" voice "squeaks," Felice intimates that Castilio's failure at wooing and his related effeminacy are a consequence not just of the high-pitched nature of his voice but of its screeching quality, which indicates his failure to manage his body's vocal systems.[81]

Male mastery over the physiological production of voice is put to the test in 5.2, when Rosaline, upon her own request, judges a singing contest that stalls her cousin Mellida's forced nuptials. Having granted Rosaline the authority to preside as "umpiress" over the competition for "music's prize," a gilded harp, Piero turns to several pages and commands, "Boys, clear your voice and sing" (5.2.6–8). According to Galenic theory, the "ahem" one uses to clear the voice before singing improves vocal sound by sweeping away humors that may have accumulated on the vocal organs. Piero's imperative, "clear your voice," thus gestures toward the humoral bodies of the singers, demanding from them what could be a difficult state of physiological readiness. If the young singer's humoral system is not balanced, then he will need much more than a cough to bring order to his vocal instruments, particularly if he wishes to prevent his voice from squeaking when he sings in a higher range.

The conversation that follows the first page's song reflects further on the unstable voice. Rosaline, taking hold of the authoritative golden harp, presents her judgment:

ROSALINE. By this gold, I had rather have a servant with a short nose and a thin hair than have such a high-stretched, minikin voice.
PIERO. Fair niece, your reason?
ROSALINE. By the sweets of love, I should fear extremely that he were an eunuch.
CASTILIO. Spark spirit, how like you his voice?
ROSALINE. "Spark spirit, how like you his voice?"—So help me, youth, thy voice squeaks like a dry cork shoe. (5.2.9–16)

Although Rosaline is charged with judging the voices based only on their singing merit, her first comment raises the stakes. A "high-stretched, minikin voice" renders the youth's performance unsatisfactory not only for Rosaline the music judge, but also for Rosaline the desirable woman—after all, Rosaline has been auditioning men to be her "servants" for much of the play. She begins by explaining that what disturbs her about the voice is not the sound per se but what the voice might indicate about the state of the man's genital instruments: a man with this kind of voice might lack significant male anatomy. At first, the exchange seems to turn on what Callaghan describes as a correspondence of vocal sound, the phallus, and castration anxiety. But Castilio's interjection shifts away from this theme, reminding Rosaline that the subject at hand is the page's voice, not his genitalia. The function of Castilio's sudden comment is unclear, particularly since this is the only line he speaks in the entire act. Perhaps Rosaline's assessment of the singing youth's voice is portrayed as having personal ramifications for Castilio's character. Castilio has been trying to woo Rosaline since the play began, and he is on the verge of discovering what his beloved likes and dislikes in a man. If so, Rosaline's evaluation of the page's voice—"So help me, youth, thy voice squeaks like a dry cork shoe"—mocks Castilio for his own unstable voice. Whether the "thy" of Rosaline's line refers to Castilio or the singing page, Rosaline's derisive comment has consequences for Castilio's sense of masculine honor. When asked to describe what she doesn't like in a man's voice, Rosaline offers Castilio's marked vocal characteristics—recall the earlier description of Castlio's "treble minikin squeaks"—as examples. At issue again is not simply the pitch of the voice but its jarring, uneven quality, compared here to the embarrassing sound a shoe makes as it brushes the ground awkwardly. As she describes these unpleasant, squeaky male voices as "stretched," Rosaline implicitly recalls the uncontrollable physiological process that is to blame for this unpleasant sound, the windpipe cracking as rising body heat causes it to expand and stretch. Given that the restoration of Castilio's masculine honor depends on his being able to win Rosaline's affections (thereby legitimizing his otherwise foolish wooing escapades), Rosaline's comments seal his failure: he cannot win her affection because, as is registered in his uncontrollable voice, he is unmanly. Not surprisingly, Castilio, who remains onstage for the rest of the play, does not say another word.[82]

Rosaline's comments about voice are borne out further in her own lengthy speeches, which serve to usurp her uncle's command over the aural register of the play.[83] Piero's inability to master Rosaline's voice (and her matrimonial course) is a prelude to his final emasculation. Not only is he outwitted by his archenemy, Andrugio, but he loses possession of his daughter to Antonio. Having refused to listen to Felice's earlier warning against the use of "public power" to bolster "private wrong" (1.1.85), Piero suffers defeat in both spheres. The humiliation of these losses is figured as grounds enough for a sequel to the play, *Antonio's Revenge*, a drama motivated by

Piero's desperate attempts to restore honor to his family and state. Compellingly, Piero's downfall in *Antonio's Revenge* is marked by a loss of vocal control: his tongue, an organ of speech, is ripped out by his enemies. Like *Antonio and Mellida* (albeit in a more gruesomely literal fashion), *Antonio's Revenge* reminds its audience that male voices, even those belonging to powerful dukes, have the propensity to fail, leading to (or at least being consequent with) a breakdown in masculine control in other respects.[84]

This message would have been underscored when *Antonio and Mellida* was performed by the Children of Paul's, for whom vocal instability was an inescapable condition. "Anxious masculinity," to recall Mark Breitenberg's terminology, results when the fictional world of the play (in which controlling the voice is a masculine imperative) and the material space of the theater (in which the physiological vagaries of the voice elude the actors' command) intersect. The collusion between thematic fiction and performative reality is most evident in the induction to *Antonio and Mellida*. The induction simulates a backstage conversation among the play's actors. With their "parts" in hand, the actors discuss their apprehensions about not being ready for the production. Successful vocal performance is central to their concerns. "Piero" complains, "Faith, we can say our parts. But we are ignorant in what mould we must cast our actors" (3–4). From there, the characters advise one another about how to gesture, walk, pronounce—how to style their lines and movements. The actor most apprehensive about his capacity to play his part, however, is "Antonio," whose character must disguise himself as an Amazon for the first part of the play. Playing this "hermaphrodite" (65) role causes not only frustration but confusion, the actor explains, twice referring to this role as "I know not what" (65, 68–69). But the actor's primary source of distress is that he does not have the voice to play the woman's part: "I a voice to play a lady! I shall ne're do it" (69). If he cannot successfully mimic a woman's voice, he will be, like Flute in Hoffman's *A Midsummer Night's Dream*, the laughingstock of the stage. But the even greater anxiety is that he may mimic female sound so effectively that he'll forget how to be a man and will fail to perform masculinity effectively when he has to play a man: "[w]hen use hath taught me action to hit the right point of a lady's part, I shall grow ignorant, when I must turn young prince again, how but to truss my hose" (74–76), a reference to breeching—a signature of manliness. "Antonio" worries, in other words, that he will become so "use[d]" to faking a "lady's part" that he will unable to perform on demand masculine acts that should come naturally. The risks of impersonating a woman are professional and personal. Should he fail to act the part of the "young prince," it can be only because he has become "ignorant" about what it means to be male. But "Antonio" need not worry, his colleagues counsel him, for the woman's part that he must impersonate is not categorically different from the part of a man: gendering an Amazon is not so difficult, they explain, for some women "wear the breeches still" (77), and an Amazon's voice is "virago-like" (70). The gender identity of an Amazon, they point out, is like that of a "hermaphrodite" (65), neither man nor woman, but both, and this blurriness of gender lines is evinced in part by the Amazon's voice.

It would be difficult to argue with W. Reavley Gair's reading of the induction as a metatheatrical reference to Paul's acting company, who, he submits, may have used *Antonio and Mellida* to announce their revival: "Marston is pointing out one of the special properties of the chorister company, that their physical condition, on the verge of puberty, allows them to be both sexes at once. The audience is made intensely aware that this performance is a debut for the Children of Paul's. In the ensuing action Antonio's inarticulate emotional crises will be a manifestation of the inexperience the cast admits to in the Induction."[85] But the "propert[y]" that makes Paul's company "special"—that its actors are "on the verge of puberty"—also makes the company vulnerable. This vulnerability is not only their inexperience but their precarious physiological state. The liminal status of the boy actor may be a tool—enabling him to "be both sexes at once"—but this seems for Antonio less the solution to than the cause of his performance anxieties. If the actor playing Antonio is, indeed, "on the verge of puberty," he has no assurance that his voice will remain virago-like for the entirety of the performance, let alone that he will be able to switch voluntarily between the "right point of a lady's part" and the right point of a man's. If the "virago" voice, like the categories of hermaphrodite and Amazon, blurs sexual difference, then how will "Antonio" enact the sexual identity of his male role? How will he portray manliness if he fails to keep his voice in order?

The induction links the vocal instability of Paul's actors with a breakdown in masculine identity explored further by the rest of the play. When Antonio reunites with Mellida for the first time, he feels unmanned by his Amazon disguise and by his passion for his beloved: "double all thy man" (1.1.161), he mutters to himself. Impersonating an Amazon, Antonio feels incompetent, out of control; without a clear sense of his manly identity, he wishes to increase the portion of himself that is "man." Significantly, Antonio's masculinity is not communicated by the pitch of his voice, where a low voice denotes a man and a high voice denotes a woman. These categorical descriptions, the play insists, are not stable indicators of gender identity: an Amazon and a man can share vocal characteristics. Rather, it is the ability to control the voice that signals manhood. Antonio lacks that from the onset. Even in the induction, the actor who plays him is plagued by stuttering. Describing the difficult part that Gallazeo must enact, he stammers: "Now as solemn as a traveller and as grave as a puritan's ruff; with the same breath, as slight and scattered in fashion as . . . as . . . as . . . a . . . a . . . anything. . . . Now lamenting, then chafing, straight laughing . . . then. . . . Faith, I know not what" (117–24).

The link between Antonio's vocal breakdown and a disruption in gender differentiation is perhaps best articulated by a page who, witnessing Antonio and Mellida erupt into Italian, turns to the audience and remarks, "I think confusion of Babel is fallen upon these lovers that they change their language; but I fear me my master, having but feigned the person of a woman, hath got their unfeigned imperfection and is grown double-tongued" (4.1.209–12). Although the page explicitly refers to a regendering of Antonio's language, in the context of a play concerned with the physiology of speech, the lines also allude to the instability of Antonio's physical voice. The observation that Antonio has adopted the traits of a woman after having "feigned the person of a woman" alludes to the play's induction even more acutely than most critics, who have discussed the strong relation between the induction and the play proper, have realized. The term "person" is derived from the Latin *persona*, meaning literally "through sound" (*per sona*).[86] The challenge of personating a woman is the risk involved in characterizing her voice: as the page points out, when a man performs womanliness through sound, he risks effeminization in other respects. No wonder "Antonio's" primary concern about acting success is portraying the voice of an Amazon woman. For it is at the site of vocal production that the masculinity of Antonio, as a character and as an actor, is most vulnerable.

Though we cannot know precisely how theater audiences reacted when a boy actor's voice squeaked midperformance, it is clear that Marston's narrative builds up pressure around this moment of potential vocal instability, preparing audiences for its inevitability by scripting characters' vocal failure. I have argued that through this dramatic exhibition of vocal failure,

Marston explores the link between vocal instability and gender identity: the induction sets forth in explicit terms that the cracking male voice disrupts not simply aural aesthetics but the clarity of gender categories, the line between "Lady" and "young prince." The squeaking, cracking male voice in Marston's play, as in the plays discussed earlier in the chapter, points to a breakdown of male control not only of the voice and the body that produces it but of the social and political spheres that "ideal" men are supposed to dominate. Marston's metatheatrics in the induction underscore, moreover, the extent to which masculine control over these spheres is an act, a function of performance. Marston presents male identity as literally a role to be played. And insofar as the male body is subject to physiological flux—the voice being symptomatic of that state—the successful performance of male identity is by no means assured.

Modern Displacements of Unstable Voice

Marston's willingness to stage the unstable male voice helps point to epistemic differences between early modern and modern perspectives on gender and sexuality. Such differences become especially evident when we can examine *Antonio and Mellida*'s modern performance history. When Peter Barnes revived the play in his 1979 adaptation *Antonio* (Nottingham Playhouse), his production suppressed "Antonio's" vocal instability by having the character played by a mature (mid-thirties) Alan Rickman[87]—an actor whose most renowned asset is his deep, mellifluous, and controlled vocal sound. Fans, reviewers, and interviewers of Rickman inevitably comment on his voice as central to his magnetism as an actor. Rickman's voice has been called "a remarkable instrument—deep, soft and relaxed to the point of langour"; a "clipped clear voice tinged at once with authority and ennui"; "seductive, disdainful, imperious."[88] One *Guardian* reviewer, recalling a Rickman performance from 1985 (over a decade earlier than the review she writes) remembers in vivid detail the seductive power of Rickman's voice at the start of his career: "What I remember of Rickman's performance as Valmont is that his body seemed to be hinged in all sorts of unexpected places, enabling him to fold and unfold it at will. That voice—poised, cadenced, raw and yet musical—came out of a mouth like a cave, creating these tilts of sound and body. He was frightening. Frightening, not because he was immoral, but because he made you want him. Within the moral vacuum that surrounded him—and that nothing could penetrate—he was irresistible."[89] What distinguishes Rickman and accounts for his sex appeal is a voice that appears *naturally* controlled and powerful. Rickman seems to exert absolutely no effort into crafting this "imperious" sound; if anything, Rickman comes across as vocally reserved, even lazy: "He gives an impression of having to crank his vocal chords into motion in order to answer my questions," writes one reviewer.[90] The implication is that Rickman seduces listeners with his voice despite what appear to be efforts on his part to remain languid, and nothing is sexier, reviewers intimate, than an actor who doesn't flaunt the source of his sexuality. The appeal of Rickman's vocal style can best be understood in terms of what Judith Halberstam describes as the "nonperformative" style that characterizes representations of mainstream white masculinity.[91] Like the laid-back white men Halberstam observes in advertisements for Dockers pants, Rickman's male masculinity is defined by understatement, the sense that male masculinity, in contrast to femininity, is natural and unstaged. With Rickman's "poised, cadenced" and relaxed voice delivering the lines, "Antonio's" anxieties about vocal failure could hardly have been taken seriously by the audiences of Barnes's production, if they were performed at all.[92]

By deemphasizing anxieties about voice expressed by "Antonio," Barnes's production distanced its theater audience from the potentially uncomfortable implications of the unstable male voice. With the self-assured Rickman at the helm, masculinity hardly could have appeared as a performance vulnerable to failure at any time. The squeaky voices in the fiction of Marston's play were safely confined to that arena, linked to Marston's early modern sensibilities and disarticulated from the modern actor's—and modern audience's—immediate preoccupations. If anything, Barnes's use of Rickman would have enabled him to stage a triumph *over* the volatile male voice: "Antonio's" concerns about his vocal control would have been put to rest by placing the part in the capable hands—or, more accurately, the steady vocal tract—of Rickman.

Barnes is not alone among late twentieth-century directors in staging this kind of triumphal displacement of the unstable male voice. A similar dynamic is at work in the Shakespeare films I discussed at the start of this chapter. Like Barnes, directors Madden and Hoffman displace the squeaky male voice from the theatrical stage, albeit in these cases a stage that is represented in a film. The ideological implications of this displacement are more easily legible in the case of the films, though, insofar as both Madden and Hoffman go to great lengths to write the squeaky male voice into their scripts, using its presence and subsequent displacement to achieve dramatic effects at key moments in their respective narratives. Hoffman's *A Midsummer Night's Dream* manufactures tension around Flute's vocal performance, tensions that are not portrayed in Shakespeare's play-script. In Hoffmann's film, Flute's squeaky impersonation of a woman's sound during the mechanicals' performance turns the tragic climax of the play-within-the-play into comedy. Yet Hoffman's Flute bravely overcomes this vocal inadequacy, thereby ensuring the success of his speech and of the play as a whole. Similarly, in *Shakespeare in Love*, Sam's vocal breakdown is presented as an impossible obstacle; the play, it seems, may have to be canceled. The obstacles are surmounted, however, when Viola, with her reliable female voice, takes over the part, literally setting the stage for Viola and Will's climactic and well-received performance. Although Madden and Hoffman banish the squeaky male voice and its disruptive effects from the stage, they go to great lengths to *stage* this foreclosure. What is accomplished aesthetically and ideologically in this theatrical *fort-da*? Why dramatize the volatile voice only to steady it and foreclose its disruptive potential?

In both films the victory over male vocal instability ushers in not only successful theater but a successful theatrical representation of heterosexual love. For the audience that watches the mechanicals' play-within-the-film, the epic romance of Pyramus and Thisbe is nothing but a joke whose final punch line is Thisbe's absurdly vocalized eulogy. With his silly squeaky voice, Flute fails not only to represent a female character effectively but to portray with the seriousness it ostensibly deserves Thisbe's deep love for Pyramus. This epic story of heterosexual love is on the verge of deteriorating into slapstick comedy. When Flute suddenly stabilizes his voice midspeech, he does more than restore dignity to the mechanicals' theatrical efforts; he restores dignity to heterosexual love—something this film is concerned to do on all counts. Hoffman's *Midsummer* needs to stage Flute's vocal failure—and his troubled representation of femininity—in order to stage a satisfying story of heterosexual romance.[93]

A similar strategy is at work, though in more complex ways, in Madden's *Shakespeare in Love*. In this film the unstable male voice is presented as yet another moment of gender blurring in a film full of gender-bending antics. Ultimately, however, the film moves its audience toward a resolution of gender ambiguity in order to produce a moving and seamless portrayal of heterosexual love. Though the film takes pleasure in playing with gender categories, it works hard to ensure that even if characters within the fiction confuse men and women, the film's conventional audience always knows the difference; indeed, quite a number of the film's jokes involve moments when the audience is prompted to exercise this knowledge of clear gender binaries. As is often true in popular entertainment, humor helps enforce ideological conformity. The audience is led to echo the chuckles of the Lord Chamberlain's Men when Viola deLesseps as Thomas Kent steps to the "ladies'" side during a dance rehearsal at the cue, "ladies downstage, gentlemen upstage." The audience is prompted to laugh especially at the Master of the Revels when he mistakenly concludes that the "real" woman on the stage is the male actor playing Juliet's Nurse. Gender ambiguity is cause for laughter, the film insists, and by laughing at these appropriate times, the audience demonstrates its knowledge of "correct," binary gender categories. As Sujita Iyengar observes, this binary is produced through the film's privileging of a rigidly defined gendered body: gender difference in this film is presented as a function not of theatrical properties (such as costumes or gendered behaviors) but of "biological sex—sexual acts and secondary sex characteristics—which are seen as fundamental and unchanging."[94] Indeed, repeatedly the film relies on bodily difference to remind us of Viola's "authentic" female identity and, as a consequence, Will's "authentic" heterosexual orientation. Will's passionate sexual embrace with Thomas Kent backstage includes an elaborate defrocking, with the real body of Viola exposed beneath the manly costume. This gendering is enacted on a grander scale at the end, when Viola sheds her manly garb for good, embracing her "authentic" femininity as she takes the stage to play, to great acclaim, a woman's part. As Valerie Traub argues convincingly, the result is a liberal feminist story of Viola's self-assertion used to "to prop up and enforce" the displacement of male homoeroticism.[95]

What remains curious, however, is why the volatile male voice plays such a prominent role in this displacement. Iyengar implicitly suggests that voice is just one more of those "apparently inevitable forces of biological sex-difference" that structure the film's conception of gender. "[S]ex organs give [Viola] away when Webster then reports to Tilney and the assembled cast: 'I seen 'im [Shakespeare] kissing 'er bubbies [breasts]!' *In a similar way,* the boy-actor Sam Gosse is rendered unable to perform as Juliet at the last minute when his voice breaks."[96] Traub, similarly addressing the film's "privileging of the gendered body over disguise" writes that "the trajectory of the film is to persuade that boys and women are *not* interchangeable, either on stage or in bed. Not only is Sam Go[s]se, the boy actor, not particularly convincing as a girl; at the critical moment, his voice breaks. *In a parallel manner*, the breasts of Viola, the woman disguised as a boy actor, are revealed."[97] But how similar is Sam's voice change to the film's visual spectacles of gender difference? As I've been arguing throughout this chapter, voice does not fall as neatly into gender categories as might Viola's "bubbies," and it seems worth asking why it is voice, and not a more stable, more obviously *embodied* signifier of gender identity, that serves the critical turning point in this film.

It is, I'd submit, *because* voice does not conform as easily to neat gender categories that *Shakespeare in Love* explicitly stages a narrative about that conformity. Unlike more embodied signifiers of gender identity, voice resists binary schemes of presence versus absence, possession versus lack. As such, voice blatantly upsets gender dichotomies, concomitantly troubling binary erotic categories as well. Voice, in other words, is the exception that threatens to expose the unfeasibility of the rule. It is no wonder that *Shakespeare in Love* uses its narrative turning point as the moment to confront this final frontier. As the film barrels toward its inevitable heterosexual romantic comedy climax, the audience has little time to question whether Sam's voice change will be as disruptive to the theater audience as Will and his colleagues assume; narrative satisfaction depends on the film audience getting to see Viola and Will play against each other, to stage publicly their affair—a resolution to the film's intersecting personal and professional plotlines. When the "crisis" of Sam's breaking voice is presented, the audience is led to focus not on the particular meanings of this event but on what narrative possibilities it creates. There is no moment in the film, as there is in Marston's play, when the actors reflect on what the volatility of the voice means for the representation of gender; under the mantra "the show must go on," the film covers over complex ideological questions the voice raises by embracing what Traub calls a "logic of sequence" through which "certain ideologically freighted terms are cannily delegitimized and replaced by others. . . . This synchronicity of realignment is overdetermined, propelled by the quiet strength of ideological conviction masquerading as necessity."[98] Voice, I'd argue, provides modern filmmakers with an ideal forum for propagating this narrative logic, for the story of pubescent voice changes can be easily articulated as a story of gender "progress": boys, the conventional story goes, become men when their voices change. The seemingly inevitable and necessary temporal unfolding of the human gendered body, signaled by these changes in vocal sound, bolsters the film's attempts to provide a seamless narrative of gender and, consequently, erotic "progress." Sam Gosse is represented as progressing seamlessly from boyhood to manhood so that Will and Viola's queer love can progress seamlessly into a great, indeed epic, heterosexual romance.

In this, the film reveals epistemic differences between its modern perspectives on gender and erotic difference and those of the early modern period it attempts to represent in so much apparent historic detail. As we have seen, in the early modern period, vocal changes were understood to be part of a temporally protracted and unsteady process, far different from the straightforward, linear narrative of vocal change that is dramatized in *Shakespeare in Love*. Whereas *Shakespeare in Love* and Hoffman's *A Midsummer Night's Dream* use voice changes to tell a story of progress—in which overcoming vocal instability helps actors and lovers achieve their "ideal" state—early modern playwrights like Marston revel in the dramatic possibilities presented by the moment of vocal instability itself. The consequence, and indeed also the cause, is that we have in the early modern Marston a more fluid notion of gender and sexuality than we find in mainstream films and many modern theatrical productions.

This is not to suggest that Marston and his audiences were any more comfortable with the implications of this fluidity. By using boy actors to demonstrate the extent to which the humoral body is a liability for men, Marston is able to distance his adult male audiences to some degree from the locus of discomfort.[99] Nevertheless, there is an important difference between Marston's distancing and modern directors' displacements. In Marston, the squeaky male voice is not sufficiently overcome but returns repeatedly to plague male characters and audiences throughout the play. Unlike Hoffman's and Madden's films and Barnes's production, Marston's play does not tell the story of men's triumph over the unstable voice.

This difference between Marston and these modern directors is partly driven by historical shifts in the way gender and sexuality are understood. But the fluidity of gender difference and erotic choice that we see in early modern plays is also generated and accentuated by the material conditions in which these plays were performed. In Marston's case, the actors who stage vocal instability are in the throes of pubescent change; their squeaky voices cannot be dramatized and then safely stowed offstage, courtesy of film editing or careful casting. Marston cannot count on the propulsion of his plot to displace the unstable male voice, for that voice threatens to reemerge at any point during a live performance. Unlike modern directors, Marston copes with the volatility of performance by inviting his audiences to contemplate it. Even from a relatively safe distance, Marston's early modern audience is prompted to consider the ways the precarious voice, as a function of the unstable body, problematizes gender and erotic categories.

Words Made of Breath: Shakespeare, Bacon, and Particulate Matter

When Philip, the conflicted French monarch of Shakespeare's *King John*, swears to a peace agreement with England, he gives weight to his words by emphasizing their material composition. It is the physical breath Philip uses to swear his oath of peace that lends authorizing force to his words: "The latest breath that gave the sound of words / Was deep-sworn faith, peace, amity, true love / Between our kingdoms and our royal selves" (3.1.230–32).[1] Despite his best intentions, however, Philip breaks his vow mere moments later, renewing a conflict with England that will rage and subside repeatedly for the rest of the play. The matter that "gave the sound of words" turns out to be, as *King John*'s Constance puts it, "vain breath" (3.1.8), nothing but wind. As these brief passages from *King John* begin to demonstrate, breath can index multiple and conflicting ideas about vocal agency for early moderns. On the one hand, writers describe breath as a crucial ingredient in vocal communication; breath is the air that, according to natural philosopher Francis Bacon "*maketh* the Voice."[2] A range of authors maintain that the shape of the vocal organs is determined by their function as conveyers of breath. Robert Robinson's pronunciation manual describes how the throat provides "the greater or lesser restraining of the ayre," and anatomist Alexander Read notes that "The roofe of the mouth is vaulted, that the aire being repercussed, the voice may be the sharper."[3] Given widely held views of breath as having a key role in producing vocal sound, it is entirely fitting that Shakespeare's Coriolanus insists on the right of his "lungs [to]/ Coin words" (*Coriolanus* 3.1.81–82) and that Falstaff describes the word "honour" as but "Air" (*1 Henry IV* 5.1.133–34). As is evident in Falstaff's quip, however, breath may be not only essential to, but paradoxically disruptive of, vocal agency. In Falstaff's catechism the air that comprises "honor"—the matter that "is in that word"—underscores the futility of honor as a concept: like the air of which it is composed, honor is "insensible," not heard or felt by the living and therefore not worthy of Falstaff's attention (5.1.133–37). The very pronouncement of the word "air," with its homophonic pun on "heir," underscores this point, insofar as it evokes the spectral presence of the heir Hal; much more than he realizes, Falstaff's impossible social aspirations are neatly captured by the unaspirated "h."[4] Longaville of *Love's Labour's Lost* also recalls the material form of words as a way to mark (conveniently) their failure. As he rationalizes his decision to violate the oath he has sworn to his friends, he claims, "vows are but breath, and breath a vapour is. / . . . / If broken then, it is no fault of mine" (4.3.63; 66). Insofar as breath is an ephemeral vapor, its capacity to work as an agent on behalf of the thoughts and intentions of a speaker is inherently suspect.

Such doubts about the communicative power of the voice should sound familiar, for as we have seen in Chapter 1, early modern plays interrogate vocal agency by dramatizing ways the physical attributes of the voice compromise its power. But whereas *Antonio and Mellida* stages vocal failure as occurring at the site of its production, the unstable humoral body, other plays, like *King John*, go further to suggest that even if the voice can be produced successfully and articulated strongly, without squeaking, the voice is not assured of success as it travels from speaker to listener. Like the cracking vocal organs of pubescent boys, the unpredictable flow of breath exposes tensions in early modern thought about the agency of voice: when breath leaves the speaker's body, does it still belong to its producer? Since breath is essentially air that interacts with air, can breath be trusted to perform its communicative task when it is no longer under the speaker's direct command? What accounts for the ability of this vaporous current to transmit voiced sounds from speaker to listener? In short, can matter as transient and ephemeral as breath be choreographed? If reader-response theory prompts critics to question the degree of an author's control over the meaning of a text and to investigate the social contexts that shape reception, then early modern plays raise similar queries, albeit based not in the relationship between readers and a written text but between listeners and heard sounds. These plays prompt the critic to apply what we might call a "listener-response" theory, an approach that takes into account how the particular material processes of vocal transmission destabilize a speaker's control over an utterance.

There is much at stake for male identity in this destabilization of a speaker's voice, for one key component of early modern masculinity, as I've argued, is the capacity to display authority through vocal control. As the substance of which voices are made, breath puts pressure on such an ideal of vocal control, for, marked by unpredictable movement and an ephemeral form, breath problematizes the possibility that men, let alone anyone else, can control voice. Breath, like (and, indeed, *part of*) the unstable humoral body, troubles the performance of masculinity by King Phillip, Longaville, and Falstaff. This chapter goes further than the previous, however, in examining the implications of the unstable voice for women. While the ephemerality and unpredictability of breath threatens the authority of men like King Philip, these attributes have different implications for characters already lacking vocal authority, like Constance. Insofar as early modern discursive constructions of femininity associate women, by nature, with an incapacity for vocal control, there is less at stake for most early modern women in the recognition that the voice is composed of ephemeral breath. In fact, I shall suggest that such a recognition sometimes works to the advantage of female speakers: female characters that embrace breath's volatile attributes—calling attention to its unpredictability and transience—are able to practice a subtle but robust form of vocal agency. Attention to the flow of breath in a range of Shakespeare's plays—including *Richard III*, *Titus Andronicus*, *Othello*, and especially *King John*—prompts us to challenge certain modern assumptions about the relationship between voice and agency. Where a traditional view of potent, transgressive speech might emphasize a bond between voice and body—the speaking agent having "a voice of her own"—in these plays the *disarticulation* of voice from body generates vocal power. I find, moreover, that this more capacious model of agency is especially available to, and practiced by, female characters.

The transformative work of this model is made possible in large part by the theater, the space through which this breath moves. When we read plays on the page, we can be tempted to treat breath as a mere metaphor for speech, voice, or language. In fact, that is largely how breath has been discussed by prior critics.[5] Yet in the theater, breath is not only a metaphor, but, indeed simultaneously, the physical substance that enables the actors to convey to audiences the language of the script. One of the most important materials of the actor's craft, breath is "material" to the actor's voice in the broader early modern (now obsolete) sense of "materials" as the "the constituent, intrinsic, or essential parts of something."[6] Breath signifies on stage in ways that can complement but may also counter the verbal language of a play-text. Multivalent meanings of breath and their implications for vocal agency emerge in particularly sharp relief in the public theater where plays like *King John* were first performed. For, as we shall see, the marginalized characters that tend to embrace breath's unstable form—women, as well as youths—were originally played by boy actors, whose capacity (and incapacity) for vocal control already provoked fascination and concern. When the marginalized characters of Shakespeare's plays underscore the precarious materiality of their utterances, they establish a parallel between the challenges of vocal agency that face them as characters in the fiction of a play and the challenges that face actors in the theatrical performance of a play.

Breath's Obstacles in *King John*

Though this chapter will examine a range of texts concerned with breath—including a book of anatomy, treatises on acoustics, writings about environmental air, and several of Shakespeare's plays—the center of our analysis will be *King John*, the Shakespeare play that uses breath more pervasively than any other to interrogate the relationship between voice and agency. Jane Donawerth observes that *King John* ranks second among Shakespeare's plays for oral speech imagery (including tongue, mouth, throat, ear, air, and breath), and she points out that the play's descriptions of language tend to be more physical than in other plays that emphasize linguistic imagery, with "breath" being the most frequent metaphor for language.[7] It is partly through meditations on the physicality of breath that *King John* grapples with an issue that has dominated criticism of the play since the late twentieth century: language and authority.[8] Language in *King John* has been described as an "agent of dissolution" in a world devoid of a single external base of authority and a "manifestation of the corruption in political ambition."[9] For most critics who address linguistic instability in *King John*, speech in the play is interesting insofar as it intersects with a range of historical practices and cultural ideologies that were the site of early modern debates about authority, including patrilineal descent, historiographic methodology, patriotic values, religious providentialism, and Machiavellian individualism.[10] Yet despite extensive work on the relationship between the play's speech and the forces generating early modern culture, scholars have neglected a central material practice that the speech of the play addresses:

the composition of the voices that *produce* speech. In its frequent references to breath, *King John* emphasizes breath not simply as a metaphor for language or an "image" for speech but as the material ingredient that enables spoken words to be heard—to recall Bacon, the ingredient that "*maketh* the Voice."

By shifting emphasis from styles of speech to the materiality of voice, from language to "language machines," I am able to interrogate the story *King John* seems to tell about gender and vocal agency.[11] To be sure, as in many of Shakespeare's plays, in *King John* characters' styles of speech code gender differences and establish hierarchies: the play's competing male leaders attempt to shore up their political power by using types of speech that seem to convey authority and superiority, like boasting and swearing oaths; by contrast, *King John*'s marginalized women, especially Constance and Eleanor, seem to sustain their marginalization through types of speech that convey helplessness and deference, such as pleading, speaking softly, and lamentation. Yet as *King John* underscores breath's role in producing all of these speech genres, it troubles the basis for such gender differences. Particular linguistic expressions and verbal styles may signal a priori positions of power, but the breath engaged to produce these expressions reveals the unsteady *conditions* of power. Ephemeral, unpredictable, and transient, breath puts pressure on the boundaries between oaths and pleas, boasts and laments. As I will argue in the next section of this chapter, the volatility of breath opens up opportunities for disenfranchised figures to intervene vocally in the play's masculinist political culture. Constance, Eleanor, and Arthur take advantage of ambiguities concerning the nature of vocal matter, discovering the power that can inhere in the unsteady material composition of the voice. Breath's peculiar material attributes are less generative for *King John*'s male leaders, to whom we will first turn. Insofar as they need to demonstrate vocal control in order to sustain political power, they are threatened by breath's capacity to destabilize vocal transmission.

At the center of the struggle for power in *King John* is a question of who masters men's voices. Throughout the play, male leaders iterate their authority by claiming they can control breath, a substance that by its very material nature resists such mastery. For instance, when the Pope's legate Pandulph demands that John answer to charges of slighting Rome, John views the demand as an attempt to seize control of his breath. Instead of responding to the query, John challenges Pandulph's right to interrogate a divinely appointed monarch: "What earthy name to interrogatories / Can task the free breath of a sacred king?" (3.1.147–48). His response and the stand-off it initiates dramatize what Gail Kern Paster has recently described as the "pneumatics of power" that structure early modern male social interactions: "movements of breath and air between characters as signaling relations of power and preeminence—especially as breath is expended aggressively in laughter, anger, or scorn."[12] In the exchange between John and Pandulph, the movement of breath graphs male political clout as the leaders struggle to gain rhetorical and physical advantage in a touchy diplomatic negotiation. For these men, moreover, power inheres in the capacity to control and discipline breath—as opposed to (as in the examples Paster discusses) the right to release breath at will. John frames his refusal to submit politically as a resistance to expending his breath in speech: answering to Rome requires relinquishing on command breath that should be "free" to be withheld. The folio version of the play underscores what is physically and politically at stake for John in preventing his breath from undergoing circulation. In place of "task," the folio uses the more sensual "tast"—which similarly means "to put to test."[13] It is as if John bristles at the implication that his "free breath" will, if it enters the space beyond his body, be *tasted*, and thus possibly consumed, even possessed, by his rival.[14]

Pandulph fights back not only by excommunicating John but by using his vocal authority to convince the French to wage war against England in the name of the Church. Like John, Pandulph maintains that his political power is a function of his capacity to control the physical movements of his breath. Later in the play, he persuades the French leadership to remain engaged in the war by boasting that the material attributes of his voice are powerful enough to deliver England's throne to the Dauphin Lewis:

Now hear me speak with a prophetic spirit,
For even the breath of what I mean to speak
Shall blow each dust, each straw, each little rub
Out of the path which shall directly lead
Thy foot to England's throne. (3.4.126–30)

Imagining that he can clear the way for Lewis's political future through the local motion of the very breath he uses to speak, Pandulph represents his vocal command as not only analogous to, but constitutive of, his power over world events. His persuasive power is not simply a matter of rhetorical craft or even of spiritual authority but a function of his voice's material form, which enables him to sweep aside even the most persistent and minute of obstacles. Pandulph considers his dominion over his breath so complete that when John finally apologizes to Rome and asks the legate to pressure France into peace, Pandulph confidently declares himself able to change Lewis's mind: "It was my breath that blew this tempest up / . . . / My tongue shall hush again this storm of war" (5.1.17–20).

Impediments to Pandulph's fantasies of vocal mastery surface, however, when Lewis challenges Pandulph's authority by deconstructing the legate's arrogant claims about his breath. Refusing to lay down his arms, Lewis redefines Pandulph's "holy breath" (5.2.68) as simply hot air:

Your breath first kindled the dead coal of wars
Between this chastised kingdom and myself
And brought in matter that should feed this fire,
And now 'tis far too huge to be blown out
With that same weak wind which enkindled it. (5.2.83–87)

To undermine Pandulph, Lewis testifies to the unpredictable nature of breath, which no man can really master. Lewis recalls how Pandulph's breath encouraged the fires of war by bringing in "matter," a term that refers simultaneously to the physical composition of Pandulph's voice as well as its weighty, litigious content. Pandulph's voice has stirred up Anglo-French conflict, bringing in politico-religious pressures. Yet Lewis, adapting the early modern proverb "a little wind kindles, much puts out the fire,"[15] goes on to counter that Pandulph may once have produced enough breath to reignite tensions between the nations, but this "weak wind" cannot dissipate a full-fledged, blazing fire already in progress. Fires obey laws of nature that exist beyond even the most steady and controlled human action—something audiences who attended the Globe's eventful 1613 performance of *Henry VIII* would have observed.

Despite his rhetorically effective claim that no human being has the capacity to direct natural phenomena, Lewis shares Pandulph's audacious belief that he can keep the flames of war moving to his own advantage. In the same breath that he challenges Pandulph's agency, he flaunts his own. Using the personal pronoun "I" almost a dozen times in his thirty-line riposte, he claims the victories of war to be his own, the progress of this "fire" to be a consequence of his actions—the self-guided work of one who is "too highborn to be . . . [an] instrument" (5.2.79–81) of Rome. Nevertheless, as recollections of the material world teach Pandulph his lesson about the contingency of voice, so they show Lewis the limits of personal agency in a tumultuous world. As the next scene unfolds, we learn that the ships Lewis assumes will clinch his victory against England crash to pieces, falling victim to unpredictable weather patterns that endanger the movement not only of words but of ships.

In its simultaneous acceptance of and suspicion about the agency of the breath, *King John* is in good historical company. Early modern anatomists and natural philosophers embrace similarly ambivalent positions on the nature of breath—an ambivalence I would argue is animated in part by their uneasy commitment to Aristotelian physics. Following Aristotle, early modern theorists of acoustics imagine breath as a significant material cause for voice. Franciscus Suàrez's 1621 translation of Aristotle's *De Anima* explains, "voice is the sound of animals that breathe. . . . voice is a sound, and sound does not exist except in air, and so neither does voice."[16] Simply put, Aristotle holds that vocal sound is produced when the breath produced by the lungs strikes against the speaker's windpipe during exhalation. The collision effects a compression of air, resulting in the production of sound as a kind of motion of the air. Writes Aristotle, "[a]ir in itself is, owing to its friability, quite soundless; only when its dissipation is prevented is its movement sound."[17] The human body is a particularly effective sound-producing device because, as Francis Bacon observes, "the *Voices of Men*, and Living Creatures, passe through the throat, which penneth the Breath" (no. 116). Ultimately, the transmission of sound is complete when the air carrying the speaker's voice reaches the listener's ears, which are filled with an inbred air, naturally still and prepared to be moved by the vibrations of the air that reach it. For Aristotle, then, vocal sound is, in its physical essence, a striking of air that sets into motion further movements of air. Breath is so central to Aristotle's definition of voice that he cites it as the material cause for the lack of voice among fish: "It is clear also why fish are voiceless; they have no windpipe. And they have no windpipe because they do not breathe or take in air."[18]

Early modern theories of acoustics, on the whole, follow Aristotle closely, recognizing breath as a key material cause for voice and air as an essential medium for the transmission of vocal sound. Yet as Bruce R. Smith points out, ancient explanations for voice were refined repeatedly in the early modern period through dissections and experiments conducted, respectively, by anatomists and natural philosophers.[19] Indeed, I would suggest, as anatomists and natural philosophers attempt to reconcile Aristotelian acoustic theory with their practical observations about sound, they (often unwittingly) expose Aristotle's limitations. Specifically, Aristotle's theories imply that a range of physical obstacles may impede the transmission of vocal sound, yet the theories fail to explain in material terms how vocal communication succeeds in the face of these challenges.[20] Early modern writings on the transmission of vocal sound tend to touch on three kinds of problems that Aristotelian physics raises but doesn't sufficiently explain: problems of spatial disparity, temporal delay, and environmental disruption. Each of these variables deserves brief discussion, especially insofar as they recur in Shakespeare's representations of failing vocal communication.

First is the problem of distance between the sounding object and the receiver. In *Sylva Sylvarum*, Bacon follows Aristotle in maintaining that for a sound to be heard, there must be some distance between the sounding object and the ear. Simply the "cave of the ear" itself can provide this necessary distance, helping to protect the fragile organs of hearing from damage by sound (no. 272). Yet when Bacon puts such theories to the test through various empirical demonstrations, he discovers that if the space between speaker and listener is "over-great," then "Distance confoundeth the *Articulation of Sound*." When, for example, an audience member stands too far away from the pulpit where a preacher speaks, Bacon writes, "you may heare the *Sound* of a Preachers voice, or the like, when you cannot distinguish what he saith" (no. 194).

A second essential but troubling feature of acoustics is temporal delay. Helkiah Crooke follows Aristotle when he notes that sound travels more slowly than sight: "when two hard bodyes are smitten the one against the other, we see the purcussion before we heare the sound, for we do not heare the sound before the ayre that was moved do bring the sound with it to our eares, neither is that motion made in a moment but *in time*."[21] Bacon similarly notes that "the *Impression* of the *Aire* with *Sounds*, asketh a time to be conveighed to the *Sense*" (no. 122). A shot fired twenty miles away "will come to the Eare; Not in the Instant of Shooting off, but it will come an Houre, or more later" (no. 208). In fact, as Bacon notes, it is only because sound is delayed in its medium that we are able to hear it at all. Thus, if a bullet moves especially quickly, it will be inaudible (no. 122). Delay may be essential to hearing, but it also leaves sounds vulnerable to disruption during their slower transmission. Bacon observes that since sounds move in "Oblique and Arcuate lines, [they] must needs encounter, and disturbe the one the other"; so "one *Articulate Sound* will confound another when many speake at once" (no. 224 and no. 194). It doesn't take much to interfere with the flow

of sound. Bacon and Crooke maintain that a speaker's voice will reach listeners most successfully if listeners hold their breath. This is because "in all
Expiration, the Motion is Outwards; And therefore, rather driveth away the
voice, than draweth it" (no. 284).[22] In other words, vocal sounds may be diminished or altered by a listener's breathing because that breath pushes
away the incoming air that carries a voice.

Even if a speaker can overcome auditors' expirations and competing
sounds, the medium of air threatens to disperse sound, subjecting it to any
number of environmental disruptions—a third factor that impedes vocal
communication. Like the other variables that compromise vocal sound, the
medium of air, what early moderns call the "externall" air (as opposed to
"internall" air, which resides in the ear), is as troubling as it is necessary.[23]
Though early modern writers debate the superiority of air over water as an
external medium for sound, they generally follow Aristotle in maintaining
that air is more efficient, since "in water the Sound is but dull."[24] While air
provides a crucial medium for sound's production and transmission, the
quality of the air—its density, temperature, and local motion—can also endanger sound. Crooke writes that "pure-thin and cleere ayre" will "receive
the sound" more quickly than "Ayre which is contained in a concavous or
hollow place."[25] Bacon, though he sometimes vacillates on whether the quality of local air can affect sound, maintains that we hear better at night or in
the evening as well as when the southern winds are blowing because the
thickness of the air at these times "preseveth the *Sound* better from Wast[e]"
(no. 218).[26] Perhaps the most disruptive of these local air conditions is wind.
When Bacon observes that "*Audibles* doe hang longer in the Aire, than those
of *Visibles*," he notes that this is not only "because of the Distance of the
Time" but because audibles "are carried up and downe with the Winde" (no.
274).[27] Crooke uses the example of bell-ringing to demonstrate the effect of
such environmental agents: "when the winde bloweth towards us we shall
heare [the bells] very lowd . . . ; when the ayre is whiffed another way, the
sound . . . of the bels will be taken from us."[28]

The effects of these obstacles—spatial, temporal, and environmental—
could be observed not just in scientific demonstrations but in the laboratory
of the theater, a space, as Smith and Wes Folkerth remind us, that was dominated by sound.[29] Indeed, for Shakespeare the unpredictable conditions of
sound's transmission make for good drama. In *3 Henry VI* the effects of
wind that Crooke describes become the basis for an elegant conceit concerning the viability of men's vows. When the imprisoned Henry tries to con-

vince his jail-keepers that they are not bound by oaths of loyalty they have sworn to the new king, Henry demonstrates how the breath used to produce these oaths is vulnerable to environmental winds. At first Henry invokes his breath only to remind the jail-keepers that, in line with theories of the king's two bodies, Henry remains the rightful monarch as long as he is alive; when the keepers refer to Henry as a *former* king, he asks rhetorically, "Why, am I dead? Do I not breath a man?" (3.1.81). Quickly, however, Henry shifts from using breath as a signifier of life to one of voice, proceeding to devalue the keepers' vows to the new king:

Ah, simple men, you know not what you swear.
Look as I blow this feather from my face,
And as the air blows it to me again,
Obeying with my wind when I do blow,
And yielding to another when it blows,
Commanded always by the greater gust—
Such is the lightness of you common men. (3.1.82–8)

While the jail-keepers insist on the meaningfulness of their oaths of loyalty, Henry uses the feather to demonstrate that if the men's vows are made of breath, a substance as easily blown by external winds as a feather, then the vows cannot promise unshakable commitment.[30] Henry demonstrates that the men and their breathed vows are, like the feather, vulnerable to the winds of circumstance, "commanded always by the greater gust."[31]

If voice is air, vulnerable to destruction by the environment through which it moves, then how, at the most basic level, do speakers ensure the transmission of their voices? For those who have the power to manipulate the material conditions of sound transmission, vocal success can be achieved more easily, of course. Seventeenth century acoustic science is replete with human attempts to shape vocal sound, mastering its movements to achieve certain effects. Bacon discovers that he can create the illusion of distant voices by speaking from inside a bucket submerged halfway under water (no. 155). He also notes that the best way to achieve the "delation of sounds" is by enclosing them, for instance, in "Roules of Parchment, or Trunckes": when "the Mouth [is] laid to the one end of the Rowle of Parchement, or Truncke, and the *Eare* to the other, the *Sound* is heard much further, than in the *Open Aire*" (no. 129). Scientist-inventor Athanasius Kircher demonstrates these principles at work in his illustrations of acoustic contraptions, one of which demonstrates Bacon's principle of enclosure (see

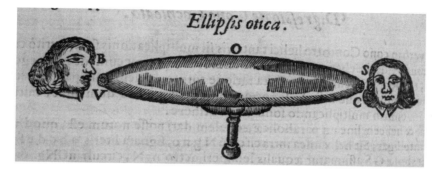

Figure 1. Instrument that demonstrates how enclosed elliptical objects amplify sound. Athanasius Kircher, *Musurgia Universalis sive Ars Magna Consoni et Dissoni* (Rome, 1650), 304. Photo courtesy of The Newberry Library, Chicago.

figure 1). Kircher's confidence in the capacity to manipulate sound is evident perhaps most fantastically in his speaking statues, whose open mouths emit sounds that are drawn via grand megaphone systems from another room or even from the town square (see figure 2). The choreography of vocal sounds was carried out effectively in less grandiose ways as well. Bacon explains, for instance, that pulpits are elevated above audiences so as to facilitate a superior acoustic arrangement: sounds move more efficiently downward than upward (no. 205). And Smith has shown how early modern theater spaces were designed to improve the flow of sound between actors and audience, not to mention between audience members.[32]

While steadily working on ways to direct sound's movements, early modern theorists of acoustics accept the limits of their task. Even Bacon admits that sound, by nature, is difficult to control. "The *Reflexion* of *Species Visible*, by *Mirrours*, you may command; Because passing in Right Lines, they may be guided to any Point: But the *Reflexion of Sounds* is hard to master; Because the *Sound* filling great Spaces in Arched Lines, cannot be so guided" (no. 242). From a material perspective, vocal sound seems resistant to human choreography, "commanded always by the greater gust." As Bacon and Crooke, along with Shakespeare, highlight the instabilities of communication through their meditations on the transmission of vocal sound, they throw into historical relief certain modern theoretical presuppositions about voice. These writers do not presume the voice to be, in Jacques Derrida's famous term, "transcendent presence"—a presumption that prompts

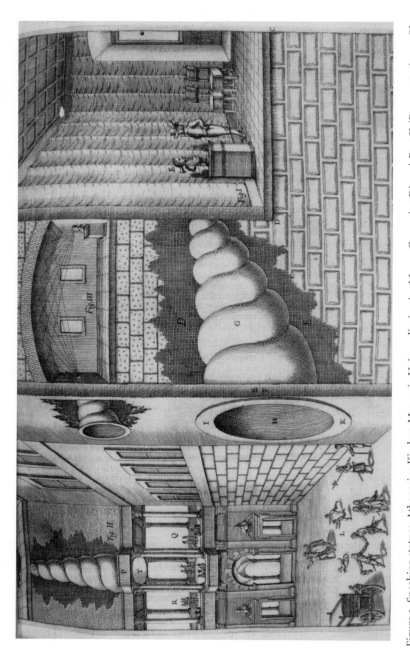

Figure 2. Speaking statues. Athanasius Kircher, *Musurgia Universalis sive Ars Magna Consoni et Dissoni*, Part II (Rome, 1650), 303. Photo courtesy of The Newberry Library, Chicago.

Derrida to turn to writing as a privileged medium for the project of deconstruction. Insofar as early moderns call attention to the material attributes
of the voice, its composition as breath, they define voice the way Derrida defines writing: as always conducive to rupture—by distance, delay, and environmental interference.[33] For Bacon and Crooke, such rupture is a source of
scientific curiosity. For the oath-swearing men of *3 Henry VI*, however, it is
a considerable source of anxiety. Demonstrating an ability to guarantee
oaths, to keep one's word, is an important marker of early modern manhood not only for these "common men" but also, indeed especially, for nobles and aristocrats like Henry.[34] Their sustained political authority is
contingent upon a seamless reiteration of vocal control, a perceived ability
to uphold their vows.

John and Pandulph in *King John* evince one method for grappling with
the uncertain material nature of breath: they claim an ability to control
breath's elusive movements, John gripping hold of his "free breath" and Pandulph claiming to clear political obstacles with his "holy breath." Though
they both possess significant spiritual authority—a "sacred king" and a
legate with a "prophetic voice"—neither assumes that his innate connection
to the sacred is enough to secure his utterances against physical obstacles.
Perhaps paradoxically, men in the play who lack clear spiritual authority
adopt a different strategy: they disavow breath's materiality, emphasizing
more strongly its spiritual nature. Philip does just that when, as he defies the
command of his spiritual leader, the Catholic Church, he insists his vow of
peace with England is spiritually binding:

This royal hand and mine are newly knit,
And the conjunction of our inward souls
Married in league, coupled and linked together
With all religious strength of sacred vows;
The latest breath that gave the sound of words
Was deep-sworn faith, peace, amity, true love
Between our kingdoms and our royal selves. (3.1.226–32)

Philip claims that the "breath that gave the sound of words" embodied not
simply the physical but the spiritual ethos of its speakers. The joining of
hands may have been symbolic of an agreement, but the exchange and cou-
pling of the leaders' breath enacted a deeper commitment, a "conjunction
of . . . souls." [35] Composed of breath, the monarchs' vows were "sacred,"
bounded by "religious strength." The point is underscored when Pandulph

commands Philip to prove the peace treaty broken by dropping John's hand; Philip responds by reminding Pandulph that the bond breath created between two souls is less easily fractured than that between two hands. Recalling the "deep-sworn faith" that was sounded by his breath, Philip maintains, "I may disjoin my hand, but not my faith" (3.1.262). Philip endows the "sound of words" with stability and certainty by representing those words as composed of soulful breath. Similarly, when Salisbury and the other noblemen of *King John* discover Arthur's dead body and, believing this to be John's work, vow revenge against the sacred King, Salisbury appeals to the spiritual nature of his breath as the source for the steadfastness of his oath: "Kneeling before this ruin of sweet life [the dead body of Arthur], / And breathing to his breathless excellence / The incense of a vow, a holy vow" (4.3.65–67). Echoing Salisbury's sentiment that the breathing of a vow is equivalent to spiritual commitment to the matter at stake, Pembroke and Bigot solemnly recite together, "Our souls religiously confirm thy words" (4.3.73).

Philip and the nobles can appeal to the sacred content of their voices, even while defying their principal religious leaders, in part because the Christian tradition to which they claim continued subscription had long associated breath with spiritual authority. The Latin term *spiritus* derives from the Proto-Indo-European base *(s)peis*, "to blow" and comes into English as *spirit* primarily through the Vulgate, where it serves as a translation for the Greek *pneuma* and the Hebrew *ruach*—used in the Hebrew Bible to refer to the breath of life that animated Adam in the book of Genesis. As the concept of *spirit* was developed by Christian theologians, it became understood as the divine force—or divine in*spir*ation—that inhabits the bodies and voices of earthly believers, an idea that is codified theologically through the entity of the Holy Spirit. Breath's connection to voice, notably, is central to Christian definitions of the Holy Spirit. According to Acts 2, the Holy Spirit revealed itself to believers through a miraculous aural event (commemorated annually in England through the festival of Whit Sunday and by Pentecostal Christians who "speak in tongues" when they claim to be inhabited by the Holy Spirit). As the story goes, when Jesus' disciples convened on the day of the first Pentecost, they suddenly heard "a sound from heaven, as of a rushing mighty winde" and appearing above them were "cloven tongues, like as of fire": "And they were al filled with the holy Ghost, and beganne to speake with other tongues, as the spirit gave them utterance." The miracle was that the multilingual crowd present could understand the disciples, as "every man heard them speake in his owne language."[36] Working in large part from this story of the first Pentecost, Christian theologians would come to interpret the Holy Spirit as a kind of great communicator, a mediator between God and earthly persons.

This Christian sense of spirit as the sacred breath that miraculously delivers meaning through vocal sound pervades much early modern philosophizing about vocal transmission. The occult philosopher and theologian Heinrich Cornelius Agrippa von Nettesheim claims that it is "spirit," carried by the breath expelled during speech, that ensures the speaker's intended meaning will be grasped by a listener. "Sound is a breath, voyce is a sound and animate breath; Speech is a breath pronounced with sound, and a voyce signifying something: the spirit of which proceedeth out of the mouth with sound and voyce; Chaludius saith that a voyce is sent forth out of the inward cavity of the breast and heart, by the assistance of the spirit."[37] While recognizing that breath produces all sorts of vocal sounds, Agrippa distinguishes "voyce" as sound that is "animated" by spirit, which leaves the mouth along with breath to convey the message of the speaker's heart. The roots of this concept of an "animate" breath are deeper than Christian theology, however. The connection between breath, voice, and divine presence develops in part from the writings of Philo of Alexandria (c. 15 B.C.– c. A.D. 50), who fused Greek and Jewish thought. Philo's concept of *pneuma*, breath or wind, encompasses a range of meanings: *pneuma* infuses the body; provides the "directive principle" that evinces reason; moves through the windpipe to produce speech; and is associated with divine inspiration.[38]

Yet to understand how breath comes to convey authority and intentionality for early modern writers, we need to go back even further to Aristotle. As noted above, in *De Anima* Aristotle maintains that the human voice acquires its capacity to create meaning when the soul stirs the air within the body, causing that air to strike the vocal organs and the speaker to expel the breath that carries words.[39] Soul, or form, is effectively transmitted in the breath expelled during voiced speech. *Anima*, like the terms *pneuma* and *spiritus*, signifies a range of ideas we associate with living creatures—including, mind, soul, feeling, and living being more generally—but is most fundamentally connected to breath, from the Proto-Indo-European *ane-*, "to blow, to breathe."[40] As ancient and medieval philosophers and theologians would continue to reiterate, the capacity to breathe in and out with intention evinces animate life and, most particularly where voice is concerned, a rational mind. Aristotle maintains that the presence of the soul helps us distinguish actual from imitated speech, or beastly sound from human voice. A parrot may be able to replicate human vocalization, but that sound does not qualify as "voice," which can only be produced by a creature in possession of a rational soul. The soul is responsible for not only the production but also the successful transmission of a vocal utterance. Aristotle emphasizes that the sound conducted through the air between speaker and listener is not a corporeal mass moving from one place to another but rather an echo of form.[41] By way of explanation, Aristotle offers the example of ice slowly developing across a lake: the ice appears here, then there, and there, producing the illusion of movement, when in fact there is only a chain of resounding form.[42] The same is true of sound. The air breathed by the speaker resonates with the airy medium, which resonates with the air in the listener's inner ear.

Through this association of breath with soul or form, Aristotle supplements his material explanations for vocal sound, discussed above, with more immaterial ones. This emphasis on immaterial explanations is not surprising given Aristotle's basic distrust of matter. Like other ancient medical authorities, Aristotle views material bodies as composed of four elements (air, earth, fire, and water) in a constant state of disruption. Bodies need to attain equilibrium in order to resist disintegration, but that equilibrium is constantly thrown off by the precarious environment to which bodies are so responsive. To explain what appears to be the stability of matter all around us, authorities from Aristotle to Galen presented soul or form as an "active cause" of persistence.[43] For Aristotle, the material composition of breath renders it inconstant and communication unpredictable, but insofar as breath facilitates the motion of the speaker's soul, it can secure acts of vocal communication.

Early modern theorists of acoustics echo Aristotle's perspective on the ensouled voice partly through their use of the concept of a sensory "species." As Crooke explains, when two objects collide, the sound they produce is translated into a form that the perceiver will be able to sense, an "audible species." The sound we hear is not the original sound produced by the collision of objects but rather a re-presentation of that sound, what Bacon also calls an "image" of the sound. The concept of species helps explain how a sound can have such an intense impact on a hearer's thoughts and feelings. It explains, to take one popular example, why music is capable of causing one to weep or of lifting one's mood.[44] Bacon explains that audible species are "incorporeall" and are "of so *Tender*, and *Weake* a *Nature*, as they affect onely such a Rare, and Attenuate *Substance*, as is the *Spirit* of *Living Creatures*" (no. 938). The species' incorporeal and "attenuate" nature, similar in constitution to the soul of the listener, has a special ability to work as an intermediary between the souls of speaking and listening subjects.[45] Bacon uses the theory of spirits further to explain how sound can penetrate through hard objects. Proposing that all material bodies contain pockets of trapped spirits, or "pneumatical parts," Bacon maintains that when sound (in the form of the spiritual species) passes through a hard body, the body's pneumatic parts, which have a similar constitution as the audible species they encounter, "co-operate" with the species. Sound is thus able to move through what seems an impenetrable body (nos. 136, 150, 167, and 213). The movement of sound within an object thus follows the same principles of sound transmission in the ambient, outside air: the spiritual essence of the sound is transmitted through an airy substance that shares and thus cooperates with the sound's tenuous, spiritual constitution. Bacon's theory of spirits, the complexities of which I have only begun to address here, is an eclectic mix of philosophical traditions, as much a divergence as an adaptation of Aristotle. Yet the key point is that for Bacon, as for Aristotle, sensory perception involves the transmission of an immaterial substance. Whether it be called soul, form, image, or species, this incorporeal substance acts as an ambassador for the "original" vocal sound, carrying the kernel of that articulation through the volatile air that separates the auditor from the speaker.[46]

Balthazar Gerbier's lecture *The Art of Well Speaking* (1650) provides an elegant explanation for how the spiritual essence of a thought remains constant while being transmitted through the external air:

[T]he life of a humane voyce, the very Spirituall Soule of that voyce, that is to say, its sence, is partly Spirituall, and partly Intelectuall; its that which enters into the pores by permission of the corporall ayre, where it remaines; and having knockt at the doore, and obtained entrance, the spirit then of humane speech, which is the speeches sence, bereaves its selfe of that Corporeall robe, and is conveyed unto our intelectuall parts, and there manifests it selfe, as in a true draught, the very being, thoughts, conceptions, desires, inclinations, and the other Spirituall passions of him that speaketh.[47]

Gerbier imagines that when a voice is released by a body, its "Spiritualle Soule"—the essential sense of the message—is clothed in a "Corporeall robe." In this form the message is able to enter the air that fills the space between the speaker and listener and ultimately to arrive at its destination: the ear or "doore" of the listener. Upon arrival, the message divests itself of its carriage, its "Corporeall robe," and proceeds in naked spiritual form to the "intelectuall parts" of the hearer, where the act of communication—the transfer of the speaker's "thoughts, conceptions, desires, etc."—occurs. For Gerbier, the real power of an utterance is its "Spiritualle Soule," which, transmitted virtually intact ("as in a true draught"), enables a voice to affect a listener in the way the speaker intends. We can see why *King John*'s noblemen would so frequently summon a spiritual discourse of breath, for according to this view, the effectiveness of speech is virtually entirely dependent on the intentions of the speaker, intentions that can be efficiently conveyed to others through the vehicle of breath.[48] Through its connection to the soul, breath promises to stabilize and authorize an otherwise precarious process of communication.[49]

While arguments about "formal" causation provide a theoretical, temporary retreat from the uncertainties of the material world, they do not provide a practical, permanent escape. Like Philip, the oath-swearing men of *King John* are quickly disabused of their confidence in promises uttered, as the material conditions of speaking undermine the spiritual authority of oaths. However passionate their commitments, the English nobles are just as incapable of keeping their "holy vows" against John as they were in keeping their initial oaths of loyalty to him. As soon as they hear that Lewis has secretly vowed to execute them after they help him win the war, they return to John, swearing their allegiance—to use Henry's words, "blown always by the greater gust." Significantly, Lewis's threat of execution plays on the language the nobles had used when they first articulated their oaths. According to the dying Melun, who relates Lewis's words, Lewis has sworn that

even this night, whose black contagious breath
Already smokes about the burning crest
Of the old, feeble, and day-wearied sun—
Even this ill night your breathing shall expire. (5.4.33–36)

The night's approach is imagined as rapidly spreading black air, "contagious breath" surrounding the men whose lives will end as their "breathing . . . expires." Once we recall that the nobles highlight breath in their original swearing of oaths against John—"breathing to [Arthur's] breathless excellence / The incense of a vow, a holy vow" (4.3.66–67)—we can more easily observe Lewis's pun on *expire*. The figurative description of dying as losing one's breath is analogous with the physical act of speaking—both involve the expulsion or *expiration* of breath.[50] Moreover, "expire," etymologically related to *spirare* and *spiritus* (from the same Proto-Indo-European root *[s]peis*, meaning "to blow") invokes the language of religiosity that so marked the nobles' initial swearing ceremony. The pun effectively mocks the solemnity of the noble's earlier oaths, underscoring, in contrast, the fragile material form of even the most heartfelt and sacred utterances.

"Breath of Soft Petitions": Women's Windy Words

I have argued so far that breath, as it accentuates the unpredictable nature of voice, underscores the volatility of speech and its consequent potential for failure. It is not surprising that when *King John*'s male leaders invoke breath, they disavow its material features or insist they can control the movements of this ephemeral, mercurial substance; their positions as leaders, indeed their very identities as men, are contingent upon a seamless reiteration of their vocal authority. *King John*'s female characters, to whom I'll now turn, have less at stake in this respect. Early modern constructions of femininity, as Paster has shown, naturalize women's failures to control a variety of bodily flows.[51] And *King John*, in keeping with early modern ideologies of women's leakiness, represents female characters as incapable of controlling the flow of their breath. To be sure, such representations reaffirm problematic gender hierarchies, reinforcing a sense that women's bodies and voices require disciplining. Yet the volatility of breath is not always a source of crisis.[52] Indeed, breath's unpredictable movements and subtle material nature lend power to certain speakers. *King John*'s female characters, when they embrace the material composition of their voices, are, in fact, able to take advantage of breath's capacious meanings. As I shall suggest, female characters in this play, along with some other histories and tragedies, mobilize the dense philosophical, etymological, and theological connections breath (as *anima, pneuma, spirit*) affords, exploiting breath's myriad manifestations in and as air, wind, life, soul, spirit, and, of course, voice. As they associate the female voice with breath's peculiar material features, the plays fortify seemingly weak genres of speech, offering marginalized characters—and the boy actors who embodied these characters—surprising access to vocal power.

Take, for instance, Eleanor's first utterance of the play, a whisper. When Eleanor reprimands her son John for boasting too boldly in public that England is his by right, she does so quietly:

Your strong possession much more than your right,
Or else it must go wrong with you and me;
So much my conscience whispers in your ear,
Which none but heaven and you and I shall hear. (1.1.40–43)

Eleanor subtly subverts the power structure of the court by exploiting a tension between the rhetorical and physical significations of her breath. As Juliet Dusinberre argues, Eleanor's whispered rebuke may be construed within the fiction of the play as a private utterance, but the speech actually appeals strategically to the theater audience, who clearly are also party to Eleanor's remark.[53] Breath links, but also underscores the disparity between, these two audiences. For while the character of Eleanor uses her breath to whisper the lines, the actor playing Eleanor must engage both breath and larynx to project these lines, incorporating visual markers of the *aside* to indicate private speech. Eleanor may figure her critical maternal voice as breath—gentle in its tone, inaudible to anyone but John—but she *performs* her voice loudly to the theater audience, wryly reminding them that she holds the royal reins. Eleanor's use of breath exposes her power as rooted in her public theatrical presence, not simply, as many other critics have assumed, in her character's outspokenness.[54] For Eleanor shows that women may seize vocal authority even when their voices are, as King Lear puts it, "soft, / Gentle, and low, an excellent thing in a woman" (*King Lear* 5.3.246–47).

Insofar as Eleanor recognizes that breath need not be commanded and direct in order to work effectively on behalf of its speaker, she is well positioned to judge the potential vocal impact of her rival Constance, who believes her own son Arthur to be the rightful heir to the English throne. Without the authority to threaten violent action or swear ominous oaths (like Pandulph, John, and the nobles), Constance's sole course of verbal action is to plead to France for support. The pleas work initially, helping incite France's war against England. But as the French and English forces prepare to battle for Angiers, Hubert, in a bold speech that witnesses compare to "cannon-fire" (2.1.462), persuades the feuding kings to consider a peace plan. Pleased by these developments, which benefit her family, Eleanor fears that the greatest threat to peace will be further supplications from Constance—supplications John considers feeble. But Eleanor urges her son not to underestimate Constance's vocal power, and thus to shore up a treaty with the French quickly:

Lest zeal now melted[,] by the windy breath
Of soft petitions, pity, and remorse,
Cool and congeal again to what it was. (2.1.477–79)

Drawing attention to the "windy breath" that comprises Constance's soft petitions seems, on the one hand, to mock Constance the way Beatrice mocks Benedick in *Much Ado About Nothing*. Beatrice submits that Benedick's "foul words" with Claudio are useless, for "Foul words is but foul wind, and foul wind is but foul breath, and foul breath is noisome" (5.2.43–44). Reduced through syllogism to windy breath, Benedick's acts of vocal aggression are rendered meaningless, their ephemeral physical nature revealing their impotence.[55] Yet where Constance is concerned, such windiness signals not a failing, but a surprisingly powerful, voice. Eleanor worries that should Constance manage to interrupt the peace proceedings and, with her "windy breath / Of soft petitions" remind the French of their obligation to Arthur, the French will realize how unethical it is to abandon Constance and Arthur and will break the treaty with England, committing with even more ardent zeal to Arthur's cause. Should Constance be successful, John will encounter much more difficulty mitigating French support for Arthur in future negotiations, for France's "zeal" will become like steel—iron that, once heated, melted, and cooled, becomes fortified. Eleanor argues that John must intervene before Constance's breath can "cool and congeal" France's "now melted" commitment to Arthur.

This interpretation of Constance's vocal power has eluded modern critics of the play, in part, I would argue, because they have not read Eleanor's lines in light of early modern views of the material attributes of breath.[56] Early modern natural philosophers had established that liquefied substances congeal and harden when they cool, and that breath could alter the temperature of a substance with which it comes into contact. Indeed the breath's ability to act as an agent of both warming and cooling is a source of amazement to Thomas Wright, who writes, "Some men wonder (and not without reason) how it commeth to passe, that out of the same mouth should issue a cold wind to coole the hot pottage, and a hot breath to warme the cold hands."[57] Dramatist Francis Beaumont, like Shakespeare, loses little time drawing parallels between the breath used to change the temperature of a substance like porridge and the breath, or wind, used to produce speech. So Mistress Merrythought in *Knight of the Burning Pestle* observes when she mocks Venturewell for his unwelcome lecture: "[L]et him keep his wind to cool his porridge."[58] From this perspective Constance has the vocal power to effect change without needing, like Hubert, to "speak . . . plain cannon-fire" (2.1.62) Her circuitous, undirected pleading can, like the air that cools porridge or melted iron, congeal and harden that which has become softened by heat: Constance's breath can reconstitute France's enfeebled support for Arthur.

Eleanor further underscores the strength of Constance's pleading by gesturing—as do Wright, Beaumont, and many of their contemporaries—toward the correspondence between breath, wind, and speech. In Wright's passage, breath and wind are interchangeable terms; Beaumont's passage invokes the correspondence more subtly, substituting "wind" for Venturewell's voice. The slippage between these terms has its roots, in large part, in ancient Greek medical theories, in which a correspondence between external winds and the body's internal vital breath helped explain the etiology of disease. Although the Greeks used different words for breath, air, and wind, all were considered a form of *pneuma* (breath, *physa*, is in the body; *aer* is outside the body; and *anemos*, related etymologically to the Latin *anima*, is the flow of air, or wind).[59] As Paster has shown, the close association between these various movements and forms of air signaled for the ancients, as well as for the early moderns who retain these ideas, the porousness of the body and the reciprocity between bodily experienced emotions and the environment.[60] Lynn Enterline has also examined the implications of this slippage between terms, arguing that it enabled lyric poets to comment self-reflectively on the evanescent craft of poetry and the pressures of producing such poetry through the medium of writing.[61] I am primarily interested, however, in how the correspondence of terms extends to, and has particularly resonant implications for, the representation of the spoken voice. Note, for instance, in *Othello* the description of the Cyprus coast storm as "the wind [that] hath spoke aloud at land" (2.1.5) and Cassio's prayer to Jove on behalf of Othello's voyage at sea: "swell his sail with thine own powerful breath" (2.1.79). Cassio's "thine own" underscores that he makes a comparison between his own breath, used to vocalize this prayer, and Jove's auspicious winds. Emilia, too, invokes an analogy between her voice and the powerful force of the wind when she refuses to obey Iago's command that she be silent: " 'Twill out, 'twill out. I

peace? / No, I will speak as liberal as the north" (*Othello* 5.2.225–26)—
a reference to the northern winds, known for their vigorous, "lively"
nature.[62]

The slippage between breath, wind, and voice is common enough that
natural philosophers seeking greater precision in definition warn against it.
Bacon's *Sylva Sylvarum* insists that although speech—"one of the gentlest
Motions of *Aire*"—is produced by expelling breath with force, the sounds of
the voice are different from "*Locall Motion* of the Aire, (which is but *Vehicu-
lum Caussae, A Carrier of the Sounds*)" (no. 125). Bacon argues more vigorously for a distinction between breath and wind in his treatise devoted fully
to the latter. In *The Naturall and Experimentall History of Winds* (trans.
1653), Bacon takes issue with ancient writers who imagine wind to be an "exhalation": "But all impulsion of the Aire is winde; and Exhalations mixed
with the aire contribute more to the motion than to the matter."[63] That is,
the "exhalations" that ancients thought made up the wind are merely helpers
in its motion, not the wind's material itself.

Though Bacon is careful to distinguish the various forms of *pneuma*,
even he resorts to comparisons of breath to wind in order to underscore the
power that inheres in breath's peculiar material form: "The breath in mans
Microcosmos, and in other Animals, doe very well agree with the windes in
the greater world: For they are engendred by humours, and alter with moisture as winde and rain doth, and are dispersed and blow freer by a greater
heat. And from them that observation is to be transferred to the winds,
namely, that breaths are engendred of matter and that yeelds a tenacious
vapour, not easie to be dissolved; as Beanes, Pulse, and fruits; which is so
likewise in greater windes."[64] Breath, like wind, may be invisible, dispersed,
and mercurial, but insofar as it is "engendered of matter," it is "tenacious"
in its impact on its environment. Indeed, as is the case with wind, the qualities of breath that seem to compromise its power—unpredictable, fleeting,
and ungovernable—are precisely the qualities that render it dangerous.
Levinus Lemnius offers a similar perspective in his opening to *The Secret
Miracles of Nature* (originally published in Italian in 1563), which describes
dramatically the destruction breath of animals can wreak. The basilisk secretly kills men with the "hurtfull breath that proceeds from him"; the wolf
can inflict hoarseness on anyone he meets "by the gaping of his mouth, and
his venomous breath."[65] The most dangerous breath is that of other men,
which is why, Lemnius explains, one needs to avoid the breath of sick people. Lemnius underscores the qualities of the breath that render it such a

threat: "This breathing and flowing out, although it doth not present it self to our eyes, and lesse declared to our seeing sense, yet it bears it self into our nostrills, ears, brain, vocall artery, and the strings of the lungs. So I have observed some with such a stinking damp and strong smelling breath, that unlesse you stand farther off they would strike every one that they meet, with the contagion of their breath, and kill them. But every one may perceive how largely the breath of living creatures may stretch it self, how far a contagious disease may extend it self."[66] What makes breath powerful is not just its diseased content but its invisibility ("it doth not present it self to our eyes") and its mobility (how it "may stretch its self"). Notably, it is on similar grounds that Shakespeare's Pisanio credits slander with destructive power. Slander's

> breath
> Rides on the posting winds and doth belie
> All corners of the world. Kings, queens, and states,
> Maids, matrons, nay, the secrets of the grave
> This viperous slander enters. (*Cymbeline* 3.4.34–38)

The power of slander lies not only in its linguistic content but in its airy material form, which enables it to be swept far and wide by "posting winds." Because slander is made of breath, it can be picked up and moved effortlessly by environmental drafts, achieving an uncanny degree of distribution and effect.[67] Pisanio describes slander as seeping into its victims, paying little heed to social identity, gender, even to mortal status—harming the dead as well as the living. The very attributes of the breath that would seem to undermine its agency—particularly its vulnerability to dispersion by wind— are the qualities that account for breath's eerie power. As it "rides on positing winds," breath levels social difference, rendering kings and maids equally vulnerable to the effects of slander.

In *King John,* breath accomplishes a related equalizing feat. As we've seen, Eleanor imagines that breath lends surprising power to marginalized vocal acts, so that Constance's "windy breath of soft petitions" can effect political change as readily as Pandulph's "breath that blew this tempest up." Constance confirms the extended agency of her breath later in the play. When her son Arthur is lost and presumed dead, her cause so utterly defeated that even pleading becomes futile, Constance turns to the one remaining genre of speech available to her, lament. Constance's use of lament, one of the most common forms of female expression in Shakespeare's histories, seems to substantiate and iterate her marginalization from public political discourse. In comparison to her earlier supplications, which, however apparently feeble, were able to incite a war between two world powers, her laments for the loss of her son seem completely insignificant. At least that is how these laments appear to Pandulph, Philip, and Lewis, who label Constance's insistent cries a symptom of madness and try to quiet her rants by belittling her "too heinous a respect of grief" (3.4.90).[68]

This reaction to Constance's grief is typical by early modern standards. Uncontrollable expressions of woe, according to many writers, are to be expected from women and can even signal the comparative healthfulness of women's bodies. Early modern medical writers often sanction expressions of grief as therapeutic, helping to purge the body of harmful humors and to generate heat in a heart that has been frozen and desiccated by sadness.[69] Breath essentially operates as the body's ventilation system, securing the health of the heart. Hamlet's "windy su*spir*ation of forced breath" (*Hamlet* 1.2.79, emphasis mine) is not only a conventional sign of grieving but serves a physiological purpose. Similarly, in *Macbeth* Malcolm counsels Macduff to vent his sadness, "Give sorrow words. The grief that does not speak / Whispers the o'erfraught heart and bids it break" (4.3.210–11). Malcolm views the uses of lament, however, to be temporary, limited, and ultimately unsuitable for men. Moments later he encourages Macduff to suppress his sadness: "Let grief / Convert to anger: blunt not the heart, enrage it" (4.3.230–31). In urging Macduff to "Dispute it like a man" (221), Malcolm suggests that the conscious choice of angry words and vengeful deeds over effete lament is the gender-appropriate and the more effective response.[70] In *Richard III* Elizabeth makes the same point. As the women of the play gather to lament the loss of their loved ones, the Duchess wonders about the agency of lament. "Why," she asks, "should calamity be full of words?" (4.4.126). Elizabeth responds to her in much the way Malcolm responds to Macduff. Words, Elizabeth explains, are

Windy attorneys to their client woes,
Airy recorders of intestate joys,
Poor breathing orators of miseries.
Let them have scope. Though what they will impart
Help nothing else, yet do they ease the heart. (4.4.127–31)

The wind, air, and breath that comprise lament help "ease the heart," but though laments can make one feel better, they "help nothing else." Elizabeth's representation of lament as healthy but essentially futile in its effects confirms Ian Moulton's claims about the gendered physiology of grief in the case of Richard III. Moulton argues that Richard becomes a powerful but maniacal villain in *Richard III* partly as a consequence of his failure to cry at the end of *3 Henry VI*—a failure that simultaneously shores up his masculinity. Richard's incapacity to cry helps him conserve the heat of his heart so that it may be used for revenge and political scheming—a plan that works, albeit ultimately costing Richard his humorally balanced body and thus his life.[71] I would add that crucial to Richard's transformation is not only the failure to cry but the failure to express grief orally, through lamentation. As he contemplates the death of his father at the end of *3 Henry VI*, the wind he should use to speak lament is otherwise preoccupied, stirring fires of anger:

Nor can my tongue unload my heart's great burden,
For selfsame wind that I should speak withal
Is kindling coals that fires all my breast,
And burns me up with flames that tears would quench. (2.1.81–84)

Suppression of lament may be unhealthy and ultimately fatal for Richard, but it also emboldens him, like Macduff, to redress wrongs through action in a way that lamenting Elizabeth and Constance cannot.

Yet *Richard III* and *King John* provide an additional, contradictory reading of the usefulness of lament, suggesting that insofar as lament is made of breath, its effects may not always be so easily dismissed. When Elizabeth denigrates words as "windy attorneys" that do nothing but "ease the heart," the Duchess interprets this deflated resignation, surprisingly, as a call to action. Responding to Elizabeth, the Duchess charges, "If so, then be not tongue-tied; go with me, / And in the breath of bitter words let's smother / My damnèd son, that thy two sweet sons smothered" (4.4.132–34). Elizabeth's characterization of breath as "windy" provides the Duchess with a rationale for defiance. The Duchess does not, like Malcolm and Richard, differentiate clearly between lamenting and angry words. Her opening, "If so, then," implies a logical connection between Elizabeth's "poor breathing" laments and her own "breath of bitter words." The Duchess effectively reduces these rhetorically distinctive types of speech to their common material form, exploiting breath's ambiguous meaning.[72] Using the same word, "smother," to describe the physical destruction of Elizabeth's sons and the proposed verbal destruction of Richard, the Duchess reinterprets Elizabeth's "airy recorders" as weapons with fatal potential. The female body's unobtrusive, natural disposition toward ventilation is not contrary to but foundational for fighting words.

In the next scene, the Duchess deploys that weapon, delivering a curse on Richard that haunts him until his dying day. Although Richard attempts to still his mother's "breath of bitter words" in much the same manner that he derailed Margaret's curses in 1.3—by drowning out the women's vocal sounds with his own—he fails to maintain complete control over his acoustic environment.[73] Between the drums and trumpets Richard summons to block out the sounds of others, the Duchess clears an aural space for her curse. Her words seem to have no immediate effect on the malevolent Richard, but they weigh heavily on him the day before battle, dragging him to defeat while spurring his enemies on to victory. Richard's raging confidence famously dips the night before battle, when his mother's parting words plague his conscience. Notably, the last words Richard hears in his nightmare—"dream on, of bloody deeds and death; / Fainting, despair; despairing, yield thy breath" (5.5.125–26)—echo the words his mother uttered earlier: "Bloody thou art, bloody will be thy end; / Shame serves thy life, and doth thy death attend" (4.4.195–96). Richard's death involves a "yield[ing]" of "breath" in several ways. Most obviously, the presence of breath in the body indicated the presence of life—thus, Lear's anxious efforts to determine if Cordelia's lips can mist a mirror. And the fact that "breath" and "death" rhyme provides playwrights and poets extra motivation to bring these concepts into conversation in early modern literature. Yet in the context of a play that figures breath as constantly in conflict with an unpredictable acoustic environment, Richard's "yielding" implies that he not only cedes his own breath but cedes *to* the breath of others, the way Bacon describes one person's exhalations being halted by those of another. When Richard "yield[s his] breath" in battle, it is as if the Duchess has succeeded in smothering him with her "breath of bitter words."[74]

The Duchess's use of breath to manipulate her acoustic environment suggests that critics may underestimate the extent to which Richard III's female characters are open to a more transgressive reading. Certainly, as Jean E. Howard and Phyllis Rackin point out, women's voices in the play tend to take the form of lament, the usefulness of which Elizabeth herself questions.[75] Yet female characters' status as stereotypical mourners does not inevitably preclude their agency. The Duchess demonstrates that women's laments directed inwardly for the purpose of bodily health can, in fact, metamorphose into violent, effective curses. Made of the same material form, the curse and the lament are closer in constitution than they seem. Margaret says as much when she argues that grief is a key ingredient in the curse: "Thy woes will *make* [words] sharp and pierce" (4.4.124; emphasis mine). It is this material link between lament and curse that provides Margaret, and then the Duchess, with a robust model of vocal agency.

The Duchess's reaction provides a helpful context for interpreting Constance's laments in *King John*. For the Duchess shifts away from a humoral and toward what we might call a more mechanical discourse of breath, implying that the real potency of this airy substance stems from its capacity to be *detached* from the body, to be wielded like a weapon.[76] Constance pursues a similar strategy when she ignores Philip's recommendation that she suppress her grief:

No, no, I will not, having breath to cry.
O that my tongue were in the thunder's mouth;
Then with a passion would I shake the world,
And rouse from sleep that fell anatomy
Which cannot hear a lady's feeble voice. (3.4.37–41)

Reading this passage too quickly, we might conclude that Constance expresses only frustration about the ineffectiveness of her "lady's feeble voice." Yet like Eleanor's whisper, Constance's lament works on multiple levels. For while she rhetorically declares herself vocally powerless, in the theater she is a dominant presence, her pathos the center of attention in this scene. So wracked with grief that she seems unable to control her dramatically engaging utterances, Constance is well positioned to condemn the play's men of power: she exposes Philip's hypocrisy and penetrates Pandulph's lofty spiritual guise, declaring him "too holy" (3.4.44). The source for her resilient and resistant voice, Constance claims, is nothing more than life itself: simply by living, she has breath to cry out her censure. Constance underscores the disjunction between her meek rhetorical and potent theatrical postures by figuring her voice as most effective when it is disconnected from her body, beyond her command. Rather than claiming ownership of and control over the elusive, mercurial voice, as we've seen Pandulph, John, and Phillip do, Constance desires to relinquish her voice to the unpredictable environment outside her body—to the mouth of the thunder.[77] Constance embraces the material conditions of vocal articulation with all their uncertainties. Indeed, Constance's representation of her breath subtly corrects King Philip's assessment of her moments before: "A grave unto a soul, / Holding th'eternal spirit against her will, / In the vile prison of afflicted breath" (3.4.17–19). L. A. Beaurline, recalling the early modern commonplace metaphor of the body as a prison or grave for the soul and the notion that breath is a signifier of life reads the "vile prison of afflicted breath" as analogous with the "grave" of Constance's body; each "afflicted" matter signals mortality as it holds captive Constance's soul. This reading, however, as it favors the figurative over the material meaning of breath, overlooks the association of breath with speech. Indeed, Constance's "afflicted breath" is not merely a sign of a deteriorating body and mind, but an efficient instrument through which she criticizes men of power.

Recognizing that Constance's breath thrives beyond the "grave" of her body is important if we want to appreciate the vocal agency Constance exhibits even when she is no longer present mentally and physically. Since Constance's body disappears from the stage and from the fiction of the play in 4.2 (when her death is reported), critics often assume that erased with Constance's body is her poignant interrogation of the play's dysfunctional, masculine political culture.[78] However, as director Deborah Warner's 1988/89 Royal Shakespeare Company production of the play demonstrated, the absence of women's bodies does not inevitably preclude their ability to serve as a subversive force.[79] Constance's "afflicted breath," hardly reducible to being, as one editor phrases it, an "attribute"[80] of her body, seems to linger on as an agent of critique even when, perhaps especially when, her body is absent. Indeed, her strategic deployment of breath resurfaces later in the play through the voice of her son Arthur, who, I shall argue later, saves his life by highlighting breath's detachable and unpredictable nature.

In the model of vocal agency that Constance and Eleanor point us toward, breath's vulnerable material form, that which renders the voice conducive to failure, also creates the conditions for communicative power. Much as Derrida suggested about writing, vocal communication is *constituted* by disruptions in transmission: by spatial gaps, temporal delay, and environmental obstacles. Unlike the men of *King John*, who attempt to secure their utterances by emphasizing the spiritual underpinnings of the voice, Constance and Eleanor embrace breath's material attributes in all their chaos and unpredictability. In so doing, the female characters of *King John* cue a different way of thinking about the matter that makes up the voice. They suggest that the chaotic constitution of breath facilitates, instead of compromises, communicative agency.

"Progress by Diffusion": *Titus Andronicus* and Particulate Matter

The notion that breath's strength and communicative force is a function of its invisible and unpredictable material nature may appear counterintuitive: even if we accept that something invisible can be counted as "material," how can a substance that cannot be tracked secure vocal agency for a speaker? How can an utterance be imbued with constancy and stability if it is composed of an erratic, tenuous material like breath? Early modern scientists tended to be less troubled by paradoxes like these. Indeed, some provided ready answers to such questions by positing that voice is comprised of indestructible and unpredictable units of matter so small that they cannot be sensed. Examining their atomic styles of explanation helps shed light, I would argue, on the seemingly peculiar models of vocal agency that emerge in *King John* and other early modern plays.

Early modern ideas about particulate matter grew out of a range of ancient writings: Aristotle theorized the existence of *minima naturalis*, indivisible units of matter; related notions of seminal particles were elucidated by diverse philosophers, from Plato to Paracelsus; for Lucretius and Epicurus these minuscule particles were "atoms" that move unpredictably in a void, swerving from their paths to clash against each other and recombine, thereby creating different kinds of substances. Whatever the term used to describe them or the specific mechanisms by which they were thought to work, invisible and indivisible particles were imagined by some ancients to be the material foundation of everything that exists. Seventeenth-century experimental scientists adopted, adapted, and fused these ancient ideas. Bacon, for instance, though he balked at blind acceptance of Lucretius and Epicurus, refers to atoms in *Principles and Origins*, describing the atom as a "true entity, having matter, form, dimension, place, resistance, appetite, motion and emanation. Likewise, amid the destruction of all natural bodies, it remains constant and eternal."[81] Where atomic styles of explanation are concerned, Bacon's eclectic combination of critique and application is evident to some degree in *Sylva Sylvarum*, which vigorously argues against ancient atomism's claims while still employing corpuscular language ("minute particles," "minute bodies") to refer to both tangible and intangible matter.

In thinking about the particulate matter of sound and the implications of such ideas for theorizing vocal agency, we are better served, however, by shifting away from Bacon, whose *Sylva Sylvarum* dismisses the notion that sound is a corporeal entity, and toward the English experimental scientists who followed in Bacon's wake.[82] In particular, I want to turn to the work of Walter Charleton, whose *Physiologia Epicuro-Gassendo-Charltoniana: Or A Fabrick of Science Natural Upon the Hypothesis of Atoms* (1654), as is evident in its title, provided the most recognizable fusing of ancient and emerging early modern ideas about particulate matter. Charleton follows the ancient atomist writings of Epicurus fairly closely in his description of the role of breath in the production of vocal sound. Epicurus maintains that speech is produced when a "blow which takes place inside us, when we emit our voice, causes at once a squeezing out of certain particles, which produce a stream of breath, of such a character as to afford us the sensation of hearing."[83] The "blow" is familiar from Aristotle's *De Anima*, but the production of a "stream of breath" composed of "certain particles" adds a twist. Epicurus goes on to explain that each of the particles in this current of sound is identical in its qualities: "[The] current . . . carried off from the object speaking or sounding . . . is split up into particles, each like the whole, which at the same time preserve a correspondence of qualities with one another and a unity of character which stretches right back to the object which emitted the sound: this unity it is which in most cases produces comprehension in the recipient, or, if not, merely makes manifest the presence of the external object. For without the transference from the object of some correspondence of qualities, comprehension of this nature could not result."[84] For Epicurus, the successful transmission of vocal sound is a consequence of two key assumptions. First, the atoms that leave the speaker's body remain whole and durable during the transmission process. Though speaker and listener are separated by a wide expanse of air, the matter "carried off from" the speaker is essentially identical to the matter received by the listener, for each atom has a "unity of character which stretches *right back* to the object which emitted the sound." We can see this kind of emphasis on the preservation of particles in Charleton's explanations: "Whe[n] a Voyce is emitted from the mouth . . . the Contexture of the minute bodies effluent is so comprest, and confracted into smaller contextures, that of the Original are made swarms of Copies, or lesser masses exactly consimular in their Formation: and that those are instantly dispersed sphaerically . . . still conserving their similitude to the Original, or General voyce, or sound, till their arrival at the Eare; and so retaining the determinate signature of their Formation, are distinguisht accordingly by the sensory."[85] Charleton proposes that the "smaller contextures," dispersed as a consequence of the force of the blow, conserve their likeness to the original vocal sound as they travel to the ear of the listener.

In effect, a speaker's voice, contained as durable atoms, arrives in unaltered form at the listener's sensory apparatus, with the atoms "retaining the determinate signature of their Formation."

Charleton's description emphasizes a second key point concerning the success of sound transmission: that each particle transmitted is just like every other particle in the mass, "exactly consimular," and is a faithful copy of the original. This synecdochal relationship between dispersed particles of sound and their source ensures that each particle has the power to carry the essence of a message intact. Whereas Aristotle and his followers maintain that the air that moves sound is "a single mass . . . continuous up to the organ of hearing," Charleton posits that sound is dispersed into multiple masses.[86] So long as one particle reaches its destination, the communicative act will have been successful. And given how many such particles are released at one time, the chances of transmitting a single atom successfully are significantly improved. While Charleton does not depart from Aristotle entirely, his theory of vocal sound differs from Aristotle's in its claim that effective vocal transmission is a function of—rather than impeded by—sound's material form.

This is not to say that Charleton ignores the significant obstacles to sound's transmission that we've seen Bacon and Crooke describe. He points out, in fact, that audibles, in comparison to visibles, are especially vulnerable to variations of their medium, because, made of "grosser particles," they move more slowly in the medium. Like Bacon, Charleton imagines winds to be among the most disruptive variables in the medium. The impact of winds on sound can be observed, Charleton maintains, by the shape a current of audible particles assumes as it leaves the speaker or sounding object. "[E]very sound make[s] a Cone, or Pyramid in the medium, whose Base consisteth in the extreme of the body producing the sound, and cone in the ear of him that hears it."[87] This cone is similar in shape to the spherical diffusion of visibles, except that audibles conform a little less to the conical shape because "the grossness of their Particles, as less velocity of their motion, are easily injured and perturbed by Winds."[88] In other words, sound particles move slowly enough that they are jostled out of their trajectory by passing winds. Charleton represents the transmission of sound as a chaotic, mercurial process, in which "configurated small masses of aer fly off from bodies compulsed or knockt each against other, with some violence; and progress by Diffusion in round." Confusion and uncertainty prevail, as each particle moves "where it finds the freest egress."[89]

Charleton thus cites the same problems with vocal transmission that we've seen Crooke and Bacon raise: spatial disparity, temporal delay, and environmental disruption. And like Crooke's *Mikrokosmographia* and Bacon's *Sylva Sylvarum*, Charleton's *Physiologia* explains the voice's vulnerability to its medium as a consequence of sound's material attributes—the "grossness of the Particles" slows them down, leaving them prone to disruption by winds and other obstacles in the medium. Nevertheless, Charleton's emphasis on particulate matter leads him to different explanations for why such problems exist and how they might be overcome. Charleton credits the robustness of sound—its ability to overcome material obstacles—to sound's corporeal nature. While by no means dismissing spiritual and formal causes entirely, he emphasizes a greater role for matter in his explanations of communicative power. In effect, sound's unpredictable, transient material nature does not simply compromise, but in fact makes possible, sound's successful dispersion.

Charleton explicates this seeming paradox when, citing the ways wind interferes in the transmission of sound, he observes that wind will not affect all particles equally: "Adverse wind, though it may indeed disturb a sound, or weaken it by suppressing some of its particles . . . yet do all the particles that remain uninterrupted, permeate the medium with equal velocity."[90] Crucial to Charleton's confidence in the transmission of sound is his assumption that each of the sound particles emitted is identical to the others and each possesses, to use Epicurus's words, a "character that stretches *right back* to the object which emitted the sound." As long as one particle in the mass can reach a listener, it will deliver the original sound precisely. Charleton offers the example of voices to underscore the point. Insofar as the original voice is split up "into myriads of minute vocal configurations or Particular voyces" then no two auditors will receive exactly the same voice.[91] But, he points out, auditors will still manage to agree on what they have heard, because the air leaving the speaker's mouth is the same air that reaches them. There will, of course, be some differences between listeners' experiences, for the closer one is to the source of sound, the greater the number of sound particles in one's vicinity. But the essence of the sound remains constant, having come from the same source: "[A]ll the Aer efflated from the mouth of the speaker [is] the same Aer; though the Particular Voyces, delated to particular Ears, are not the same Numerically."[92] In effect, it is the very chaos and mobility that mark acoustic transmission that account for sound's capacity for wide, effective dispersion.

Although Charleton published his writings years after the heyday of the English public theater, his writings provide the modern critic with a useful set of terms for understanding the way early modern plays explore the materiality of vocal sound.[93] For one thing, the notion of sound as composed of particulate matter helps to destabilize a binary of matter versus figure that, as Jonathan Gil Harris argues, has often plagued studies of Shakespeare and materiality. Theories of particulate matter (Harris's focus is Epicurean atomism in particular) underscore that matter is always apprehended through figure. What Harris calls this "double-helix"[94] of matter and figure is, I would argue, the key to understanding how breath functions in Shakespeare's plays, particularly in a live theater where, through the speech of actors, the matter and figure of breath are necessarily intertwined. Moreover, corpuscular perspectives reinforce how a history of materiality is a history of things in motion, things moving through time and space. This "dynamic, diachronic dimension of materiality"[95] is particularly important to histories of the theater, a form of art predicated largely on movement—of bodies on the stage and of voices through the theater. Significantly, the substance of breath embodies the dialectic at the heart of particulate matter theories: that something transient, invisible, and subject to dispersal by unpredictable forces can be, for these very reasons, durable and powerful. Charleton's explanations for sound are useful, then, for understanding how early moderns represented tensions in the nature of matter and, consequently, the material conditions of vocal power, because he theorizes matter as agency amid vulnerability and stability amid chaos. Such explanations prove especially useful for thinking about female voices in Shakespeare's plays—voices that even when present only figuratively on an all-male stage, and even when assuming the form of mere lament or plea, have the potential for significant agency on account of their mobile, unpredictable material constitution.[96] The Duchess, Eleanor, and Constance, we have seen, figure their voices as comprised of uncontrollable, ephemeral, and transient breath—a substance that is durable and powerful not in spite but *because* of its ambiguous form. Agency is available to these female voices regardless of the genre of speech characters use, for, as the plays remind us, all types of vocalized speech—bold boasts and confident oaths *as well as* unassuming whispers, desperate pleas, and defeated laments—are composed of breath.

Stretching this concept to its limits opens up interesting possibilities for studying female vocal agency in drama. If voice can be reduced to breath, then to what extent might breath alone constitute or signal voice? And what might this mean for our interpretations of moments in a play when a character is stripped of speech—a recurring trope in early modern dramatic and nondramatic literature—but still in possession of breath? Shakespeare stages such a scenario in *Othello*. Hovering over Desdemona as he contemplates murdering her, Othello pauses, sighing: "O balmy breath, that dost almost persuade / Justice to break her sword!" (5.2.16–17). Desdemona may not speak in any conventional fashion, but, as Othello's remarks emphasize, Desdemona does expel a key ingredient of voice: breath. And this agent makes a case for her innocence, prompting Othello to hesitate and reconsider his plans. As moments like these set up a tension between the absence of speech and the presence of breath—between the lack of verbal language and the persistence of vocal matter—they suggest that breath be read as virtually sufficient for voice.

This redefinition of voice has profound implications for our readings of the "silenced" female characters of the stage, the most exemplary of which, perhaps, is Lavinia in *Titus Andronicus*. When Lavinia's rapists Chiron and Demetrius cut off her hands and excise her tongue, they render her apparently unable to communicate her trauma, mercilessly mocking Lavinia for her disabilities: "So, now go tell, an if thy tongue can speak, / Who 'twas that cut thy tongue and ravished thee" and "She hath no tongue to call nor hands to wash, / And so let's leave her to her silent walks" (2.4.1–2; 7–8). Most critics have been as quick as Chiron and Demetrius to assume that when Lavinia loses her tongue, she loses all capacity for vocal expression and all access to agency. Lavinia has become for many feminist readers in particular the archetype of a link between voice and agency; her narrative enacts intersections between women's sexual and political subjection and their loss of voice.[97] As important as it is to reveal the brutality of Lavinia's mutilation, it is also important to observe the limits of Chiron's and Demetrius's horrific act. For although Lavinia "hath no tongue to call," her rapists, I would maintain, fail to silence her completely. Lavinia goes on to engage in a form of dramatic dialogue with Marcus when he finds her in the woods and prompts her for her story:

> Why dost not speak to me?
> Alas, a crimson river of warm blood,
> Like to a bubbling fountain stirred with wind,
> Doth rise and fall between thy rosèd lips,
> Coming and going with thy honey breath.
> But sure some Tereus hath deflowered thee
> And, lest thou shouldst detect him, cut thy tongue. (2.4.21–27)

Marcus's question "Why dost not speak to me?" is followed by recognition, "alas," a formulation that implies that somehow the blood flowing from Lavinia's "rosèd lips," carried by her "honey breath," serves as Lavinia's response. Despite lacking a tongue to articulate words, Lavinia answers Marcus's query by expelling this telltale blood. From the response, Marcus concludes, correctly, that Lavinia has been "deflowered" by "some Tereus," her tongue removed to prevent her from informing on her assailants. Lavinia may have "no tongue to call," but an act of vocal communication has, in effect, taken place.[98] Chiron and Demetrius conflate Lavinia's speech, language, voice, and agency, but Marcus encourages distinctions between these terms. The tongueless Lavinia may be denied scripted lines, but she performs certain gestures that, from an early modern perspective, denote voice: she produces breath, which leaves her lips, communicating her message to an auditor.

In particular it is the movement of Lavinia's breath, its "rise and fall," "coming and going," that point up to her performance of voice—something that has been underscored in modern productions of the play (at least those that resist the urge to cut the speech). Many directors, including Peter Brook, Pat Patton, and Gerald Freedman, accentuate this movement by depicting Lavinia's blood as red streamers or ribbons that "seemed to flow out of the wounded figure."[99] In Deborah Warner's 1987 production, Marcus's description cued Lavinia to dribble red liquid from her mouth, causing the audience to gasp in reaction.[100] These figurations of moving blood capture provocatively a perspective on sound that was commonly articulated by early modern theorists of particulate matter: that motion and sound, in the words of Kenelm Digby, are "one and the same thing."[101] Digby investigates the phenomenon whereby a deaf man may perceive music by touching his teeth to a stick that lies on a musical instrument. Do we not find, he observes, that the "shaking of the sticke (working a like dauncing in the mans head) did make a like motion in his braine, without passing through his ear?"[102] As the deaf can perceive sound by sensing motion, so the blind can sense motion by perceiving sound. Digby describes a blind schoolmaster who was able to direct his students' gestures as they rehearsed a play simply by listening to their voices. "[W]hen he taught his schollers to declame . . . or to represent some of Senecas Tragedies, or the like, he would by their voice know their gesture, and the situation they putt their bodies in: so that he would be able, as soone as they spoke, to judge whether they stood or sate, or in what posture they were."[103] Digby and other writers interested in hearing- and speaking-impaired individuals also tell of deaf persons who are able to perceive the words of another simply by watching the gestures of the speaker's mouth, that is, by lipreading. By the same token, they tell of mute persons who communicate through gesture.[104] What Shakespeare gives us in the scene from *Titus* is essentially a dramatization of similar phenomena, accomplished with Lavinia's "rosèd lips" and flowing breath.

Shakespeare's comparison of Lavinia's breath to a wind that pushes forth her blood "[l]ike to a bubbling fountain" further reinforces the peculiar agency of Lavinia's voice.[105] We have seen that for many early moderns, winds represent the power of the chaotic and the "tenacious" nature of the invisible. Shakespeare's fountain metaphor attaches similarly multivalent, conflicting meanings to the breath Lavinia expels. The significance of the fountain metaphor becomes clearer if we compare the way the figure of the fountain is used in Charleton's writings on sound. Like Shakespeare, Charleton explains the voice's capacity for wide transmission through a comparison between air expelled from a mouth and water from a fountain: "the greater Drops of water being in their trajection through the aer, broken, by reason of the impulse of the breath, that discharged them in distress, into swarms of less drops, and those again into less, successively in the several degrees of remove, until they attain such exiguity, as we observe in the particles of a mist: and that small proportion of Aer, emitted from the mouth of him that speaks, being dispersed into a dense mist of voyces, replenishing the whole sphere of Diffusion."[106] As when water sprays from a fountain, when voice is expelled from a speaker's mouth, matter is released into the air as a result of some impulsion at the source. As these "swarms" move outward, they become less and less concentrated. But dispersion by no means undercuts successful vocal transmission. Like the mist from a fountain, a "small proportion of Aer, emitted from the mouth of him that speaks" can have wide-reaching effects on a "whole sphere of diffusion." Similarly, compared to a fountain's mist, Lavinia's breath is imagined to have a significant impact, despite being ephemeral and virtually invisible.

Charleton's passage is especially pertinent to our reading of Lavinia's voice because Charleton, to clarify and underscore his point about the dispersion of air, goes on to set his analysis of voice in the context of the theater, an ideal laboratory in which to observe acoustic phenomena. Certainly, Charleton submits, proximity to an orator improves an auditor's ability to hear clearly: "[T]he Voyce of an Orator in a Theatre is more strong and distinct to those of his Auditory, that fit neer at hand, than to those far off." At the same time, though, in "a whole Theatre of Auditors, each one shall distinctly hear [the orator's voice]: insomuch as onely a mouthful of Water blown from a Fullers mouth, is so diffused as to irrigate the aer replenishing a room of considerable amplitude."[107] In the same way that a spurt of water from a fountain can dampen a vast room, so a mere mouthful of air can convey the orator's voice to multiple auditors dispersed throughout the theater space. As Charleton seems to recognize, and as I'll go on to demonstrate further in the next section, the theater is as an especially privileged space in which to query the uncanny material workings of vocal sound.

Staging Scandalous Breath

The significance of the theatrical idiom is compellingly evident at the end of *Othello*, when, like Lavinia, Desdemona loses an organ of speech—in this case her breath, which is stifled when Othello suffocates her. Yet Othello's control over the flow of Desdemona's breath is not as absolute as he later implies in his comments to Gratiano: "There lies your niece, / Whose breath indeed these hands have newly stopped" (5.2.208–9). For Desdemona's breath, like Lavinia's, proves momentarily resilient. Just when Othello believes Desdemona to be dead, she find the breath to call out "falsely, falsely murdered" (5.2.126), summoning Emilia into the room to discover the deed.[108] Desdemona's sudden revival, from the perspective of its linguistic content, seems disappointing. Having declared her innocence, she goes on to iterate the misogynistic logic that women are to blame when men err: asked who is responsible for her state, Desdemona uses her final moments of life to respond, "I myself." But what if we bracket the linguistic content of these remarks and reduce them to the material form they would assume in the theater, breath? Trevor Nunn's Royal Shakespeare Company video production does just that. In place of the text's lines "falsely, falsely murdered," Imogen Stubbs's Desdemona exhales and coughs dramatically—as if her body still contains some unextinguished breath that emerges unexpectedly, carrying her voice along. Despite its inarticulate nature, Stubbs's expulsion of breath accomplishes the same feat as the verbal articulation in the script: the sound calls Emilia to the crime scene, allowing Desdemona's story to be publicized. By substituting the actor's breath for the lines of the play, Nunn effectively dramatizes Constance's view that voice may persist as long as a woman has "breath to cry."[109] Of course, Desdemona's breath does not persist for long. What is more, she does not die with the haunting, verbal eloquence of Richard II. By the same token, Lavinia does not deliver a tortured soliloquy declaring her innermost grief the way Hamlet does. Nevertheless, the presence of breath in and especially out of these characters' bodies undercuts the assumption that they are completely silenced. Indeed, these characters perform surprisingly effective vocal acts, albeit ones that are temporary and easily overlooked (by fellow characters as well as by critics).

The ideological and political work of breath would likely have been even more obvious in the theaters in which these plays were first performed. For on England's all-male public stage, Desdemona and Lavinia would have been played by actors who already embodied the challenge of controlling breath's flows. As the boys who played Shakespeare's female parts went through puberty, their windpipes were imagined to crack, a physiological condition that affected not only the vocal organs, as we saw in Chapter 1, but the breath moving through and beyond these organs. Detritus on the surface of the windpipe, for instance, would create a rougher passage for the breath, resulting in a more halting, scratchier sound. Unevenness in the quality of a boy's vocal sound signaled his struggles to master the breath necessary for vocal articulation. In effect, early modern gender ideologies that fueled, and were fueled by, representations of women as lacking control over their breath were mirrored by a theatrical institution that used the most vocally precarious of actors to play women's parts. Boy actors could thus underscore through vocal performance the problems of vocal authority raised in the fictions of Shakespeare's plays, for the plays' most marginalized and vulnerable characters were impersonated, fittingly, by the theater's most marginalized and vulnerable voices.

Evidence for this correspondence between dramatic fiction and theatrical conditions may be found by examining how the plays treat not simply female but also boy characters. For boy characters were played by some of the same pubescent actors who filled the roles of Desdemona and the other female characters I have been discussing. It is no coincidence, then, that the young Arthur of *King John* figures breath in similar terms as his mother and Eleanor. When Arthur realizes that Hubert, the man he believes to be a kindhearted protector, in fact plans to burn out his eyes with hot iron, Arthur, like his mother Constance, can do little more than plead to Hubert to take pity on him. The pleas have an effect, albeit not necessarily the one explicitly intended: Arthur's "innocent prate" (4.1.25) draws on so long that Hubert's iron cools, and the coals that could be used to reheat the iron burn out. Arthur provocatively suggests that this is God's way of relieving Hubert of his wretched task: "The breath of heaven hath blown his [the coal's] spirit out" (4.1.109). The "breath of heaven" is, in its strictest sense, the air of the atmosphere, which has lowered the temperature of the coals in much the same way human breath, to recall Wright, can cool porridge. Arthur goes further to imply that this material phenomenon has spiritual import, invoking the philosophical, theological, and etymological connections between breath and spirit that I discussed above. God's guiding agency, Arthur maintains, makes itself known through this most physical of acts, the extinguishing of hot coals. Arthur represents the miraculous event as involving a reciprocity between material and divine animation: the coals die out as their "spirit" responds to the "breath of God."

Hubert, like so many of the adult male characters of *King John*, attempts to reestablish his authority by insisting on control over breath. Adapting for his own strategic purposes Arthur's etymological and physical link between breath and life, Hubert threatens that should he blow on the coals "with my breath," he can "revive" their spirit (4.1.111). Arthur counters by using the same logic of matter that Constance and Eleanor articulated. He argues that insofar as breath must leave Hubert's body in order to work, its effects cannot be predicted so easily. Instead of rekindling the fire, Hubert's breath may cause the fire to "sparkle. . . . / And like a dog that is compelled to fight, / Snatch at his master that doth tarre him on" (4.1.114–16). Arthur proposes that when Hubert uses his breath to encourage the agency of the coals, he may unintentionally surrender his own agency, becoming a victim to the very forces he sets into motion. *King John* has already dramatized such a scenario through the figure of Pandulph, who discovers that the effects of breath may conflict with the intentions of the subject who produces the breath. No doubt, as critics have observed, Hubert wavers in carrying out the violence in part as a consequence of his growing compassion for Arthur.[110] Yet Hubert's decision seems to be informed also by his recognition of the limits of his control over breath. For it is Arthur's rhetorically astute demonstration of the dispersal of human agency in a mercurial material world that immediately precedes Hubert's capitulation.

Although Hubert's breath in this scene is imagined to be used only for the purposes of blowing air on coals, the significance of Arthur's comments to the representation of vocal agency in *King John* cannot be ignored, especially given the frequency with which the play associates breath with speech.

Insofar as Arthur takes comfort in the surrender of breath to the vagaries of the air, he can be differentiated from *King John*'s adult male characters, who either disavow the materiality of breath completely, insisting upon its figurative, spiritual significance, or deny the precariousness of breath's material form in their claims that they can command the uncommandable movements of this airy substance. Arthur, by contrast, articulates a view of breath that resembles Constance's and Eleanor's, arguing that breath's agency is a function of its transience and detachability from the body. Like Constance and Eleanor, Arthur appeals strategically to these attributes of breath in order to exercise agency in a situation in which his voice carries little authority.[111]

I have suggested that similarities between Arthur and *King John*'s female characters point to more than a fictional correspondence: these similarities draw directly on the performance conditions of the early modern public theater, where boy actors played all of these roles. These performance conditions help explain why references to breath by the Bastard Falconbridge—who, like Arthur, is marginalized in the fiction of the play but, *unlike* Arthur, would have been played by an adult actor—differ so markedly from those of Arthur, Constance, and Eleanor. Certainly the Bastard is more canny about vocal power than the other male characters in the play, for, as many critics have noted, he discovers quite quickly that the spoken word carries little authority in a world where oaths are just another "Commodity" (5.1.274) to be used at whim by wily politicians.[112] Yet unlike these other marginalized characters, the Bastard does not emphasize how the breath he uses to produce voice deconstructs vocal authority. The Bastard's speech works more like Hubert's "cannon-fire" than Constance's "windy" petitions; Austria, for instance, complains that the Bastard is a "cracker . . . that deafs our ears / With this abundance of superfluous breath" (2.1.147–48). Later in the play when the Bastard and Pandulph negotiate on behalf of John and Lewis, respectively, the Bastard expressly maligns breath as the empowering force for voice. Lewis's declaration not to lay down arms is, according to the Bastard, "fury breath'd" by this "youth," whereas the Bastard's own speech is authorized by the English King, whose "royalty doth speak in me" (5.2.127–29). By comparing the Bastard and Arthur, we can see that appeals to unpredictable breath and the particular forms of vocal agency these afford are the province of figures marginalized not only thematically, but *theatrically*.[113]

With their developing, precarious voices, the boy actors who played the roles of Constance, Eleanor, and Arthur made manifest challenges of vocal control and aural command that were undoubtedly present for all the male actors on Shakespeare's stage. Like the writings of acoustic theorists, plays foreground the degree to which the agency of breath is a function of its distance from the speaker. The breath must leave the actor's body to work, but once it leaves, it becomes vulnerable to the forces of the theater air, and, as we will see in Chapter 3, to the whims of audience members who receive it. At the same time, when actors' voices worked successfully on the stage—as they must have for audiences to have heard the pleas of Constance and Arthur, the whispers of Eleanor, and the groans of Desdemona and Lavinia—these actors helped illustrate through performance a generative model of vocal agency. Their performance, in W. B. Worthen's words, did "material and theoretical work."[114]

The nature of this vocal agency is, to be sure, ambiguous. Does Desdemona strategically wait to exhale her call until the moment Emilia is near at hand to hear the cries? Or does Desdemona's breath seep out from her body uncontrollably, the way it did when she slept? By the same token, does Lavinia open her mouth and push the blood from it in order to alert Marcus to her wounds? Or does that blood move on its own accord, riding the wave of Lavinia's ordinary exhalations? The plays leave unresolved such questions. And I would maintain that it is precisely this ambiguity that is the key to breath's transgressive potential on the stage. Because it is so difficult to establish the intentions behind the flow of breath and because breath is inherently disjoined from the bodies that produce it, breath problematizes the speaker's body as a site of agency, dispersing accountability for an utterance. Detached, ephemeral, and unpredictable, breath exemplifies what Shoshana Felman in her psychoanalytic reading of J. L. Austin's speech-act theory calls the "scandalous" relationship between speech and the body.[115] Insofar as speaking is a bodily act, Felman argues, speech exposes the subject as never in full control of its articulations: "the [speech] act cannot know what it is doing."[116] In Judith Butler's reading of Felman, "[T]he speaking body signifies in ways that are not reducible to what such a body 'says.' "[117] For Felman and Butler, the volatility of the speaking body—the fact that it is always poised to do more, say more than the speaker may intend—explains its uncanny power. A speaker's intentions, encoded in the language s/he speaks, are never the full story; the repressed or disavowed meanings embedded in a particular utterance may unpredictably manifest themselves.

Like the body in Felman's account, the meanings of breath are not reducible to the meanings a speaker seems or even intends to verbalize: Eleanor and Constance may speak defeatedly, Lavinia and Desdemona not at all, but they persistently produce breath, the meaning of which exceeds the more limited significations of these characters' verbal language. Perhaps most importantly, these speakers cannot be held fully accountable for their vocal excesses. Desdemona exhales persuasive breath because she happens to have her mouth open while sleeping, something that early modern physiologists recommend for physiological well-being.[118] Constance breathes her critique of male hypocrisy while in the process of lamenting the loss of her son, a vocal act that is culturally acceptable for women, regardless of how much it bothers Pandulph and Philip. In this sense, breath is even more "scandalous" than the body Felman describes. For whereas bodies can to a large extent be tracked, their performances of resistance measured and thus often disciplined or curtailed, the breath—ephemeral, mobile, unpredictable, indeed invisible—defies supervision and resists choreography, often slipping beneath the radar of patriarchal regulatory schemes.[119]

As we have seen, the theater is a ripe venue in which to witness the scandalous voice. And this is particularly true for the public theater in which Shakespeare's plays were first performed.[120] Through its use of pubescent boy actors, Shakespeare's theater accentuated the material workings of vocal sound, foregrounding breath's ambiguous material nature and its excesses of meaning. As *King John* and other plays performed in this theater reduce a range of genres of speech to their common material denominator, breath, the plays, like contemporaneous physiological and acoustic texts, destabilize gender differences in speech. Taking the form of breath, a mother's lament may accomplish as much, sometimes more, than a king's oath. I have argued that such ambivalence around vocal agency is a source of anxiety for many male characters, who have much at stake in demonstrating their control over voice and whose political and social power is supposed to guarantee vocal authority and reiterate superiority. But such ambivalence can serve the interests of early modern women and youths, for the breath used to produce even the most conventional forms of speech—like laments, whispers, and pleas—is difficult to monitor and discipline. To be sure, granting agency to the breath of Lavinia, Constance, and the others does not mean ignoring how these characters and the worlds they inhabit promote the subjugation of and violence against women. With the exception perhaps of the Duchess in *Richard III*, the "voice" these characters exercise is clearly not enough in the end. Nevertheless, produced in the form of breath, these voices sometimes elude supervision and discipline. Diachronic, invisible, and always in motion, the breath provides some marginalized figures, especially women, a generative foundation for vocal power.

Chapter 3

Fortress of the Ear: Shakespeare's Late Plays, Protestant Sermons, and Audience

An expanded political conception of voice needs Artaud's theatre to liberate it from its incarceration in the mouth. . . . The particular force of this theatrical insight for progressive politics is that it recalls us to the demands of active audition.

—Peggy Phelan, "Performing Talking Cures"[1]

DeFlores:	*Justice invites your blood to understand me.*
Beatrice:	*I dare not.*
DeFlores:	*Quickly!*
Beatrice:	*O, I never shall!*
	Speak it yet further off, that I may lose
	What has been spoken and no sound remain on't.
	I would not hear so much offense again
	For such another deed.

—The Changeling[2]

When Beatrice, the chaste and compromised heroine of Middleton and Rowley's *The Changeling*, slowly realizes that the servant DeFlores is proposing that she give up her virginity to compensate him for killing the man she didn't want to marry, she desperately wishes that she could stop herself from understanding his meaning. Once she is made to hear and admit she understands, she will have taken the first step toward losing the chastity that, according to the play's patriarchal logic, is her most important possession. To mitigate her fear, she recalls that DeFlores' voice is made of sound, like all spoken voices; thus, there is some chance, she imagines, that the distance that separates her from DeFlores will delay his voice from reaching her and corrupting her chaste sensibilities. Given my discussion in the last chapter of how female characters in early modern drama are able to exploit to their advantage representations of the voice's physical form, it is not surprising that Beatrice should describe DeFlores' voice in such vividly acoustic terms. Having few other options, Beatrice lays her hopes on the possibility that DeFlores' meaning, because it is conveyed by a voice made of sound, will not remain intact as it moves across the space between their bodies. Of course, DeFlores does not abide by her request "to speak it yet further off," and she is "quickly" made to "understand." Once she "hear[s] these words" (3.4.129), submitting aurally to De Flores, she believes she has little choice but to submit to his sexual advances.

The scene presents a limitation to the theory of agency I have presented in the previous chapter. If an abusive voice cannot be dispersed by environmental factors, if it isn't in the air long enough to be countered and dissipated, then a vulnerable woman like Beatrice can easily be victimized, aurally and sexually. Such a conclusion assumes, however, that a voice that reaches the listener has no other obstacles to overcome. And this is not a conclusion that can be drawn from all early modern representations of hearing. Indeed, as I shall show in this chapter, many early modern authors, in and out of the theater, represent the listener's body as an effective—or, from a different perspective, a frustrating—obstacle to vocal transmission. We need not wait, as Peggy Phelan maintains, for Artaud to "recall . . . us to the demands of active audition." As I hope to prove, such an "expanded political conception of voice" is dramatized in the early modern theater and in moral and religious writings of the period.

Acoustic Subjectivity in Protestant Sermons

This principle of "active audition" is defined with particular urgency by early modern Protestant preachers, whose sermons instruct parishioners in how to attain salvation through hearing God's Word. In sermons on the biblical parable of "the sower and the seed," the Word is imagined as a generative germ that enters parishioners' ears and, if sowed effectively, takes root in their hearts, helping them produce the "fruit" of good deeds. Salvation is thus contingent on parishioners' aural receptivity—the extent to which their ears can be penetrated and their hearts fertilized by the seed-Word. Drawing from an agricultural discourse that was frequently used in this period to describe human sexual reproduction, the sermons suggest that salvation can be achieved if the Christian is fully open to the aural penetrations of the fertilizing Word.[3]

At the same time that Protestant sermons advocate receptive organs of hearing, however, they also express concern that ears are the bodily organs through which evil enters. John Donne preaches, "Take heed that you heare them whom God hath appointed to speake to you; But, when you come abroad, take heed *what* you hear; for, certainely, the Devill doth not cast in more snares at the eye of man, then at the eare."[4] As God provides grace by sending his seed into the hearer's heart, so the devil can, in the words of preacher Thomas Taylor, sow "the seed of the wicked" into a "fit and friendly soyle."[5] Thus, whereas one may willingly open oneself to the seed of God, one must persevere to shut out the seed of the devil which, like a cagey seducer, can overwhelm good Christians, penetrating them when they least expect it. In sum, Protestant sermons on hearing characterize the ideal Christian as a womb that is both receptive to the implantation of God's Word and vulnerable to being pillaged by the devil.

Representing hearing as a multivalent transformative practice, Protestant sermons, along with contemporaneous religious and moral texts concerning personal and spiritual well-being, suggest productive directions for my study of historical forms of vocal agency. I have argued in the previous chapters that a more capacious understanding of agency becomes available when we question the conflation between vocal expression and power. Sermons complicate this thesis, for the metaphor of voice they use rests solidly upon the very conflation I have been questioning. As God's voice incarnate, the seed is not imagined to be subject, for instance, to the kinds of crises of production discussed in Chapter 1. In the case of pubescent boy actors, the fragile state of the speaker's body threatens to undermine the potency of the voice produced, but in the case of sermons, the originator of the voice is imagined to be omnipotent God—the human preacher acts as a mere messenger or intermediary, delivering the seed-Word from its unwaveringly authoritative site of production. And unlike the breath discussed in Chapter 2—the efficacy of which can be compromised by its ephemeral form—a seed is capable of transformative acts mostly *because* of its material form. Seeds, sermons remind us, are inherently generative objects that produce changes in the ground on which they fall. Moreover, the seed-voice metaphor imagines a single voice as multiplied; the essence of God's message is contained in the multitude of seeds cast on the ground where auditors stand. Although some seeds may be blown off course like the breath of kings in Chapter 2, sermons imply that the sheer number of germs produced ensures that God's message will reach every parishioner. Somewhat like the atoms described by early modern acoustic theorists I discussed in the previous chapter, the seed-Word seems largely impervious to environmental disruption.

Nevertheless, the seed does face obstacles in its successful transport of a message from speaker to listener, not because its authority is compromised by an unstable site of production or because its medium renders it vulnerable but because it is subject to unpredictable conditions of reception. As preachers teach their auditors, even if the seed reaches the "soil" of a listener and even if it manages to implant itself, it may not be able to produce the kinds of changes in the listener that the speaker hopes for or expects. Placing the onus of salvation upon parishioners and upon the act of listening in church, the sermons locate agency in the bodies of hearers, defining spiritual subjectification as an acoustic feat. As sermons shift the conditions of subject formation away from speaking and toward listening, they complicate to an even greater extent than have previous texts I have examined the conflation of speaking and agency. It is the act of audition, not vocalization, that attests to one's position in relation to God and one's potential for salvation.[6]

As Protestant sermons explicate the act of audition, they help theorize a form of agency and a process of subjectification that are dramatized in early modern plays.[7] The argument that sound—verbal and nonverbal—shaped in fundamental ways the processes of subject formation in early modern England, especially in the context of the theater, has been convincingly argued in different ways in recent book-length studies by Bruce R. Smith, Kenneth Gross, and Wes Folkerth. Gross and Folkerth, focusing on Shakespeare in particular, point to the frequency with which plays figure sound as invading the vulnerable ears of the auditor, who is psychologically and even physically transformed through an auditory experience. Whether the listener in question is part of the theater audience or a fictionalized character on the stage, sound penetrates listeners to their core, producing "deep" (Folkerth) and sometimes "liberating" (Smith) subjectivity or "troubled interiority" (Gross).[8] Often for these critics, the emergent subject's relationship to sound is figured as one of subordination. Folkerth and Gross focus extensively, for instance, on early modern representations of the ear as open and vulnerable—a receptive orifice (Folkerth) or "vortex" (Gross) that, because it is always poised to be invaded, is the site of moral edification as well as abuse. Folkerth maintains that in Shakespeare's plays and, notably, in Protestant sermons, growth of the self is figured as contingent on one's having a "willing" or "receptive" ear.[9] Gross describes how in Shakespeare and early modern discourses of defamation a "space of human privacy gets discovered precisely by being invaded."[10] And Smith argues that the theater is a privileged site for the formation of early modern subjects in part because of the way theatrical sounds can surround the auditor, "penetrating his or her body through the ears."[11] Each of these theories implies that the acoustic subject, on and off the stage, emerges in part through a process of aural subjugation.

This scholarship has been immensely valuable to my own pursuits in that it highlights the centrality of hearing to the process of subject formation and situates auditory activity at the center of early modern cultural life.[12] Yet these studies are limited by their lack of sufficient attention to the role gender difference plays in representations of hearing. Based often on analyses of male characters (generally with an emphasis on the protagonists of Shakespeare's tragedies), these prior accounts of acoustic subjectivity unwittingly universalize the auditory experiences of male characters and leave untheorized the different cultural pressures that weighed on male and female auditors in the early modern period.[13] More thorough attention to gender is crucial when analyzing representations of hearing in early modern drama, in which aural penetration is often associated with impregnation and, thus, sexual reproduction. As a consequence of the plays' fixations on female chastity, aural vulnerability is figured as a particularly fraught state for women. We might note in *Hamlet* the contrary advice given to Laertes and Ophelia. Whereas Laertes is counseled to improve himself through aural generosity—"Give every man thine ear" (1.3.68)—Ophelia is warned to keep her ears shut: "Then weigh what loss your honor may sustain / If with too credent ear you list his songs, / Or lose your heart, or your chaste treasure open / To his unmastered importunity" (1.3.29–32). For the gentlewoman, aural generosity compromises honor. If aural vulnerability is theorized as a *condition* of acoustic subject formation, as prior studies have implied, then proper, chaste women are essentially prevented from emerging as agentive subjects.

The limitations of prior models of acoustic subjectification become especially evident when applied to Shakespeare's "late plays" *Cymbeline*, *Pericles*, *The Winter's Tale*, and *The Tempest*, which, performed at roughly the same time as the sermons I've been describing, share with these sermons an understanding of hearing as the key to salvation.[14] And like sermons on the parable of the sower and the seed, in particular, these plays employ metaphors of penetration and fertility to describe the benefits as well as the risks of aural vulnerability. But in the plays, where a thematic interest in family lineage results in an overriding concern with female reproduction, the benefits and risks of receptivity become polarized more explicitly in terms of gender. Indeed, auditory practice becomes in the plays a site of gender differentiation. The plays define male identity in terms of aural openness, echoing a critique of deafness that Folkerth finds articulated in *Coriolanus*: the "destruction of [Coriolanus's] self" is brought about by the character's "sustained period of deafness" to "the claims of the Other."[15] As I'll discuss in the following section, the male protagonists of Shakespeare's late plays achieve personal growth and restore political order when they abandon their aural resistance and allow the words of subordinates to penetrate their ears. Yet, as I'll argue in the subsequent section, for female characters the same kind of vulnerability is imagined to upset the social order, leading good women into moral turpitude. Buoyed by early modern misogynist assumptions about women's excessively porous bodies, the late plays define chaste femininity in terms of aural closure: it is by carefully regulating and sometimes resisting what enters their aural organs—and by implication their reproductive bodies—that the female characters of the late plays can prevent personal as well as political disaster. Aural obstructions thus signify differently for male and female characters: for female characters, aural obstructions are defensive in nature, and thus constructive for the social order; for male characters, such blockages are a sign of problematic deafness, disruptive if not overcome.

The establishment of these gender differences in hearing would seem to delimit if not impede female subjectivity in these plays. If we extend Gail Kern Paster's influential critical argument about the effect of bodily disciplining on female identity, pressures upon the chaste female body to remain enclosed and impermeable to sound would seem to problematize women's emergence as acoustic subjects.[16] However, as I shall go on to demonstrate later in the chapter, the line between what I call *constructive defensiveness* and *disruptive deafness*—a line that helps maintain early modern gender hierarchies and a patriarchal social order—is unstable in this period, with the two states of hearing virtually indistinguishable in practice. As constructive defensiveness slides into disruptive deafness, women's hearing can undermine the smooth functioning of the social order depicted in these plays. Thus in the process of shoring up female difference through a discourse of aural closure, the plays ultimately imbue female characters with a method of resisting authority and challenging social hierarchies. It is through their resistance to aural subjugation, rather than their surrender to it, that female characters in these plays emerge as agentive subjects.[17]

The auditory agency dramatized by female characters in the plays lays bare a transformative practice that is available not only to characters on the stage but also to audience members in the early modern theater. As I shall suggest toward the end of this chapter, the dramatization of auditory agency in the plays reflects, as it is informed by, the kind of hearing in which audience members could be engaged during a performance. Given that one of the few major roles women could occupy in the early modern English commercial theater was that of audience members, auditory agency constituted women as a force in this important site of English cultural production.

"Hearing for Profit" in Shakespeare's Late Plays

Protestant sermons on the parable of the sower and seed are a rich site of investigation for an analysis of receptive agency because they shift much of the responsibility for salvation to their listeners. In his sermon entitled *The Difference of Hearers* (1614), William Harrison tells his parishioners that the work of salvation lies not in his transmission of the Word of God but in their ability to receive that Word effectively. "This seed [of God's Word] doth fructify, or not fructify; according to the qualitie & disposition of the ground into which it is cast. If the ground be bad, the seed perisheth; if the ground be good, it encreaseth."[18] In the bluntest of terms, if churchgoers do not profit from the preached doctrine, "the fault is in the hearers not in the teachers."[19] In Protestant sermons the importance of the parishioner's role in salvation results in a privileging of aural over visual sensory experience. Donne elevates hearing above seeing in his sermon about the conversion of St. Paul, who was brought to God by a voice: "Man hath a natural way to come to God, by the eie, by the creature; so *Visible things* shew the *Invisible God*: But then, God hath super-induced a supernaturall way, by the eare. For, though hearing be naturall, yet that faith in God should come by hearing a man preach, is supernatural."[20] Vision can bring one closer to God—

one can see God's invisible hand in the visible details of the natural world—but hearing instills faith through "supernatural" means. Donne's insistence on a difference between natural and supernatural sensory activity and his emphasis on hearing over vision are grounded in early modern Protestant ideas about salvation. Implicit in Donne's comment that there must be "supernatural" forces at work if "faith in God should come by hearing a man preach" is an understanding of the preacher as a natural vehicle for God's supernatural communications. A mere man in the service of God, the Protestant preacher differs from the Catholic priest, who claims to be endowed by God with the capacity to bestow grace.

It follows logically that Protestants who imbue hearers with responsibility for their own salvation would privilege the ear as the holiest of bodily organs.[21] For Donne the site where natural and supernatural processes meet is not the preacher's tongue but the listener's ear—an organ that performs *both* secular and spiritual tasks. Robert Wilkinson's *A Jewell for the Eare* (1605) submits that although the ear is used for earthly activities, it is created for a holy purpose: "God hath planted the eare for spiritual uses," he writes, here gesturing toward the commonplace pun on ears as organs of hearing and stalks of corn.[22] Sermons like Wilkinson's evince an almost fetishistic focus on the "fleshiye instrument of hearing."[23] Wilkinson insists it is better to lose an eye, an arm, or a leg than the use of one's ears: "[I]f God take away the use of hearing, it is a signe he is angry indeede," for "the soule feedeth at the eare, as the body by the mouth: therefore better loose all then loose it." Wilkinson's sermon argues that ears are the bodily conduits through which God touches the human soul: "God never cometh so neere a mans soule as when he entreth in by the doore of the eare, therefore the eare is a most precious member *if men knewe how to use it*."[24]

The conditional clause at the end of Wilkinson's statement serves as a kind of scare tactic. Having set up the dependence of grace upon the ears, Wilkinson reminds his congregation that although they have the organ of understanding that enables salvation, they cannot take for granted that the organ will work effectively. As is evinced in the oft-iterated biblical proverb, "though wee have all eares, yet all have not eares to heare,"[25] Protestant sermons recognize that good hearing can be a painstaking practice. "Hearing with your ears," a seemingly redundant phrase that recurs frequently in early modern sermons, is, according to preachers, "a tallent" and an "arte."[26] Stephen Egerton's sermon *The Boring of the Eare* (published in 1623) calls hearing an "exercise" of some "difficultie."[27] M. G. Gifford's *A Sermon on the*

Figure 3. Thomas Taylor, *Parable of the Sower and the Seed*, 2d ed. (London, 1623), engraved title page. This item is reproduced by permission of The Huntington Library, San Marino, California.

Parable of the Sower (1582) compares the "hard and painful" task of good hearing with field labor.[28] Proper hearing cannot be accomplished through passive receptiveness; it requires actively working to absorb the seed of God's Word through one's ears and more deeply into one's heart. Indeed, proper hearing is represented in sermons as a process occurring over time, beginning well before the sermon starts and continuing for days after it has ended. Hearing for profit requires not only energy and time but space. Gifford writes, "my heart be softned in such sorte, that I feele the roote goeth *deepe*, yea, so deepe, that it can never be rooted out."[29]

To underscore the challenging nature of the work of hearing and to demonstrate the spiritual consequences for those who fail to receive the Word properly, Protestant sermons describe in great detail what it means to be a "bad hearer." Because spiritual hearing is a temporal and spatial practice—not an instantaneous act one chooses or refuses to perform—bad hearers may disrupt the inception of the Word at a range of stages during the hearing process. These stages of disruption are illustrated compellingly on the frontispiece to Thomas Taylor's *The Parable of the Sower and of the Seed* (1623) (see figure 3).

At the top of the image stands a preacher, holding what appears to be a box but clearly represents a book in the third edition. The small black dots that cascade down the page on either side of the preacher represent God's Word—they are seeds being dispensed by the preacher with the aim of fertilizing the parishioners who gather to listen to the oration. As is elucidated in the sermon text, the four emblems below the preacher represent four kinds of hearers who vary in their degree of receptivity to the seed of God's Word. The first group, the huddled masses standing before a barren ground strewn with seeds, are like highway ground into which the seed has no entry. To their right is a depiction of the second type of hearers; their ground has produced small sprigs of crops, but because this earth is hard and stony, the plants cannot take deep root and will flourish no further. The bottom-left quadrant shows a group of auditors who have allowed the seed to penetrate and take root, but because they failed to nurture the planted seed, weeds have invaded their ground. The frontispiece illustrates only one successful kind of hearer: standing beneath the banner "Centuplum" (many or multiple) appear a small group whose seeds have been entirely converted into the garden before which they stand. These, the sermon tells us, are the best sort of hearer of God's Word, for they let the Word penetrate them deeply, and having nurtured it, turn the seed into bountiful crops, good deeds.

Taylor's sermon develops this frontispiece representation of hearing as a multistage process. He, like other preachers, explains that in order to achieve salvation through hearing, one must attend the service in order to be exposed to the Word; and one must concentrate on the sermon, so that the Word enters one's ears effectively. But this is not enough, for one must also find ways to retain the preacher's message in one's mind after leaving the service; and further, one must process the message carefully so as to fully understand it and absorb it into one's heart. Disrupting the seed's movement during any one of these stages results in a "bad crop." The purpose of sermons about listening, then, is not only to inform Christians, especially what Harrison calls the "simpler sorte," about the importance of hearing "for their profit,"³⁰ but also to instruct them in how to choreograph their own salvation: to guide the movement of the seed-Word through their ears and into their hearts.³¹

Learning to hear for profit is a constant theme in Shakespeare's plays, which share many of the sermons' tropes of hearing. Falstaff, in his typically blasphemous fashion, parodies the salvational rewards of proper hearing when he leaves Poins with the task of convincing Hal to participate in the next day's adventures: "Well, God give thee the spirit of persuasion and him the ears of profiting, that what thou speakest may move and what he hears may be believed" (*1 Henry IV* 1.2.134–36). The idea that "profitable" hearing occurs when words take root in the ear and bear fruit there is articulated by the King of France in *All's Well That Ends Well*, when he, employing the pun on ears of corn and ears of hearing, describes Bertram's father's talent for oratory: "Methinks I hear him now; his plausive words / He scattered not in ears, but grafted them / To grow there and to bear" (1.2.53–55). In *Twelfth Night*, Viola conjoins fertility and aural receptivity when petitioning to woo Olivia in private: "My matter hath no voice, lady, but to your own most pregnant and vouchsafed ear" (3.1.80–81). Earlier Viola also insists upon the idea that the ears play a significant role in creating the meaning of an utterance. Requesting again to be left alone with Olivia, she says: "What I am and what I would are as secret as maidenhead; to your ears, divinity; to any others', profanation" (1.5.189–91). Rosaline expresses similar sentiments in *Love's Labour's Lost* when she teaches Biron that even the best verbal art depends for its success upon listeners: "A jest's prosperity lies in the ear / Of him that hears it, never in the tongue / Of him that makes it" (5.2.838–40).

But of all Shakespeare's plays, it is the late plays—widely viewed by

critics as staging narratives of human salvation[32]—that explore most intently the transformative power of hearing.[33] For many of the male characters of these plays, transformation is predicated on aural subjugation. As
Peggy Muñoz Simonds has argued, in *Cymbeline* auditory acts induce the
collapse and the restoration of King Cymbeline's family and state. Both
Cymbeline and his son-in-law Posthumous fall prey to the poisonous
words of false allies and can rebuild their social and political worlds only
when they open their ears and hearts to the truthful utterances of those
they have ignored throughout the play.[34] The stubborn male protagonists
of *Pericles* and *The Winter's Tale* undergo a similar process of salvation
through aural receptivity. The closed-minded and closed-eared Pericles
and Leontes can transform their crumbling worlds into fertile and regener-
ative systems when they listen to the voices of subordinates. In effect, the
male rulers of these late plays must be willing to be subjugated by the
sounds of subordinates (especially women), before their selves and kingdoms can be rejuvenated.

For Leontes, Pericles, and Cymbeline, political and personal problems
stem from an inability to hear effectively and thus to render advantageous
judgments for their subjects and families. Pericles' troubles begin in the
palace of Antioch, where Pericles' failure to engage his hearing faculties renders him incapable of recognizing the truth about Antiochus's incestuous
relationship with his daughter. Captivated by the silent daughter's beauty,
Pericles is dumbstruck with love. Maurice Hunt, who focuses on the recurring trope of speechlessness in the late plays, argues that the palace scene is
indicative of "the failure of certain extraordinary words to warn him [Peri-
cles] of a lethal threat" and of Pericles' "antiverbal attitude."[35] But the emphasis of the scene seems to be not that words fail to be spoken, but that, as
a consequence, they cannot be heard; the Daughter's and Pericles' muteness
prevent Pericles from using his most vital organs, his ears. Pericles is able to
decipher the astonishing truth about Antiochus and his daughter only when
he reads *aloud* the puzzling riddle. Sounding out for his own ears the content of the riddle, Pericles achieves understanding, corroborating preacher
Richard Gouge's position that "[o]f all the Senses, none is more needfull, or
use-full, then *Hearing*."[36] Pericles signals his new understanding by shifting
from visual metaphors, which dominate his first reactions, to aural ones.
Whereas his eyes might have been tricked by the daughter's virtuous face
and appealing apparel, his ears clearly sense her corruption. Pericles discovers the daughter's sinfulness through a conceit of her sound:

You are a fair viol, and your sense the strings,
Who, fingered to make man his lawful music,
Would draw heaven down and all the gods to hearken;
But, being played upon before your time,
Hell only danceth at so harsh a chime. (1.1.82–86)[37]

The daughter's sensual appetite is compared to the strings of a viol that will create heavenly music when played solely for "lawful" pleasure, her husband's. Because she has been "played on" by her father, the music the daughter produces is vile and dissonant; the instrument plucked before its time is as distasteful as a fruit picked before it is ripe. When Pericles overcomes deafness and hears the daughter's music, he is able to engage his skills of judgment and plan an escape.

In the late plays, as in sermons on the parable of the sower and seed, forms of disruptive deafness are organized as if on a continuum from superficial inattention to deep, active resistance. As does the Taylor frontispiece discussed above, the plays represent hearing as a multilayered process: the effectiveness of a sound is measured by the depth it is able to travel, the innermost layer being the heart. Pericles' auditory challenges in the beginning of the play lie on the superficial end of this spectrum. He lacks access to sensory information in the same way that Christians who are not present in church for the sermon are beyond the range of the salvational Word. Leontes' failures of audition in *The Winter's Tale* occur at a deeper level, however: Leontes is too distracted by his own internal monologue of suspicion to listen to the many voices that insist on Hermione's innocence. Leontes' hearing problems confound his judgment, with fatal results. Refusing to listen to Hermione, he loses her; unwilling to heed the oracle, he induces the death of his son; and refusing to attend to Paulina, he almost brings about the death of his daughter.

Leontes' aural obstinacy is particularly clear in these cases, because the orators he ignores are described elsewhere as being overwhelmingly persuasive. Hermione deftly convinces Polixenes to stay in Sicilia despite his repeated insistence to the contrary; although he tells Leontes, "There is no tongue that moves, none, none i'th' world / So soon as yours, could win me" (1.2.20–21), it is Hermione's, not Leontes', tongue that is victorious. And yet Hermione's tongue has no such effects on Leontes. He is unmoved even by the supernatural commands of the oracle. Cleomines describes the oracle's voice as so "ear-deaf'ning" that it "surprised my sense / That I was nothing" (3.1.9–11); and yet Leontes ignores the oracle's powerful prophecies. Simi-

larly, Paulina is described as the only "lady living / So meet for this great er-
rand" (2.2.48–49) of persuading the king of Hermione's innocence. Paulina's
oratorical prowess seems proven at first when she comes to Leontes "with
words as medicinal as true, / . . . to purge him of that humour / That presses
him from sleep" (2.3.37–39) and pleads, "I beseech you hear me" (2.3.53).
Leontes lends an ear at first, allowing her to begin her oration with "Good
my liege, I come—" (2.3.52) and to speak for almost seven lines. But the king
is quickly sidetracked by Paulina's invocation of "good queen" (58), a term
that captures his attention so profoundly that he can listen no further.
"Good queen?" he repeats and very shortly demands Paulina be removed
from his presence. Although Paulina continues to argue her case, unfazed by
his harsh rebukes, she is unable to bring the king to accept her point of view
because Leontes stops listening.

Leontes exercises a particular form of bad hearing described by Gifford's sermon, which complains of those auditors who initially attend to a
sermon but lose its message entirely when they seize hold of "some word or
sentence which they heard uttered, and are carried so far, that they cannot
of long time recover their minde to bring it again to the matter." These
churchgoers might begin as good auditors, but they are just as doomed as
those who do not attend church at all, for when they become captivated
with a particular detail and allow their minds to free-associate, they miss the
rest of the sermon and remain in "confused opinion."[38] Gifford presents
these auditors as examples of the first sort of bad hearers, into whose hearts
the seed cannot penetrate because they are like the ground of the "way side,
where the path is trampled & beaten smooth & hard, by mens feet." The seed
of the Word does not penetrate deeply into these listeners, but rather "lyeth
above the ground altogether uncovered" easily carried off by passing birds.[39]
This, Gifford explains, is the etiology of the expression "it went in at the one
eare, and out at the other."[40] For even obedient Christians who come to
church and intend to listen may not achieve understanding and be saved,
because the Word is barely given entry into them before it is carried away by
the distracting devil. Leontes' heart has, in a similar sense, become hardened
against his wife, and no matter how persuasive Paulina's rhetoric, no matter
how strongly she argues Hermione's innocence, the words will not penetrate
deeply enough to take root; they go in one ear and out the other. Blocked
against Paulina's truthful words, Leontes' ears admit only the weak, soft
voices of flatterers, who "tender o're his follies" and confirm his rigid opin-
ions when they "sigh / At each his needless heavings" (2.3.34–35).

Leontes recovers his trust in Paulina when he discovers that by slandering Hermione, he has (to the best of his knowledge) killed her. That he has reversed his opinion of his wife and begun to tread a path toward salvation is signaled by his dedication to opening his ears to Paulina's harsh harangues. "Go on, go on," he replies as Paulina rebukes him for causing Hermione's demise, "Thou canst not speak too much. I have deserved / All tongues to talk their bitt'rest" (3.2.212–14). No longer is Paulina the "mankind witch" (2.3.68), "intelligencing bawd" (69), or "callat / Of boundless tongue" (91–92) whose criticism was tantamount to treachery moments before. Now her piercing words contain a "truth" that he is willing and even anxious to "receive" (3.2.231). He is so receptive, in fact, that when all rational thinking points to the necessity for him to find a new wife (and thus produce an heir for the throne), Leontes bends his ear to Paulina's contrary advice. Regretting the consequences that ensued the last time he refused her "counsel" (5.1.52), he realizes that he has no choice but to open himself up aurally to Paulina, whose words of truth may cause great danger if not admitted. He fears that were he to close his ears to Paulina's advice and take another wife, Hermione would haunt him, causing violence, not coincidentally, upon his organs of hearing: "Were I the ghost" of Hermione, Paulina warns, "I'd shriek that even your ears / Should rift to hear me, and the words that followed / Should be 'Remember mine'" (5.1.63–67). One cannot help but be reminded of the Ghost of King Hamlet, whose haunting call "remember me" (1.5.91) is accompanied by or, as in Campbell Scott's film version of *Hamlet*, constitutive of an act of aural violence.[41] The threat of an aural haunting that would split his organs of hearing keeps Leontes mindful of Paulina's counsel, and he swears, "We shall not marry till thou bidd'st us" (5.1.82).

As critics often have noted, *The Winter's Tale* and the other late plays combine tragic happenings with a comic ending wherein the social and political order is reconstituted through the arrangement of marriage(s) and the full promise of future heirs to the throne. One of the differences between the endings of these plays and the endings of most of Shakespeare's comedies, however, is that this rebirth of lineage is accompanied by (or precipitated by) the rebirth of the male hero.[42] Traditionally, critics have read these stories of suffering and redemption within a universal and male Christian narrative of salvation.[43] The problem with such a reading is not only that, as recent scholars point out, it overlooks the plays' engagements with pagan myths of regeneration and, concomitantly, women's fertility,[44] but it also overlooks historical, religious, and cultural differences in the ways the Christian narrative of redemption is expressed. I am suggesting that the rebirths dramatized in these plays need to be examined in light of early modern Protestant representations of redemption as the crop yielded through productive hearing. As Protestant sermons on the parable of the sower and the seed underscore the importance of hearing to salvation, they help highlight not simply the spiritual but the social, political, and personal benefits that ensue from male heroes' recovery of their aural senses. Just as Leontes' cured deafness enables him to be reunited with his daughter and wife and thus recover an heir, Cymbeline and Pericles find their long-lost daughters and, in the case of the latter, an assumed-to-be-dead wife when these aurally stubborn kings open their ears to receive oral counsel. In a somewhat literal fashion, the male heroes of the late plays dramatize the process of aural salvation described in sermons: when these rulers desist from disruptive deafness and open their ears, they are fertilized by words and able to bear "fruit."

At the ends of *Cymbeline* and *Pericles*, various personal and political rebirths follow from men's recovery of their hearing. As Leontes' recognition of his failure to hear provokes him to open his ears to the least approved of advisors (a woman), Cymbeline's shocking discovery encourages him to listen to "Fidele," a youth who is known to him only as a former servant of his enemies (albeit Innogen in disguise). When Fidele—who embodies salvation in his very name (the Latin *fides* meaning "faith")—asks the king to "give me hearing" (5.6.116), Cymbeline, without having any reason to trust the youth, grants the request heartily, promising to "lend my best attention" (5.6.117). Throughout the final scenes of the play, Cymbeline is more than an attentive listener; he is an active, hungry auditor, increasingly eager to hear the truth from Fidele and the other captives. "Renew thy strength," he commands the fainting Giacomo, "I had rather thou shouldst live while nature will / Than die ere I hear more. Strive, man, and speak" (150–52). And as Giacomo relates the story of his trickery, Cymbeline demonstrates the hunger of his now-open aural organs, interrupting Giacomo to urge him on: "I stand on fire. / Come to the matter" (168–69) and "Nay, nay, to th' purpose" (178). One would be hard-pressed to describe Cymbeline as submitting peacefully and passively to the role of listener; indeed, he occupies this new position with vigor, commanding his orators to continue feeding him knowledge.[45] When he discovers that his long-lost sons are alive and stand before him, Cymbeline is overcome with the desire to hear all the details of their plight. "O rare instinct! / When shall I hear all through? This fierce abridgement / Hath to it circumstantial branches which / Distinction should be rich in" (382–85).

Pericles also develops ears hungry for the truth when he finally overcomes his state of deafness. When Pericles appears on the stage in act 5, he is a shell of the man he once was. Unshaven and dressed in rags, he has alienated himself from the world around him—"A man who for this three months hath not spoken / To anyone, nor taken sustenance / But to prorogue his grief" (5.1.20–22). Although most critics have focused on Pericles' refusal to speak as indicative of his antisocial condition,[46] it is important to note that the king's muteness is a symptom of a much more profound state of isolation: Pericles will not speak to those who approach him because he seems not to *hear* them. His trials at sea and extreme grief have resulted in his loss of fine hearing, the sense that was necessary for him to judge events and avoid danger in the beginning of the play (when he confronted the incestuous Antiochus). The only way to bring Pericles back from his state of alienation, his friends maintain, is to "make a battery through his deafened ports / Which now are midway stopped" (5.1.39–40).

Doreen Delvecchio and Antony Hammond, the New Cambridge editors of the play, can largely be justified in their choice of the quarto's "defend" ("defended" in Q2) in place of "deafened" in this line, not just because the words are virtual homonyms (as they point out), but because of a popular early modern understanding of the ears as an individual's defense system.[47] There is much at stake in editorial disagreements about Pericles' hearing, a point to which I shall return later. For now, let us simply observe that if Pericles is defended, rather than deafened, his self-imposed alienation may be read as somehow necessary and self-sustaining, a constructive practice rather than as some sort of deficiency to be overcome. Representations of the ears as self-protective fortresses appear in a range of early modern moral treatises. In *Essaies Upon the Five Senses* (1620), Richard Brathwaite writes that "a discreet *eare* . . . cheeres the affections, fortifying them against all oppositions. [T]hose be the best *Forts*, and impregnablest, whose feats, most opposed to danger, stand in resistance against all hostile incursion."[48] Pierre de la Primaudaye, echoing an observation about the ears that appears in early modern anatomy books, notes that the very composition and placement of the ears supports their role as "watchmen over the whole body": as important to surveillance as the eyes, the ears are placed "hard by the eyes on each side"; not only are they made of "gristles," which are far firmer than flesh, sinews, and other substances in the body, but they are also placed near the body's "hardest and firmest bones . . . whereby the eares are strongly fortified."[49] In short, the ears are built to serve as defenders of the body and the mind.

This is not to say that every aural fortress is beneficial to the self. Sometimes, the aural fortress is represented as excessive or misplaced, and thus defensiveness becomes more disruptive rather than constructive. In the first scene of *Hamlet*, Barnardo appeals to this notion of misplaced fortresses when he begs the skeptical Horatio to listen to his narrative about the ghost's appearance the previous night: "Sit down a while, / And let us once again assail your ears, / That are so fortified against our story" (1.1.28–30). The weapon in this case is a true story of which Horatio needs to be informed, and thus aural fortifications must be beaten down. As is evident in the example from *Hamlet*, the ears—in addition to being considered essential defense mechanisms for the body-castle—are simultaneously entry-points of knowledge. In Bartolomeo del Bene's epic poem *Civitas Veri sive Morum* (1609), where the mind is a walled city, the journey of knowledge upon which del Bene and his companions embark begins at the gate that symbolizes hearing.[50] The poem illustrates a concept generally recognized by an array of early modern texts: where learning is concerned, hearing is the most crucial of the senses. In Thomas Tomkis's university drama *Lingua* (1607), the title character, who has been trying to lodge a petition to be included as one of the senses, accuses Auditus (the sense of hearing) of devising "dayly subtile plots . . . To stop me from the eares of common Sense," a high official in the state of Microcosm.[51] Lingua disputes Auditus's control over the information Common Sense receives, for by obstructing Lingua's voice, Auditus undermines Common Sense's capacity to judge her case fairly: "a plaintife cannot have accesse, / But through your gates," and thus Common Sense is "informed" with "nought els / But that thy crafty eares to him convaies."[52] When Pericles' supporters claim that the king's blocked ears require "battery," they suggest that, in this case, the fortifications are inappropriate: in closing his ears to protect himself from further dangers, Pericles has shut out knowledge as well, including the essential knowledge of his state's political disorder. Vital, beneficial sounds are being disrupted "midway" (5.1.40) in the hearing process, preventing Pericles from performing his political duties.

Pericles' deafness is a consequence of his profound grief over the demise of his wife and daughter, Marina—a grief as much political as it is personal, for with the deaths of his loved ones, Pericles has lost his opportunity to produce an heir to the throne. It is fitting that Pericles is prompted to open his ears by the speech of a maid (unbeknownst to him, Marina) who reports being uprooted, of being denied her place as an heir. Summoned for her eloquence and superb singing voice, Marina fails at first to break through Pericles' aural obstructions: he does not seem to have "[m]arked" (73) her song, and when she addresses him in a typical oratory fashion, "Hail sir! My lord, lend ear" (75), he still refuses her—perhaps violently.[53] What opens Pericles' ears, allowing for their fertilization, is the language of regeneration. Pericles responds to Marina directly after she declares that "time hath rooted out my parentage" (83). Notably, the first articulate words he speaks after three months of muteness echo Marina's: "my fortunes— parentage— good parentage—/ To equal mine. Was it not thus? What say you?" (88–89). Although the scene builds toward recognition and salvation for Pericles, these first words are a climax in and of themselves, for by echoing Marina, Pericles demonstrates not only that he has arrested his prolonged state of muteness, but that on some level he has heard Marina's speech and thus made permeable his aural fortress. From this point forward, he transforms quickly from a reclusive, passive, despondent man to, like Cymbeline, a demanding listener. To the maiden before him, "Another Juno; / Who starves the ears she feeds and makes them hungry / The more she gives them speech" (102–4), he fires a barrage of question and commands to hear more: "Where do you live?" (104), "Where were you bred?" (106), "how achieved you these endowments" (107), "Prithee speak" (110), "Report thy parentage" (120), "Tell thy story" (125).[54] Once Pericles' ears are open, he becomes impatient to put them to use as discriminating judges. Indeed, Pericles becomes so sensitive to sound and so adept at auditory perception that he claims to be able to hear the "[m]ost heavenly music" (220) of the spheres, sounds that no one else can sense.[55]

Pericles describes this rarefied music as affecting him less spiritually than physically: "It nips me unto listening" (221) he exclaims, as he is induced into sleep. C. L. Barber associates the word "nips" with sublime moments in Shakespeare's late plays, arguing that in this instance the word introduces maternal imagery—the "nips" that forge intimate bonds between mother and child.[56] As it was used in the sixteenth and seventeenth centuries, however, the word carries a more aggressive physical resonance: it means to painfully squeeze the neck or head of someone, thereby overwhelming and reducing him to a state of helplessness.[57] The music that "nips [Pericles] into listening" does not waft over him like the soft touch of a mother's love but assaults him painfully. The reading may suggest that when Pericles collapses on the stage, he does so out of not exhaustion but shock. His ears are not passive receptacles into which sound enters fluidly and unobserved. Pericles battles physically with the sounds that assault him and, like other male rulers of the late plays, is happily overcome.

In sermons the pleasures and rewards of being aurally penetrated by God's Word, of overcoming spiritual deafness, are sometimes represented in erotic terms. Gifford's description of good hearing implies that salvation is a form of intercourse with God, an orgasmic experience with the character-istics of a *petit mort*: "Those are a thousand times happie, which feele melt-ing heartes & soft affections, so that Gods word doth pearse into them, and causeth them to tremble at the majestye & power of the same: their tender heart doth sigh and *mourne* for their iniquitie." With soft hearts, hearers will be prepared for God to "digge in them, and thrust in his spade to the bot-tome."[58] But, explains Gifford, the true pleasures to be gained from this en-counter between the seed and the auditor's receptive heart are the offspring produced as a consequence. Being penetrated by God's Word is valuable only if the interaction results in "fruit": "[I]t is not inough to heare the word, & to receive it with ioy, & to let it grow in us, unlesse it bring forth reasonable and timelye fruit in us."[59]

Adopting a similar logic, *Pericles* and *Cymbeline* link the salvation that follows from aural penetration with procreation. When the male rulers of *Pericles* and *Cymbeline* open their ears and allow themselves to be pene-trated aurally, their bodies are endowed with women's reproductive capaci-ties, enabling them to give birth to a lineage. Cymbeline compares his reunion with his three heirs as a maternal birthing: "O, what am I? / A mother to the birth of three? Ne'er mother / Rejoiced deliverance more" (5.6.369–71). Cymbeline's "deliverance" of three children follows directly from his willingness to be aurally inseminated by the speeches of his cap-tives, his disguised daughter being one of them. Similarly, Marina's implan-tation of the seeds of truth in Pericles' ear produces a reborn king who, realizing he has found his daughter, calls for his royal robes and reenters po-litical society. Pericles figures his restoration as a birth when he says to Ma-rina, "Thou that beget'st him that did thee beget" (5.1.185). In effect, both Cymbeline and Pericles produce heirs after having been aurally impregnated by, among others, their daughters.

The incestuous implications of these metaphors of rebirth have troubled some critics, who wish to discriminate between, for instance, the heroic, renewed Pericles who ends the play and the Pericles who begins it with a narrow escape from the world of incest. Delvecchio and Hammond insist, for instance, that "[t]he 'begetting' in question is wholly spiritual: there is *no* connotation of sexuality or incest implied."[60] Pericles' spiritual state is certainly at issue here, but the editors' anxious bracketing off of *all* physical implications is misguided. Insofar as *Pericles* and the other late plays are concerned with the regeneration of a family line and with locating a fertile womb to produce future heirs, the reproductive body is very much at stake.[61] Moreover, as we have seen, the period's own discourses of salvation link spiritual generativity with reproductive processes.

Given the extent to which the late plays valorize the fertile maternal body, it is perhaps not surprising that critics have often read the plays as exhibiting protofeminist leanings. Sometimes in part as an effort to refute the characterization of Shakespeare as a misogynist, critics have argued that these plays signify a turning point in the playwright's career: as the artist matures in his later years, the masculine bloodshed and violence of the tragedies give way to a feminine emphasis on healing and rebirth and an elevation of female characters to more powerful positions.[62] While I concur that the late plays embrace some traditional feminine values, I question the extent to which this valorization of feminine attributes signifies a more generous portrayal of women.

For one thing, arguments for the late plays' feminist ethos have been based partly on the assumption that the plays evince their celebration of the feminine by representing female characters as articulate, convincing speakers.[63] Simon Palfrey writes, for instance, that in these plays "emotional investment and often narrative organization are, almost unremittingly, feminized. A foolish or venal male hegemony is altered and humanized by the incorporation, as a persuasive instrument of power and decision-making, of a 'feminine principle' based not only in the faithfulness of chastity but the eloquence of the female tongue."[64] Referring to the scene in which Marina is imagined to feed the truth to her father, Palfrey maintains that the association between "educational speech" and food underscores that "[t]o possess public rhetoric is to control the bread"; "the circulation of speech and food offers a graph of power."[65] Critics maintain that the late plays' rhetorically persuasive female speakers are emblematic of a shift in the balance of power away from male rulers and toward their daughters and wives. It is true that all the late plays feature outspoken and/or disobedient female characters who challenge the authority of male rulers and, indeed, by the end of each play, are credited with enabling male salvation.[66] However, this portrayal of effective female orators does not necessarily imply an elevation of female characters to positions of power. Although Marina, Innogen, and Paulina speak persuasively at crucial moments, their vocal power has diminished currency in plays that figure salvation as *aural*, rather than *oral*. If the plays celebrate not the piercing rhetoric of speakers but the receptive posture of listeners, as I have argued, then when female characters step into a space of vocal authority, that space has already been vacated of much of its value. In terms of their capacity to dramatize female agency, the late plays' representations of women's persuasive speech are thus a red herring. Enacting a modified version of the Pauline principles of female behavior often reiterated in the period, the late plays are concerned with keeping women not silent, but deaf.

There are also limitations to the contention that the late plays valorize women by celebrating traditional feminine attributes. At first glance this would seem to make sense, for the correlation of salvation with fertility, which I have traced in the plays, seems to privilege women's experiences. Pericles' comment to Marina that if her story of suffering prove as poignant as his own, "thou art a man, and I / Have suffered like a girl" (5.1.127–28) suggests that men must undergo a sex change of sorts in order to shore up their identities. However, male appropriation of the female body is not always benign and does not necessarily translate into a celebration of women.[67] As Katharine Eisaman Maus has shown in her work on male writers and womb imagery, male writers can appropriate the positive meaning of a female symbol while reiterating and displacing onto women its more negative significations; they can identify with the womb as a symbol of generative, male creativity but continue to denigrate its duplicitous, licentious nature.[68] In the late plays, representations of hearing—which also carries multivalent meanings in the period—work in a similar way. For male characters, as we have seen, aural openness displays a heroic capacity for leadership as well as personal and political fortitude. Yet, as I shall discuss in the next section, in female characters such openness functions as a sign of lasciviousness. This is not to say that the late plays deny women power entirely. To the contrary, they dramatize a most provocative model of female agency, albeit one that locates agency in aural, rather than oral, acts and that, at the same time, does not assume auditors' vulnerability to sound.

Constructive Aural Defense

Religious and moral discourses on hearing can help us begin to create such a model. We have seen that Protestant sermons call for a vulnerable auditor who is poised to receive God's salvational Word. But while sermons propose that receptive hearing is the mark of a good Christian, they simultaneously warn about the dangers of the ears being too impressionable. The problem, preachers explain, is that the ears are entryways not only for God but for the devil. Harrison preaches to his congregation: "[A]s you must take heed how you heare, so also take heed what you heare. It is the word of God, not the word of the Divell . . . that must make you fruitful. . . . Beleeve not everie spirit; but try the spirits whether they bee of God."[69] As is suggested in Harrison's solution—"*try* the spirits"—sermons, along with contemporaneous religious and moral texts concerning spiritual and personal well-being, propose that auditors deploy their ears as a first line of defense against evil, which often assaults by way of sound. In effect, the aural obstructions that preachers argue to be so disruptive to salvation can at times be constructive for the spiritual self.

Arguments for the ears as constructive organs of defense for the body and the soul appear in a wide range of early modern moral and religious texts. We have already seen la Primaudaye and Brathwaite describe the ears as a fortress. Brathwaite further advises that when confronted with dishonorable sorts, "my *eare* must be tuned to another note, that my edifying Sence may discharge her peculiar office, not to affect novelties, or chuse varieties, but to dedicate her inward operation to the mindes comfort (to wit) the *Melodie of heaven*."[70] In Stephano Guazzo's *The Civile Conversation* (translated into English in 1581), Guazzo is told by his fictional tutor Anibel that a "wise man" takes on "solitarinesse of the mind" when "in the company of the evil: from hearing whose talke hee ought to stop his eares."[71] Such arguments follow in the vein of Seneca, whose epistle 31, translated by Thomas Lodge in 1614, advises, "thou shalt be wise, if thou knewest well how to close up thine eares, which it sufficeth not to damme up with waxe: thou must close stop [*sic*] them after another manner."[72] The biblical figure associated most strongly with such constructive defensiveness is David, who is cited for being "as deafe and dumbe at reproach, as any stock, or stone."[73]

Early modern writers figure closed ears as especially important for the maintenance of female chastity. In Elizabeth Cary's *The Tragedy of Mariam*, the association of open ears with an open body fuels Herod's suspicions about Mariam. As Reina Green argues, Herod and others fault Mariam not simply for her "unbridled speech" but for her willingness to listen to men other than her husband, an act Herod construes as evidence of her adulterous affair with Sohemus.[74] Salome, too, exploits the ideological link between open ears and an open body when she urges Pheroras to be suspicious of his new wife's seeming virtue. Recalling the "wicked words" that Graphina has already failed to defend against—the seductions of Pheroras himself—Salome doubts that the "porter" at the gates of Graphina's mind can effectively fend off harmful words: "But of a porter, better were you sped, / If she against their entrance made defence."[75] Antitheatricalists Stephen Gosson and William Prynne similarly prey on men's anxieties about female hearing when they recommend that women practice vigilant aural defensiveness. Gosson urges women, "if you perceive your selves in any danger at your owne doores, either allured by curtesie in the day, or assaulted with Musicks in the night; Close up your eyes, stoppe your eares."[76] Prynne touts the virtues of Hiero Syracusanus, who insisted his wife be protected from wanton poetry: "[H]ee would that in his house not onely other parts of the body should be chaste, but the eares also, which be unto other members of the body instead of a tunnell, to be kept, *sartas tectas*, that is, defended and covered."[77] If the ears are a "tunnel" into Hiero's wife's body, then preserving her chastity means ensuring that she has strong aural fortresses.

To be sure prescriptions like Prynne's for female aural defensiveness are grounded in misogynist assumptions about female aural vulnerability—assumptions that were used throughout the period to justify women's subordinate positions in social and political hierarchies. Yet, I submit, it is because the ears are understood to be a site of female vulnerability that the performance of aural defense comes to constitute a form of agency for women. John Weever's *Ancient Funerall Monuments* (1631) suggests as much in its report of a wife who valiantly defended herself against a licentious Abbot. Alone with the woman, the Abbot "began to sollicite her chastitie" by tempting her with promises of greater wealth. But the woman frustrated the Abbot's attempts, "giving no eare to his libidinous motions." Despite his cunning efforts, "she still resisted all his encounters, promises, and perswasions."[78] The character of the militantly chaste woman who resists persuasions by turning a deaf ear to dangerous solicitations recurs throughout the literature of the period. For instance, in Phillip Massinger's play *The Bond-*

Man (1624) Cleora fulfills her vow of fidelity to her beloved by fending off the petitions of another suitor who begins his solicitation: "The Organs of your hearing yet are open; / And you infringe no vow, though you vouchsafe, / To give them warrant, to convey unto / Your understanding parts the story of / A tortur'd and dispairing Lover."[79] By contrast, Cleora's true beloved proves his genuine devotion by maintaining that he has never attempted to batter down the fortress of her ear. "I ne're tun'd / Loose Notes to your chaste ears; or brought rich Presents / For my Artillery, to batter downe, / The fortresse of your honour."[80] And of course, among the most famous of literary examples of heroic female aural defensiveness is the chaste Lady in Milton's masque of *Comus*.[81]

Acts of valiant aural defensiveness help define female heroism in Shakespeare's late plays as well. When Marina in *Pericles* is captured by pirates and enslaved in a brothel, she similarly succeeds in guarding her chastity. Diverse critical readings of Marina in the brothel have focused primarily on the character's impressive oratorical talents, which enable her to dissuade interested clients from procuring her services.[82] The audience witnesses two gentlemen exiting the brothel and declaring that Marina's speeches—"divinity preached" (4.5.4)—have led them "out of the road of rutting for ever" (4.5.9); and we look on as Marina's skillful speaking not only deflects the lewd propositions of Lysimachus, but even induces him to offer her gold to support her continued good works. But before Marina can preach divinity, she employs her ears, eluding the seductive and sinful life of a prostitute by practicing aural defense. The brothel's bawd, like the Abbot of Weever's story, tempts Marina with the promise of material wealth and sexual pleasure. In response Marina turns a deaf ear, leading the bawd to express disbelief that such a life does not appeal to Marina: "What, do you stop your ears?" (4.2.74).[83] The answer to such a question is self-evident from the perspective of ideologies of female aural defensiveness, which explains Marina's simple response, "Are you a woman?" (75). In Marina view, stopping one's ears to such talk is the very definition of chaste womanhood. That the bawd should query Marina for closing her ears throws into doubt the bawd's very identity as female: one can be, according to Marina, either "[a]n honest woman, or not a woman" (77). As she slowly realizes that the bawd confounds her definition of womanhood, Marina solicits heavenly assistance, "The gods defend me!" (81), and is promptly reminded by the bawd that the work of the gods is fulfilled by earthly men who have earthly needs: "If it please the gods to defend you by men, then men must comfort you, men must feed you, men stir you up" (82–83). Indeed, Marina cannot rely on men to defend her chastity in the brothel; like other female characters of the late plays, she is left to her own devices—the first of which is aural obstruction. Later when the bawd tries again to corrupt Marina, claiming that a virgin's display of modesty will merely elevate her price, Marina again resists persuasive rhetoric—this time by articulating a well-established formula of the bad hearer, "I understand you not" (114). As the Protestant preacher Taylor explains, the worst kind of hearer is he who "understands not" and does not "apply his mind so to understand" (26). Marina appropriates this form of disruptive deafness, reconfiguring it as a defensive strategy to keep her impervious to the bawd's rhetoric. This defensive victory launches Marina as a political force: she becomes so famous for her heroic chastity that she is commissioned to counsel a King.[84]

Of course, Marina's valiant defense of her chastity serves a larger political and narrative purpose. For the heroine to be able to deliver "sacred physic" (5.1.67) to her father, enabling his personal and political salvation, she must remain a maid. Moreover, as in all the late plays, women's chastity, insofar as it secures a lineage, is necessary for the political restoration of male leaders. As important as chastity may be to the patriarchs of these plays, however, it is not simply co-opted by them. *Pericles* suggests as much when it presents Diana as the governing force of the play. As Suzanne Gossett notes, for early moderns Diana embodied the seemingly contradictory imperatives of *Pericles*: she is goddess of fertility as well as chastity and is thereby able to "protect Marina's chastity and restore Thaisa and Pericles to matrimony."[85] Mary Zimmerman's 2004–5 production of *Pericles* underscores the significant power of "chaste fertility" when she has Diana's person preside triumphantly over the reconciliation scene, standing imperiously on a balcony above the action as if guiding the play's characters through to the conclusion she desires.[86] Marina serves Diana most explicitly perhaps by employing persuasive rhetoric to escape the brothel, but her ability to launch this verbal offensive, the play suggests, is predicated on her earlier success at protecting her chaste body and mind from abuse.

Like Marina, Innogen's capacity to deliver words of truth to her father is predicated on her earlier success in using her ears to defend her chastity. Her first assault comes from Giacomo, who gains a hearing by appealing to Innogen's concern for Posthumous. Capitalizing on her desire for news of her banished husband, Giacomo manipulates Innogen into becoming an eager listener by offering only short, cryptic answers to her increasingly urgent questions about Posthumous. ("Continues well my lord? / His health, beseech you?" [1.6.57–58]; "Is he disposed to mirth?" [59]; "Will my lord say so?" [74].) Without appearing the aggressor, Giacomo subtly suggests that Innogen has reason to be concerned about her husband and to be pitied, prompting her to ask anxiously: "What do you pity sir?" (83); "Am I one, sir?" (84); "what wreck discern you in me / Deserves your pity?" (85–86); "Why do you pity me?" (90). By inducing Innogen to solicit answers, Giacomo leads her to commit to the position of listener—all the while depicting himself as a reluctant orator. Once he has tricked her into a receptive position, Giacomo begins the slow task of leading Innogen to trust him, and not to trust Posthumous.

This is not the only time that Innogen is shown to be aurally vulnerable to Posthumous and his purported agents. Several times she places herself in danger when she listens too intently to news about her beloved. Unaware that by heading to Millford-Haven for a rendezvous with Posthumous she will speed her demise, she urges Pisanio to deliver quickly the directions. She underscores her voluntary aural vulnerability through the terms she uses to describe to Pisanio her eagerness for information: "speak thick—/ Love's counsellor should fill the bores of hearing, / To th' smothering of the sense" (3.2.56–58). Innogen wishes to be overwhelmed by sounds related to her hoped-for reunion; Pisanio's "thick" (both quick [Norton] and dense) speech will, she hopes, enter her ears so rapidly that they will clog. The conceit draws on anatomical discourses about the ears as holes, or "bores," that are filled with speech. Moreover, as we saw in the previous chapter, early modern theorists of acoustics hold that just as sound that moves too slowly may not be heard accurately, sound that moves too quickly or too intensely will overwhelm the hearer, causing deafness.[87] The differences between Innogen's aural hunger and that which we have seen in Pericles and Cymbeline is notable, for Innogen's aggressive receptivity leads her directly into danger.

Innogen's unflinching devotion to Posthumous is signaled by her willingness to let down her aural guard. It is because she is so willing to open her ears to any matters concerning Posthumous that when she discovers his accusations against her, she feels particularly "wounded" and gives only grudging attention to Pisanio, who wishes for her to "Hear me with patience" (3.4.111). "I have heard I am a strumpet," she tells him, "and mine ear, / Therein false struck, can take no greater wound, / Nor tent to bottom that" (112–14). She has been shaken by Posthumous's accusations, which are figured as pounding blows that enter through her ears. At least where Posthumous is concerned, the Queen's characterization of Innogen is appropriate: "a lady / So tender of rebukes that words are strokes, / And strokes death to her" (3.5.39–41). Giacomo gains access to Innogen by launching his seduction when her ears and heart are in this particularly receptive state.[88]

Giacomo's strategy resembles that of the devil as he is described in Protestant sermons. Preachers warn that blocking the devil's wiles is more challenging in a church than in less godly places, for like the crows that circle fields where planting occurs, "[a] whole flight of Divels follow Gods Seeds-man, and frequent the Ministery, that where the Word is sowne."[89] These devils, who reside in the air, have "subtill, slye, and invisible natures" and thus can "easily over-match our grosse, heavy, and earthly mold." The only way to deal with these evil forces is "by incessant watch against them."[90] Such watch is most crucial during the times when the ears are most vulnerable and open, when "his adversary [is] most secure, and least expecting it"—that is, while the parishioner is listening to the sermon, hoping to be saved by the ears. Most frightening about the devil is that he has the potential for most success when God's hearers are most receptive, as they are supposed to be during the sermon.[91] Likewise, Giacomo attempts to penetrate Innogen while she is open to his influence.

But Innogen's vulnerability lasts only until she becomes aware that she, as an eager auditor, has been tricked into taking responsibility for Giacomo's discourse. When Giacomo exclaims, that " 'tis your graces / That from my mutest conscience to my tongue / Charms this report out" (1.6.116–18), Innogen recognizes the danger of her receptive position and erects an aural fortress, responding, "Let me hear no more" (118).[92] From this point on, the implicit correspondence between aural and sexual violation becomes pronounced, and Giacomo's subtle hints transform into overt sexual propositions. No longer is this a conversation between a man and a woman with common interests; now it is a ravishing of Innogen's ears that threatens to lead to a ravishing of her body. Once Giacomo is characterized as the unwelcome speaker, he slips easily into the role of pursuer, trying desperately to convince Innogen that she should sleep with him so as to be revenged on Posthumous for his alleged infidelity.

Although Innogen's responsiveness has left her vulnerable to Giacomo's efforts to penetrate her ears, he is unable to proceed further to corrupt her heart and her body because Innogen marshals her aural defenses.

Although she continues to listen to Giacomo, she becomes more guarded, as is evident in the way she deploys the metaphor of hearing in her tentative response: "If this be true—/ As I have such a heart that both mine ears / Must not in haste abuse—if it be true, / How should I be revenged?" (130–32). Innogen signals growing uncertainty through the repeated conditional, "if this be true." Innogen's ears have, in one sense, failed to work as her defenders. But, as her conceit of hearing illustrates, a final step in the process of hearing has yet to be completed, and Innogen locates her resistance in this space. Though her ears "have / So long attended" (142–43) Giacomo, she is still capable of halting the abuse that her heart may suffer should it begin to believe Giacomo's claims. Giacomo's words have penetrated her ears, but because they must still complete their process of inception, they can still be prevented from taking root. Innogen pleads to herself to stop this inception by slowing down the process of hearing—"both mine ears must not *in haste* abuse." Innogen can "condemn [her] ears" (142) for being too open to Giacomo's speeches and still engage her fuller aural faculties in defending both her heart and body from abuse.

Innogen's aural defense skills only improve as the play proceeds. In the next act, she repels even more efficiently the seductions of Cloten, whose attack comes by way of a serenade. Arriving at her bedchamber with musicians, Cloten divulges his plan to entice Innogen: "I am advised to give her music o' mornings; they say it will penetrate" (2.3.10–11). Cloten may be most interested in penetrating Innogen's sexual organs—as is evident in his bawdy comment to his musicians, "If you can penetrate her with your fingering, so; we'll try with tongue too" (2.3.12–13). But it is Innogen's aural organs that present the most immediate challenge. Cloten recognizes as much when he speculates about the success of his serenade: "If this penetrate I will consider your music the better; if it do not, it is a vice in her ears which horse hairs and calves' guts nor the voice of unpaved eunuch to boot can never amend" (2.3.24–27). Echoing the sentiments of frustrated preachers, Cloten admits that neither the best of musical instruments nor the most potent of voices (here, the voice of the eunuch) stand a chance if the listener is unreceptive.[93] Innogen's strategies of aural defensiveness, as Cloten perceives them, correspond closely with the strategies advocated by preachers. The similarities become particularly clear when we note how Cloten's explanation of the failure of his serenade—"it is a vice in her ears"—reads in the play's folio version. In the folio the word "vice" reads "voyce," so that the explanation for Innogen's resistance is: "there is a *voyce* in her ears." The folio phrase is not as unintelligible as editors of the play have thought. According to the logic of the folio line, the reason Cloten cannot get through to Innogen is that her mind and her ears are otherwise occupied; they attend to another voice and are thus too distracted to be affected. Protestant sermons on hearing help make sense of this reading. Describing how churchgoers must learn to tune out the voices of evil that sometimes speak simultaneously with the voices of good, preacher Wilkinson advises the very tactics that Innogen practices: "*[H]eare* not what the world saith, not what the flesh saith, not what the divell saith, but what the spirit saith, thus if both speak at once we should listen to the spirit, and turn the deafe side to the divell."[94] Wilkinson suggests that it is possible to maintain an open channel of communication with the voice of the spirit even while engaging one's aural defenses against the devil. Innogen seems to practice this simultaneous receptivity and defense, for despite being a captive audience to the serenade, she remains unmoved by it. Cloten indirectly recalls the fortress imagery often associated with this kind of defensive hearing when he reluctantly reports to Cymbeline that he has "*assailed* her [Innogen] with musics, but she vouchsafes no notice" (2.3.35–36; emphasis mine).

Female aural defensiveness is not without its disadvantages, however. In the process of maintaining chaste ears, the female characters of the late plays, like the "bad hearers" of sermons, are barred from opportunities to develop skills of judgment and to achieve the salvation that follows full reception and understanding of the Word. Expected to call up their aural defenses immediately when they sense danger, chaste female characters rarely have a chance to make productive mistakes. For instance, because Innogen raises her aural defenses to block Giacomo's seduction, she loses the opportunity to grasp completely the degree of danger he poses. As a consequence of failing to understand fully his motives, she does not question his request to leave a trunk in her bedroom and remains vulnerable to violation that very evening, when Giacomo infiltrates her bedroom by hiding in the trunk. Innogen's constructive defensiveness thus risks becoming disruptive to her personal and political welfare.

Shakespeare's male characters, by contrast, are shown to be capable not only of experiencing but recovering from aural assaults. Unlike Innogen, who avoids immediate danger by halting Giacomo's words before they affect her heart, Posthumous falls prey to Giacomo's devilish mistruths and, as a result, loses faith—in Innogen, in their marriage vows, and in women more generally. Posthumous's too easy acceptance of Giacomo's false stories are a result of the overly receptive hearing that Innogen is conditioned to halt. As Pisanio observes of Posthumous, "O master, what a strange infection / Is fall'n into thy ear! What false Italian, / As poisonous tongued as handed, hath prevailed / On thy *too ready* hearing?" (3.2.3–6; emphasis mine). Giacomo's words tumble easily into Posthumous's ears, and because Posthumous does not engage his aural defenses when evil approaches, he is readily "prevailed" upon. Posthumous's fallen ears do not condemn him for the entirety of the play, however—he, like Cymbeline, is ultimately saved. As in the case of Pericles, this redemption is marked by a communiqué with supernatural forces; Posthumous has a prophetic dream wherein his parents and brothers return from the dead to beg Jupiter's assistance. He awakes from his dream renewed and knowledgeable about the future, having been realigned with a lineage: "Sleep, thou hast been a grandshire, and begot / A father to me" (5.5.217–18).

Protestant preachers might say that it is because the men of the late plays are allowed to falter that they may later be redeemed, able to bear the fruit of salvation. Taylor explains that aural receptivity, whatever its costs in the short run, ultimately works to the benefit of the Christian: "God hath appointed hearing for the engendring of Faith: For as by hearing the divels voyce, we lost our faith and happinesse: so the Lord hath appointed by hearing his voyce againe, as the most convenient meanes, to recoverour [sic] faith and salvation."[95] Although keeping the ears open increases the risk that evil may intrude and wreak havoc, such openness ensures that God can enter as well and battle the devil's influence. Thus, not despite, but *because* Posthumous fails to defend his ears from being pillaged by evil, he now is positioned to attain redemption and undergo rebirth. The same can be said of *Pericles*' men of Miteline, who initially are led easily by the ears. When Boult orally advertises the brothel's newest beautiful virgin, the men of Miteline open their ears and hearts widely. "I have drawn her picture with my voice" (4.2.87), Boult reports, and the young auditors "listened to me as they would have hearkened to their father's testament" (90–91). It is because they have succumbed to aural temptation that the men of Miteline come to the brothel and receive, to their surprise, spiritual rejuvenation. In *Cymbeline* and *Pericles*, male characters grow stronger because they have encountered and conquered weakness, whereas female characters are assumed to be unable to recover from "too ready hearing." Innogen may initially seem capable of filtering out harmful sounds, but when danger becomes too acute, it is necessary that she, like Marina, shut her ears completely to shield herself from violation. Because the line between depravity and rectitude is, for female characters as for early modern women, clearly drawn, they are prevented from reaping the full rewards that ensue from "hearing for profit." Nevertheless, as the plays construct a climate of fear around female hearing, they represent female acoustic subjectivity as emerging less from the conditions of aural subjugation than from the practice of aural insubordination.

Deafened/Defended Auditors

As I have mentioned, in the cases of Innogen and Marina, aural defensiveness is constructive not only of personal but social order, the maintenance of chaste ears constituting a victory not only for particular female characters but for the larger patriarchal system that depends on their continued chastity. In this respect the plays delimit the transgressive potential of aural defensiveness: Innogen and Marina may successfully block their ears to challenge figures who have power over them, but their aural defensiveness is recuperative of patriarchal social norms. Indeed, the figures whose authority they balk—the bawd, Giacomo, and Cloten—are derogated by the plays for interfering in the construction of ideal families and kingdoms. *Cymbeline* and *Pericles* thus propose a careful distinction between the aural defensiveness performed by chaste female characters—which serves the patriarchal social order—and the disruptive deafness exhibited by male characters. To what extent, we are left to wonder, is female aural defensiveness a truly disruptive practice? We can begin to address that question by examining Judith Butler's work on hate speech. In *Excitable Speech*, Butler gestures toward the potential agency of defensive hearing when she argues that even the most powerful and potentially most harmful speech acts cannot be guaranteed to hit their mark—to produce the kind of injury in the hearer that they intend. Butler explains this failure of vocal abuse as a consequence of the temporal framework through which language gains performative power. The potency of an insult, Butler argues, is not arbitrary and is not established in the single instance of its use: a bigoted name-call, for instance, has efficacy because it has been repeated again and again as an abusive utterance, thereby accumulating harmful meaning. This view of linguistic agency as temporally mediated enables Butler to "question . . . the presumption that hate speech always works," thereby "loosening . . . the link between act and injury."[96] As a consequence, Butler is able to theorize ways in which a victim of hate speech, instead of being paralyzed by a verbal attack, may disrupt the potency of the threat and speak back to the attacker: "failure is the condition of a critical response."[97] For Butler, the subject produced through this exercise of language is neither "a sovereign agent with a purely instrumental relation to language, nor a mere effect whose agency is pure complicity with prior operations of power."[98] In other words, subjectivity is not a prerequisite for "talking-back" but is produced in concert with or even as a consequence of the act itself.

While Butler locates agency and the emergence of subjectivity in this moment of "unexpected and enabling response,"[99] she does not explicitly address the agentive capacities of hearing, which is understandable given that her focus in *Excitable Speech* is the transformative potential of verbal language. Nevertheless, her work implies that an act of aural defense theoretically precedes the speaker's counteroffensive response: it is only because the hearer is *not* fully victimized by harmful words that she is capable of "counter-speech."[100] Butler assumes a defense against injurious words but leaves unexplained and overlooked the practical applications of this idea. The agency of audition is, in Butler, an implied step in a symbolic process of linguistic transformation, not a social act informed by material conditions.

What in Butler is only theoretical potential becomes in early modern moral, religious, and theatrical discourses on hearing a material act, what Pierre Bourdieu would call a "practice." Indeed, as Bourdieu provides a material analog to Butler's primarily linguistic conception of agentive response, his ideas can help elucidate how the practice of hearing represented in Shakespeare's late plays constitutes a robust model of agency that is productive for female subjectivity.[101] Bourdieu offers the concept of *habitus* to describe the dialectic wherein cultural forces are inscribed on the body at the same time as individuals actively shape the way they live through inscribed norms. Central to Bourdieu's theory of agency as emerging from constraints or disciplinary norms is the concept of *le sens pratique*, often translated as a "feel for the game." In effect, the game's rules—for instance, the norms of gender identity—become internalized to such a degree that they feel "natural" to those who inhabit them. Bourdieu does not see these norms as steadily inculcated in the way Foucault does. Rather, he suggests that bodily "dispositions" are reified and internalized through the *practice* of them. To extend the analogy, one gains a feel for the game through playing it.[102] Bourdieu, more successfully than Foucault, theorizes a balance between the forces of cultural inscription and the work of agents. For Bourdieu, it is the actions of the players, who jostle for preeminence and power, that give the game, or what he calls the "field," form. Ideology is less, per Foucault, an overarching system propagated by institutions than it is a cultural production that human agents help create. Even without consciousness of the effects of their actions, these agents help determine what the "field" will look like at any given moment. Thus while gender dispositions, among many other social norms, are encoded on bodies, their inscription is mediated *by* bodies that practice inscriptive codes in sometimes surprising, unpredictable (though not unlimited or arbitrary) ways.[103] Bourdieu's ideas can help explain how the practice of hearing enables bodies—particularly, in Shakespeare, *female* bodies—to negotiate the pressures of patriarchal institutions and misogynist discourses. Hearing bodies, I would suggest, can practice inscriptive codes in surprising ways, sometimes transforming constructive aural defense into *disruptive* deafness.

One key reason this slippage is possible is that plays and other texts concerning the ethics of hearing struggle to differentiate constructive defensiveness and disruptive deafness. Even as authors work to discriminate the two states, their efforts often break down, consequently destabilizing not only the distinction between auditory practices but also the gender hierarchies this distinction supports. We have already seen evidence of the slippage between disruptive deafness and constructive defensiveness in *Pericles*, where its significance risks being overlooked in the editorial conflict concerning "deafened" versus "defended." Perhaps modern editors of the play discount the latter word choice because it would lend an uncomfortable positive valence to Pericles' aural closure: if "defended" is allowed to stand, Pericles' inability to hear others may be read as an act of self-protection and, thus, constructive of Pericles' identity. Malone's substitution of "deafen'd" for "defended" may clarify the play's ethical stance concerning Pericles' need for transformation but at the cost of recognizing the play's more complex engagement with early modern cultural discourses of hearing. To ask whether Pericles is deafened or defended is to assume that these states can be distinguished clearly. I am not trying to suggest that Pericles' cure is unnecessary but rather urging analysis of the ways *Pericles* and the other late plays blur the boundaries between deafness and defensiveness.

The plays are in good historical company. Early modern religious and moral meditations on the role of hearing encourage the slippage between disruptive deafness and constructive defensiveness when they employ the same metaphors to define both states. In sermons on the parable of the sower and the seed, for instance, metaphors of fertilization and reproduction are used to illustrate the processes of aural salvation *and* damnation. Just as God's words are represented as generative seeds, so the devil's words are "wicked seeds, which having found a fit and friendly soyle, come up so fast."[104] As God's seeds can produce the fruit of good deeds when they are planted in a receptive heart, so evil seeds sown in a receptive soil will produce weeds that propagate quickly and kill off desired plants. In another example the phrase from scripture "to have ears but hear not," so frequently used by preachers to describe the sinful deafness of those who refuse God's message, is also used to describe the practice of defending oneself against the devil. Richard Young's treatise *The Victory of Patience* (1636) urges readers, "though they be railed on and reviled by their enemies, yet *have eares, and heare not.*"[105] Prynne, who argues so vehemently for aural closure, also rebukes readers for stopped ears and hard hearts—at least when such aural obstructions interfere with *his* message: "But if you will yet stop your eares, and harden your hearts against all advice proceeding on stil in this your ungodly trade of life, *in which you cannot but be wicked*, then know you are such as are marked out for Hell."[106] Brathwaite, whose *Five Senses* (1610) urges the wise man to use his "edifying Sence" to tune out injurious sounds, prays in *The Penitent Pilgrim* (1641) that God will help him avoid shutting his ears at the wrong time: "O let mee bee no such *Hearer* as is the *deafe Adder*, which *stoppeth* her *eares*, charme the Charmer never so wisely."[107]

The metaphor of the deaf adder exemplifies the kind of slippage of meaning characteristic of moral and religious writings on hearing, for the adder symbolizes *both* constructive and destructive aural closure. Working from the biblical association of the devil with a serpent (in biblical and early modern parlance, an "adder"), early modern writers frequently relate the serpent's natural tendency toward self-protection to the devil's and the sinner's hardhearted resistance to the Word. A religious meditation by I. B. entitled *The Psalme of Mercy* (1625) explains the analogy:

The Adder or Cockatrice, is (as some say) naturally, (as some others) cunningly deafe, laying the one eare close to [the] ground, & stopping the other with his tayle, purposely to prevent the skill of the Charmer, who seekes to enchant him in such sort, as he shall not be able, either to bite, or sting.

So man, in his pure, or rather impure naturals, is either sencelesly deafe, and can-

not, or voluntarily deafe, and will not heare any voice, that tends to the spirituall sol-
ace of his soule.[108]

In Robert Greene's *The Repentence* (1592), the speaker draws on this biblical
metaphor as he laments, "I have long with the deafe Adder stopt mine eares
against the voice of Gods Ministers, yea my heart was hardened with Pharao
against all the motions that the spirit of God did at any time worke in my
mind."[109] The deaf adder becomes a symbol for not only spiritual but also
civil disruption. Greene's *The Second Part of Conny-Catching* (1591) reviles
its subjects of study, who "with the deafe Adder . . . stop their eares against
the voice of the charmer," proceeding to blaspheme and cozen without remorse.[110] And John Donne, in a sermon before King James at Whitehall,
preaches, "if we will not hear . . . we might be no subjects. *By the Law*, he
that was willing to continue in the service of his Master, was willing to bee
boared in the eare, willing to testify a readinesse of hearing and obedience. . . . *David* describes the refractary man so, *He is like the deafe Adder*,
that stoppeth her eare."[111] He who is deaf to the voices of authority, be they
heavenly or earthly, is as spiritually bereft as the serpent.

Yet even the deaf adder, the embodiment of Satan himself, is not stable
as a symbol for disruptive deafness. Sometimes, as John Downe explains in
Certain Treatises (1633), we need to imitate evil in order to combat it: "[T]he
Serpent, as wee have shewed, stops his eares because hee will not heare the
enchanters charme. So should wee also turne the deafe eare unto the crafty
insinuations of false & treacherous *Sinons*."[112] Thus, the deaf serpent is a
model of wisdom for the chaste maid depicted in Hadrian Dorrell's *Willobie
His Avisa. Or the True Picture of a Modest Maid* (1594). Fending off the "al-
luring intisements" of her suitor, the modest Avisa declares,

Well now I see, why Christ commends,
To loving mates the Serpents wit,
That stops his eares, and so defends
His hart, from luring sounds unfit,
If you your madnes still bewraye,
I'le stop my eares, or goe my way.[113]

For Downe, as for Dorrell, the adder's obstruction of sound displays the animal's "instinct" for self-preservation, something, writes Downe, that God
has instilled in all his creations—from the hound and partridge to the substance of fire. Similarly, God has "instilled into a man love towards his owne

selfe" and thus a desire to protect the self from harm. Downe recalls indirectly the imagery of the ear as fortress, declaring, "*Feare* is as it were the sentinell of the heart."[114]

Downe admits that there are perils to aural closure. His sermon, which elucidates Christ's message "Be yee therefore wise as Serpents and innocent as Doves" (Matt. 10:16), emphasizes that such a practice must be limited: "*I doe indeed advise you for avoiding of danger and securing of your selves to bee as wise and wari[e] as serpents: but least yee should mistake mee, knowe that I permit not unto you an unlimited wisdome to compasse your designes by what meanes soever. No, I would have you so to be serpents as yee cease not to be Doves, so to be wise as yee remaine also innocent.*"[115] In other words although it is important to shut one's ears, it is equally important not to allow constructive defensiveness to slide into sinful deafness. Plutarch's essay "Of Hearing," translated in 1603 by Philemon Holland, issues a similar warning. The essay insists that young men's ears be "defended against corrupt and leawd speeches," but it stresses that this does not mean one should "deprive them altogether of hearing, and to commend deafenesse."[116] Shakespeare uses the image of the adder itself when he plays with the slide between defensiveness and deafness to achieve dramatic irony. When in *2 Henry VI* King Henry, having just learned of Gloucester's assassination, turns in grief and anger away from Queen Margaret, she rebukes him for ignoring her speech, asking whether he has, "like the adder, waxen deaf" (3.2.76). What she presents and maligns as his improper, unhusbandly deafness is, as the audience knows, warranted *defensiveness*, given that her performance of grief is, indeed, of some danger to him.

Given the imprecision of the line between defensiveness and deafness, it is no wonder that Downe devotes almost an entire sermon to the subject of how to differentiate between the two. Yet Downe himself is unable to keep these states clearly distinguished. Even his terms for that ideal state of balance between deafness and defensiveness are nothing but a restatement of the paradox: "*Bee you Serpent-like Doves and Dove-like Serpents, wisely innocent, and innocently-wise.*"[117] He admits that what his auditors need is some "direction" in how to achieve this balance, but admits that "*Hic labor, hoc opus est,* this indeede is the point of difficulty."[118] In answering the question "how then can wee be both wise and innocent at once?" he returns to the language of paradox: "[A] man cannot be truly *innocent* except hee be *wise* . . . [and] neither can a man bee *wise* without *innocence.*"[119]

The paradoxes and puzzlements of Downe's sermon may well be, as

Bryan Crockett argues about Protestant sermons more generally, the preacher's rhetorical technique intended to create a productive spiritual quagmire for auditors.[120] But the effect of this rhetoric is to represent aural defense as a necessary but dangerously imprecise practice—one that may unwittingly lead auditors down the path to evil. When auditors are invested with this kind of agency, the sermon suggests, one cannot predict to what ends they will employ their power. Auditors may defend themselves so vehemently that they fall into sinfulness, becoming the serpent that they have tried only to mimic. Carried to its logical ends, Downe's sermon thus raises concern that the practice of proper aural defense may imbue listeners with the capacity for aural disobedience.

Such concerns are similarly echoed by the male authorities of Shakespeare's late plays. On the one hand, female aural defensiveness helps maintain the patriarchal systems depicted in the plays: stopped ears and a closed body keep the eloquent daughter eligible to be married off to the mate who will deliver beneficial alliances to royal fathers. On the other hand, cultivating defensive hearing in women is risky. If female auditors are expected to practice aural defense, then isn't it possible that they will engage these skills when they *should* be listening? If women need to be kept from understanding in order to remain chaste, then how can their understanding be guaranteed when it is necessary? The spectrum of levels of bad hearing I have discussed—from inattention and distraction to misunderstanding and obstinacy—has the potential to collapse: daughters trained not to hear have the propensity to become subjects who refuse to listen.

This slide from productive defensiveness to disruptive deafness is particularly evident in the case of Innogen. The female character of the late plays who is submitted to the harshest test of audition is also the character who most significantly pushes the boundaries of patriarchal control. Indeed, the play opens with a report of Innogen's insubordination—her secret marriage to Posthumous that contravenes her father's expressed wishes—and goes on to dramatize her subsequent disregard for authority: her continued correspondence with Posthumous and her final decision to flee her father's court. Advocating female aural defensiveness exacts a cost for male authorities, like Cymbeline, whose political and social positions necessitate they be *listened to* by subordinates. It is no wonder that Cymbeline becomes enraged when he discovers that Innogen and his wife have conspired against his wishes to facilitate one last rendezvous for Posthumous and Innogen— "They were again together; you have done / Not after our command"

(1.1.152–53). Cymbeline's fury reaches greater heights, though, when Innogen's disobedience is figured in sensory terms. When Cymbeline scolds Innogen for disobeying his orders, she responds, "I beseech you, sir, / Harm not yourself with your vexation. / I am *senseless* of your wrath. A touch more rare / Subdues all pangs, all fears" (1.1.134–37; emphasis mine). The only person Cymbeline affects with his heated words is himself, Innogen insists, for her attentions are placed elsewhere; her mind is touched by far more pressing thoughts (of Posthumous), leaving her with no sensory energy to receive her father's message. She is literally sense-less when confronted with his words of rage. As we have seen, later in the play this practice of sensory disruption will be framed more explicitly as aural when Innogen defends herself against Cloten's serenade by listening to a different "voyce in her ears." Yet even that socially legitimated act of aural defense carries overtones of disobedience, manifested when editors render Innogen's listening to another "voice" as a disruptive "vice."

The male authority of the late plays who is most troubled by the slippage between constructive defensiveness and the vice of deafness is Prospero, not coincidentally the patriarch most invested in aural domination. Prospero assumes that he can command his daughter's obedience as an auditory subject, that her ears—and her heart—can be counted on to be receptive. When he is ready to tell his story in 1.2, he instructs Miranda, "The very minute bids thee ope thine ear, / Obey, and be attentive" (*The Tempest* 1.2.37–38). Yet despite being the sole authority figure in Miranda's life and despite having a story that "would cure deafness" (1.2.106), Prospero struggles—or at least believes he struggles—to keep the attention of his daughter. Throughout his narrative, he expresses concern that Miranda tunes him out: "I pray thee mark me" (1.2.67); "Dost thou attend me?" (78); "Thou attend'st not!" (87); "I pray thee mark me" (88); "Dost thou hear?" (106); "Hear a little further" (135). Whether Miranda actually loses interest or Prospero merely fears that she does, Prospero's questions evince an anxiety that his dovelike daughter has become the recalcitrant serpent.

Prospero has good reason to be concerned, since he is responsible for instilling in Miranda this adder-like instinct for aural closure. In an effort to maintain Miranda's chaste ears and body—the female difference that will enable his political restoration—Prospero has conditioned his daughter to practice constructive aural defensiveness. Prospero seems to have accomplished this aim by frequently tempting Miranda's ears with stories of her history and then denying her the answers she craves; recalls Miranda, "You

have often / Begun to tell me what I am, but stopped / And left me to a boot-
less inquisition, / Concluding 'Stay; not yet'" (1.2.33–36). That Prospero has
been successful in training the curiosity out of Miranda is clear by her ad-
mission, "More to know / Did never meddle with my thoughts" (1.2.22–23).
But Prospero's interest in keeping Miranda blissfully ignorant and unmoti-
vated to overcome ignorance creates a challenge for him when he decides to
educate her. Rather than teaching Miranda how to "hear for profit"—how
to filter out harmful voices and engage her aural defenses when necessary—
Prospero has effectively trained his daughter to close her ears as soon as she
encounters the unfamiliar. It is no wonder that when in 1.2 Prospero finally
chooses to inform Miranda of her history, he cannot trust her capacity to
listen, to understand, and as a consequence, to obey. Because of his own
anxieties of familial and self-preservation—the need for a chaste heir and,
thus, chaste ears—he has taught his daughter to imitate the serpent without
helping her understand the balance of the dove.

Critics and directors of the play, unattuned to the ways audition can be
a source of agency for Miranda, have largely overlooked the degree to which
the early moments of 1.2 present Miranda as resistant to her father's manip-
ulations. David Sundelson's observation is paradigmatic: "Throughout
[Prospero's] long narration, Miranda is the ideal listener; she has no critical
faculty of her own, and her responses are invariably just what her father
wants."[121] Those critics who argue for a more defiant Miranda character locate the foundation of that defiance in Miranda's desire for Ferdinand,
which emerges only at the end of the scene. David Lindley's argument for "a
rather more assertive Miranda" concludes that "it is her love for Ferdinand
which most obviously provokes her to thoughts of self-assertive opposition
to her father."[122] But well before Miranda meets Ferdinand, she is presented
as a threat to Prospero's authority. Indeed, as Stephen Orgel points out, the
early exchange between Prospero and Miranda has the potential to disturb
idealized readings of Prospero as the benevolent patriarch who is beloved by
his passive, innocent daughter—so much so that sections of the scene have
often been removed from productions.[123] For those critics and directors interested in representing Miranda's deeper resistance to her father's will, the
first part of 1.2 has proved crucial. Heather James, for instance, uses the
scene to argue for the subversive potential of Miranda's piteous response to
Prospero, which, like other sympathies inspired by tragedy, cannot always be
governed or channeled in predictable ways. Miranda's potential for subversion is actualized in some theatrical productions, like George Wolfe's 1995

The Tempest, which represents Miranda as a rebellious teenager, in this scene bored by her father's stories of the past.[124]

One need not go as far as Wolfe to recognize the agentive nature of Miranda's auditory acts. As Bourdieu maintains, agentive practices need not be voluntary or even reflexive; resistance to subjection can work at the same unconscious or semiconscious level as forces of subjection. As I have argued, the play sets up Miranda's aural resistance as a response to Prospero's own oppressive methods of inscription. Prospero has carefully controlled his daughter's receptiveness so that when he is ready, he, and no one else, will be able to inscribe cultural codes upon her. Yet by teaching Miranda the virtues of aural defensiveness, Prospero unwittingly orchestrates her resistance to aural subjugation and her emergence as an acoustic subject. This is not to suggest that Miranda escapes being inscribed by Prospero entirely. Miranda's disobedience, like Innogen's, ultimately is channeled to suit her father's political goals. But Prospero's power over Miranda, even before she meets Ferdinand, is more unstable than critics have often assumed. Perhaps that instability explains Prospero's elaborate efforts to assert control over Miranda's union with Ferdinand, a match that appears ready to flourish with or without his intervention. It is not enough for Prospero to have his will fulfilled; he must have an active hand in the process. That Miranda enacts her father's plan in the end is not the point; the point is that Prospero has to go to extreme lengths to secure the obedience of his daughter, who, to his great fear and by his own fault, has stopped listening to him.

From Auditor to Audience

Thus far, my examination of acoustic subjectivity in the theater and the role aural defense performs in its production has been limited to analysis of play-scripts: I have examined how characters, especially in Shakespeare's late plays, represent the material practice of hearing. As I have argued throughout this book, however, the thematization of communicative agency in early modern plays meditates on—and may even have been inspired by—the theatrical conditions in which these plays were staged. In Chapters 1 and 2, we surveyed the particular impact of pubescent boy actors on the plays' representations of vocal production and transmission. Extending these insights, let us now consider how historical conditions of theatrical reception intersected with representations of hearing on the stage. To what extent could the resistant audition enacted by Innogen, Marina, and Miranda offer insight into the ways plays shaped and reflected the acoustic subjectivity of audiences in the theaters in which these plays were originally staged? Exploring these connections, I will suggest, helps broaden our understanding of the sort of role women were imagined to play in England's professional theater.

Representations of the act of hearing provide us with a different view of audience practices than has heretofore been recognized by studies of early modern theatrical reception, which have traditionally perceived ideal audiences as overwhelmingly receptive to the effects of plays.[125] Studies of early modern audiences have generally based their conclusions on representations of playgoers in diaries, antitheatrical and protheatrical tracts, and prologues or plays-within-a-play, as well as on the characterization of audience members advanced in the discourse of rhetoric. These sources often distinguish ideal audiences from those disruptive audiences who are removed, rude, or critical of a performance. In the theater, the latter troublesome group includes gentlemen and law clerks who attended plays so that they might strut the latest fashions, smoke their tobacco pipes, and demonstrate their wit at the players' expense. Ben Jonson's *Every Man Out of his Humour* describes, for instance, a gallant who "Sits with his armes thus wreath'd, his hat pull'd here, / Cryes meaw, and nods, then shakes his empty head."[126] This is the kind of audience we find at the end of *Midsummer Night's Dream*. While Theseus and his companions watch the mechanicals perform, their primary source of entertainment is trading witty quips about the actors' lack of talent. At the other end of the socioeconomic scale of disruptive audiences are apprentices and servingmen, the young men of the city, described by one author as "lewd mates" who often come to the theater drunk and seeking an excuse to fight. Henry Chettle's *Kind-Harts Dreame* (1592) describes these as "men beside all honestie, willing to make boote of cloakes, hats, purses, or what ever they can lay holde on in a hurley burley."[127] Like the empty-headed gallants, these playgoers are frequently the source of playwright's complaints as well as of the wrath of antitheatricalists, who portray the theater as a haven for vice and civic disruption.

Set in contrast to these irritating playgoers are those audience members who are thoroughly engaged in the performance—so engaged that they lose themselves to the fiction. This is the sort of audience evoked in early modern rhetoric books, which theorize successful oratorical performances as a stacked battle: good rhetors mesmerize their listeners with captivating speeches. Surveying the combative metaphors (of seizure, ravishment, and capture, for instance) that appear frequently in early modern writings about rhetoric, Wayne Rebhorn concludes that early modern "rhetoricians consistently imagine [the orator's] words as an invasion force, a kind of imperial, colonizing army which, entering people through their eyes and ears, plants its flag of conquest on the terrain of their souls."[128] Effective theater was often described as capable of such conquest. Thomas Heywood's *An Apology for Actors* (1612) famously cites several female playgoers who were driven to confess the murder of their husbands after seeing similar plots enacted in plays.[129] Whereas Heywood describes such incidents in order to prove drama's moral purpose, antitheatricalists invoke the topos of auditor conquest to demonstrate the dangers of theater. When an audience is that susceptible, antitheatricalists insist, plays do not inculcate morality but jeopardize it. Prynne writes, "there can be found no stronger engine to batter the honesty as well of wedded Wives, as the chastity of unmarried Maides and Widdowes, then are the hearing of common Playes." He challenges his reader to find a single instance of a woman whose lust is not "inflamed even unto fury" by these "spectacles of strange lust."[130] Whether held up as evidence of theater's threatening power or of its salvational capacities, these sources echo rhetoric books in representing audiences as vulnerable, passive consumers—their eyes, ears, and wills easily seized by powerful theater.[131]

As Dympna Callaghan points out, the period's association of this engaged audience type with women has been read by some critics as indicative of the power female theater consumers might have held. Although the public theater industry excluded women from roles of production, it welcomed, indeed depended, on the ostensibly weaker sex for its hypervulnerability to plays. However enticing such a proposition of female receptive agency might be, it has significant drawbacks. As Callaghan importantly explains, such arguments are predicated on a problematic fantasy about female vulnerability, wherein women are ideal audiences because they so readily surrender their wills to the mimetic power of the stage. It is not surprising that such a fantasy would emerge from those who had much at stake in proving that theater was effective, whether valuable for its pedagogical possibilities or dangerous as a sinful pastime. Both views are predicated on assumptions about theater's ability to seize the will of audiences.

Given that "receptiveness is a heavily freighted ideological construct," it is difficult to argue that representations of women's vulnerability to theater are indicative of women's power as theater consumers.[132] Callaghan's intervention presents a challenge for feminist work on audience. If we want to recognize audiences as agents in the process of theatrical production and, concurrently, map out a significant role for women in a public theater industry from which they were otherwise excluded, we must buy into early modern fantasies about women's vulnerability. In effect, the theatrical ideal (of receptive playgoers) seems incommensurate with a political ideal (agentive female audiences).

But to what extent can we assume that receptive, engaged playgoers were, for early moderns, the sole theatrical ideal? To be sure, this view of audiences as succumbing easily to the powerful sway of good orators is presented in many early modern texts that treat audience response. But modern critics, eager to read plays, as well as sermons, through the terms set up by early modern rhetoric books, have been too quick to adopt rhetoricians' narrow definition of an ideal audience. For example, in *Shakespeare's Art of Orchestration*, Jean Howard writes, "I argue that in the largest sense drama is one of the rhetorical arts. . . . And, as with all types of rhetoric, an underlying premise is that audiences are not static entities, but are shaped by the skill of the artist and made malleable to his control."[133] Crockett's more recent study of the relations between stage-plays and sermons goes further, arguing that plays and sermons, like oratory, seduce and mesmerize audiences, creating a "cult of the ear." Both the sermon and the play, Crockett argues, "achieve their effect in part by evoking a sense of wonder" in the audience; and Shakespeare in particular capitalizes on the theater's "linguistic potential for spellbinding the audience."[134]

Although the rapt and malleable audiences that Crockett and others describe were undoubtedly one ideal in the early modern period, they were not the only ideal. When we examine the way plays represent the phenomenological aspects of theatergoing—hearing being one such crucial part of the theatergoing experience[135]—then an alternate view of ideal playgoing emerges. According to the plays and sermons I have discussed, ideal auditors are not necessarily expected to surrender their wills to the sounds they encounter; rather, they are encouraged to judge carefully what they hear and close their ears when they believe defensiveness is warranted. In the late plays, we've seen aural defensiveness is constructive not only of an individual auditor's subjectivity but of smoothly functioning social and political systems. Insofar as these plays, like so many early modern dramas, gesture through their fictions to the material world of the theater, the plays suggest that such auditory practices can be similarly efficacious to the production of acoustic subjectivity in the theater and to the smooth functioning of a theatrical system. At least one director has recognized the ways in which the late plays extend their lessons on audition beyond the stage and to their audience. In Giorgio Barberio Corsetti's *La Tempesta* (performed at Teatro Argentina in 2000), Miranda listens to Prospero's lecture from one of the seats in the theater auditorium.[136] Miranda's ears become the ears of the audience, and Prospero's repeated anxieties about being heard by his daughter are linked to the actor's (and perhaps the playwright's) concerns about the wandering interests of playgoers.[137]

Staging the inattention of audience members may seem counterproductive to the purposes of playing, which at the most basic material level must involve capturing the interest of consumers. Yet, as Prospero's own example illustrates, creators of theater risk losing an audience entirely when they take for granted its receptivity. Prospero assumes that the combination of his authoritative position and the engaging substance of his narrative will keep his audience attuned. Perhaps this is the reason that his character, while repeatedly expressing concern about losing his audience's attention, does little to cultivate it. Indeed, as Prospero explains his history to Miranda in 1.2, he largely ignores her needs as an auditor, often leaving her confused. For instance, told "twelve year since, . . . / Thy father was the Duke of Milan, and / A prince of power" (1.2.53–55), the confounded Miranda asks, "Sir, are not you my father?" (55). As Prospero proceeds with his story, he ceases allowing time for Miranda's questions. Rather than waiting to see how she responds and taking into account shifting circumstances of reception—the kinds of techniques deployed by good storytellers—Prospero pushes forward with his long narration, pausing only to request perfunctory assurances from Miranda that she is listening. Prospero's history lesson is an extended monologue that masquerades unconvincingly as a dialogue. That Miranda should doze off at the end indicates not necessarily that Prospero's magic has lulled Miranda into a slumber—the most common critical explanation for Miranda's exhaustion—but that she has become completely disengaged from Prospero's performance. Prospero loses his audience because he employs none of the strategies that Shakespeare's other narrators use to present the backstory of a play in a compelling manner.[138] Overconfident in his vocal power and in his daughter's aural submission, Prospero overlooks the degree to which the attentions of auditors need to be courted. Through the negative example of Prospero, *The Tempest* suggests that producers of theater cannot simply command audiences to listen, as Prospero commands Miranda "ope thine ear, / Obey, and be attentive" (1.2.37–38). They would do better to assume an auditor might not be willing to hear and then work for the audience's attention.[139]

Given that *The Tempest* dramatizes, through Miranda, a model of resistant hearing, it is particularly troublesome that the play is so often used by critics to argue for theater's spellbinding effects on its audiences. Scholars consistently describe *The Tempest*, as well as *Pericles, Cymbeline,* and *The Winter's Tale*, as "bewildering" and "awe-inspiring" "miracle plays," full of "wonder."[140] Audiences of the late plays are often compared to Prospero's island visitors—so captivated by the miracles staged before them that they are stunned into submission. The plays are assumed to control audience emotions and reactions with great precision, primarily through a process of engagement.[141] Indeed, some critics have argued that the true meaning of the late plays can only be gleaned by audiences who submit fully to the power of these plays, dropping their critical guard. Elizabeth Bieman tells her readers that one of her ideal audiences is her five-year-old daughter, who, after viewing *The Winter's Tale*, did not question Hermione's forgiving treatment of Leontes at the end of the play. Bieman writes that Shakespeare's late plays can be appreciated best when audiences resist "taking expectations of a commonsensical sort into the theater": "[I]f we meet [the plays] with a childlike acceptance, the Romances will make us all feel better."[142] Fawkner offers a more sophisticated rendering of what is ultimately a similar claim: he contends that "groundlessness" is the "ontological climate and spectatorial condition" of these plays, and thus dialectical processes (such as psychoanalytic investigation) are fruitless ways into the dramas. Because the "miraculous" prevails, we must, according to Fawkner, surrender our familiar modes of critical response and embrace the awe-inspiring late plays on their own terms.[143] Although a number of critics recognize the ways the plays promote the audience's detachment and invoke a distance between the stage and spectators—indeed, this has been a key point of debate in scholarship on *Pericles*[144]—such detachment is understood to be carefully directed by the playwright.[145]

When critics attribute so much power to the producers of theater, positing as ideal those audiences who give up their defenses and allow themselves to be "seized," these critics ignore a key model of audience activity that

Figure 4. Hercules Gallicus, the orator—his mouth chained to the ears of his listeners. Andrea Alciati, *Emblematum Liber* (Paris, 1536), 97. Photo courtesy of The Newberry Library, Chicago.

the plays themselves present. As we've seen, when the late plays dramatize the material practice of hearing, they suggest, like sermons, that an audience's aural resistance can be constructive of an ideal theatrical economy. When Miranda tunes out Prospero during his self-involved monologue, she silently but effectively critiques Prospero's disruption of this theatrical economy. Of course, neither the plays nor sermons conclude that aural defensiveness should go unchecked, as it approaches becoming in the case of Miranda. They advocate defense not as a means for the auditor to wrest total control away from the speaker but as a method of striking a balance between the powers of "creators" and the powers of "receivers."[146] The theater and church are represented, in effect, as contractual spaces whose vitality is ensured by cooperation between these agents. Such an ideal is an undercurrent

even in the speaker-centered rhetorical discourse of the period. In his discussion of the emblem of Hercules Gallicus—which (see figure 4) depicts
subjects chained by their ears to the tongue of the rhetor-ruler—Rebhorn
observes that although many writers and artists use the emblem to illustrate
the orator's/ruler's power to use rhetoric to enslave audiences/subjects, in
fact, the figure of the chain can be read "against the grain" of interpretation
forwarded by rhetoric book writers: whatever meaning rhetoricians may as-
sign it, visually, the chain becomes a "sign of linkage, of mutual attachment,"
underscoring the dependence of orators on their auditors (and the dependence of rulers on their subjects).[147]

We do not need only to read against the grain of early modern texts in
order to find models of this sort of mutuality. The plays I've examined
dramatize and enact the cooperation between audiences/receivers and ora-
tors/creators, suggesting that their successful interdependence is contingent
on both sides maintaining some leverage: for orators, that leverage is the capacity to seduce; for audiences, it is the capacity to resist seduction. Aural resistance, then, need not be read as hostile to, but rather as constitutive of,
theater's aims.

Most interestingly for feminist analysis of early modern audiences, the
ideal of constructive aural resistance is enacted in plays by female characters,
whose auditory practices intersected (directly and indirectly) with those of
female audience members in the theater. Insofar as the late plays dramatize
widespread cultural attitudes toward chastity and hearing, their ideas about
hearing must have been familiar to at least some of the women who attended performances of the plays, perhaps even providing such women with
models of agency that could be practiced, reflexively or not, outside as well
as within the theatrical space. Or perhaps the plays invoke a parallel between
female audiences and the boy actors who played female auditors on the
stage, both groups to some extent marginalized in early modern England.
Regardless, the stability of early modern gender hierarchies—hierarchies
that affected characters on the stage as well women in the theater—is at
stake in the late plays' representations of hearing. As we have seen, the plays
attempt to police gender hierarchies by positing a clear moral distinction
between disruptive and constructive aural defensiveness. Good men are defined by their willingness to abandon aural defenses, good women by their
ability to keep such defenses in place. Yet like some sermons and moral treatises, the plays also recognize the costs of encouraging women to practice
aural resistance. Constructive aural defensiveness can slide into disruptive

deafness, as women taught to keep their ears closed may, purposefully or not, fail to listen. The blurring of the line between constructive defense and destructive deafness has spiritual consequences in sermons; in plays the consequences are social and political: gender differences and the logic of gendered hierarchies break down when the boundaries between these auditory practices become indefinite. The plays dramatize how the cultural work of differentiating the sexes and policing female conduct produces conditions for female auditory agency—and for the emergence of a different kind of acoustic subject.

Chapter 4
Echoic Sound: Sandys's Englished Ovid and Feminist Criticism

> DELIO.   Hark, the dead stones seem to have pity on you
>   And give you good counsel.
> ANTONIO.   Echo, I will not talk with thee,
>   For thou art a dead thing.
> ECHO   Thou art a dead thing.
> —The Duchess of Malfi[1]

In this scene from John Webster's *The Duchess of Malfi*, Delio's advice that Antonio avoid visiting the Cardinal is reiterated by an eerie echo that Antonio admits is "very like my wife's voice" (5.3.26). Earlier in the play, the Duchess unexpectedly revives from (presumed) death by strangulation to call for "Antonio" and "mercy" (4.2.342, 345) in an echo of Desdemona's tell-all cry from her deathbed, "falsely, falsely murdered" (*Othello* 5.2.126). And yet even when the Duchess's death is final, her body buried, her sound seeps forth in act 5, reverberating the men's voices and warning Antonio that his life is in danger. The Duchess's echo offers us a most compelling example of the disembodied voice as a source of female agency. The headstrong Duchess, as it turns out, needs neither head nor body to continue to voice her concerns about the Cardinal's plot to destroy her family. Her body absent, her voice lingers on, offering wisdom and guidance for those she loved while she was alive. What is especially interesting about the Duchess's echoic voice is that it demonstrates how the *auditory* agency we examined in Chapter 3 can, with little effort on the part of the hearing subject, be converted into the kind of *vocal* agency we explored in Chapter 2. The echo in Webster's play does not simply halt sounds, preventing them from penetrating a listener's body; it throws sounds back to their producer, creating what appears to be an independent vocal act. The echo's capacity to "speak" is precipitated by its capacity to "hear," as hearing and speaking become two sides of the same disembodied vocal process, virtually indistinguishable from each another. Moreover, like the squeaky voice, breathed words, and fortressed ears (discussed in Chapters 1, 2, and 3, respectively), echoic sounds are defined by ambiguity and instability. Disjoining vocal sound from the speaking body and dispersing accountability for an utterance, echoes straddle the line between human voice and mere sound. Could this actually be the voice of the Duchess? the play asks. Or is this simply a sonic reverberation? Like other plays I've examined throughout this book, *The Duchess of Malfi* leaves that question unresolved and, in doing so, intimates that the Duchess, even in death, possesses startling vocal power.

The scene in Webster is interesting, moreover, for its dramatization of male reactions to the presence of a disembodied, ambiguous voice, a concern also explored in previous chapters. When the echo states hauntingly that Antonio will never see his wife again, Antonio and Delio are troubled. How can a sound reverberating off of a wall approximate so closely an intentional voice? To cope with the uncomfortable implications of this question, Delio and Antonio dismiss the phenomenon as nothing more than "fancy" (5.3.46). "I'll be out of this ague" (5.3.47), Antonio declares. Antonio and Delio's reactions to the echoic voice in this scene typify those of other early moderns, especially men, around the disembodied and uncontrollable voice. As the echo problematizes a binary between expressive *voice* and mere sound, it throws into question one of the central ways in which human beings in this period (and perhaps in our own) defined themselves against animals and objects. As we've seen, such distinctions were of particular importance to early modern men, whose claims to be able to control voice, their own and that of subordinates, iterated and perpetuated social and political hierarchies. Previous chapters have diagnosed how these anxieties emerge in relation to dramatic representations and other live performances of voice, which often underscore the unpredictability of communicative practices. This chapter follows a different, but parallel, trajectory by examining how one early modern poetic text deals with these anxieties. We shall consider how George Sandys—seventeenth-century poet, traveler, and mythographer—tackles the mythical figure of Echo in his 1632 translation of and commentary on Ovid's *Metamorphoses*.

My focus on Sandys calls for some explanation, given the emphasis of previous chapters on drama and texts connected to live performance. Unlike texts discussed so far, Sandys's *Ovid's Metamorphosis: Englished, Mythologized, and Represented in Figures* bears no relationship to live performance. It was not even the source-text for Shakespeare's dramatic forays into Ovidianism, for Shakespeare consulted Arthur Golding's translation of Ovid, not Sandys's. Yet Sandys's text is valuable to my study because it illustrates efficiently the ideological tensions existing at the intersection of voice, body, and gender. In Ovid's figure of Echo, Sandys confronts the kind of unpredictable and disembodied voice that early modern dramatists (not to mention acoustic scientists and Protestant preachers) confront in their respective crafts. And like these authors, Sandys must present that voice to audiences who are uncomfortable with the ways the disembodied voice destabilizes vocal authority and gender hierarchies. In wrestling with the figure of Echo and her disembodied vocal sound, Sandys's text engages with the same cultural forces and contradictions—science, philosophy, Christianity, classicism, and gender ideology—that put pressure on the representation of voice in plays and other texts concerned with live vocal performance. But the 1632 edition of Sandys's *Metamorphosis* is especially useful for investigating early modern concerns about the voice because, unlike many of these other texts, Sandys's text presents itself overtly as an ideological project that is invested in resolving conflicting cultural perspectives. In its efforts to choreograph the unruly female voice Ovid's Echo represents, Sandys's text makes explicit representational strategies that are at work more subtly in performance spaces like the theater.

Sandys frames his project as part of a long tradition of *Ovide moralisé*. Dealing seriously with Ovid's mythography at a time when Ovid's popularity was waning or controversial among devout Christians,[2] Sandys carefully argues his case for the applicability of Ovid's stories to early modern mores, claiming that the stories provide access to philosophical and moral truths despite having been narrated by a pagan writer. Sandys's preface foregrounds the instructional objective of his translation: "For the Poet not onely renders things as they are; but what are not, as if they were, or rather as they should bee."[3] This justification of the Poet's artistic license seems directed toward the poetic practices of both Ovid and Sandys. Just as Ovid's poetry can bend the truth of "things" in order to represent them "as they are," so Sandys's text is authorized to "render . . . things" as he, the poet, sees fit. Armed with the argument that poetry is always on some level a craft of translation, of representing reality, Sandys defends his manipulation of Ovid's original: he explains that he has made Ovid's stories fitting and useful for seventeenth-century readers "by polishing, altering, or restoring, the harsh, improper, or mistaken" (9). The 1632 edition illuminates especially well Sandys's ethical investments, for to ensure that Ovid's "sacred stories afford the clearest direction" (8) to "the ordinary Reader" (9), Sandys not only takes editorial license with Ovid's poem but also appends to his translation of each of Ovid's books an extensive commentary section in which he propounds the moral lessons of each tale. Sandys's translation and commentary thus work in collaboration to "English" Ovid's depiction of Echo—a figure who dramatizes what many early modern men fear most about the unruly (especially when female) voice. As Sandys chooses which elements of Ovid's story of "Narcissus and Echo" need "polishing, altering, or restoring," his text exposes the pressures inherent in male efforts to control the motion of the voice. For echoic sound, as it disrupts the unity of voice, body, and subjectivity, undermines such efforts and produces the conditions for uncanny female vocal agency. Sandys's handling of Ovid's Echo reveals much concerning not only early modern anxieties about the disembodied voice but the particular strategies by which a text negotiates and allays these concerns.

Synchronizing Voice and Body: Sandys's Translation of Ovid

Ovid's figure of Echo bears much in common with characters like Lavinia and Desdemona, not to mention the Duchess of Malfi. Like these characters, Echo continues to produce voice after having been stripped of her capacity for normative speech. As her name indicates, Echo's only mode of "speech" is the repetition of the sounds of others; a reverberation by definition, her vocal sound is produced seemingly without her volition and irrespective of her body (as becomes evident when her body disintegrates later in the myth, leaving behind her echoic voice). Though disembodied and disconnected from her person, Echo's voice is rendered as able to express the nymph's desires. When Echo repeats the ends of Narcissus's words, her resonating language implies meanings alternate to the ones intended by Narcissus; despite her supposed inability to speak of her own accord, she articulates an erotic interest in the youth. Ovid's wittiest use of this echoic trope occurs when the lost Narcissus mistakes Echo's sounds for the voices of the friends he has been trying to locate:

perstat et alternae deceptus imagine vocis
"huc coeamus" ait, nullique libentius umquam
responsura sono "coeamus" rettulit Echo (III.38587)

(He stands still, deceived by the answering voice, and "Let us come together here," he cries. Echo, never to answer other sound more gladly, cries, "Let us come together.")[4]

For Echo's resounding response, "coeamus," to Narcissus's call, "huc coeamus," Ovid plays with the Latin double meaning of *coetus*—"to meet" and "to have sexual intercourse." From the perspective of the reader, the lost Narcissus requests a meeting, and the smitten Echo agrees to a copulation. When Ovid has Echo repeat back "coeamus," capitalizing on its sexual connotations, he not only enables her to express interest in erotic conversation with Narcissus but also suggests that this meaning was embedded in Narcissus's call. It is as if Echo's active audition underscores Narcissus's lack of control over his own vocal sound. Echo, the poem goes on to dramatize, believes that Narcissus reciprocates her affections: she is so convinced that Narcissus intended the sexual undertones of the word "coeamus" that she rushes out of the forest and embraces him. Intention, Ovid's poem suggests, matters little once speech leaves the speaker's body and enters a communal realm where it is subject to reinterpretation and redirection. Echo's words are not mere reflections of Narcissus's speech, but are copies that alter the stability of the "original" they supposedly mimic. Jonathan Goldberg articulates this point elegantly: "In Narcissus, the solicitude of the mirror, in Echo, the disturbance of the mirror of reflection."[5] By uncoupling meaning and intention, Ovid's poem offers the eerie possibility that echoic sound may be read as the nymph Echo's volitional voice.

Whereas Ovid's Latin poem merely *suggests* that echoic sound can constitute voice, Sandys's translation more clearly represents aural reverberations as Echo's self-expression. Perhaps most tellingly, Echo's first word in Sandys's translation is the pronoun "I." Ovid's Narcissus asks "ecquis adest?" ("is anyone here?" [III.380]) and Echo answers, "adest" ("here"), but Sandys translates the lines as follows: "The Boy, from his companions parted, said; / Is any nigh? I, *Eccho* answere made" (III.381–82). By translating the Latin *adest* as "nigh," Sandys sets himself up for an echoic pun (aye/I) that personalizes Echo's response. Through her articulation of "I," Echo declares her personhood using the grammatical signifier of subjectivity. Sandys's choice of this particular translation is not a result of his formal constraints of rhymed couplets, as the "nigh? I" appears in the middle of the line and has the same rhythmic effect as "here, here" would have. Sandys, in other words, could have translated this exchange as "here, here," a direct translation that foregrounds the physical location of the subject.[6] Instead, he plays with the possibilities offered by the English language in much the same way as Ovid plays with the possibilities of Latin. Sandys could also have had Echo resound "nigh," Narcissus's exact word, and achieved the effect of Ovid's text; the word "nigh" would still have given Echo a mysterious aural presence. But Echo's first word, though it sounds much like "nigh," is different both in textual appearance *and* in meaning. Changing the word in appearance amplifies Echo's vocal independence, and the use of "I" as her first word emphasizes her status as a subject who, though unable to choose her words, constitutes her personhood through the words which are available to her. In Sandys's translation, Echo emerges as a locatable "I" by using the very voice she has been denied. No longer upsetting the line between voice and sound, Sandys's Echo speaks loudly on her own behalf.

The provocative pun is only one among a number of Sandys's enhancements to Ovid's original poem. Indeed, the format of the 1632 edition, with translation interspersed by commentary, provides its author with two spaces in which to pursue his revision of Ovid. The translation grants Echo grammatical and linguistic "ownership" of the voice she produces, lending her a greater aura of personal expression and of intentional articulation than is posited in Ovid's original. However, as I will explore later in the chapter, Sandys's commentary on the translation revokes the potentially human origins of echoic sound, defining echoes as mere aural curiosity.[7] The two approaches might at first glance seem incomprehensibly at odds: where the translation personifies echoic sound, attaching it to the speaking subject Echo, the commentary disqualifies echoic sound from categories of voice and speech. The first of these methods, linking Echo's voice to her body, might lead us to contrast the dehumanizing, scientific commentary with a translation that seems proleptically feminist. Judith de Luce's work on the silenced women of Ovid's *Metamorphoses* considers Echo a pathetic figure whose loss of speech signals her degradation into beastliness; if we follow de Luce's argument, we may be tempted to applaud Sandys's translation for restoring "human" identity to Ovid's vocally disabled nymph.[8] But, as we have seen throughout this book, an embodied voice is not necessarily more potent and effective than a disembodied one. Indeed, Sandys's rereading of Ovid's Echo is less transgressive than it appears.

When Sandys's translation links Echo's voice with her body, the resulting normalization of speech compromises, instead of facilitating, Echo's vocal power. To understand this dynamic, we might look by way of analogy to modern efforts to synchronize female voice and body, as is the case in classical Hollywood films. As Kaja Silverman argues in *The Acoustic Mirror*, classical film directors' efforts to conjoin sound and image are ideologically fraught. On the one hand, directors grant interiority to female characters, bolstering their authenticity of character by naturalizing their capacity for speech. But such interiority is far from liberating where female subjectivity is concerned. As the disembodied voice is given a "definitive localization," it "loses power and authority." A far more potent female voice, according to Silverman, is the one presented by feminist filmmakers, who blur or eliminate "corporeal assignation" for the cinematic female voice.[9] So, too, the localization of the disembodied voice in Sandys humanizes echoic sound at a cost. With her capacity (intentional or not) to manipulate disembodied voice, Ovid's Echo is able to inhabit what Silverman would call a space of "enunciative authority" in the story. Like the male voice-offs (voices sounding from offscreen) of classical Hollywood films, the echoic, disembodied voice allows Ovid's Echo the "invisibility, omniscience, and discursive power" that, according to Silverman, is not available to female characters in these classical films.[10] Like the Hollywood films Silverman discusses, Sandys's poem evinces anxiety about the potential powers of this disembodied female voice. When Sandys turns Echo's reverberating, disembodied sound into self-expression, he practices his own form of *synchronization*; in contrast to Ovid's original Latin poem, Sandys's Englished translation sets up a "definitive localization" for echoic sound by representing it as intentional speech and emphasizing Echo's interiority. Rather than offering a "feminist" revision of Ovid, then, Sandys's translation directly undermines Ovid's more provocative representation of the female voice. In Ovid's poem, Echo emerges as a subject not in spite of, but *because of,* the indeterminate nature of her vocal power. The uncanny ability of echoic sound to construct linguistic meaning on the nymph's behalf enables Echo to announce her desires but to remain beyond the reach of censure. Sandys's text, by naturalizing Echo's sound and realigning it with her body and self, places echoic sound within the range of male surveillance.

Whereas Silverman theorizes the anxieties of her artists and texts through the discourse of psychoanalysis, for my reading of Sandys's practice of synchronization, I would emphasize the historically specific variables that shape Sandys's representations of the female voice. The eerie vocal power of

Ovid's Echo would have been met with particular consternation by early modern audiences, many of whom embraced an ancient Aristotelian understanding of speech contrary to the view personified by Ovid's Echo. Aristotle views voice as the definitive trait of human identity: "Voice then is the impact of the inbreathed air against the windpipe, and the agent that produces the impact is the soul resident in these parts of the body. Not every sound, as we said, made by an animal is voice . . . ; what produces the impact must have soul in it and must be accompanied by an act of imagination."[11] This perspective on voice was prevalent throughout the Tudor and Stuart periods, extending well into the late seventeenth century. William Gearing similarly defines voice as a product of the human soul and, more specifically, its God-given capacity for reason. He opens *A Bridle for the Tongue: Or A Treatise of Ten Sins of the Tongue* (1663): "As Man is a reasonable creature, so is speech given to him by God to express his reason . . . Brute creatures can make a noise, but man only can articulate his voice."[12] A half century earlier, music theorist John Dowland, translating Andreas Ornithoparcus's *Micrologus* (1609), remarks that only "sensible creatures" can articulate voice: "A *Voyce* therefore is a sound uttered from the mouth of a perfect creature."[13] That is, vocal production becomes proof of a "man's" perfection in the eyes of God and nature. Robert Robinson iterates the claim when he explains in *The Art of Pronunciation* (1617) that the primary cause of voice is spiritual: the "Microcosmos of mans body" contains a mind that was created in God's image, and this mind is the cause of the voice.[14] These writers suggest tautologically that we can know that the producer of a sound is human if the sound it produces is voice. The disembodied sound of an echo, a "voice" that is not rooted in any clearly locatable subject, would be disconcerting to those who follow this definition of humanness because echoic sound violates seemingly straightforward assumptions about the relation between speech and the human body, between voice and selfhood.

If the capacity for vocal expression is the primary trait that defines "humanness," then how does one apprehend the message delivered by a voice that has no locatable origin, let alone no human one? Moreover, that such unconventional vocal power is depicted as belonging to a *female* figure would have compounded the shock value of Ovid's poem for early modern readers. Ovid's poem raises doubts about early modern efforts to restrict and regulate female speech, for how can one monitor a voice that does not emerge from a locatable body? Ovid relieves the echo phenomenon of some of its eerie nature and unsettling implications by imagining that the sounds closely approximating human speech may be the vocal products of a human entity, but he allows his Echo figure to straddle the line between intentional "human" speech and merely imitative, "inhuman" sound. As Joseph Loewenstein writes, Ovid, through personification, "regulates . . . the threat to consciousness implicit in the phenomenon of echo," but ultimately he "restrains" this personification.[15] That is, although Ovid creates the figure of Echo to depict more comfortably the strange echo phenomenon, the poem disarticulates the link between subjectivity and voice, between personhood and agency. In Ovid, echoic sound is given material form through the figure of Echo, but just when that "voice" seems to achieve an aura of stability through its connection to an embodied, speaking subject, the voice suddenly eludes our grasp, dissolving into unlocatable, untrackable sound.

A key part of Sandys's effort to correct that which is "harsh, improper, or mistaken" in Ovid is mending Ovid's uncertain, incomplete personification of echoic sound. Where Ovid's poem revels in the indeterminate nature of the voice, Sandys's Englished edition clarifies and polices the line between human and inhuman sound. What Ovid leaves ambiguous, Sandys "polishes," thereby normalizing the eerie vocality that Ovid's Echo possesses. Faced with the task of moralizing Ovid's example of echoic vocal production, Sandys ultimately finds a way to uphold Aristotelian logic about the relation between voice and subjectivity—but not without implications for the representation of early modern gender systems. For when Sandys's translation anchors echoic sound more firmly to Echo's personage, it not only imbues the nymph with a sense of interiority but represents her as having access to more conventional forms of vocal power. Caught between the exigencies of early modern voice philosophy and ideologies of gender, Sandys works hard elsewhere in his text to undermine the vocal power his own translation grants Echo. As I'll argue later, the text's success in revoking the agency of echoic sound exposes the insufficiency of certain modern conventional models of vocal power and the value of feminists theorizing alternate models.

By paying attention to the details of Sandys's "Englishing," I counter two trends in scholarship on the translated Ovid. First, though many scholars read Ovid's *Metamorphoses* in translation, few account for the sociohistorical circumstances of a particular translation and the effect these have on the representation of Ovid's stories.[16] The importance of factoring in history is particularly evident in the case of the "Narcissus and Echo" episode, for in an early modern culture so preoccupied with marking the boundaries of expression, especially where women are concerned, the figure of Ovid's Echo and her startling vocal capacity resonate deeply. Secondly, while the methodology and content of Sandys's commentary have received serious attention from scholars, the Englished translation has been seen as less worthy of analysis, perhaps because, in the words of Deborah Rubin, it is "notably literal and unbiased" in comparison to other "Englished" classics."[17] Rubin's characterization of Sandys's translation merits further investigation. Because the semantic range of Latin words and the language's flexible syntax are almost impossible to represent fully in English, Sandys makes translation choices in places where Ovid's text is more ambiguous. Whether his choices result from the demands of poetics (for example, Sandys's scheme of rhymed couplets) or from the pressures of an ideological project (*Ovide moralisé*), these changes metamorphose Ovidian representations of female vocal agency into a narrative that would be comprehended and accepted more readily by seventeenth-century readers.

How does Sandys grant Echo interiority, a sense of personhood, through sound—or, if you will, *per son*? We need to begin by examining how Ovid's original story destabilizes Echo's personhood. Ovid narrates that Echo received her liminal vocality as a punishment from the goddess Juno, whom Echo had enraged. Before Echo earned her name, she was like all other nymphs, complete with body and self-expressive voice. On Jove's order, Echo would distract Juno, engaging her in conversation so that the goddess would not discover Jove's infidelity:

fecerat hoc Iuno, quia, cum deprendere posset
sub Iove saepe suo nymphas in monte Iacentis,
illa deam longo prudens sermone tenebat,
dum fugerent nymphae. (III.362–65)

(Juno had made her thus; for often when she might have surprised the nymphs in company with her lord on the mountainsides, Echo cunningly held the goddess with her long speeches until the nymphs had fled.)

When Juno becomes aware of Echo's trickery, she curses the loquacious nymph: "huius . . . linguae . . . potestas / parva tibi dabitur vocisque brevissimus usus" ("that tongue of yours shall have its power curtailed and have the briefest use of speech" [III.366–67]). Echo's tongue, the instrument that stands in for her vocal capacity, will no longer work as efficiently after Juno's punishment: Echo will be restricted from owning her speech and will now merely have *usus* (use) of it. The term *usus* emerges from ancient legal discourses about property that, among other things, explain the conditions under which one may profit from the handling of another person's belongings. As Echo has only "use" of speech, she reaps the benefits of a property that is not hers; Narcissus's speech passes through her momentary possession, and she profits from it, even though she does not officially own it. Loewenstein points out, moreover, that the legal notion of utility from which the term *usus* arises, "challenges the boundary between object and subject. . . . Usus is a Janus-concept at the limits of property, sometimes splitting an object's utility off from its essential status of being-owned, sometimes revising ownership." As a *usable* property, Echo's speech stands on what Loewenstein calls "a weird frontier."[18] It is neither an embodied feature that inherently belongs to her (as speech, per Aristotle and his early modern followers, would otherwise be assumed to be), nor is it a movable property entirely separable from her. Echo's speech is a product or tool of which she—whether owner or vehicle—temporarily claims possession. Even before Echo's punishment, Ovid's descriptions of her speech convey its instrumental nature through corresponding grammatical form: the ablative of means. When narrating the history behind Juno's anger at Echo—"illa deam longo prudens sermone tenebat" ("She [Echo] cunningly held the goddess *by means of her long speeches*")—Ovid represents Echo's lengthy speeches to Juno in the ablative, "sermone," distinguishing and separating the speech from the nominative agent Echo. Speaking, in the Ovidian original, is grammatically the *tool* that Echo, the agent, deploys skillfully to fool Juno.

When Sandys translates this moment, he shifts Echo's "discourses" into the nominative position, into the position of the sentence's subject: "*Her long discourses* made the Goddesse stay" (III.365; emphasis mine). Discourses that once were employed by Ovid's Echo become, for Sandys, the primary agents of the sentence. This grammatical change, though it does not significantly alter Ovid's meaning and conforms closely to the original Latin, modifies the overall sense of this line and distinguishes Sandys from his predecessors. Arthur Golding, whose translation choices Sandys usually follows, retains Ovid's ablative construction, translating this phrase, "This elfe wold *with her tatling talke* detaine her [Juno] by the way."[19] The ablative appears as well in Thomas Howell's 1560 translation: "This Ecco *wyth a tale*, the goddes kepte so longe."[20] In Sandys the engaging discourses, rather than being the instruments that Echo uses to fool Juno, operate as metonymies for the nymph, indicating her power over Juno. Moreover, when Sandys grants agency to "her long discourses," he grammatically (through the inclusion of the possessive pronoun "her") yokes the speeches more closely to Echo; the trickery is performed by "discourses" that Echo inherently owns.

The significance of differences between Sandys's and Ovid's poetic choices become especially evident at the point in the poem when Echo discovers Narcissus wandering in the forest and falls in love with him. While he tries to locate his friends with his voice, she is provided with the phrases to articulate her interest in him. Ovid's language suggests that the words that Echo speaks in response are the combined result of her planning and good fortune. The Latin poem sets up these seemingly contradictory circumstances for echoic speech:

natura repugnat
nec sinit, incipiat, sed, quod sinit, illa parata est
exspectare sonos, ad quos sua verba remittat.
forte puer comitum seductus ab agmine fido
dixerat: "ecquis adest?" (III.376–80)

(Her nature forbids [her expression of desire for him], nor does it permit her to begin, but as it permits, she is ready to await the sounds to which she may give back her own words. By chance the boy, separated from his faithful companions, cried out: "Is anyone there?")

Though she is by nature incapable of initiating speech, "illa parata est /exspectare sonos," she is ready to await the sounds. Ovid's Echo does not merely hope that Narcissus will provide her with the opportunity to speak; she prepares herself for the event, *expecting* that such an occasion will present itself. And it does in the very next line. In his typically ambiguous style, however, Ovid prefaces the fulfillment of Echo's expectations with the word "forte," by chance. The effect of this combination of anticipation and surprising luck is that Echo is represented as both an agent of her own desires *and* a victim of destiny who happens to benefit from the cards (or, to be more specific, the words) fate deals her. When Sandys translates these lines, however, the latter characterization falls away as Sandys sets "forte" aside:

But, Nature no such liberty affords:
Begin she could not, yet full readily
To his expected speech she would reply.
The Boy, from his companions parted, said;
Is any nigh? (III.378–82)

Omitting any translation of "forte," Sandys's text moves directly from Echo's state of preparation to the conversation that allows her to fulfill her expectations. The effect of this elision, which differentiates Sandys from his predecessors,[21] is that Echo expects Narcissus to provide her with auspicious words, and he seems to speak at her passive bequest. Narcissus's initial words, the words that allow Sandys's Echo to announce her person ("I"), narratively proceed not "forte," by chance, but as anticipated. Narcissus's "nigh" is rendered as "expected speech." With less vacillation than Ovid, Sandys portrays Echo as exercising some measure of control over vocal expression and communication.

Echo's role in communication processes is figured generally as more active in Sandys than in Ovid. Ovid's Echo is defined as the eternal respondent, never initiating discourse but involuntarily reflecting its close: "haec in fine loquendi / ingeminat voces auditaque verba reportat" ("she doubles the phrases at the end of a speech and returns the heard words" [III.368–69]). Unable to do more than "return" heard words, Echo's speech is the borrowed property of another. When Ovid's Echo speaks, she moves that property *back* into the possession of its ostensible owner, the previous speaker. Some essence of this sense of movement back is retained in Sandys when he translates "reportat" as "relates": "she yet ingeminates / The last of sounds, and what she hears relates" (III.369–70). Perhaps Sandys chooses this meaning to strike a rhyme with "ingeminates," and his phraseology conveys the repetitive form of Echo's speech in accordance with Ovid's general description of her vocal posture. Yet in using the term "relates," Sandys's text delivers a slightly different sense of vocal property: as early as the fifteenth century, the term "relate" is "to recount, narrate, tell, give an account of," and, according to the *OED*, this is still a primary meaning today.[22] To a greater extent than the speaker who "reportat" (the definition of which is "to give back information" or, as in this case, words), the speaker who "relates" participates in the conveyance of information; she does not merely act as a receptacle but actually shapes the story. The focus of Ovid's "reportat" is on the initial source of the information, the speaker acting as siphon; the focus of Sandys's "relate" is on the task of narration itself. Thus, in Sandys's description of Echo as one who "relates," she is less an aural mirror returning what belongs to someone else than a messenger who offers selected information to a present and eager listener.

By virtue of this word choice, Sandys's introduction of Echo links her to a tradition of echoic gossips or personified rumors who famously exaggerate the accounts that they relate. We might recall the echoic rumor that Warwick describes in Shakespeare's *2 Henry IV*, when he reassures the king that the enemy's numbers cannot be as large as they are alleged to be, for "Rumour doth double, like the voice and echo, / The numbers of the feared" (3.1.92–93). While Warwick summons the echoic trope in order to pun on "double," the association of echoes with errant gossip was long-standing. As a product of rumors, Warwick's echo does more than just repeat news; it can manipulate information, or, like Rumor who opens *2 Henry IV*, even manufacture falsehoods. The more active participation of Sandys's Echo in shaping the words that reach her might be further noted in Sandys's translation of Ovid's phrase "auditaque verba reportat" ("and she returns heard words"). When Sandys translates this phrase as "and what she hears relates," he not only alters the definition of *reportat*, as I have noted, but also turns the modifying participle "audita" into the verb "hear." The words that Sandys's Echo ostensibly reiterates are taken in and incorporated by her hearing body, and only then are they converted into vocal articulations. In grammatical terms, Echo's body is thus the site of a form of hearing as active as the feat of speaking. Echo emerges as, what I termed in the previous chapter, an *acoustic subject*. She practices auditory agency.

In sum, Sandys's translation renders Echo as an agent of her own desires, practically accountable for the words that issue forth from her body. Though Sandys does not (and, by virtue of the genre of translation, cannot) go so far as Ben Jonson in restoring Echo with independent speech and a visually recognizable body,[23] his translation still accentuates the personification of Echo that is only ambiguously suggested in Ovid. As such, readers of Sandys's Englished translation would have encountered a depiction of voice in Ovid more commensurate with that of Aristotle and many of his early modern followers—that is, a "voice" expressive of human consciousness and will. In the process of aligning Ovid's tale more closely with this voice philosophy, however, Sandys's text aggravates early modern social anxieties about the relation between gender and vocal expression. To be sure, Sandys's Echo flouts Pauline strictures of chastity, silence, and obedience and seems to escape regimes of discipline to which early modern women—in fiction and in reality—were subject often. But before we leap to the conclusion that Sandys's text betrays protofeminist commitments, it is important to note that the text frames this transgressive rereading of personalized voice not as Sandys's but as Ovid's. The English words might be Sandys's, but the essence of Echo's story—Sandys, the translator, insists—belongs to the heathen

Ovid. This distinction and its strategic purpose become more evident when we consider the contrast between the translation and the moralizing commentary that follows it. While Sandys's translation emphasizes Echo's personhood, his commentary reduces Echo to an inhuman phenomenon, with a "debility" (156) in speech and a notable lack of vocal control.

"Only the Repercussion": Sandys's Commentary

Sandys's commentary is only one among a number of additions/improvements to the 1632 edition, but it is certainly the most notable and is partly responsible for the author's popularity as an Ovid translator. Much as Golding had dominated the sixteenth century with his Englished *Metamorphoses*, so Sandys dominated English readings of Ovid's poem in the seventeenth, publishing at least eight editions of his full translation.[24] The 1632 edition was the most glamorous, accompanied by fifteen full pages of new illustrations depicting mythological figures, marginal glosses that highlight the names of the central figures of each story, and the extensive commentary, organized by narrative episode. The composition and placement of the commentary strongly suggest that readers of the 1632 edition would have attended as much (if not more) to the commentaries as to the translation itself: the commentary sections are equal in length, sometimes even longer, than the Englished poem, and they take the form of pedagogical/philosophical essays, placed conspicuously between translated books.

Sandys justifies his commentary as a necessity "since divers places in our Author are otherwise impossible to be understood but by those who are well versed in the ancient Poets and Historians" (9). Having traveled to various worldly destinations and having settled for some time in Virginia, Sandys is indeed "well versed." The commentary evinces not only its author's experiences as a voyager but also his encyclopedic knowledge of classical history and philosophy, of mythography, and of science. The sources Sandys cites, whether these are stories relayed from scholastic traditions or observations drawn from his own experiences, assess the credibility and value of Ovid's myths by appealing to scientific or historical precedent.[25] The format of the commentary, like contemporaneous commentaries, positions Sandys as a capacious collector, not selective editor, of historical opinion. He draws on a variety of sources, rarely offering his overt views except when he affirms the moral message of each tale. The commentary, one might say, presents Sandys as a "mere" echo, reporting the ideas of others without much mediation. It is clear, however, that the commentaries provide a forum for reflection on, and corrections to, the content of Ovid's tales. In addition to delivering the ethical lesson of the stories, announced with verbal cues such as "now to the morall" (160), each commentary draws on a limited selection of sources among the vast array from which Sandys could cull. By the time Sandys compiled his commentary on "Narcissus and Echo," Echo had received centuries of attention from writers with diverse interests in her as a mythical figure, literary trope, metaphoric emblem, and, of course, natural phenomenon.[26] In its selection of citations, Sandys's commentary tells a very particular story about Echo, with hardly negligible ideological consequences.

In its discussion of Echo, Sandys's commentary relies predominantly on the discourse of natural philosophy. Exploring at length the nature of echoes as acoustic phenomena, the commentary appeals to empirical observations to dispute the "human" quality of Echo's sound. From the perspective of acoustic theory, echo, though sometimes uttered "without failing in one sillable" (156) is not an original voice, and the commentary emphasizes the source that creates the initial sound: "Now *Eccho* signifies a resounding: which is only the repercussion of the voice, like the rebound of a ball, returning directly from whence it came: and that it reports not the whole sentence, is through the debility of the reverberation" (156). Here Echo is reduced to object status, an "it" that helps explain the material operation of repercussion. Distinguished from expressive human voice, echoic sound is compared to a rebounding ball that has no control over its movements and, by its nature, can only return back to its place of origination.[27] Where the translation had described an Echo who actively "relates" what she hears, the commentary strictly interprets the verb *reportare* that Ovid had used to characterize Echo's voice. In the commentary, Echo returns the voice "directly from whence it came"; she does not actively hear words, process the information, and relate what she chooses like a messenger but "reports" the heard words like a mindless resonator. The commentary explains away any hint of Echo's vocal intentionality. Her auspicious reverberations of only the ends of sentences, which in the translation had given Echo the opportunity to declare her subjectivity, are here figured as the result of faulty reverberation. By emphasizing the echo as a purely acoustic phenomenon, the commentary disqualifies Echo's sound from the category of human voice.

Although elsewhere in his commentary on the *Metamorphoses* Sandys incorporates the mythological along with the scientific, his commentary on Echo primarily cites natural philosophy. Elucidated thoroughly by the empirical criteria of the "new" science, Echo, in the commentary, loses her peculiar vocal powers. The impact that this explanatory apparatus has on Sandys's presentation of Echo becomes clear when we consider how the commentary draws on Francis Bacon's scientific writings about echoes. Scholars have recognized that Sandys's 1632 edition registers the extent to which the poet was influenced by Bacon, especially by Bacon's mythography, *De Sapientia Veterum* (translated into English in 1619).[28] Yet references to *De Sapientia* are absent in Sandys's commentary on Echo. The allusions to Bacon that Sandys does include seem to derive from Bacon's *Sylva Sylvarum* (1626), the assortment of empirical studies about the nature of sound that I discussed in Chapter 2. In several of the demonstrations that appear in *Sylva Sylvarum*, Bacon discusses echoes, distinguishing between simple echoes, what he calls "reflexion iterant," and echoes of echoes, or "super-reflexions." In order to explain an observation about "super-reflexions" reported to have been heard in a chapel outside of Paris, Bacon draws a parallel between visual and aural reiterations:

Like to *Reflexions* in *Looking-glasses*; where if you place one *Glasse* before, and another behinde, you shall see the *Glasse* behinde with the *Image*, within the *Glasse* before; And againe, the *Glasse* before in that; and divers such *Super-Reflexions*, till the *species speciei* at last die. For it is every Returne weaker, and more shady. In like manner, the *Voice* in that *Chappel*, createth *speciem speciei*, and maketh succeeding *Super-Reflexions*; For it melteth by degrees, and every *Reflexion* is weaker than the former. (no. 249)

With his technical nomenclature and hints at an experimentally based logic, Bacon empties echoes of their eerie potential. Sound operates in predictable patterns, Bacon insists in this instance.[29] Sandys's commentary reaches a similar conclusion, using virtually identical language. Sandys also refers to the chapel in Pavia where Lambinus heard "not fewer then thirty" echoes answering one another, and comments: "The image of the voice so often rendred, is as that of the face reflected from one glasse to another; melting by degrees, and every reflection more weake and shady then the former" (156).

Filtered through scientific discourse, Echo's liminal speech is reduced to predictable sound that, if given the time, will dissipate like the "super-reflexions" at Pavia. Such conclusions were a staple of scientific discourse on

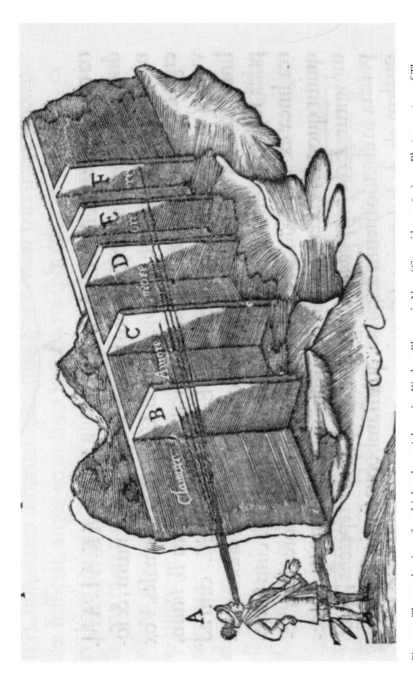

Figure 5. The production of multiple echoes. Athanasius Kircher, *Phonurgia Nova* (Campidano, 1673), 47. Photo courtesy of The Newberry Library, Chicago.

echoes, their implications captured well in Athanasius Kircher's illustration of the echo phenomenon (see figure 5).

Kircher's drawing demonstrates how the acoustic experimenter, by placing resonant surfaces at just the right distances and precise angles, can control the production of echoic sound, to produce the illusion of speech. The sounded word "clamore" is shown to break down by degrees, with each produced sound uncannily resembling a comprehensible word ("amore," "more," "ore," "re"). But the lines drawn to and from the words mark out explicitly that these are mere reflections of an original utterance voiced by a particular gentleman. Standing in for the acoustic scientist invited to reproduce this phenomenon, this man is represented as clearly in control of the sounds that return. From the perspective of scientific discourses of echoes, the echoic phenomenon is anything but eerie; it is a provable and reproducible acoustic effect. Referencing such experiments, Sandys's commentary offers a similarly sober perspective. The strangeness of echoes can be easily explained and even manufactured by men well-versed in the scientific principles of reflection. What is more, including scientific evidence on the nature of reflections in a commentary on the "Narcissus and Echo" myth links Echo's aural reverberations with the mirror images that mislead Narcissus. Through this analogy, Echo's presence is rendered as illusive and fictive as Narcissus's visual reflection, nothing more than a reverberation he produces and misrecognizes.

A markedly different sense of Ovid's nymph appears in Bacon's mythographic writings about echoes, which Sandys does not cite or mention in the commentary on Echo. Bacon's *De Sapientia Veterum* (1619) follows a different mythographic tradition, which couples the nymph not with Narcissus but with Pan. According to *De Sapientia*, Pan desires Echo because she represents "true philosophy," the only thing that Pan (the World) lacks: "[T]hat alone is true philosophy, which doth faithfully render the very words of the world, and is written no otherwise then the world doth dictate, it being nothing els but the image or reflection of it, not adding any thing of its owne, but onely iterates and resounds."[30] In Baconian mythography, Echo symbolizes the purity of philosophical discourse, the most transcendent form of the human voice.[31] Bacon's laudatory views of Echo extend from the writings of Macrobius, who had depicted the nymph as the representative of the celestial realm. Sandys certainly knew of this traditional reading of Echo, being a known scholar of Bacon's *De Sapientia*, yet the commentary privileges Bacon's scientific over his mythographic explanations.

A skeptical reader might posit that Sandys excludes the Baconian mythographic allusions because Bacon's Echo is derived from a mythological tradition that differs significantly from Ovid's. The story of Pan and Echo switches the roles of pursuer and pursued: Pan is captivated by Echo's song and yearns for her, unlike Ovid's poem in which Echo desires and seeks Narcissus. The Echo of the Pan-Echo story pines for no man and courageously fends off her pursuer. In one rendition of the narrative, Pan becomes so enraged with Echo's refusal to surrender her chastity that he calls on wild animals to tear her limbs apart; under the guidance of the Muses and the nymphs, however, Echo's invisible, scattered body parts retain their ability to produce captivating music, keeping Pan in a state of frustrated desire.[32] This account of Echo as defender of chastity, ally of nymphs and Muses, and desirable representative of the celestial heavens underlies Baconian notions of Echo as the representative of philosophical discourse. One might reasonably maintain that it was not appropriate for an Ovid commentator to muddy his commentary with discussions derived from a different mythological genealogy.

Yet at least one other commentary on Ovid's "Narcissus and Echo," published the same year as Sandys's expanded edition, does draw on the tradition of celestial Echo. Mythographer and rhetorician Henry Reynolds follows his translation of Ovid's poem with a moralizing commentary in which he condemns Narcissus for not listening to Echo's "Divine voice." Citing Pythagorus's notion *"while the winds breathe, adore Ecco,"* Reynolds reports that Echo has been considered the "Reflection of this divine breath," since the wind is "the Symbole of the Breath of God."[33] Reynolds's inclusion of a reference to the tradition of celestial Echo and her relationship to Pan results in a commentary that celebrates the uncanny, disembodied nature of Echo's speech. Her sound is not a simple reverberation of the human voice but a celestial prophecy that imitates and thus articulates the voice of God. Engaged in the same project and published at the same time, Sandys's and Reynolds's perspectives on Echo could not be more different.

Rather than cite the tradition of celestial Echo, Sandys's commentary includes a translation of Ausonius's Epigram XXXII, in which Echo speaks to a painter, calling herself "a voice without a mind" and "of judgment blind / the mother." In Ausonius's poem Echo taunts the painter about his artistic limitations, challenging the painter to try to represent the "Daughter of aire and tongue," and goading him: "If therefore thou wilt paint me, paint a sound" (157). Echoes, she reminds him, can be processed only as aural experiences, and a visual medium, like painting, can never fully portray an aural phenomenon. Representing Echo is quite impossible, the poem suggests, for Echo has no existence outside of her medium of sound.

Defining Echo as "mere" sound is not inherently a slight against the figure. As we have seen, many early moderns believed sounds to be incredibly powerful—for some writers even more powerful than images. Bacon's own *Sylva Sylvarum* asserts the primacy of hearing over sight, claiming that sounds more directly and more materially affect the spirits of a listener than sights affect a visual observer. In comparison to other forms of sensory perception, Bacon writes, "*Objects* of the *Eare*, doe affect the *Spirits* (immediately) most with *Pleasure* and Offence . . . So it is *Sound* alone, that doth immediately, and incorporeally, affect most" (no. 700). And Echo's sound is especially potent given its pervasive nature—she is not found in one place but is rather "omnibus auditur" ("heard by all" [401]). In the context of Sandys's commentary, however, Ausonius's poem *is* a disparagement of the vocal nymph. Elsewhere in his commentary, Sandys undermines the efficacy and the materiality of sound, questioning, contra Bacon, whether sound has any power at all. In commenting on the bodily decay of Echo, Sandys writes that Echo "consumes to an unsubstantiall voice." She "converts into a sound; that is, into nothing" (156). The syntax of the latter sentence implies not only that Echo's body becomes "nothing," but that sound in general is "nothing."

The sober scientific and historical reality about Echo related in Sandys's commentary, like the personification of Echo in his translation, curbs the potential power of the disembodied voice—the translation by synchronizing voice and body, and the commentary by disqualifying echoic sound from the category of voice. In its multiple, conflicting depictions of echoic sound, the 1632 edition exhibits the degree to which its representation of female voice is subject to competing cultural discourses. And it is through this dual structure, translation conjoined with commentary, that the text negotiates conflicting cultural mandates. The translation counteracts Ovid's classical reading of Echo as an eerie, unlocatable voice by creating a vocally empowered nymph who subsequently troubles the early modern ideological connection between femininity and silence; the commentary appeals to scientific and Christian moral discourses to neutralize the threat to early modern gender ideologies that the translation has aggravated.

Notably, the text's two representations of voice do not carry equal authority. Sandys presents the translated poem and its ideas as belonging more directly to Ovid, Sandys being "only" the translator, whereas he underscores that he himself has compiled and composed the commentary. The 1632 edition does not simply distinguish Ovidian fiction from early modern truth, as Rubin maintains;[34] it asserts the preeminence of the latter and secures Echo's conventional vocal agency (the unity of her voice, body, and subjectivity) in the domain of the former. For the Echo that Sandys offers early modern readers is either the expressive human agent created by the pagan Ovid or the "modern" scientifically validated, inhuman phenomenon presented by the Christian Sandys.[35] Sandys's text not only reasserts a binary of voice versus sound, a distinction that privileges more normative forms of speech over alternate forms, but also dissociates its author from the agentive Echo who emerges from "Ovid's" poem. By emphasizing Ovid's responsibility for narrating a story of Echo's vocal power and then offering the commentary as a moral corrective, Sandys's edition protects its early modern readers from the uncanny agency that the echoic voice seems to possess in Ovid's poem.

"Now to the Morall": Echoes and Feminist Criticism

The project of *Ovide moralisé* licenses Sandys to grapple with and dismiss the agency of an ambiguous, unpredictable voice. In my epilogue, I will discuss why Sandys's text is able to successfully foreclose female vocal agency in a way that plays and other texts subject to live vocal performance could not. In closing this chapter, however, I want to reflect on what is at stake for feminist critical perspectives on voice in Sandys's treatment of Ovid's Echo.

A number of feminist critics have recognized Ovid's capacity to produce potentially subversive representations of mythic and historical women, and some of the most compelling work in this area has come from scholars who examine the reactions of early modern male writers to Ovid's characterizations.[36] Scholars interested in Ovid's representations of female speech have noted especially the depictions of women in Ovid's *Heroides*, a collection of epistles narratively figured as authored by famous women to their lovers. Elizabeth Harvey situates her treatment of the *Heroides* in the context of a discussion about ventriloquized voices, the trope whereby male writers impersonate the female voice. She argues that Ovid's ventriloquization of Sappho's voice in *Heroides* challenges "the epic and patriarchal ethos of Augustan Rome." Though Ovid's ventriloquization is motivated by a need to master the poetic legacy of Sappho, this project of anxious appropriation is self-consciously exploited in *Heroides XV*: "In a sense, Sapphic and Ovidian signatures are superimposed on one another in a palimpsestic transparency, and the usurpation that has made Ovid's ventriloquized speech possible is thus thematized in the text"; by calling attention to his ventriloquization, Ovid offers an unstable answer to the question "Who is speaking, and to whom does speaking belong?"[37] Deborah S. Greenhut similarly links Ovid's self-conscious ambiguity with subversive representations of gender identity in the *Heroides*. Assessing the rhetorical skill of female speakers in Ovid's text, Greenhut argues that Ovid creates a vital and unmoralized link between eloquence and sexuality, envisioning that the speakers of the *Heroides* articulate desire without shame and fear of social repercussions.[38] Harvey and Greenhut both note that Ovid's representations of women would have been difficult for early modern writers to accept. And both demonstrate how later adaptations of Ovid's *Heroides* alter the original to comply more easily with early modern attitudes toward female speech, thereby revealing the historical conditions that shape literary production.

Although attuned to the usefulness of Ovid for feminist literary historiography, Harvey and Greenhut, like most feminist scholars, dismiss the extraordinary potential of the echoic voice that Ovid himself suggests in the *Metamorphoses*.[39] When both of these insightful critics recall the trope of echoing, they articulate views that bear closer resemblance to Sandys's writings than to Ovid's.[40] In her definition of the male poet's "ventriloquistic appropriation" of the female voice, Harvey distinguishes echoing from the more masterful theft or "linguistic rape" that Ovid pursues: "Ovid knew Sappho's poetry and his epistle is full of its echoes, but whereas 'echo' suggests a disembodied voice capable only of repetition, Ovid's radical reinscription of Sappho bears the marks of sexual mastery and theft, ... displac[ing] the authority of her words."[41] Harvey distinguishes impotent echoing from Ovid's authoritative, even violent, reinscription of voice, thereby implying that echoes are inherently incapable of the kind of powerful appropriation of another discourse that Ovid accomplishes. Greenhut, discussing the figuration of female speech as echoic in early modern conduct books, writes that in rhetorical terms the echo "assigns polite women's speech the quality of an abstract or a digest, whose only value is in its confirmation of the original, or authoritative, sound. An echo is not original, and what it expresses is subordinate to and dependent on the original sound."[42] While importantly calling attention to the misogynist nature of these characterizations of female speech, Greenhut inadvertently reiterates conduct-book definitions of echoic speech. To be sure, many early modern conduct books use the trope of echoing to divest female speech of its potential power, but one need not thereby conclude that echoic speech is *inherently* impotent as a model of effective voicing.

The tendency for many feminist critics to view the mythical Echo as purely a victim of misogynist silencing regimes, rather than as a potential challenge to them, is emblematic of a broader problem in feminist treatments of voice, especially in early modern studies. As I have noted throughout this book, readings of early modern representations of female voice often emphasize the way in which writers prescribe women's morality through a conflation of silence and sexual continence. Although this focus, and even reactions against this focus, have enabled critics to address the relation between enforced silence and the disciplined female subject, a tendency to concentrate on the speaker's body (the site of articulation) has limited scholarly recognition of the potential power of disembodied voice. And yet early modern writers provide a wider set of parameters for their definitions of voice. How, I have asked, do certain material forms and practices of vocal communication draw attention to the detachment of voice from body? And what kind of power can the voice have after it leaves the speaker's body, before and after it reaches a listener's ears?

Theorizing how the material voice performs beyond the speaker's body can lead scholars toward a more capacious definition of female agency. We have seen Lavinia use uncontrollable breath to "narrate" her trauma, and we have seen Innogen protect her body from sexual assault by preventing voices from entering her body through her ears. Alternate readings of female agency become available when we interrogate, rather than assume, that vocal power derives from the speaker's body. With Ovid's Echo we come full circle to a figure able to express herself without a body at all. Indeed, it is precisely the disarticulation of speech from the speaker's body and person that opens up a space for Ovid's Echo to express and perform her desire for Narcissus. Transactive and dialogic, echoic speech enjoys a liminal kind of agency that is difficult to track and thus impossible to restrain fully. Ovid's Echo may speak inappropriately, expressing desires that should, according to some readers, be left unarticulated, but insofar as Echo cannot be held accountable for her sound, she cannot be consummately punished for vocal transgressions. Like Constance and Desdemona, Echo cannot be blamed for words that are not "her own." Echo thus reaps the benefits of speech, while the male subject, Narcissus, is held (anxiously) accountable.

This ambiguous and thus powerful relationship of speech to agency changes in Sandys's translation of Ovid's story. By personifying Echo's voice and yoking unpredictable words to their female speaker, Sandys places Echo firmly within the conduct-book tropology of the loquacious and lascivious woman. Sandys translates disembodied echoic sound into the willful, immodest expressions of (yet another) lusty woman. Although he grants Echo self-expressive power through her voice, he casts that power as immoral, and specifically, as indicative of a *classical* immorality that he aims to correct through his modern, scientific commentary. Shakespeare and his contemporaries sometimes adopt a similar strategy in their representations of garrulous women on the stage. Consider, among others, Eleanor in *2 Henry VI* and Katherine in *The Taming of the Shrew*—female characters who use their voices to wield power in their respective plays but who are publicly humiliated and duly punished for their boldness. Sandys, I have been arguing, needs to turn Ovid's Echo into an Eleanor or a Katherine before he can discipline her for her vocal unruliness.

Like Sandys, a generation of feminist critics risks revoking Echo's more implicit potential for vocal power by reading echoic voice through a discourse of moral instruction. But I argue that Ovid's Echo, like other figures I've discussed, offers us a way to think beyond the confines of prescriptive literature and to reassess the terms by which many feminists study "voice" as a theoretical, historical, and performative motif. The implications of this argument become especially evident if we return to *The Duchess of Malfi*. When the Duchess disobeys her brothers and proposes marriage to Antonio, she asserts her rights over her own body, her own sexuality, becoming, so it seems, a paradigmatic feminist icon of the early modern stage. Yet *The Duchess of Malfi* quickly becomes a tragedy about how the Duchess's brothers prevent her from asserting such rights; the outspoken Duchess loses her life because she claims her own voice. Expanding our definition of what constitutes voice can extend the Duchess's story, however—a story that does not end when the Duchess is strangled. In the final act of the play, the Duchess speaks again. This may not be the candid, forthright Duchess we have heard articulate forcefully her desires throughout the play. But it is because the Duchess's echoes cannot be traced clearly to her person that these sounds can successfully voice her will: the echoic sounds are beyond the command of the men who have tried and, they believe, succeeded in silencing the Duchess; the sounds even elude the control of Antonio, despite the fact that his voice helps produce them. The Duchess may be dead, but her voice carries authority at this late moment in the play and, on some level, it prevails in the end. After all, it is the Duchess's son—not Ferdinand, the Cardinal, or their chosen successor—who remains on to rule "In's mother's right" (5.5.112).

Critics who recognize agency primarily in the form of outspoken female historical and literary figures risk dismissing alternate forms of potent voicing. Other models of the relation between articulation and agency were available in early modern England, particularly to women, whose access to conventional forms of power was circumscribed by legal and social practices. Ovid's Echo exemplifies one such model—at least until Sandys refashions her in his 1632 *Metamorphosis*, granting her interiority and, in effect, a voice of her own. That Sandys's text needs to normalize, in order to dismiss, Echo's vocality indicates just how disconcerting the disembodied voice was for some early moderns and, at the same time, how compelling Echo's legacy can be for contemporary feminist theories of agency.

Performing the Voice of Queen Elizabeth

The figure of Echo captures trenchantly the guiding argument of *Voice in Motion*: that the voice's distance from, rather than presence in, the body can constitute the conditions of agency. As we saw in the previous chapter, a voice that cannot be located firmly in or connected to a speaker's body threatens men's assumptions about their capacity for vocal control, producing, instead, unexpectedly robust models of female agency. But the previous chapter also revealed the ways such vocal agency can be foreclosed. George Sandys's *Metamorphosis* weakens the eerie power of the echoic voice by normalizing it. The translation restores echoic voice to the body of an intentional, speaking subject, and the commentary frames the echo as an acoustic phenomenon that is easily explained by early modern scientific precepts. Sandys's text is not unusual in its treatment of voice. My book has examined similar efforts by men on and off the stage to stabilize volatile voices. Chapter 1 discussed the ways Marston, whose play would have been performed by boys on the verge of puberty, writes the male squeaky voice into his play-scripts, preempting its potential to surprise audiences and remind them of their own potential for vocal failure. Chapter 2 examined how male characters in Shakespeare's *King John*, recognizing that voice is made of ephemeral breath, attempt to control this elusive matter, or, failing that, disavow breath's material dimensions, emphasizing its stable spiritual attributes instead. And Chapter 3 explored how male rulers in Shakespeare's late plays, unable to control the production and transmission of voices that presumably threaten their daughters' chastity, attempt to control the female body by counseling daughters to close their ears.

But there is a notable difference between these plays and Sandys's text. In the plays, the voice proves unpredictable and thus impossible for men to manage completely. We have seen, in fact, how marginalized characters—specifically the women and youths in *King John*, *Othello*, *Titus Andronicus*, and *Richard III*—are able to exploit breath's elusiveness in efforts to express their views and desires even after being stripped of the capacity to speak in normative ways. We have also seen how female characters in the late plays transform the injunction to aural defense—so vigorously maintained in Protestant sermons—into a prerogative to practice disruptive deafness. By purposefully shutting their ears, female characters reassert control over their own bodies, turning a repressive mechanism into a site of resistance to a father's will. John Webster's Duchess of Malfi offers an especially poignant contrast with Sandys's Echo: the Duchess's echoic voice, stealing from her grave to warn her beloved of harm that may befall him, enables the Duchess to resist her brothers' efforts to silence her. Why, we might wonder, is Sandys's text successful in its foreclosure of female communicative agency in a way that the plays I've discussed are not?

To answer this question we need to attend to key differences between Sandys's printed book and plays that were not simply printed and read but performed live onstage. I have argued that the difference of the early modern theater—a space of pubescent boy actors whose voices could crack at any moment, of unpredictable acoustic conditions, and of potentially disobedient audience members—contributes significantly to the ways the voice is represented by plays. Indeed, the critical leverage of this volatile voice is evinced not only in plays but in a range of spaces of live vocal performance in early modern England, including the schoolhouse, the acoustic science laboratory, and the Protestant church. In concluding this book, I want to highlight this difference of performance by exploring one particular case in which the Echo figure was dramatized: George Gascoigne's dialogue between the Savage Man and Echo in the entertainments at Kenilworth Castle. Composed for the occasion of Queen Elizabeth's visit to the castle in 1575, the Echo episode was only one among a variety of entertainments planned for her eighteen-day sojourn. The entertainments were on the whole part of an effort by Kenilworth's residing aristocrat, Robert Dudley, earl of Leicester, to canvass Elizabeth's support for two of Dudley's chief projects: the aggressive promotion of Protestantism through England's military intervention in the Netherlands and the Queen's acquiescence to Dudley's offer of marriage.[1] It is the latter of these two projects, as we will see, that Gascoigne's Echo episode attempts boldly to influence. I close with Gascoigne's performance because it allows us to revisit and extend the key insights of *Voice in Motion*. The entertainment proves generative for two reasons. First, it stages the foreclosure of an ostensibly unpredictable female voice—that belonging to the figure Echo—in the presence of Queen Elizabeth, renown for her powerful, unpredictable voice.² Second, Gascoigne recruits the medium of print in order to gain control over a volatile performance that eludes him.

Our knowledge of the entire Kenilworth festivities comes primarily (though not exclusively) from Gascoigne, who wrote many of the episodes himself and published what he claimed was a faithful transcription approximately six months after the event. The transcription, known as *The Princely Pleasures at Kenelworth Castle*, treats the Echo figure in similar ways to Sandys's commentary on Ovid, stripping Echo of her eerie vocal power. Her lack of agency in general is evident from the moment she is introduced. Whereas Ovid's original Echo, like the Echo of the Duchess in Webster's play, arrives on the scene to promote her own interests, Gascoigne's Echo arrives only at the beckoning of the Savage Man (played by Gascoigne). She is summoned, in particular, because the Savage Man encounters utter confusion at the meaning of the entertainments that have unfolded on previous days, and yet his pleas to Jupiter for enlightenment receive no response. He calls out, instead, to Echo and receives immediate satisfaction:

> Wel Eccho, where art thou
> could I but Eccho finde,
> Shee would returne me answere yet
> by blast of every winde.
> Ho *Eccho: Eccho*, ho . . . ³

Through a resonating "dialogue" in which Echo responds to questions asked of her, the Savage Man learns all about the meaning of the entertainments and is led to realize that his interactions with Echo are, in fact, being performed before none other than the Queen herself (who, as the transcription has it, encounters the Savage Man upon her return from the day's hunt).

Although Gascoigne's text presumes to portray Echo as a bearer of unexpected news, Echo proves less a source of wisdom than a sounding board for knowledge the Savage man already has. Embedded in each of the Savage Man's questions are two possible answers, the second of which, repeated by Echo, is the correct one. Curious about the people's rejoicing, the Savage Man inquires, "is it for King or Queen," to which Echo responds "Queen" (94). Wondering about the figure of a sibyl who had met Elizabeth as she approached the castle, the Savage Man asks, "What meant the woman first, / which met hir as she came? / Could she devine of things to come, / as *Sibelles* use the same?" Echo confirms his suspicions sounding back, "The same" (98). And so it continues. Gascoigne's Echo is anything but the canny, borderline subject who emerges from Ovid and Webster. For much of the scene, she is no different from the acoustic phenomenon that Sandys describes in his commentary, a reflection without any hint of intention.[4]

Gascoigne's use of the Echo figure becomes more pernicious when Echo is recruited to speak for Elizabeth's desires, especially in regards to Dudley's marriage proposal. Later in the scene, the Savage Man pursues a series of questions about gifts that Dudley had presented to Elizabeth in an earlier entertainment, exclaiming, "Gifts? What? Sent from the Gods? / as presents from above? / Or pleasures of provision / as tokens of true love?" (99). Echo's response casts the gifts, predictably, as tokens of "true love," thereby suggesting that Elizabeth's receipt of the gifts signified not simply the royal guest's graceful courtesy but her acceptance of Dudley's affection. Echo is made to articulate Dudley's rendition of Elizabeth's voice even more explicitly when the Savage Man says of Dudley that "he gave him selfe and all / A worthy gift to be received, / and so I trust it shall," to which Echo confidently responds, "It shall." As a cipher for appropriating the Queen's voice, the figure of Echo is even more audaciously employed in another instance. Asked by the Savage Man about who is giving the gifts—"Was it not he? Who (but of late) / this building here did lay?" Echo alters her resounding response in order to utter the name of Gascoigne's patron, "*Dudley.*" Gascoigne ostensibly uses this technique of witty repetition in much the same fashion as other Ovid translators (including Sandys) do: to imbue Echo with an independent mind. But Gascoigne goes further, using this device to secure Echo's praise for his patron, who is named explicitly as the gracious, generous, and powerful host. Gascoigne's mischievous repetition proves especially impudent, as Ilana Nash notes, since Kenilworth was, in fact, owned by the crown, bestowed on Dudley by the Queen herself (as she has already reminded Dudley earlier in the festivities). Although Dudley had restored and added on to the building, his claim of familial ownership was specious at best.[5]

Dudley's audacity, made possible through Gascoigne's writing, has been well-noted by commentators.[6] But the significance of Gascoigne's inclusion of Echo in the festivities and his particular use of the figure has not received sufficient attention. Echo is more than just another character added to the mythical smorgasbord that was the Kenilworth entertainments. Rather the Echo episode captured, perhaps more transparently than any other entertainment performed at Kenilworth, Dudley's complex relationship with Elizabeth. For if Echo has to use the voice of others to express desire she cannot otherwise articulate, then she represents Dudley's fantasy of Elizabeth. Dudley continued his long courtship of the Queen in part because he was driven by a hope that Elizabeth's romantic interest in him persisted even though she did not articulate such desires clearly or consistently in public. Yet when Dudley would try to speak for Elizabeth's desires, he was often frustrated. In one incident, Dudley performed the part of a jealous lover after Elizabeth showed favoritism to his rival. Elizabeth seems to have recognized that Dudley's public display of jealousy—claiming he would beat his rival—challenged her authority; for by suggesting that his rival had usurped his rightful place, Dudley was implying that Elizabeth returned Dudley's affections, that he had a *right* to play the jealous lover. According to one report of this incident, Elizabeth responded by publicly humiliating Dudley for his impertinence and letting him sulk out of her favor until he apologized.[7] Dudley, like many others, hung precariously on Elizabeth's every utterance, which could confirm his affections and just as quickly leave him distraught. For a man who was repeatedly frustrated by his inability to control Elizabeth's unpredictable and often contradictory voice, Gascoigne's Echo is an ideal: like the conventional Echo figure, she can be interpreted as speaking her mind by using the words of others, as if she does not mind being spoken for; what's more, in Gascoigne's version, Echo's words are, in fact, controlled by her interlocutor. By convention, Echo ostensibly appropriates the voices of others, but in Gascoigne's text, it is Echo's voice that is appropriated, carefully scripted to serve the interests of Kenilworth's men. As such, Echo becomes a crucial figure for Gascoigne's efforts to inscribe what Bruce Smith calls "a political geography of sound" at Kenilworth.[8]

Gascoigne and Dudley, as it turned out, were not as successful as they'd hoped in scripting female voices at Kenilworth. Gascoigne's printed rendition of the events—the full title of which is *A Briefe Rehearsall, or Rather a True Copie of as Much as Was Presented Before her Majesti[e] at Kenelworth During Her Last Aboade There*—was, at least on several fronts, wishful thinking. There is significant evidence that some of the events that were supposed to have been performed, and which Gascoigne describes in his account, were canceled because Elizabeth, offended by their content, censored them. Gascoigne's "true copie" of what happened at Kenilworth is rendered further suspect by the appearance of another report published immediately after the entertainments and describing details that Gascoigne does not. The publication, known as *Laneham's Letter*, purports to be the eyewitness account of the Kenilworth entertainments written by Robert Laneham (or Langham) and sent by epistle to a mercer in London named Humphrey Martin.[9] The text was, in fact, an elaborate joke, the author's attempt to mock, by impersonating, a court officer named Robert Langham.[10] As Susan Frye argues, the *Letter* goes further to mock court culture more generally, taking pleasure in describing "details that dampen the glory at Kenilworth."[11] Whether such details captured the reality of the performance that Gascoigne (understandably) chose not to report or whether the author of the *Letter* embellishes his account of the festivities in order to amplify his satire of the court is less important than considering what difference such details make to the representation of Elizabeth and, for the purposes of my analysis, for the representation of female vocal agency. As Frye importantly observes, the *Letter* "grants Elizabeth a dissenting voice," using her reactions to highlight the absurdities of the festivities and particularly to distance her from "the suspiciously lavish praise heaped on Dudley."[12] Frye argues that the Queen reasserts her authority over Dudley later during the visit, when she actively shapes the representation of herself in a number of the entertainments. The *Letter* suggests, however, that it is in the Echo scene, performed much earlier than the events Frye emphasizes, that Elizabeth exercises her authority most cannily.

According to the *Letter*, the Echo scene, rather than providing gushing praise for Dudley, becomes a moment of significant embarrassment for Gascoigne and, by association, for Dudley. The *Letter* narrates how after the Savage Man, played by Gascoigne, completed his speeches, he attempted to show "submission" to the Queen, most likely by bowing. But in the process of taking his bow, he mistakenly "brake hiz tree a sunder," or broke his staff. The *Letter*'s narrator tells of how the top of the staff then flew off, almost hitting Elizabeth's horse on the head and causing the horse to become "startld." While others, including one gentleman "mooch dismayed," tried desperately to bring order to the debacle, calming the horse and attending to Elizabeth, Elizabeth remained unruffled, demonstrating much "benignitée" as she called out "no hurt, no hurt!" The *Letter*'s author calls these words "the best part of the play."[13] This record of Elizabeth's vocal reactions to Gascoigne's ridiculous guffaw is fascinating for the ways it criticizes Gascoigne's and Dudley's attempts to use Echo to speak for Elizabeth. In Gascoigne's printed version of the event, Elizabeth stands by quietly while Dudley and Gascoigne use Echo to voice the Queen's supposed desires. Elizabeth's silence, carefully scripted by Gascoigne and Dudley, is meant to signal her acquiescence to Dudley's self-flattery and impudent representation of himself as a fitting consort for the Queen. In contrast, the *Letter* emphasizes Elizabeth's "benignitée," her graciousness in putting up with the ridiculous antics that surround her. In showing Elizabeth calmly reacting to the commotion that left others "mooch dismayd," the *Letter* intimates that Elizabeth's quiet observation of events at Kenilworth signifies not her acquiescence to the representations of herself and Dudley—which are shown to be utterly laughable—but rather serves as a testament to her strength of character and tolerance for Dudley and Gascoigne's impertinence and foolishness.

Laneham's Letter has attracted the interests of critics for the ways it divulges details of royal entertainments and court culture, as well as for what it reveals about the construction of Elizabeth's image. But in its content and form, it comments powerfully as well on the volatility of live performance and the ways that volatility could be exploited to make room for social and political critique. One of the ways the *Letter* undermines Gascoigne's efforts to script praise for Dudley is by calling attention to Gascoigne's Echo episode as a theatrical failure. The Savage Man's "dialogue" with Echo appears stiff and overscripted when set against the unplanned, almost slapstick scene finale described in the *Letter*. Laneham sets up his readers for the contrast by first describing in flattering detail Gascoigne's Echo invention: "pronounced in good meter and matter, very wel indighted in rime. Echo finely framed most aptly by answerz thus to utter all."[14] We need only compare Gascoigne's Echo against her portrayal by other poets (especially Ovid) to recognize this hyperbolic praise of Gascoigne's meter and rhyme as part of the joke. Even as Gascoigne reports the dialogue in his biased *Princely Pleasures*, its echoic rhymes are silly and conventional. Such "second-rate quality" of verse is, in fact, typical of that found in country-house revels, which were often written quickly and without much advance notice so that they might respond to the aristocratic audience's whims and in situ comments.[15] In contrast to Gascoigne's aesthetically underwhelming, scripted verse, the Savage Man's unscripted misadventures with his staff are great drama, unpredictable and genuinely funny. The *Letter*'s author's preference for the latter, more spontaneous part of the performance is confirmed by his closing quip that the Queen's "no hurt, no hurt" was "the best part of the play." Using aesthetic arguments, the *Letter* criticizes Gascoigne scripting of the Kenilworth festivities, presenting the performance space as, in fact, impossible to script and showing how the volatility of live performance both improves the quality of the theatrical experience and promotes the production of unexpected, transgressive meanings. Gascoigne may be able to write a female character who dutifully repeats praise of Dudley, but once unleashed on a live stage, no character's lines or actions can be fully controlled. And this, the *Letter* intimates, is what makes theater both pleasurable and politically efficacious.

Laneham's Letter confirms its argument about the volatility of performance through its own form, an unauthorized record of a court event. It is immaterial whether early modern readers of the *Letter* believed that it provided an accurate report of what happened at Kenilworth. Simply through its existence, the *Letter* reminds readers that Kenilworth's entertainments were live performances, rendering all published accounts one step removed. In so doing, the *Letter* undermines Gascoigne's later attempt to stabilize the performance through the publication of a more "reliable" transcription. Gascoigne's *Princely Pleasures* may carry the weight of authority in the world of printed books, but *Laneham's Letter*, simply by existing as an alternate account, challenges Gascoigne's textual authority, framing Gascoigne's "true copie" as simply another competing representation. Because the Kenilworth entertainments were performed live, they elude the control even of the author who created the bulk of them. Gascoigne's efforts to script the Queen's voice after the fact in print were ultimately no more successful than the Savage Man's efforts to script her voice during the theatrical event.

Whatever its relationship to the events at Kenilworth, *Laneham's Letter* depicts their performance as unpredictable. The text proves especially generative from my perspective in that it demonstrates the way Elizabeth could take advantage of theatrical volatility to critique the Echo scene's content and expand its meanings. *Laneham's Letter* thus encapsulates the theory of vocal agency that I have outlined throughout this book. I have argued that early modern performance conditions, because they were so volatile, left room for alternative forms of female vocal agency to be described and expressed. When understood as produced by an unstable humoral body, as composed of ephemeral breath, and as received by unpredictable listeners, the voices of the early modern stage exposed the impossibility of vocal control. In so doing, these voices were a resource for women and others far less privileged than Elizabeth. Indeed, especially for those who were socially or politically policed in their efforts to "speak out," the voices in motion onstage pointed toward a model of vocal agency that resisted foreclosure.

Notes

Introduction

1. Judith Butler, *Excitable Speech: A Politics of the Performative* (New York: Routledge, 1997), 7.

2. François Rabelais, *The Histories of Gargantua and Pantagruel*, trans. J. M. Cohen (New York: Penguin Books, 1985), 569. Rabelais, in fact, is retelling a classical story found in Plutarch's *Moralia*. See *Plutarch's Moralia*, trans. Frank Cole Babbit, vol. 1 (London: Heinemann, 1927), esp. 418–21.

3. Judith H. Anderson, *Words That Matter: Linguistic Perception in Renaissance English* (Stanford, Calif.: Stanford University Press, 1996), 19. For an introduction to sixteenth-century ideas about language, and especially the Elizabethan interest in the materiality of speech, see Jane Donawerth, *Shakespeare and the Sixteenth-Century Study of Language* (Urbana: University of Illinois Press, 1984), esp. chap. 1. Donawerth captures Renaissance authors' nervousness about the material dimensions of speech, about *vox*. She argues, however, that authors imagined men could transcend physical limitations through their capacity to organize voice into rational speech, *oratio*. I share Donawerth's interest in early modern writers' concerns about the necessarily chaotic physical conditions of speech. But where Donawerth maintains that the speaker's vocal authority depends on an ability to transcend these material dimensions—through an emphasis on language as reason—I argue that, for some early modern authors, such authority can be located in the material conditions of vocal communication, no matter how unpredictable such conditions may be.

4. Other key scholarship addressing the materiality of language through a focus on writing and/or print culture includes Jennifer Andersen and Elizabeth Sauer, eds., *Books and Readers in Early Modern England: Material Studies*, Material Texts (Philadelphia: University of Pennsylvania Press, 2002); Alain Boureau and Roger Chartier, *The Cultural Uses of Print in Early Modern France*, trans. Lydia G. Cochrane (Princeton, N.J.: Princeton University Press, 1989); Roger Chartier, *The Order of Books: Readers, Authors and Libraries in Europe between the Fourteenth and Eighteenth Centuries*, trans. Lydia G. Cochrane (Cambridge: Polity Press, 1994); Roger Chartier, *Forms and Meanings: Texts, Performances, and Audiences from Codex to Computer*, New Cultural Studies (Philadelphia: University of Pennsylvania Press, 1995); Julia Crick and Alexandra Walsham, eds., *The Uses of Script and Print, 1300–1700* (Cambridge: Cambridge University Press, 2004); Martin Elsky, *Authorizing Words: Speech, Writing, and Print in the English Renaissance* (Ithaca, N.Y.: Cornell University Press, 1989); Juliet Fleming, *Graffiti and the Writing Arts of Early Modern England*, Material

Texts (Philadelphia: University of Pennsylvania Press, 2001); Jonathan Goldberg, *Writing Matter: From the Hands of the English Renaissance* (Stanford: Stanford University Press, 1990); David Scott Kastan, *Shakespeare After Theory* (New York: Routledge, 1999); Harold Love, *Scribal Publication in Seventeenth-Century England* (Oxford: Clarendon, 1993); Arthur F. Marotti, *Manuscript, Print, and the English Renaissance Lyric* (Ithaca, N.Y.: Cornell University Press, 1995); Arthur F. Marotti and Michael D. Bristol, eds., *Print, Manuscript, and Performance: The Changing Relations of the Media in Early Modern England* (Columbus: Ohio State University Press, 2000); Evelyn B. Tribble, *Margins and Marginality: The Printed Page in Early Modern England* (Charlottesville: University Press of Virginia, 1993); Wendy Wall, *The Imprint of Gender: Authorship and Publication in the English Renaissance* (Ithaca, N.Y.: Cornell University Press, 1993); H. R. Woudhuysen, *Sir Philip Sidney and the Circulation of Manuscripts, 1558–1640* (Oxford: Clarendon, 1996).

5. On the differences between speech-act theory and conversation analysis and for excellent applications of the latter approaches to early modern literature, see Lynne Magnusson, *Shakespeare and Social Dialogue: Dramatic Language and Elizabeth Letters* (Cambridge: Cambridge University Press, 1999); David Schalkwyk, *Speech and Performance in Shakespeare's Sonnets and Plays* (Cambridge: Cambridge University Press, 2002); and Heather Dubrow, "'The tip of his seducing tongue': Authorizers in *Henry V*, 'A Lover's Complaint,' and *Othello*," in Shirley Sharon-Zisser, ed., *Suffering Ecstasy: Essays on Shakespeare's "A Lover's Complaint"* (Aldershot, Hampshire: Ashgate, forthcoming). My thanks to Heather Dubrow for sharing with me her work and her fruitful insights into speech-act theory.

6. Wayne A. Rebhorn, *The Emperor of Men's Minds: Literature and the Renaissance Discourse of Rhetoric*, Rhetoric & Society (Ithaca, N.Y.: Cornell University Press, 1995). See also Patricia Parker, *Literary Fat Ladies: Rhetoric, Gender, Property* (London: Methuen, 1987).

7. Leslie C. Dunn and Nancy A. Jones, eds., *Embodied Voices: Representing Female Vocality in Western Culture* (Cambridge: Cambridge University Press, 1994), 1–2.

8. Roland Barthes, "The Grain of the Voice," in *Image, Music, Text*, trans. Stephen Heath (New York: Hill and Wang, 1977), 181–82. On music, gender, and vocal performance, see Jacquelyn Fox-Good, "Other Voices: The Sweet, Dangerous Air(s) of Shakespeare's *Tempest*," *Shakespeare Studies* 24 (1996): 241–74; Leslie Dunn, "Ophelia's Songs in *Hamlet*: Music, Madness, and the Feminine," in Dunn and Jones, eds., *Embodied Voices*, 50–64; Linda Phyllis Austern, *Music in Children's Drama of the Later Renaissance* (Philadelphia: Gordon and Breach, 1992); Linda Phyllis Austern, "'No Women Are Indeed': The Boy Actor as Vocal Seductress in Late Sixteenth- and Early Seventeenth-Century English Drama," in Dunn and Jones, eds., *Embodied Voices*, 83–102; Susan McClary, *Feminine Endings: Music, Gender, and Sexuality* (Minneapolis: University of Minnesota Press, 1991).

9. This is not to suggest that such factors are irrelevant to the study of song; but concerns about sound transmission and audience are, as I argue, a persistent thematic feature in early modern plays, regardless of whether they include song.

10. Barthes, 188; emphasis mine.

11. I borrow the term from Jeffrey Masten, Peter Stallybrass, and Nancy Vickers,

Language Machines: Technologies of Literary and Cultural Production (New York: Routledge, 1997). This excellent collection represents a rare scholarly effort to recognize voice as one of a number of media technologies. In their introduction, the editors discuss the early modern body as a voice-producing machine; the essays in the section "Voice" focus on the modern period, however.

12. Bruce R. Smith, *The Acoustic World of Early Modern England: Attending to the O-Factor* (Chicago: University of Chicago Press, 1999), 18.

13. See, for example, the essays in Andersen and Sauer's collection, and the seminal work by Chartier cited above.

14. Goldberg, *Writing Matter.*

15. Smith, *Acoustic World,* 12. On the deconstructive potential of voice, see Jonathan Goldberg, "Shakespearean Inscriptions: The Voicing of Power," in *Shakespeare and the Question of Theory,* ed. Patricia Parker and Geoffrey Hartman (New York: Methuen, 1985), 116–37. For Goldberg, however, the voice's deconstructive potential is textual in nature: "When speech occurs, when the voice sounds, there is always another in the voice, an otherness that accompanies the utterer. . . . [T]hat voice may be called the text" (130).

16. Smith, *Acoustic World,* 18. On how early modern discourses of sound inform Shakespearean drama, see also Wes Folkerth, *The Sound of Shakespeare,* Accents on Shakespeare (New York: Routledge, 1992). Smith's and Folkerth's arguments participate in a broader critical movement that challenges Walter Ong's influential conception that a culture is either predominantly oral or predominantly literate. Walter Ong, *Orality and Literacy: The Technologizing of the Word* (London: Methuen, 1982). Critics attuned to the medium of sound have found evidence of significant overlaps of oral and literate forms of expression, especially among nonmodern and non-Western cultures. In addition to Smith, see Sylvia Scribner and Michael Cole, *The Psychology of Literacy* (Cambridge: Cambridge University Press, 1981); Ruth H. Finnegan, *Literacy and Orality: Studies in the Technology of Communication* (Oxford: Basil Blackwell, 1988); Brian V. Street, *Literacy in Theory and Practice* (Cambridge: Cambridge University Press, 1984). There is increasing evidence, for example, that many early modern English texts were constructed to be read aloud, implicating the voice in what was once considered a purely "literate" act. See, for example, Elsky. Critical work on aurality reminds early modern scholars of listeners' persistent presence and of the importance of sound to early modern modalities of perception and cognition. For an excellent overview of the orality/literacy binary and the place of aurality studies, see Joyce Coleman, *Public Reading and the Reading Public in Late Medieval England and France* (Cambridge: Cambridge University Press, 1996).

17. Jonathan Gil Harris and Natasha Korda, eds., *Staged Properties in Early Modern English Drama* (Cambridge: Cambridge University Press, 2002), 7. A number of scholars have addressed these problems. See, for instance, Natasha Korda, *Shakespeare's Domestic Economies: Gender and Property in Early Modern England* (Philadelphia: University of Pennsylvania Press, 2002), which I discuss further below; Margreta de Grazia, Maureen Quilligan, and Peter Stallybrass, eds., *Subject and Object in Renaissance Culture,* Cambridge Studies in Renaissance Literature and Culture (Cambridge: Cambridge University Press, 1996); Patricia Fumerton, *Cultural Aesthetics:*

Renaissance Literature and the Practice of Social Ornament (Chicago: University of Chicago Press, 1991); Patricia Fumerton and Simon Hunt, eds., *Renaissance Culture and the Everyday* (Philadelphia: University of Pennsylvania Press, 1999); Lena Cowen Orlin, ed., *Material London, ca. 1600* (Philadelphia: University of Pennsylvania Press, 2000); Douglas Bruster, *Drama and Market in the Age of Shakespeare* (Cambridge: Cambridge University Press, 1992); Andrew Sofer, *The Stage Life of Props* (Ann Arbor: University of Michigan Press, 2003); Peter Stallybrass and Ann Rosalind Jones, *Renaissance Clothes and the Materials of Memory*, Cambridge Studies in Renaissance Literature and Culture (Cambridge: Cambridge University Press, 2000); Will Fisher, *Materializing Gender in Early Modern Literature and Culture*, Cambridge Studies in Renaissance Literature and Culture (Cambridge: Cambridge University Press, 2006); Holly E. Dugan, "The Ephemeral History of Perfume: Scent and Sense in Early Modern England" (Ph.D. dissertation, University of Michigan, 2005).

18. Douglas Bruster, *Shakespeare and the Question of Culture: Early Modern Literature and the Cultural Turn*, Early Modern Cultural Studies (New York: Palgrave, 2003), 204. Bruster argues that a more efficacious form of "new materialist" scholarship would attend more carefully to sixteenth- and seventeenth-century materialist thought. An exemplary essay, cited by Bruster, is Henry S. Turner, "Nashe's Red Herring: Epistemologies of the Commodity in *Lenten Stuffe* (1599)," *ELH* 68, no. 3 (2001): 529–61.

19. Korda, *Domestic Economies*, 7.

20. As Korda writes, "it is because matter is not entirely malleable, because its movements do not always obey prescribed paradigms of ownership and exchange, that it does matter. For it is often the forms of resistance or agency to which these movements point that produce ideological change" (ibid.).

21. On the theater's location in the liberties, see Steven Mullaney, *The Place of the Stage: License, Play, and Power in Renaissance England* (Chicago: University of Chicago Press, 1988); on playwrights, see Paul Yachnin, *Stage-Wrights: Shakespeare, Jonson, Middleton, and the Making of Theatrical Value* (Philadelphia: University of Pennsylvania Press, 1997); on props, see Harris and Korda, *Staged Properties*; and Sofer.

22. Mary Thomas Crane makes a similar point: "If we are able to view discourse and embodiment, representation and experience, as mutually constitutive aspects of performance rather than assuming that discourse and representation subsume the other two, a way is cleared for a broader view of the evolving concepts of theater and performance in early modern England." Mary Thomas Crane, "What Was Performance?" *Criticism* 43, no. 2 (2001), 171.

23. The great range of texts featuring sound is demonstrated in Smith, *Acoustic World*.

24. This is particularly true when the texts and events we study elude archival memory. As Mark Franko and Annette Richards suggest, "If texts are no longer the containers of truth, and if events remain unavailable in their visceral facticity as 'done deeds,' then act and text can be summoned to redefine one another in or as the performative presence of interpretation." Mark Franko and Annette Richards, eds., *Acting on the Past: Historical Performance Across the Disciplines* (Hanover, N.J.: Wesleyan

University Press, 2000), 2. An excellent example of this kind of approach to performance is P. A. Skantze, *Stillness in Motion in the Seventeenth-Century Theatre*, Routledge Studies in Renaissance Literature and Culture (New York: Routledge, 2003).

25. I cite from L. A. Beaurline, ed., *King John*, New Cambridge Shakespeare (Cambridge: Cambridge University Press, 1990). Unless otherwise noted, all other citations of Shakespeare's plays follow Stephen Greenblatt, ed., *The Norton Shakespeare*, 2d ed. (New York: W. W. Norton, 1997).

26. Michael C. Schoenfeldt, *Bodies and Selves in Early Modern England: Physiology and Inwardness in Spenser, Shakespeare, Herbert, and Milton*, Cambridge Studies in Renaissance Literature and Culture (Cambridge: Cambridge University Press, 1999), 11–12.

27. Schoenfeldt refers here specifically to Thomas Laqueur, *Making Sex: Body and Gender from the Greeks to Freud* (Cambridge, Mass.: Harvard University Press, 1990); and Gail Kern Paster, *The Body Embarrassed: Drama and the Disciplines of Shame in Early Modern England* (Ithaca, N.Y.: Cornell University Press, 1993).

28. Gary Spear, "Shakespeare's 'Manly' Parts: Masculinity and Effeminacy in *Troilus and Cressida*," *Shakespeare Quarterly* 44, no. 4 (1993). For a helpful introduction to masculinity in Shakespeare and the early modern period, see Bruce R. Smith, *Shakespeare and Masculinity*, Oxford Shakespeare Topics (Oxford: Oxford University Press, 2000).

29. In her recent book, Paster offers a somewhat different argument, maintaining that some elite men perform a *lack* of control (primarily of their emotions, though this may be expressed through volatile speech) in order to assert their individuality and their higher status. They demonstrate their superior social position by claiming the "humoral right of way," the prerogative to be more emotionally volatile because of their hot-bloodedness. Gail Kern Paster, *Humoring the Body: Emotions and the Shakespearean Stage* (Chicago: University of Chicago Press, 2004), 231. Notably, however, Paster also emphasizes, like Schoenfeldt, the ways male impulsiveness is given form through rules and structures. See her astute analysis of the querulous vapors game in Ben Jonson's *Bartholomew Fair*, which figures "emotionally embodied life as a difficult, fluid, but rule-bound form of play with opposition itself as its event, structure, and goal" (240).

30. This is not to suggest that such instruction was given *only* to women. Indeed, early modern authors offer lessons in vocal conduct to men as well. Nevertheless, there seems to be significantly more anxiety in the period around women and when and how they should speak. For some of these perspectives, see Katherine Usher Henderson and Barbara F. McManus, *Half Humankind: Contexts and Texts of the Controversy about Women in England, 1540–1640* (Urbana: University of Illinois Press, 1985).

31. Interestingly, Paster reaches a related conclusion in her recent work. See the discussion of virgin melancholia in *Humoring the Body*, chap. 2. Paster argues that when humoral discourse represents a young woman's body as heating up as she reaches sexual maturity, it normalizes the "aggressive agency such heat entails" (87). The forms of agency I trace are equally powerful, albeit more elusive insofar as they do not manifest themselves as aggression.

32. It is with some hesitation that I rely on these categories of feminist thought,

"liberal," "cultural," and so forth. The approaches are not easily defined, mutually exclusive, or fully representative of the range of theorists. I offer them, however, simply as a guiding rubric to the diverse ways that "voice" has been used in feminist thought.

33. National Organization for Women, "Statement of Purpose," in *Feminist Theory: A Reader*, ed. Wendy Kolmar and Frances Bartkowski (Mountain View, Calif.: Mayfield Publishing Company, 1966), 169–71.

34. Carol Gilligan, *In a Different Voice* (Cambridge, Mass.: Harvard University Press, 1982).

35. See, for example, Hélène Cixous, "The Laugh of the Medusa," *Signs: Journal of Women in Culture and Society* 1, no. 4 (1976): 875–93; Luce Irigaray, *This Sex Which Is Not One*, trans. Catherine Porter (Ithaca, N.Y.: Cornell University Press, 1985).

36. See, for example, Norma Alarcon, "The Theoretical Subject(s) of This Bridge Called My Back and Anglo-American Feminism," in *Making Face, Making Soul: Haciendo Caras*, ed. Gloria Anzaldua (San Francisco: aunt lute, 1990), 356–69; Maria C. Lugones and Elizabeth Spelman, "Have We Got a Theory for You! Feminist Theory, Cultural Imperialism and the Demand for 'The Woman's Voice,'" *Women's Studies International Forum* 6 (1983): 573–81.

37. Kathleen Donovan, *Feminist Readings of Native American Literature: Coming to Voice* (Tucson: University of Arizona Press, 1998); Sybil Sheridan, *Hear Our Voice: Women in the British Rabbinate*, Studies in Comparative Religion (Columbia: University of South Carolina Press, 1998).

38. Voice is used in such ways in areas outside feminist theory as well. In particular, literary critics have used the term "voice" to describe poetic subjectivity, often intimating the kind of presence I am problematizing.

39. J. L. Austin, *How to Do Things with Words*, ed. J. O. Urmson and Marina Sbisà, 2d ed. (Cambridge, Mass.: Harvard University Press, 1975), 60.

40. Andrew Parker and Eve Kosofsky Sedgwick, eds., *Performativity and Performance* (New York and New York: Routledge, 1995), 7.

41. See Butler, *Excitable Speech*, esp. 10–11.

42. Ibid., 152.

43. See Jacques Derrida, "Signature Event Context," *Glyph: Johns Hopkins Textual Studies* 1 (1977): 172–97. See also Jacques Derrida, *Speech and Phenomena and Other Essays on Husserl's Theory of Signs*, trans. David B. Allison (Evanston, Ill.: Northwestern University Press, 1973).

44. See, for example, Linda Bamber, *Comic Women, Tragic Men: A Study of Gender and Genre in Shakespeare* (Stanford, Calif.: Stanford University Press, 1982); Lynda E. Boose, "Scolding Brides and Bridling Scolds: Taming the Woman's Unruly Member," *Shakespeare Quarterly* 42, no. 2 (1991): 179–213; Paster, *The Body Embarrassed*; Peter Stallybrass, "Patriarchal Territories: The Body Enclosed," in *Rewriting the Renaissance: The Discourses of Sexual Difference in Early Modern Europe*, ed. Margaret Ferguson, Maureen Quilligan, and Nancy Vickers (Chicago: University of Chicago Press, 1986), 123–42.

45. See, for example, Maurice Charney and Hanna Charney, "The Language of Madwomen in Shakespeare and His Fellow Dramatists," *Signs* 3 (1977): 45–60; Debo-

rah T. Curren-Aquino, "Toward a Star That Danced: Woman as Survivor in Shake-speare's Early Comedies," *Selected Papers from the West Virginia Shakespeare and Renaissance Association* 11 (1986): 50–61; Christy Desmet, "Speaking Sensibly: Feminine Rhetoric in *Measure for Measure* and *All's Well That Ends Well*," *Renaissance Papers 1986* (1987): 43–51; Inga-Stina Ewbank, "Shakespeare's Portrayal of Women: A 1970's View," in *Shakespeare: Pattern of Excelling Nature*, ed. David Bevington and Jay L. Halio (Newark: University of Delaware Press, 1978), 222–29; Joel Fineman, "The Turn of the Shrew," in *Shakespeare and the Question of Theory*, ed. Patricia Parker and Geoffrey Hartman (New York and London: Methuen, 1985), 138–59; Carole McKewin, "Counsels of Gall and Grace: Intimate Conversations between Women in Shake-speare's Plays," in *The Woman's Part: Feminist Criticism of Shakespeare*, ed. Carolyn Ruth Swift Lenz, Gayle Green, and Carol Thomas Neely (Urbana: University of Illinois Press, 1980), 117–32; Betty G. Norvell, "The Dramatic Portrait of Margaret in Shakespeare's Henry VI Plays," *Bulletin of the West Virginia Association of College English Teachers* 8 (1983): 38–44; Patricia Parker, *Shakespeare from the Margins: Language, Culture, Context* (Chicago: University of Chicago Press, 1996); Edward Snow, "Language and Sexual Difference in *Romeo and Juliet*," in *Shakespeare's "Rough Magic": Renaissance Essays in Honor of C. L. Barber*, ed. Peter Erickson and Coppélia Kahn (Newark: University of Delaware Press, 1985), 168–92; Valerie Wayne, "Refashioning the Shrew," *Shakespeare Studies* 17 (1985): 159–87.

46. Christina Luckyj, *"A Moving Rhetoricke": Gender and Silence in Early Modern England* (Manchester: Manchester University Press, 2002), 8. Other perceptive feminist studies that trouble the silence/speech binary include Heather Dubrow, *Echoes of Desire: English Petrarchism and Its Counterdiscourses* (Ithaca, N.Y.: Cornell University Press, 1995); Lynn Enterline, *The Rhetoric of the Body from Ovid to Shakespeare*, Cambridge Studies in Renaissance Literature and Culture (Cambridge: Cambridge University Press, 2000); Mary Ellen Lamb, "The Countess of Pembroke and the Art of Dying," in *Women in the Middle Ages and the Renaissance: Literary and Historical Perspectives*, ed. Mary Beth Rose (Syracuse, N.Y.: Syracuse University Press, 1986), 207–26; and Katharine Eisaman Maus, *Inwardness and Theater in the English Renaissance* (Chicago: University of Chicago Press, 1995). On the productive work of silence in Shakespeare's plays, see Philip C. McGuire, *Speechless Dialect: Shakespeare's Open Silences* (Berkeley and Los Angeles: University of California Press, 1985).

47. Many of the insights these scholars have offered are central to my own methodology, especially their astute discussions of loss of voice as a condition of female subjectivity and their emphasis on male anxieties about the voice's dislocation from self. See Lynn Enterline, *The Tears of Narcissus: Melancholia and Masculinity in Early Modern Writing* (Stanford, Calif.: Stanford University Press, 1995); Enterline, *Rhetoric of the Body*; Goldberg, "Shakespearean Inscriptions"; Elizabeth D. Harvey, *Ventriloquized Voices: Feminist Theory and English Renaissance Texts* (New York: Routledge, 1992); Carla Mazzio, "Sins of the Tongue," in *The Body in Parts: Fantasies of Corporeality in Early Modern Europe*, ed. David Hillman and Carla Mazzio (New York: Routledge, 1997), 53–79. Other fruitful approaches include Emily C. Bartels, "Strategies of Submission: Desdemona, the Duchess, and the Assertion of Desire," *SEL* 36 (1996):

417–33; Frances E. Dolan, "'Gentleman, I Have One Thing More to Say': Women on Scaffolds in England, 1563–1680," *Modern Philology* 92, no. 2 (1994): 157–78; Dubrow, *Echoes of Desire*.

48. Dympna Callaghan, "The Castrator's Song: Female Impersonation on the Early Modern Stage," *Journal of Medieval and Early Modern Studies* 26, no. 2 (1996): 321–530. An expanded version of the essay appears in Dympna Callaghan, *Shakespeare Without Women: Representing Gender and Race on the Renaissance Stage*, Accents on Shakespeare (New York: Routledge, 2000).

49. Callaghan, "Castrator's Song," 324.

50. For an influential argument on this point as it relates to the emergence of transgressive ideas in the theater, see Jean E. Howard, *The Stage and Social Struggle in Early Modern England* (New York: Routledge, 1994).

Chapter 1

1. Stephen Orgel, *Impersonations: The Performance of Gender in Shakespeare's England* (Cambridge: Cambridge University Press, 1996). Although Orgel devotes some attention to the voices of boy actors, the study privileges visual signifiers of gender performance, such as costuming. The centrality of the visual is suggested by half of the chapter titles: "The Eye of the Beholder"; "Masculine Apparel"; and the concluding essay, "Visible Figures." There is, notably, great debate in the period itself about whether playgoers should privilege their eyes over their ears in the theater. See Andrew Gurr, *Playgoing in Shakespeare's London*, 2d ed. (Cambridge: Cambridge University Press, 1996), 86–104.

2. John Madden, dir., *Shakespeare in Love* (Miramax Films, 1998); Michael Hoffman, dir., *William Shakespeare's A Midsummer Night's Dream* (Fox Searchlight Pictures, 1999).

3. Here the film takes artistic license with historical evidence. Although female stage performers were disparaged by early modern writers concerned with morality and theology, scholars have not discovered legal statutes prohibiting women from performing.

4. It is conceivable that boys whose voices began to squeak held on to their roles longer than is suggested by Madden's film. Theater companies requested money from the crown for the care of boys whose voices had fully cracked, representing these boys as a financial burden. See E. K. Chambers, *The Elizabethan Stage*, 4 vols., vol. 2 (Oxford: Clarendon, 1923). But records from the period do not confirm that boys abandoned their performance careers when their high voices began to squeak at puberty, and there is even less evidence concerning how the theater dealt with male voices while they were in the process of changing.

5. The term "male masculinity" is not redundant. As Eve Kosofsky Segwick reminds us, "when something is about masculinity, it is not always 'about men.'" Eve Kosofsky Sedgwick, "'Gosh, Boy George, You Must Be Awfully Secure in Your Masculinity!'" in *Constructing Masculinity*, ed. Maurice Berger, Brian Wallis, and Simon Watson (New

York: Routledge, 1995), esp. 12. For interesting work on female masculinity, see Judith Halberstam, *Female Masculinity* (Durham, N.C.: Duke University Press, 1998). Although masculinity is not the exclusive property of men, in early modern England *ideal* men are defined (in a range of cultural discourses) in terms of their exhibition of masculine traits, such as courage and control, especially, I argue, as these pertain to voice. Work on early modern masculinity that informs my approach to the subject in this chapter includes: Rebecca Ann Bach, "Tennis Balls: *Henry V* and Testicular Masculinity; or, According to the *OED*, Shakespeare Doesn't Have Any Balls," *Renaissance Drama* 30 (1999–2001): 3–23; Mark Breitenberg, *Anxious Masculinity in Early Modern England* (Cambridge: Cambridge University Press, 1996); Donald Hedrick, "Male Surplus Value," *Renaissance Drama* 31 (2002): 85–124; Ian Frederick Moulton, "'A Monster Great Deformed': The Unruly Masculinity of *Richard III*," *Shakespeare Quarterly* 47, no. 3 (1996): 251–68; Smith, *Shakespeare and Masculinity*; Spear. My discussion of aging and masculinity is indebted to Judith Kegan Gardiner, "Theorizing Age with Gender: Bly's Boys, Feminism, and Maturity Masculinity," in *Masculinity Studies and Feminist Theory: New Directions*, ed. Judith Kegan Gardiner (New York: Columbia University Press, 2002), 90–118.

6. Recent scholars have begun to turn much needed attention to children's companies and the full representational possibilities of the boy actor. Lucy Munro, *Children of the Queen's Revels: A Jacobean Theatre Repertory* (Cambridge: Cambridge University Press, 2005) provides a thorough study of one particular children's company; for a useful discussion of the ways boys performed not only gender- but age- and class-transvesticism, see chap. 1. See also Will Fisher, "The Renaissance Beard: Masculinity in Early Modern England," *Renaissance Quarterly* 54, no. 1 (2001): 155–87, which examines the prop of the beard as it was used to distinguish young and old men, and thus fashion masculinity, in children's company plays.

7. Sir Francis Bacon, *Sylva Sylvarum: Or a Naturall Historie* (London, 1626), no. 180.

8. Levinus Lemnius, *The Touchstone of Complexions Generallye Appliable, Expedient and Profitable for All Such, As Be Desirous & Carefull of Their Bodylye Health* (London, 1576), 45v.

9. Smith, *Acoustic World*, 100–101.

10. Robert Herrick, *Hesperides, or The Works Both Human & Divine* (London, 1648), 169.

11. Bacon, *Sylva Sylvarum*, no. 117; no. 237.

12. John Dolman, trans., *Those Fyve Questions, Which Marke Tullye Cicero, Disputed in His Manor of Tusculanum: Written Afterwardes by Him, in as Manye Bookes, to His Frende, and Familiar Brutus, in the Latine Tounge. And Nowe, Oute of the Same Translated, & Englished* (London, 1561), book 5 (no pagination).

13. William Gamage, *Linsi-Woolsie: Or Two Centuries of Epigrammes* (London, 1621), epigram 54.

14. Thomas Heywood, *The Fair Maid of the West. Or, a Girle Worth Gold* (London, 1631), 13.

15. James Shirley, *Changes: or, Love in a Maze* (London, 1632), 25.

16. John Marston, *The Malcontent and Other Plays*, ed. Keith Sturgess, The World's Classics (Oxford: Oxford University Press, 1997), 5.2.35–36. Unless otherwise indi-

cated, all citations of Marston's plays follow this edition and will, henceforth, appear in my text. The editors of the *Norton English Renaissance Drama* read this as evidence that the gallant is "evidently fond of pinching ladies' behinds and hearing the ladies squeak in reaction." David Bevington et al., eds., *English Renaissance Drama: A Norton Anthology* (New York: W. W. Norton, 2002), 5.5.41 n. 4. As seen in other references to men making women squeak, there is, however, a more explicitly bawdy implication to this term.

17. Paster, *The Body Embarrassed*. Paster offers a different argument in *Humoring the Body*, esp. chap. 4; see my discussion in the Introduction, n. 29.

18. Pace Schoenfeldt's insistence that the model of inwardness he traces is not gendered, I would maintain that the gender of the primarily male subjects he examines is not incidental to, but constitutive of, the emancipatory control they pursue. Moreover, attending to the gender differences at stake in humoral physiological models of identity does not necessarily entail privileging the genitals as a locus of identity, as Schoenfeldt maintains (*Bodies and Selves*). Indeed, as we have seen, gender differences in voice, according to the humoral paradigm, are a function of differences in the body's degree of heat. In their impact on the voice and its variability, changes in heat levels were imagined to have more sweeping implications for male rather than female bodies: early modern texts, especially those of the stage, exhibit far more interest in the voice changes that accompany male, rather than female, puberty.

19. Breitenberg, 53.

20. For a discussion of the role of humoral ideologies in perpetuating male anxieties, see Breitenberg, especially chap. 1.

21. On the social significance of the female voice, see, for example, Boose; Patricia Parker, "On the Tongue: Cross Gendering, Effeminacy, and the Art of Words," *Style* 23, no. 3 (1989): 445–65; and Stallybrass, "Patriarchal Territories." On visually oriented readings of the theatrical production of gender difference, see, in addition to Orgel (discussed in n. 1), Howard, *Stage and Social Struggle*, which also privileges the sights of the theater over its sounds. Howard's astute analysis of theatrical media focuses, for instance, on the "spectacle" of female cross-dressing.

22. Callaghan, "Castrator's Song," 323.

23. On liminal states of being and the production of gender difference in Renaissance tragedy, see Susan Zimmerman, "Marginal Man: The Representation of Horror in Renaissance Tragedy," in *Discontinuities: New Essays on Renaissance Literature and Criticism*, ed. Viviana Comensoli and Paul Stevens, Theory/Culture (Toronto: University of Toronto Press, 1998), 159–78. See also Smith, *Shakespeare and Masculinity*, chap. 3.

24. Richard Mulcaster, *Positions Wherin Those Primitive Circumstances Be Examined, Which Are Necessarie for the Training up of Children, Either for Skill in Their Booke, or Health in Their Bodie* (London, 1581). Citations will appear in my text. For a modern edition that includes a useful introduction to this eclectic work, see William Barker, ed., *Positions Concerning the Training Up of Young Children* (Toronto: University of Toronto Press, 1994).

25. Examining Marston's play in relation to Mulcaster's treatise is especially attractive given that both writers were in some way affiliated with St. Paul's. Although St.

Paul's grammar school, where Mulcaster taught, and the theater company Children of Paul's, for which Marston wrote, were entirely separate operations, there may have been some interaction between the two institutions. Michael Shapiro notes that Nathan Field, an actor in the Children of Paul's, claimed to be a student of Mulcaster's. Michael Shapiro, *Children of the Revels: The Boy Companies of Shakespeare's Time and Their Plays* (New York: Columbia University Press, 1977), 20. And scholars argue that child actors in Paul's company might have learned grammar and rhetoric at the nearby school. See Andrew Gurr, *The Shakespearean Stage, 1574–1642* (Cambridge: Cambridge University Press, 1970), 70; Adrian Weiss, "A Pill to Purge Parody: Marston's Manipulation of the Paul's Environment in the *Antonio* Plays," in *The Theatrical Space*, ed. James Redmond, Themes in Drama (Cambridge: Cambridge University Press, 1987), 81–97. Certainly the young male voices that are the subject of Mulcaster's education program were also a key feature of the children's theater company for which Marston wrote. The possession of some of England's finest young male voices helped children's companies like Paul's gain favor with the court and attract public audiences. For a discussion of how children's drama took advantage of these fine voices, see Austern, *Music in Children's Drama*. Austern points out that the voices of certain characters are only or primarily used in songs, indicating that there were less intensive acting roles reserved for boys who had voice training but not much dramatic training.

26. Ben Jonson, *Poetaster*, ed. Tom Cain, The Revels Plays (Manchester: Manchester University Press, 1995), 5.2.22.

27. Although many things are described as "breathing" in the period—in particular, music is often described this way, even when produced by an inanimate instrument—it is my sense that breath works analogically in these cases. Mellida's apostrophe, "O music, thou distill'st / More sweetness in us than this jarring world; / Both time and measure from thy strains do breathe" (*Antonio and Mellida* 2.1.190–92), imports from physiological/philosophical discourses about human breath a metaphor to describe the power of music to move the soul.

28. Historically speaking, careful control of the voice is not the predominant emphasis of vocal training. Many of today's British and American voice coaches offer the opposite advice: that pupils learn to "free" their voices. Indeed, for modern actors, freeing the voice effectively is very difficult and requires years of instruction and exercise. See, e.g., the writings of voice coaches, including: Cicely Berry, *The Actor and His Text* (New York: Scribner, 1988); Kristin Linklater, *Freeing Shakespeare's Voice: The Actor's Guide to Talking the Text* (New York: Theatre Communications Group, 1992); Patsy Rodenburg, *The Right to Speak: Working with the Voice* (London: Methuen, 1992).

29. Charles Butler, *The English Grammar, or the Institution of Letters, Syllables, and Words in the English Tongue* (London, 1633), 54.

30. Robert Robinson, *The Art of Pronunciation* (London, 1617), sig. A10r–A11v.

31. John Playford, *A Brief Introduction to the Skill of Musick: For Song and Viol* (London, 1658), sig. A2r–v.

32. Charles Butler, *The Principles of Musick, in Singing and Setting: With the Two-Fold Use Therof, (Ecclesiasticall and Civil)* (London, 1636), sig. 3r.

33. John Dowland, trans., *Andreas Ornithoparcus His Micrologus, or Introduction: Containing the Art of Singing* (London, 1609), 22.

34. Ibid., 21.

35. Ibid., 22.

36. Ibid., 90 [misprinted as 80].

37. See Barker. Shapiro counts eight recorded performances, as does Richard L. De-Mollen, "Richard Mulcaster and the Elizabethan Theatre," *Theatre Survey* 13, no. 1 (1972): 28–41.

38. See DeMollen. Credit for the revival of the Children of Paul's is usually given to Thomas Giles, who was in charge of the choir at St. Paul's. DeMollen points out, however, that several plays were performed under the name of Children of Paul's before Giles's contract began, suggesting perhaps that Mulcaster brought the children to court for these plays—one of which might have been *Antonio and Mellida*. Mulcaster has not been given credit because his name is not associated with the company during this period, but there is evidence that boys from Mulcaster's grammar school participated in plays (Nathan Field, e.g., was impressed by Blackfriars while he was a student at Mulcaster's grammar school).

39. Mulcaster has been called the best-known pedagogue of the period. Considered the archetype of the demanding schoolteacher, his name is alluded to explicitly in one play (Beaumont and Fletcher's *Knight of the Burning Pestle*), and DeMollen even argues that Mulcaster would have been the recognizable model for Holsefern in Shakespeare's *Love's Labour's Lost*.

40. Mulcaster is best known by literary scholars for his progressive ideas about education—that is, his belief that boys of all class positions should be educated in a uniform curriculum at a truly public school and that women should be educated to proficient levels of reading and writing. See Barker.

41. Note entrances involving running and walking as well as the staging of wrestling matches (e.g., *As You Like It*) and dancing scenes.

42. For an overview of ancient medical theories of vocal exercise, see Gretchen Finney, "Medical Theories of Vocal Exercise and Health," *Bulletin of the History of Medicine* 40, no. 5 (1966): 395–406.

43. Johann Vesling, *Anatomy of the Body of Man* (London, 1653), 45.

44. Helkiah Crooke, *Mikrokosmographia: A Description of the Body of Man* (London, 1615), 634.

45. Vesling, 44.

46. Henrie Cuffe, *The Differences of the Ages of Mans Life* (London, 1607) explains that male infants are born hot and wet but gradually decrease in moisture and heat until they become dry and cold in old age (115–20). There are variations on this paradigm in the period, but Cuffe's views represent the most common formulation of the relation between age and temperament.

47. Though Mulcaster believes that weeping and laughing are equally effective treatments for dislodging excess humors, he favors the latter over the former because it is more easily incorporated into a physical fitness curriculum. Mulcaster explains that a master who needs to whip his student to get him to cry risks being resented by

the student. Thus weeping, while it should not be disregarded completely, is not a preferred method.

48. Barker, xxiii.

49. Ann Brumwick, *Booke of Receipts*, Wellcome Western Manuscripts 160 (c. 1625–1700), 160.

50. On the status of evidence in theater history scholarship, see William Ingram, "What Kind of Future for the Theatrical Past: Or, What Will Count as Theater History in the Next Millennium?" *Shakespeare Quarterly* 48, no. 2 (1997): 215–25.

51. Shapiro, who discusses the theater history debate about style, points out that no single style could have been used in all plays by all characters. He halts the style debate by pointing out that children's companies likely used "different styles for different plays and parts of plays, just as directors and actors do today" (113).

52. It is on this point that I take issue with Smith's brilliant study *The Acoustic World of Early Modern England*. Bringing phenomenology to bear on historical analysis, Smith uses as evidence contemporary scientific studies of sound in order to understand what early modern theatergoers "would have heard" when they went to playhouses. I find Smith's methodology—the use of contemporary scientific discourse to shed light on early modern acoustics—to be intriguing, but I am wary of some of the positivist goals served by this methodology, with the book's overall aim of "historical reconstruction" (29).

53. Franko and Richards, 1.

54. Thomas Dekker, *The Shoemaker's Holiday*, ed. Anthony Parr (New York: W. W. Norton, 1997), 13.9–10.

55. G. Blakemore Evans, ed., *The Riverside Shakespeare*, 2d ed. (Boston: Houghton Mifflin Company, 1997), note to 2.2.428.

56. Smith, *Acoustic World*, 229.

57. Thomas Dekker, *The Honest Whore with, the Humours of the Patient Man, and the Longing Wife* (London, 1604), scene 7; sig. B2v.

58. As Ilana Krausman Ben-Amos points out, early moderns accepted a range of models of the life cycle. According to the Ptolemaic model, to take one example, there are seven phases, each of which corresponds with a planet: infancy, childhood, adolescence, young manhood, manhood and old age; the final age is a return to childishness. Ilana Krausman Ben-Amos, *Adolescence and Youth in Early Modern England* (New Haven, Conn.: Yale University Press, 1994).

59. It is important to keep in mind that these ages of transition are by no means precise. As Ben-Amos maintains, maturation was not linked clearly to the number of years someone had lived. The most important markers of maturation were determined by how an individual moved through major events, like leaving the parental home, entering into and leaving service, marriage, setting up business/managing lands (8). Such transitional events were contingent on each individual's particular circumstances, with gender and class playing a crucial role. Thus, adolescence could begin at age nine or as late as fourteen; youth could begin at ages fourteen or eighteen, even up to ages twenty-five or twenty-eight.

60. Smith, *Shakespeare and Masculinity*, 78.

61. *Oxford English Dictionary*, 2d ed. (Oxford: Oxford University Press, 1989), s.v. "crack," 7b.

62. The seminal work is Judith Butler, *Gender Trouble: Feminism and the Subversion of Identity* (New York: Routledge, 1990).

63. For an astute feminist analysis of the importance of theorizing age in terms of gender, see Gardiner.

64. Smith, *Shakespeare and Masculinity*, 85–86.

65. *Oxford English Dictionary*, s.v. "crack."

66. Ibid., s.v. "rope"; s.v. "halter."

67. Ben Jonson, *The Complete Plays of Ben Jonson*, ed. G. A. Wilkes, vol. 2 (Oxford: Clarendon Press, 1981), 2.1.3–8. Further citations will appear in my text.

68. According to Ptolemaic astrology, in which each age of life corresponds to one of the planets, childhood is associated with Mercury.

69. Thomas Heywood, *The Second Part of, If You Know Not Me, You Know No Bodie* (London, 1606), 1.1; D3r-v.

70. On Caius Martius's relationship with his mother, see, for example, Janet Adelman, *Suffocating Mothers: Fantasies of Maternal Origin in Shakespeare's Plays*, Hamlet *to* The Tempest (New York: Routledge, 1992); Coppélia Kahn, *Roman Shakespeare: Warriors, Wounds, and Women* (New York: Routledge, 1997); Madelon Sprengnether, "Annihilating Intimacy in *Coriolanus*," in *Women in the Middle Ages and the Renaissance: Literary and Historical Perspectives*, ed. Mary Beth Rose (Syracuse, N.Y.: Syracuse University Press, 1986), 89–111.

71. For a fascinating reading of the relationship between Coriolanus's masculinity and the methods by which his character achieves depth in the theater, see Cynthia Marshall, "Wound-Man: *Coriolanus*, Gender, and the Theatrical Construction of Interiority," in *Feminist Readings of Early Modern Culture: Emerging Subjects*, ed. Valerie Traub, M. Lindsay Kaplan, and Dympna Callaghan (Cambridge: Cambridge University Press, 1996). In her analysis of Coriolanus's refusal to show his wounds, Marshall argues, "*Coriolanus* shows masculinity to be, like the actor's body, a construction of surface effects that may become permeable. It shows interiority, on the other hand, to begin with permeability and to achieve meaning through the textual system in which it is read" (112).

72. Critics have noted, in particular, Marston's visual spectacles include complex blocking (e.g., the stage directions in act 3) and shocking set design (e.g., the body of Felice hung up in Mellida's window at the start of *Antonio's Revenge*).

73. For example, in one scene Marston has Balurdo enter partially costumed, his "beard half off, half on" (*Antonio's Revenge* 2.1.20). John Scott Colley explores Marston's self-conscious theatricality, arguing that Marston distances the viewer from the fiction, provoking the audience to judge the action of the stage—Brecht's alienation effect. John Scott Colley, *John Marston's Theatrical Drama*, Jacobean Drama Studies (Salzburg: Salzburg Studies in English Literature, 1974). It makes sense, as T. F. Wharton argues, that Marston's plays found their greatest admirers in audiences of Beckett and absurdist theater, where there is a premium on self-referentiality, on ensuring that audience members not forget their subject positions and that they maintain critical awareness in the theater. T. F. Wharton, *The Critical Fall and Rise of John Marston* (Columbia, S.C.: Camden House, 1994).

74. Alexander Leggatt, *English Drama: Shakespeare to the Restoration, 1590–1660.* Literature in English Series (London: Longman, 1988), 119.

75. These quotations of Marston are included in Sturgess's introduction to Marston, *The Malcontent and Other Plays* (ix). The first of the comments was in reference to *The Malcontent*; the second appears in Marston's letter to the reader that prefaces *The Fawn*.

76. On the relationship in Shakespeare between effeminacy and masculinity, see Spear, who writes of masculinity that it is "fully realized only in tension with historically and socially specific notions of effeminacy," which he defines as "a recontextualization of socially produced ideas of the feminine . . . signifying at the same time a disarticulation of masculine authority and the 'unnatural' empowerment of biologically and socially 'inferior' women" (409).

77. To make matters worse, Castilio and Balurdo are doomed to remain in this state of excessive desire, as they are unequipped to prosper in the wooing game that constitutes the subplot of *Antonio and Mellida*. Thus, they are unable to remedy their excess passion with what Breitenberg describes as the conventional early modern antidote to excess passion: marriage (41–42).

78. They gracefully put up with the jokes Rosaline delivers at their expense, such as when she scoffs that a bad smell in the room must be the result of one of them wearing socks, a sign of a nursing child (2.1.55–56). When Rosaline spits and tells Castilio to clean up her "rheum" (2.1.81), the courtier more than obliges her; he adds, "[Y]ou grace my shoe with an unmeasured honour. I will preserve the sole of it as a most sacred relic, for this service" (2.1.82–84). Castilio and Balurdo's eagerness to give up any modicum of dignity in pursuit of Rosaline leads Felice to compare them to dogs whom Rosaline allows to "lick her feet, / Or fetch her fan" (2.1.91–92). In short, their desire for Rosaline turns them into beasts over whom a woman has full control.

79. This effeminate trait is not easily separable from others in early modern representations of vocal performance. Henry Fitzgeffrey's satirical epigram about a male singer represents the cracking voice as a consequence of the man's sexual "exploits":

See how the Gentlewomen
Throng to his *Chamber doore,* but dare not come in,
Why? least he *ravish* them! Tush! Laugh ye not,
H'as done (I wosse) as great exploites as that.
(Or else he cracks) the sweenesse of his voyce
Ore-heard of Ladyes, hath procur'd him choyse
Of *Matches*: Noble, Rich: but hee'l not meddle,
And why (I pray?) for cracking of his *Treble*.
No! hee'l with better industry make tryall,
If hee can *Match* his Treble to the *Violl* (Henry Fitzgeffrey, *Satyres: and Satyricall Epigrams. With Certaine Observations at Black-Fryers* [London, 1617], sig. F6r–v).

The male singer's voice is so seductive that he can have his "choyse / Of Matches" with any of the women who hear him. Ironically, though, responding to women's sexual advances and becoming a sexual subject will cause his voice to crack, preventing him from remaining an object of women's desires. A cracking voice signals the man's transformation from a position of power over women to one of enslavement to them and the excessive sexual passion they provoke.

80. *Oxford English Dictionary*, s.v. "minikin."

81. One is tempted to read this as a description of the actual sound produced by the actor playing Castilio, helping us to construct how the actor's voice likely sounded when the play was originally performed. This, however, cannot be known with certainty. The male youth playing Castilio may, in fact, have a fine, high-pitched voice, which Felice, always the critic, simply derogates. Regardless of how Castilio's voice would have sounded in any particular performance, it is worth noting that Felice and the other characters *represent* that voice as aesthetically jarring, indicating, at least in the dramatic fiction, the vocalizer's inability to master his voice.

82. The stage directions, notably complex and detailed throughout the play, do not give Castilio an exit, as they do for Balurdo.

83. See, e.g., 5.2.45–71.

84. On tongue loss and its implications for the loss of phallocentric linguistic power, see Carla Mazzio, "Staging the Vernacular: Language and Nation in Thomas Kyd's *The Spanish Tragedy*," *Studies in English Literature* 38, no. 2 (1998): 207–32; Mazzio, "Sins of the Tongue." On the tongue's subversive volatility and early modern failed efforts to contain it, see chap. 5 in Jonathan Gil Harris, *Foreign Bodies and the Body Politic: Discourses of Social Pathology in Early Modern England*, Cambridge Studies in Renaissance Literature and Culture (Cambridge: Cambridge University Press, 1998).

85. W. Reavley Gair, ed., *Antonio and Mellida*, The Revels Plays (Manchester: Manchester University Press, 1991), 45.

86. To the Romans the term "persona" referred to a mask worn by actors. In addition to producing a visual effect, the mask (used by the Greek theaters as well) helped amplify the actor's voice via a resonating chamber in its forehead. Thus, the origins of theatrical role-playing are etymologically and performatively based in the production of voice.

87. The original cast list is available from http://members.iconn.net/~ab234/Plays/Antonio/Antonio.html (cited October 25, 2005).

88. Sean French, "Rickman's Worth," *GQ*, September 1991 (cited October 25, 2005), available from http://www.alan-rickman.com/articles/worth1.html; John Lahr, "Evil Elegance," *Lear's Magazine*, 1992 (cited October 25, 2005), available from http://www.alan-rickman.com/articles/evil_elegance.html); Steve Rea, "Free Spirit," *Knight-Ridder News Service*, June 5, 1991 (cited October 25, 2005), available from http://www.alan-rickman.com/articles/spirit.html.

89. Suzie Mackenzie, "Angel with Horns," *The Guardian*, January 3, 1998 (cited October 25, 2005), available from http://www.alan-rickman.com/articles/angel.html.

90. See French.

91. Halberstam, 234–35.

92. Weiss submits that Marston's induction was cut from Barnes's production ("A Pill to Purge Parody," 91), a point I cite in Gina Bloom, "'Thy Voice Squeaks': Listening for Masculinity on the Early Modern Stage," *Renaissance Drama* 29 (1998): 64. My

subsequent research into the reception of the Barnes production and recovery of contrary evidence renders this conclusion difficult to substantiate. (I am grateful to Weiss for trying to recover his original recorded evidence, unfortunately without success.) Specifically, Lucia Crothall recalls that the 1979 Barnes production "starts with most of the male actors grumbling about the parts they are about to play," which suggests some version of the induction was performed. Lucia Crothall, "Antonio," *Plays and Players*, December 1979 (cited October 2, 2005), available from http://members.iconn.net/~ab234/Plays/Antonio/ANPlays_Players.html. Without Barnes's original script, we cannot know, however, if "Antonio's" lines about vocal failure were among those included; reviews I consulted do not comment on particular actors' complaints, just the fact that actors *do* complain. Regardless, it is clear that Barnes's production sidelines "Antonio's" anxieties about voice, either editing them out completely or implying, with the use of Rickman in the part, that these anxieties are illegitimate and perhaps melodramatic.

93. This move is all the more paradoxical, however, given that Flute's successful performance entails describing his love for Pyramus in a manly, grave voice, thereby mapping homoerotic overtones onto this epic story of heterosexual romance. The film attempts to suppress this homoerotic potential by encouraging its audience to focus on how Flute's performance provides a satisfying theatrical experience, bringing the mechanicals' plotline (their desire to stage a play) to a successful resolution. Flute doesn't confuse or trouble the onstage audience with his deep voice; rather, he captivates them, moving them to pity the grieving Thisbe. As I'll discuss further below, *Shakespeare in Love* similarly uses narrative logic—and, specifically, a narrative of great theater's emergence—to suppress homoeroticism and pave the way for a story of heterosexual romance.

94. Sujata Iyengar, "Shakespeare in HeteroLove," *Literature/Film Quarterly* 29, no. 2 (2001): 123.

95. Valerie Traub, "The Sonnets: Sequence, Sexuality, and Shakespeare's Two Loves," in *A Companion to Shakespeare's Works*, ed. Richard Dutton and Jean E. Howard (Malden, Mass.: Blackwell, 2003), 293.

96. Iyengar, 123, emphasis mine.

97. Traub, 290–91, emphasis mine.

98. Ibid, 292.

99. My thanks to Wendy Wall for helping me formulate this final point.

Chapter 2

1. Unless otherwise noted, citations of *King John* follow Beaurline.

2. Bacon, *Sylva Sylvarum*, no. 199, emphasis mine. Subsequent citations will appear in my text.

3. Robinson, 13. Alexander Read, *The Manuall of the Anatomy or, Dissection of the Body of Man* (London, 1642), 261 [typeset mistakenly as 361].

4. I am indebted to Jonathan Gil Harris for this insight.

5. See, for instance, Theodore Weiss, *The Breath of Clowns and Kings: Shakespeare's Early Comedies and Histories* (New York: Atheneum, 1971); and Donawerth.

6. *Oxford English Dictionary*, s.v. "material."

7. Donawerth, esp. 165–66.

8. On the play's critical reception through the beginning of the twentieth century, see Joseph Candido, ed., *King John*, Shakespeare: The Critical Tradition (London: Athlone Press, 1996). On modern responses and for an extensive bibliography of scholarship and performance since 1940, see Deborah T. Curren-Aquino, ed., *King John: New Perspectives* (Newark: University of Delaware Press, 1989). Introductions to both volumes offer overviews of critical dissatisfaction with the play as well as explanations for why the play has enjoyed a revival in the late twentieth century.

9. Eamon Grennan, "Shakespeare's Satirical History: A Reading of *King John*," *Shakespeare Studies* 11 (1978): 32; and Donawerth, esp. 175. The seminal work on the play's depiction of language is Sigurd Burckhardt, "*King John*: The Ordering of This Present Time," *ELH* 33, no. 2 (1966): 133–53. Like Donawerth, I see the physicality of the play's speech imagery as crucial to play's thematization of the power of speech. However, I read *King John*'s thematization of speech in terms of the play's particular conditions of production in the early modern theater and thus view breath not as a metaphor of language but as a material substance staged in the theater and, in fact, crucial for the production and transmission of language.

10. In addition to Burckhardt, Grennan, and Donawerth, see James E. May, "Imagery of Disorderly Motion in *King John*: A Thematic Gloss," *Essays in Literature* 10, no. 1 (1983): 17–28; Barish; A. R. Braunmuller, ed., *The Life and Death of King John*, Oxford Shakespeare (Oxford: Clarendon, 1989), esp. 39–53; Edward Gieskes, "'He Is but a Bastard to the Time': Status and Service in *The Troublesome Raigne of John* and Shakespeare's *King John*," *ELH* 65, no. 4 (1998): 779–98; Dorothea Kehler, "'So Jest with Heaven': Deity in *King John*," in Curren-Aquino, ed., *King John*, 99–113; Michael Manheim, "The Four Voices of the Bastard," in Curren-Aquino, ed., *King John*, 126–35; Robert Weimann, "Mingling Vice and 'Worthiness' in *King John*," *Shakespeare Studies* 27 (1999): 109–33; Christopher Z. Hobson, "Bastard Speech: The Rhetoric of 'Commodity' in *King John*," *Shakespeare Yearbook* 2 (1991): 95–114; and Maurice Hunt, "Antimetabolic *King John*," *Style* 34, no. 3 (2000): 380–401. See also Joseph A. Porter, "Fraternal Pragmatics: Speech Acts of John and the Bastard," in Curren-Aquino, ed., *King John*, 136–43. Much critical analysis has centered on the speech of the Bastard, whose meditations on the multifarious meanings of the word "commodity" at the end of act 2 seem to index the play's figuration of "modern" ideologies of the subject's self-sufficiency. See especially Gieskes; Manheim; Weimann.

11. I borrow the term "language machines" from Masten, Stallybrass, and Vickers, *Language Machines*.

12. Paster, *Humoring the Body*, 231.

13. Most editors steer clear of the sensual significance of *tast*, usually substituting a range of alternatives, including *task*, *tax*, and *test*. My reading suggests, however, that the sensual significance of *tast* is crucial to the passage.

14. This is not the play's only reference to the relationship between tasting and hearing. When Lewis has lost all hope in France's potential for victory, he laments:

"Life is as tedious as a twice-told tale, / Vexing the dull ear of a drowsy man, / And bitter shame hath spoiled the sweet word's taste" (Braunmuller, *King John* 3.4.108–10). (I cite from Braunmuller's version, which follows the folio, rather than Beaurline's, which, as it chooses the later emendation of "world" instead of "word," elides the significance of *taste*.) Braunmuller notes that the folio *words* could also be read as plural possessive ("words' sweet taste"), which would refer to the words of the twice-told story. Additionally, when Hubert describes the way rumors of John's murder of Arthur spread through the streets, he notes one commoner "[w]ith open mouth swallowing" (4.2.195) the news. Shakespeare associates listening with the consumption of words in other plays as well. For example, Pericles describes Marina as "another Juno, / Who starves the ears she feeds, and makes them hungry / The more she gives them speech" (21.99–101). Also, Desdemona is reported to have fallen in love with Othello in the process of "devouring up" his stories with her "greedy ear" (1.3.150–51).

15. Morris Palmer Tilley, *A Dictionary of the Proverbs in England in the Sixteenth and Seventeenth Centuries* (Ann Arbor: University of Michigan Press, 1950), W424. Cited in Braunmuller, *King John*, 5.2.83–87n; and Beaurline, 5.2.83–87n.

16. Quoted in Dennis Des Chene, *Life's Form: Late Aristotelian Conceptions of the Soul* (Ithaca: Cornell University Press, 2000), 37.

17. Aristotle, in Jonathan Barnes, ed., *The Complete Works of Aristotle: The Revised Oxford Translation*, vol. 1, Bollingen Series (Princeton, N.J.: Princeton University Press, 1984), Book II, 420a, 7–9. This philosophical connection between breath and vocal sound is etymologically present in the term *anima*, which, though translated in English as soul, comes from the Proto-Indo-European base *ane-*, which means "to blow, to breathe." "Anima," available from http://www.etymonline.com/index.php?l=a&p=14 (cited August 12, 2005).

18. Aristotle, in Barnes, ed., Book II, 421a, 4–6.

19. Smith, *Acoustic World*, 98–99. My discussion of early modern acoustic theory throughout this chapter is much indebted to Smith's study.

20. Aristotle does provide an explanation for this success, but it is grounded in spiritual, not material, terms. I discuss this further below.

21. Crooke, 610 (emphasis mine).

22. Crooke notes similarly, "he that would listen & heare distinctly holdeth his breath" (700 [misprinted as 694]).

23. Ibid., 609.

24. Ibid.

25. Ibid., 610.

26. Later, Bacon argues, contrarily, that the quality of the external air *cannot* affect sound—although he does so with some hesitation: "The *Disposition* of the *Aire*, in other *Qualities*, except it be joyned with *Sound*, hath no great Operation upon *Sounds*: For whether the *Aire* be lightsome or darke, hot or cold, quiet or stirring, (except it be with *Noise*) sweet-smelling, or stinking, or the like; it importeth not much; Some petty Alteration or difference it may make" (*Sylva Sylvarum*, no. 226).

27. That Bacon is troubled by the implications of this conclusion is evinced in his waverings on the matter. He writes, "The *Unequall Agitation* of the *Winds*, and the like, though they bee materiall to the Carriage of the *Sounds*, further, or lesse way; yet

they doe not confound the *Articulation* of them at all, within that distance that they can be heard; Though it may be, they make them to be heard lesse Way, than in a Still" (no. 193). Though Bacon attempts to deny that winds can compromise the reception of vocal sound, the subsequent qualification, "though it may be," suggests he is not convinced by his own objections. And, indeed, in a separate observation, he concludes with more assurance that sound is "carried with *Wind*: And therefore *Sounds* will be heard further with the *Wind*, than against the *Wind*; And likewise doe rise and fall with the Intension or Remission of the *Wind*" (*Sylva Sylvarum*, no. 125).

28. Crooke, 610.

29. Smith, *Acoustic World*; Folkerth.

30. Macbeth similarly turns to the metaphor of breath and its characteristic fragility when he comments on the disappearance of the witches: they vanish, he marvels, into thin air, "as breath into the wind" (1.3.80).

31. If we read "the greater gust" as describing the commands of superiors that cause the oath-swearing men to switch loyalties, then the passage might gesture (as Heather Dubrow has pointed out to me) not only to the fragility and unpredictability, but also the power, of voices. As such, the passage would underscore particularly well my larger argument in this chapter about the ambiguity of breath.

32. Smith, *Acoustic World*, chap. 8.

33. See, for example, Derrida, "Signature Event Context."

34. It is not just the common men who are disabled by Henry's analogy of speech to breath. When Henry uses his own breath to blow the feather, he demonstrates that his vocal power can be compromised by its material form as well. Although the feather responds to Henry's breath at first, we see how it responds just as obediently to a "greater gust" that comes from elsewhere. By this proof, Henry's breath, despite being produced by a king, is not privileged.

35. The idea that conversation is an exchange of breath substantiates in material terms the erotic implications of "conversation," as advanced by Jeffrey Masten, *Textual Intercourse: Collaboration, Authorship, and Sexualities in Renaissance Drama*, Cambridge Studies in Renaissance Literature and Culture (Cambridge: Cambridge University Press, 1997). Some early modern writers explain that when lovers kiss, they are really conjoining their souls through the exchange of breath. Baldesar Castiglione writes that the mouth is "an issue for the wordes, that be the enterpreters of the soule, and for the inwarde breth, whiche is also called the soule: and therfore [the lover] hath a delite to joigne hys mouth with the womans beloved with a kysse: . . . bicause he feeleth that, that bonde is the openynge of an entry to the soules, whiche drawen with a coveting the one of the other, power them selves by tourn, the one into the others bodye, and be so mingled together." Baldesar Castiglione, *The Book of the Courtier*, trans. Thomas Hoby, The Tudor Translations (London: David Nutt, 1900), 355.

36. *The Holy Bible Containing the Old Testament, and the New: Newly Translated out of the Original Tongues: And with the Former Translations Diligently Compared and Revised, by his Maiesties Speciall Commandement* (London, 1613), Acts 2:2–6 (sig. D2r).

37. Henry Cornelius Agrippa, *Three Books of Occult Philosophy* (London, 1651), 258.

38. Christopher Stead, "Pneuma," *Routledge*, 1998 (cited August 11, 2005), available from http://www.rep.routledge.com.proxy.lib.uiowa.edu/article/A092.

39. Aristotle, in Barnes, ed., Book II, 420b.

40. "Anima," available from http://www.etymonline.com/index.php?l=a&p=14 (cited August 12, 2005).

41. See Terrel Ward Bynum, "A New Look at Aristotle's Theory of Perception," in *Aristotle's* De Anima *in Focus*, ed. Michael Durrant (New York: Routledge, 1993), 90–109; and M. F. Burnyeat, "How Much Happens When Aristotle Sees Red and Hears Middle C? Remarks On De Anima 2. 7–8," in *Essays on Aristotle's* De Anima, ed. Martha C. Nussbaum and Amélie Oksenberg Rorty (Oxford: Clarendon, 1995), 421–34. There has been debate about whether the sensory organ actually undergoes material alteration during sensory perception. Some philosophers (e.g., Burnyeat) maintain that for Aristotle sensory perception is wholly immaterial and involves no physiological change. Others argue that though there is no matter conveyed from the sense object, this does not mean that perception is *immaterial*. For the latter idea, see Richard Sorabji, "Body and Soul in Aristotle," in Durrant, ed., *Aristotle's* De Anima *in Focus*, 162–96; and S. Marc Cohen, "The Credibility of Aristotle's Philosophy of Mind," in *Aristotle Today: Essays on Aristotle's Idea of Science*, ed. Mohan Matthen (Edmonton, Alberta, Canada: Academic Printing and Publishing, 1987), 103–26. Nevertheless, there is general agreement that sensation involves the transmission of forms, with some modern commentators claiming that sound is *only* form.

42. Burnyeat, 430.

43. I am indebted to the discussion of matter in Gad Freudenthal, *Aristotle's Theory of Material Substance: Heat and Pneuma, Form and Soul* (Oxford: Clarendon, 1995).

44. Bacon writes, "*Harmony* entring easily, and Mingling not at all, and Coming with a manifest Motion; doth by Custome of often Affecting the *Spirits*, and Putting them into one kinde of Posture, alter not a little Nature of the *Spirits*, even when the Object is removed. . . . *Tunes* have a Predisposition to the *Motion* of the *Spirits* in themselves" (*Sylva Sylvarum*, no. 114).

45. The precise workings and definitions of Bacon's "spirits," while fascinating, are beyond the scope of this chapter's main aims. To summarize these ideas in their simplest terms: Bacon imagines a competition of sorts between inanimate and vital spirits. The latter have the desire to remain contained in the body, and it is because of their retention that a body remains alive. The former, attracted for various reasons to the ambient air, desire to escape a body, and it is the loss of these inanimate spirits that explains process of decay in all sorts of bodies. For an introduction to Bacon's theory of spirits, see Graham Rees, "Bacon's Speculative Philosophy," in *The Cambridge Companion to Bacon*, ed. Markku Peltonen (Cambridge: Cambridge University Press, 1996), 121–45.

46. This is not to suggest that early modern writers like Crooke and Bacon use Aristotle to put forward a dualism of soul vs. matter. Forms, even for Aristotelians, rely upon matter to be actualized. Form and matter are not oppositional as much as dialectical in their relationship to each other. Nevertheless, Aristotle implies that it is the soul embodied in matter that accounts for the successful transmission of voice. Bacon's notion of spirits, as I've explained, negotiates this terrain in even more sub-

tle ways through the idea of "pneumatical parts" contained in seemingly solid bodies. To complicate matters further, Bacon's theoretical writings suggest that he thought it possible that spirits were composed of minute particles, at least in theory. See Silvia A. Manzo, "Francis Bacon and Atomism: A Reappraisal," in *Late Medieval and Early Modern Corpuscular Matter Theories*, ed. Christoph Lüthy, John E. Murdoch, and William R. Newman (Leiden: Brill, 2001), esp. 242.

47. Sir Balthazar Gerbier, *The Art of Well Speaking* (London, 1650), 24.

48. Significantly, Gerbier does not refer to breath specifically here, but rather to "corporall air." While we should be careful not to conflate air and breath, it is worth remembering that this conflation was fairly common in the period, as I'll discuss further below.

49. This tension between material and spiritual meanings of breath invokes a broader tension between stillness and motion. In an argument that resonates with the claims of my chapter, P. A. Skantze demonstrates that the early modern theater complicates the story that has often been told about the gendering of stillness and motion. Traditionally, stillness—with its concomitant positive traits of firmness, steadiness, certainty—has been valued, associated with the masculine and the medium of print, whereas movement—ephemerality, unpredictability, the transitory—has been derided as feminine and associated with performance. In fact, Skantze argues, these binaries are much messier in practice, as plays engage in an "intricate dance in the aesthetic of stillness and motion" (13). Representations of breath, as we shall see especially below, perform a similar such dance and prompt a similar interrogation of gender binaries.

50. Donawerth (esp. 68) observes the frequency with which Shakespeare associates breath and death. Most interesting is the trope in which dying characters imagine their last words as physically leading them closer to death, as the very act of speaking on one's deathbed involves a sacrifice of some of the breath needed for continued life. Expiring breath thus directly causes the expiring of life.

51. Paster, *The Body Embarrassed*.

52. Interestingly, Paster reaches a similar conclusion in her more recent work. See *Humoring the Body*, esp. chap. 2.

53. Juliet Dusinberre, "*King John* and Embarrassing Women," *Shakespeare Survey* 42 (1990): 37–52.

54. Critics who discuss female speech in *King John* have generally emphasized the outspokenness of Eleanor as the source of her vocal power. Noting in particular the quarrel between Eleanor and Constance that commands much stage time, critics comment on the sheer quantity of lines given over to female voices in the play and the "irreverent" nature of these contributions. Women, Phyllis Rackin writes, "set the subversive keynote" in this particular history play, but only until the second half when, killed off, they are reduced to "the silent objects of male narration." Phyllis Rackin, "Patriarchal History and Female Subversion in *King John*," in Curren-Aquino, ed., *King John*, 76–90, esp. 82. See also Howard and Rackin, *Engendering a Nation*, chap. 7, which expands on similar material. I am suggesting, however, that if we examine the ways Eleanor and Constance gesture when they speak toward the material form of their voices, we discover that their vocal agency also can involve less overtly

aggressive, and thus less easily circumscribed, forms of theatrical verbal display. On the power of outspoken women in *King John*, see, in addition to Rackin and Howard, Levin, esp. 125; Joseph Candido, "'Women and Fools Break Off Your Conference': Pope's Degradations and the Form of *King John*," in *Shakespeare's English Histories: A Quest for Form and Genre*, ed. John W. Velz (Binghamton, N.Y.: Medieval and Renaissance Texts and Studies, 1996), 91–110; and Dusinberre, esp. 43.

55. Beatrice uses the syllogism to especially witty effect here to remind Benedick that her affections are contingent on his fulfilling his manly duty—here, his flaccid breath, used unsuccessfully in his exchange with Claudio, is literally the cause Beatrice will not kiss, or exchange breath, with him. Benedick's breath "stinks" on several levels.

56. A broader understanding of breath's peculiar attributes helps resolve a long-running debate among editors regarding to whom the "windy breath" of the passage belongs and whether *zeal* refers to France's eagerness for the peace plan or for Arthur's cause. Since the folio does not punctuate the passage, most editors put a comma after "zeal" to argue that the "windy breath" of this passage belongs to Hubert, whose bold oration in favor of peace can be read as having melted France's zealous support for Arthur. See, for example, Stanley T. Williams, ed., *The Life and Death of King John*, The Yale Shakespeare (New Haven, Conn.: Yale University Press, 1927); R. L. Smallwood, ed., *King John*, New Penguin Shakespeare (Middlesex: Penguin Books, 1974); and *The Riverside Shakespeare*. Braunmuller argues persuasively to the contrary, however, that since Hubert's speech has been anything but "soft" (the Bastard has just referred to Hubert's declamatory rant in favor of the peace settlement as "cannon-fire" [2.1.462]), the "windy breath" belongs to Constance and the "zeal" is support for the peace offer (2.1.478–80n). My reading reconciles Braunmuller's explanation of "windy breath" as belonging to Constance with other editors' interpretations of "zeal" as France's commitment to Arthur. Braunmuller believes the readings to be irreconcilable: "If *zeal* here were to mean the commitment to Arthur . . . the *soft petitions* . . . would have to be understood as Hubert's." In my reading the "soft petitions" can still belong to Constance provided that one allows "melt"—which Braunmuller must take figuratively as meaning "change"—to carry its full, material significance.

57. Thomas Wright, *The Passions of the Minde in Generall*, ed. Thomas O. Sloan (Urbana: University of Illinois Press, 1971), 162–63.

58. Francis Beaumont, *The Knight of the Burning Pestle*, ed. John Doebler, Regents Renaissance Drama (Lincoln: University of Nebraska Press, 1967), 4.184–85.

59. Shigehisa Kuriyama, *The Expressiveness of the Body and the Divergence of Greek and Chinese Medicine* (New York: Zone Books, 1999), 246. Kuriyama observes that in the period between Hippocrates and Galen, there is a gradual shift toward internalization of *pneuma*, a focus less on the outer winds and more on the breath animating from within the body. Aristotle will maintain that this "innate breath" works independently from the outer winds, giving shape to the unformed body (e.g., by helping to mold the fetus). So whereas Hippocrates would see the winds as shaping the body from without ("winds that provided . . . the *context* of human being") writers from Aristotle to Galen will say that the breath shapes the body from within ("*pneuma* as inner *content*") (261). I am grateful to Gail Paster for alerting me to Kuriyama's work.

60. Paster, *Humoring the Body*, esp. chap. 4.

61. Enterline, *Rhetoric of the Body*.

62. See the gloss on "north" as a reference to the northern winds in *The Norton Shakespeare*. On the nature of the northern winds, see Sir Francis Bacon, *The Naturall and Experimentall History of Winds* (London, 1653), esp. 55.

63. Bacon, *History of Winds*, 88.

64. Ibid., 176.

65. Levinus Lemnius, *The Secret Miracles of Nature* (London, 1658), sig. A2v.

66. Ibid., A3r.

67. On the physiological/psychological power of slander in Shakespeare, albeit not concerning *Cymbeline* in particular, see Kenneth Gross, *Shakespeare's Noise* (Chicago: University of Chicago Press, 2001), esp. chapter 2. See also M. Lindsay Kaplan, *The Culture of Slander in Early Modern England* (Cambridge: Cambridge University Press, 1997).

68. On the ways that Constance's rants have embarrassed male readers of the play—who have responded by cutting many of her lines—see Dusinberre; and Candido, "'Women and Fools.'"

69. Michael C. Schoenfeldt, "'Give Sorrow Words': Emotional Loss and the Emergence of Personality in Early Modern England," in *Dead Lovers: Erotic Bonds and the Study of Premodern Europe*, ed. Basil Dufallo and Peggy McCracken (Ann Arbor: University of Michigan Press, forthcoming). My thanks to Schoenfeldt for sharing his work with me in advance of its publication.

70. Many critics assume that lament, feminized, is a marker of powerlessness in the plays. For example, Charles H. Frey argues that in *Titus Andronicus* grief is feminized and depicted as useless: women lament, while men rage, taking violent, albeit tragic, action. Charles H. Frey, "Man's Rage/Woman's Grief: Engaging Death in *Titus Andronicus*," in *Re-Visions of Shakespeare: Essays in Honor of Robert Ornstein*, ed. Evelyn Gajowski (Newark: University of Delaware Press, 2004), 66–88.

71. See Moulton.

72. My argument about the reduction of speech to its material signifiers in essence reverses the phenomenological reduction Edmund Husserl attempts. Husserl argues that when the self speaks to the self, meaning is secured by the self's intentions, unmediated by the world. As David Schalkwyk explains, Husserl suggests that a process of reduction rids words of their materiality. David Schalkwyk, *Literature and the Touch of the Real* (Newark: University of Delaware Press, 2004), esp. 72.

73. For a fascinating reading of the acoustic dynamics of this scene, see Smith, *Acoustic World*, 230–32, which traces how Richard uses volume and pitch to gain a "firm command of the aural field." I differ from Smith, however, in arguing that the Duchess's curses are disruptive of Richard's authority, despite their softer, less aggressive aural character.

74. On *Richard III* and male characters' fascination with being smothered in the womb, see Adelman.

75. Howard and Rackin, *Engendering a Nation*, 106–8.

76. The syntax of the Duchess's threat supports this point: Richard will be smothered *in* the breath of bitter words.

77. My argument about Constance's breath dovetails with Katherine Rowe's concerning the agency of hands. Rowe argues persuasively that in "dead hand stories," the disembodied part's ability to act independently of the subject that wills it to act blurs lines between the principle (one on whose behalf an action is performed), the agent (one who exerts the power to perform the action), the instrument (the tool that accomplishes the action), and the patient (one upon whom the action is performed). She argues that the blurring of these terms can be strategically useful for making "the idea of agency both fuzzy and capacious." Katherine Rowe, *Dead Hands: Fictions of Agency, Renaissance to Modern* (Stanford, Calif.: Stanford University Press, 1999), esp. 18–20.

78. Phyllis Rackin, *Stages of History: Shakespeare's English Chronicles* (Ithaca and New York: Cornell UP, 1990), 18; Howard and Rackin, *Engendering a Nation*, 126; Vaughan, "Subversion," 72. See also Adelman, 10; and Levin, 230.

79. Warner uses "the absence of the women in the second half of the play to explore, through male characters, aspects of the mother-child relationship." See Geraldine Cousin, *Shakespeare in Performance: King John* (Manchester: Manchester University Press, 1994), 128–29. I am grateful to Deborah Curren-Aquino for bringing this to my attention. For a key critical reading that develops this theoretical point, see Nina S. Levine, *Women's Matters: Politics, Gender, and Nation in Shakespeare's Early History Plays* (Newark: University of Delaware Press, 1998).

80. Beaurline, 3.4.19n.

81. I cite from the translation of *De Principiis atque Originibus* in Graham Rees, *The Oxford Francis Bacon: Philosophical Studies c. 1611–c. 1619*, vol. 6 (Oxford: Clarendon, 1996), sig. M3r (p. 253).

82. Bacon appears to eschew atomism completely in *Sylva Sylvarum*'s sections on sound. He emphasizes multiple times that audible species are not corporeal entities (see nos. 259, 287, and 288). In pointing out that Bacon avoids atomic styles of explanation in his writings on acoustics, I do not mean to imply that Bacon's entire text is "anti-atomist," as earlier historians of science have suggested. Robert Hugh Kargon, *Atomism in England from Hariot to Newton* (Oxford: Clarendon, 1966) maintains that Bacon abandoned atomism in later works like *Sylva Sylvarum*, substituting in its place his theory of pneumatic matter. For a related position, see Paolo Rossi, *Francis Bacon: From Magic to Science* (Chicago: University of Chicago Press, 1968). More recent historians of science, however, have argued that though Bacon's ideas changed over the course of his career, he never completely eschewed the notion of corpuscular matter, at least not on theoretical grounds (see especially Manzo). This revisiting of Bacon's atomism is part of a larger effort to rethink assumptions about what counts as atomistic philosophy in the seventeenth century. As is argued in Stephen Clucas, "The Atomism of the Cavendish Circle: A Reappraisal," *Seventeenth Century* 9, no. 2 (1994): esp. 251–52, earlier historians dismiss the significant contributions of early and mid-seventeenth century English thinkers (like Bacon, Walter Charleton, Kenelm Digby, and Margaret Cavendish, among others) to the story of atomism's revival in England because the atomic theory these writers propose is so eclectic, integrating Epicurean atomism with the scholastic tradition of *minima* and the Neoplatonic "seminalism" of Paracelsus. Clucas uses the term "neo-atomism" to describe the early modern re-

vival of ancient atomic thought in an effort to encourage historians to read seventeenth-century atomic styles of explanation on their own terms, rather than as faulty derivatives of ancient philosophy. For further elucidation of Clucas's argument, see the introduction to Christoph Lüthy, John E. Murdoch, and William R. Newman., eds., *Late Medieval and Early Modern Corpuscular Matter Theories* (Leiden: Brill, 2001). I am grateful to Antonia LoLordo for calling my attention to this volume and to Alvin Snider for helping me negotiate the complex terrain of early modern theories of particulate matter.

83. Epicurus, letter to Heroditus in Cyril Bailey, ed., *Epicurus: The Extant Remains* (Hildesheim: Georg Olms Verlag, 1926), III.B (p. 31).

84. Ibid.

85. Walter Charleton, *Physiologia Epicuro-Gassendo-Charltoniana: Or A Fabrick of Science Natural Upon the Hypothesis of Atoms* (London, 1654), 217.

86. Aristotle, in Barnes, ed., Book II, 420a, 3. Of all the English neo-atomists, Charleton is perhaps the most closely associated with Pierre Gassendi, who made a point of distinguishing himself from Aristotle when defining his physics of material particles. Charleton is not consistently anti-scholastic by any means, but his passages on sound transmission in *Physiologia* evince some interesting contrasts with those of Aristotle's in *De Anima*, highlighting some of the key issues at stake in my argument.

87. Charleton, 210.

88. Ibid.

89. Ibid., 212.

90. Ibid., 222.

91. Ibid., 218–19.

92. Ibid.

93. My interest in Charleton's writings on particulate matter, then, is less historical than it is theoretical. This is not to say that early modern playwrights were unaware of the ideas that Charleton explores. Charleton draws into conversation a range of ancient and early modern writers that were certainly available to be read by Shakespeare and other early modern playwrights. Indeed, Jonathan Gil Harris points out that Shakespeare was familiar with ancient atomism. Perhaps exposed to these ideas through his readings of Montaigne, who cites Lucretius often, Shakespeare refers to atoms in several plays, defining them in terms of their mobility and minute size. Jonathan Gil Harris, "Atomic Shakespeare," *Shakespeare Studies* 30 (2002): esp. 48. On the influence of Epicurean materialism on early modern political philosophy, see Stephen M. Buhler, "No Spectre, No Sceptre: The Agon of Materialist Thought in Shakespeare's *Julius Caesar*," *English Literary Renaissance* 26, no. 2 (1996): 313–32.

94. Harris, "Atomic Shakespeare," 47.

95. Ibid., 49.

96. It seems no coincidence that, as Alvin Snider argues, seventeenth-century female writers like Aphra Behn would be attracted to atomist philosophy, which, Snider shows, allows Behn to present a more erotically empowering perspective on the body. Notably, Snider maintains that Lucretian philosophy prompts Behn to theorize an erotic agency predicated on a view of the body and its pleasures as out of our control—a perspective on gender and atomism that resonates provocatively with my

own. See Alvin Snider, "Atoms and Seeds: Aphra Behn's Lucretius," *Clio* 33, no. 1 (2003): 1–24.

97. For Sara Eaton, Lavinia represents the exclusion of women from humanism's idealistic tenets: "Lavinia, who begins the play potentially unruly in her speech and her humanist education, her writing, her teaching, is rendered a macabre and reified image of the chaste, silent, and obedient wife and daughter after her mutilation—or because of it." Sara Eaton, "A Woman of Letters: Lavinia in *Titus Andronicus*," in *Shakespearean Tragedy and Gender*, ed. Shirley Nelson Garner and Madelon Sprengnether (Bloomington: Indiana University Press, 1996), 66. Coppélia Kahn argues in a similar vein that Lavinia's loss of voice is symbolic of women's subjection to patriarchal language (see esp. chap. 3). And Sid Ray—extending arguments about the politics of language to address the play's commentary on political ideologies more generally—sees Lavinia's mutilated body as a metaphor for the mutilation of the Roman people's will. As the Roman people are forced to accept Titus's choice of emperor and denied a "voice" in the political process, so Lavinia is denied the husband of her choice and later silenced, compelled to submit to the sexual abuse of Chiron and Demetrius. Sid Ray, "'Rape, I Fear, Was Root of Thy Annoy': The Politics of Consent in *Titus Andronicus*," *Shakespeare Quarterly* 49, no. 1 (1998): 22–39. One interesting exception is Christina Luckyj, who argues suggestively that Lavinia's silence, as it renders her impossible to read, places her "beyond masculine rhetorical control" (93). Luckyj challenges the assumption that speech is equivalent to agency, arguing instead that silence can be eloquent and subversive. Even as Luckyj's argument opens up a powerful reading of Lavinia's agency, it still is built upon the problematic assumption that Lavinia, because she lacks a tongue, lacks a voice. Luckyj locates Lavinia's power in silence, not in voice, as I am arguing.

98. My reading still leaves open the question of why Marcus, despite clearly recognizing in this scene (through his invocation of Ovid's rape story) that a rape has occurred, somehow forgets what he knows, so that he and Titus wait two acts before truly "discovering" the rape. Emily Detmer-Goebel argues that the point of this recognition and forgetting is to "tease the audience with the idea that the men should know that she has been raped" thereby emphasizing, as is true about women's speech more generally in rape cases of the period, "men's ultimate reliance on Lavinia's words." Emily Detmer-Goebel, "The Need for Lavinia's Voice: *Titus Andronicus* and the Telling of Rape," *Shakespeare Studies* 29 (2001): 81. I argue that Lavinia uses her *voice* successfully in this scene, even if she does not utter *words*; that Marcus cannot retain the information she voices indicates a flaw in his listening and apprehension, not simply her expression. In this respect Marcus might be compared to the hearing-impaired male characters of Shakespeare's late plays, which I discuss in Chapter 3.

99. Cited in Alan C. Dessen, *Titus Andronicus*, Shakespeare in Performance (Manchester: Manchester University Press, 1989), 30.

100. Ibid., 60.

101. Kenelm Digby, *Two Treatises in the One of Which the Nature of Bodies, in the Other, the Nature of Mans Soule; Is Looked Iinto: In Way of Discovery, of the Immortality of Reasonable Soules* (Paris, 1644), 257.

102. Ibid.

103. Ibid., 253.

104. See George Sibscota, *The Deaf and Dumb Man's Discourse. Or a Treatise Concerning Those That Are Born Deaf and Dumb, Containing a Discovery of Their Knowledge or Understanding; as Also the Method They Use, to Manifest the Sentiments of Their Mind. Together with an Additional Tract of the Reason and Speech of Inanimate Creatures.* (London, 1670). Sibscota relates the story of someone "who being born Deaf and Dumb, constantly frequents publike Sermons, and doth as it were contemplate upon the Words of the Preacher with his eyes fixt upon him, so that he seems to receive them in at his Mouth as others do by the Ear" (44).

105. In *The Body Embarrassed*, Paster incisively points out the gendered inflections of Lavinia's blood, which, unlike the blood of the self-mutilating Titus, is unwilled and uncontrollable. "The blood flowing from Lavinia's mouth" recalls the blood of menstruation and defloration, both signs of "an immutable condition—the condition of womanhood" as well as being signs of male mastery over the vulnerable female body and its wounds that "cannot ever heal." One might extend this argument to the breath that similarly leaks from Lavinia, "coming and going" uncontrollably with her blood. Yet the presence of that breath would complicate what Paster describes as "a chain of dramatic metonymies" that deny Lavinia vocal agency. Paster writes, "Lavinia's inability to prevent her rape is equivalent to her inability to stop bleeding, is equivalent to her inability to speak her own bodily condition" (99). To the contrary, Marcus's conclusion that Lavinia has suffered the fate of Philomel, "deflowered" by "some Tereus," points to his having heard Lavinia, on some level, through the "honey breath" she expels.

106. Charleton, 218. The association of the speaker with a fountain is by no means unique to Charleton or neo-atomist writings. The fountain is a commonplace metaphor for eloquent orators.

107. Ibid.

108. Emily C. Bartels, "Strategies of Submission: Desdemona, the Duchess, and the Assertion of Desire," *SEL* 36 (1996), argues in a similar vein that Desdemona's dying moments constitute a performance of obedience. "Although critics . . . have turned her into a 'bodiless obedient silence,' Desdemona has both voice and body here" (430). Desdemona's and other female characters' "gestures of submission" (420) allow them to pursue their desires while seeming to submit to male authorities. See also Dubrow's reading of Desdemona's Barbary song in Dubrow, "'The Tip of His Seducing Tongue.'" Dubrow also finds Desdemona embracing what seem to be contradictory positions of authority.

109. If, as other critics have suggested, Desdemona's murder in effect punishes her for vocal and erotic transgressions committed at the beginnings of the play—when she disobeys her father, chooses her own husband, and is outspoken about her desires—then the model of vocal agency she exhibits at the end of the play may be considered superior in some ways to more conventional forms of vocal agency she exhibits at its beginning. Vocal transgressions must be perceptible to be disciplined, after all, and breath's ambiguous nature renders it resistant to tracking. The same might be said for Lavinia, who, like Desdemona, initially insists on her right to speak and to choose her own husband and who also, consequently, loses an organ of speech.

Chiron and Demetrius may limit Lavinia's speech, but curtailing her voice proves more challenging, for Lavinia's breath eludes their grasp. My argument thus follows but rethinks Peter Stallybrass's that Emilia in *Othello* transcends the binary Desdemona enacts: Stallbrass maintains that whereas Desdemona shifts from being an active agent at the start of the play to a figure implicated in the "problematic of the closed body" by the end, Emilia represents a "rejection of enclosure and the validation of the female grotesque" ("Patriarchal Territories," 142). I am suggesting that Desdemona's use of breath positions her more closely with Emilia than has often been assumed.

110. The claim regarding Hubert's compassion has been advanced most influentially by Burckhardt, 137–38.

111. Similarities between Arthur, Constance, and Eleanor seem to have been observed and emphasized throughout the history of the play's performance. In the nineteenth century, directors cast a female actress for the part of Arthur, a practice that, as Dusinberre argues, resolves the problem of finding a male child talented enough to perform this exacting role (49, 37n). Whatever the intended reasons for this gender switch, it approaches the effect of Shakespeare's all-male company, insofar as it links Arthur to the play's female characters through the sex of the actors playing these roles. In Shakespeare's theater the casting of apprentice boys for these parts would have served the additional purpose of helping define the play's meditations on the issue of vocal agency, for pubescent boys embodied the precarious nature of breath. When the character Arthur thematizes voice as uncontrollable breath, he invokes the physical condition of the voice of the actor who plays him—a voice that, if not already cracking, carries the potential for uncontrollability. Dusinberre assumes that the part must be played by a boy with an unbroken voice—thus the decision by directors to cast a female actress (with a high, "feminine" voice), rather than an older boy whose voice has broken. Yet, as I suggest below, a boy with a more unstable voice—for instance, a youth going through the vocal changes of puberty—would be a more apt choice in terms of highlighting the play's engagement with questions of vocal agency.

112. See, for example, Burckhardt; Donawerth; and Hobson.

113. *King John* has been widely discussed as a "metatheatrical" play. See Weimann (which I discuss further below); Dusinberre; David Scott Kastan, "'To Set a Form Upon That Indigest': Shakespeare's Fictions of History," *Comparative Drama* 17, no. 1 (1983): 1–16; Virginia Mason Vaughan, "*King John*: A Study in Subversion and Containment," in Curren-Aquino, ed., *King John*, 62–75; Douglas C. Wixson, "'Calm Words Folded up in Smoke': Propaganda and Spectator Response in Shakespeare's *King John*," *Shakespeare Studies* 14 (1981): esp. 112–21; John W. Blanpied, *Time and Artist in Shakespeare's English Histories* (Newark: University of Delaware Press, 1983), chap. 7; and Grennan, esp. 34. On the ways the theatrical style of *King John* evinces a transition from the style of the first to the second tetralogy, see Virginia Mason Vaughan, "Between Tetralogies: *King John* as Transition," *Shakespeare Quarterly* 35, no. 4 (1984): 407–20; and Rackin, *Stages*, esp. 128–29. The most oft-cited of the play's metatheatrical moments is the Bastard's speech at Angier, when he compares the warring kings to actors on a stage before the citizens of Angier, who, rather than get in-

volved in a fray, "stand securely on their battlements / As in a theatre, whence they gape and point / At your industrious scenes and acts of death" (2.1.373–76). But the play also stages more subtle meditations on its form.

114. W. B. Worthen, *Shakespeare and the Authority of Performance* (Cambridge: Cambridge University Press, 1997), 180.

115. Shoshana Felman, *The Literary Speech Act: Don Juan with J. L. Austin, or Seduction in Two Languages*, trans. Catherine Porter (Ithaca, N.Y.: Cornell University Press, 1983).

116. Cited in Butler, *Excitable Speech*, 10.

117. Ibid.

118. There is some debate in the period about open-mouthed sleeping. Lemnius expresses concern about the practice because of the bad air that might be inhaled should the mouth lie open during sleep. But most other authorities recommend open-mouthed sleeping, emphasizing not what comes in but what can be passed out. See for example, Thomas Walkington, *The Optick Glasse of Humors, or the Touchstone of a Golden Temperature, or the Philosophers Stone to Make a Golden Temper* (London, 1607) and Tobias Venner, *Via Recta Ad Vitam Longam: Or, a Plain Philosophicall Demonstration of the Nature, Faculties, and Effects of All Such Things as by Way of Nourishments Make for the Preservation of Health . . .* (London, 1628).

119. It is for this reason that the breath has greater transgressive potential than the tongue, another common early modern metaphor for speech. On how early modern writers and political authorities imagine the tongue metaphor in literal terms through torture devices like the scold's bridle, see Boose. On representations of the tongue as resistant to such discipline, see Mazzio, "Sins of the Tongue." Of course, the "fantasies" of the tongue Mazzio examines can only be fantastical, since the organ, however mobile, remains attached to the body unless violently excised. The breath, by contrast, is expected to be detached from the body, arguably lending it greater imagined freedom.

120. Enterline uses Felman to make a related argument about theatrical voicing in relation to Hermione's speaking in *The Winter's Tale*. See chap. 6 in *Rhetoric of the Body*.

Chapter 3

1. Peggy Phelan, "Performing Talking Cures: Artaud's Voice," in *Language Machines: Technologies of Literary and Cultural Production*, ed. Jeffrey Masten, Peter Stallybrass, and Nancy J. Vickers (New York: Routledge, 1997), 237–38.

2. Thomas Middleton and William Rowley, *The Changeling*, ed. Matthew W. Black (Philadelphia: University of Pennsylvania Press, 1966), 3.4.101–4.

3. On the value of receptive ears in sermons on the parable of the sower and the seed, see Folkerth, 44–51.

4. John Donne, *Fifty Sermons. The Second Volume* (London, 1627), 234.

5. Thomas Taylor, *The Parable of the Sower and of the Seed. Among Other Things*

Largely Discoursing of a Good Hart Describing It by Very Many Signes of It (London, 1634), 23.

6. Although parishioners may indicate they have heard and digested the sermon by responding orally, in these sermons such a response does not verify a parishioner's state of grace. On the way in which Protestant services were structured so as to produce an oral response on the part of the congregation, see Smith, *Acoustic World*, 261–69. For a discussion of liturgical call-and-response dynamics from the perspective of audience response theory, see Christine Callender and Deborah Cameron, "Responsive Listening as Part of Religious Rhetoric: The Case of Black Pentecostal Preaching," in *Reception and Response: Hearer Creativity and the Analysis of Spoken and Written Texts*, ed. Graham McGregor and R. S. White (New York: Routledge, 1990), 160–78.

7. On the intersection between Protestant ideologies and the early modern English theater, see Bryan Crockett, *The Play of Paradox: Stage and Sermon in Renaissance England* (Philadelphia: University of Pennsylvania Press, 1995); Huston Diehl, *Staging Reform, Reforming the Stage: Protestantism and Popular Theater in Early Modern Englan* (Ithaca, N.Y.: Cornell University Press, 1997); Michael O'Connell, *The Idolatrous Eye: Iconoclasm and Theater in Early-Modern England* (Oxford: Oxford University Press, 2000). Diehl and O'Connell examine how Protestant suspicions of spectacle affect the status of visuality in the plays. Crockett's study of sermons explores the rhetorical strategies of preachers, focusing on the verbal art of the stage and pulpit.

8. Folkerth, 26; Smith, *Acoustic World*, 270; Gross, 39. For a related argument, see chap. 5, "Vulnerable Ears: *Hamlet* and Poisonous Theater" in Tanya Pollard, *Drugs and Theater in Early Modern England* (Oxford: Oxford University Press, 2005).

9. Peter Cummings anticipates this argument in his essay on *Hamlet*, which explains Hamlet's delay as a consequence of his failure to hear: "the tragic prince is deaf." Peter Cummings, "Hearing in *Hamlet*: Poisoned Ears and the Psychopathology of Flawed Audition," *Shakespeare Yearbook* 1 (1990): 91.

10. Gross, 39.

11. Smith, *Acoustic World*, 271.

12. In addition to the above, useful essays concerning hearing in early modern drama and culture include Reina Green, "'Ears Prejudicate' in *Mariam* and *Duchess of Malfi*," *SEL* 43, no. 2 (2003): 459–74; Heather James, "Dido's Ear: Tragedy and the Politics of Response," *Shakespeare Quarterly* 52, no. 3 (2001): 360–82; and Eric Wilson, "Plagues, Fairs, and Street Cries: Sounding Out Society and Space in Early Modern England," *Modern Language Studies* 25, no. 3 (1995): 1–42.

13. This is not to say that these critics ignore gender completely; it is, however, not their central focus. Folkerth, for instance, notes repeatedly that a range of "acoustic values" (9), including obedience, receptivity, and reproduction, were coded as feminine in this period, and he touches on female audition in *Measure for Measure* and *Othello*. But he does not trace out the implications of this "feminine" coding for the figuration of gender identity in the plays. For interesting essays on gender and hearing that complement my approach to the subject, see essays by Green and James.

14. There has been great debate among critics about what, if anything, links these

plays together generically, structurally, or thematically. For a discussion of these links, see Jennifer Richards and James Knowles, eds., *Shakespeare's Late Plays: New Readings* (Edinburgh: Edinburgh University Press, 1999). On the various terms used to describe these plays—"romance," "tragicomedy," and so forth—see Barbara A. Mowat, "'What's in a Name?' Tragicomedy, Romance, or Late Comedy," in *A Companion to Shakespeare's Works*, ed. Richard Dutton and Jean E. Howard (Malden, Mass.: Blackwell, 2003), 129–49. It is for the sake of convenience, rather than an investment in the chronology of Shakespeare's artistic career, that I refer to these as "late plays." Although categorizing plays by genre is not a wholly satisfying, and often even a counterproductive, scholarly activity, there are enough overlaps between these plays to merit grouping them in this chapter. At the same time, like a number of other scholars, I find that *The Tempest* fits less neatly into this grouping, specifically in terms of its representation of hearing. It is useful, nevertheless, to understand the *ways* in which it differs, which I attempt to do in the latter part of this chapter. On the question of whether *The Tempest* is generically similar to *Pericles, Cymbeline*, and *The Winter's Tale*, see Elizabeth Bieman, *William Shakespeare: The Romances*, Twayne's English Authors Series (Boston: Twayne Publishers, 1990); H. W. Fawkner, *Shakespeare's Miracle Plays: Pericles, Cymbeline, and The Winter's Tale* (Rutherford, N.J.: Farleigh Dickinson University Press, 1992); Simon Palfrey, *Late Shakespeare: A New World of Words*, Oxford English Monographs (Oxford: Clarendon Press, 1997).

15. Folkerth, *Sound of Shakespeare*, 85.

16. Paster, *The Body Embarrassed*.

17. My divergence from Paster echoes that of Schoenfeldt, who argues that for early modern writers (particularly those influenced by Galenic physiology), "self-discipline . . . [was] imagined as a necessary step towards any prospect of liberation" (*Bodies and Selves*, 11). However, I follow Paster in holding onto gender as a key category of analysis when making claims about embodied subjectivity, for, pace Schoenfeldt, there are different issues at stake for men and women in the practice of self-fortification.

18. William Harrison, *The Difference of Hearers. Or an Exposition of the Parable of the Sower* (London, 1614), 17.

19. Ibid., 18.

20. John Donne, *The Sermons of John Donne*, ed. Evelyn M. Simpson and George R. Potter, vol. 6 (Berkeley and Los Angeles: University of California Press, 1962), vol. 6, sermon 10, ll. 459–63.

21. On the privileging of the ear over the eye in Protestant theology, see Crockett, 53–56 and Smith, *Acoustic World*, 261–69. On the persistence of iconophilia in Protestant practice, see Diehl. On the hierarchy of sight versus sound in the early modern period more generally, see Gurr, *Playgoing*, esp. 86–98, and Thomas Frangenberg, "*Auditus Visu Prestantior*: Comparisons of Hearing and Vision in Charles De Bovelles's *Liber De Sensibus*," in *The Second Sense: Studies in Hearing and Musical Judgement from Antiquity to the Seventeenth Century*, ed. Charles Burnett, Michael Fend, and Penelope Gouk (London: Warburg Institute, 1991), 71–89.

22. Robert Wilkinson, *A Jewell for the Eare* (London, 1605), sig. A5v. On Shakespeare's use of "ear" in this agricultural sense, see Folkerth, esp. 79–80.

23. Wilkinson, sig. A5r.

24. Ibid., sig. A8r, emphasis mine.

25. Ibid., sig. B1v.

26. Ibid., sig. A8v; A4v.

27. Stephen Egerton, *The Boring of the Eare, Contayning a Plaine and Profitable Discourse by Way of Dialogue, Concerning 1. Our Preparation Before Hearing. 2. Our Demeanour in Hearing. 3. Our Exercise After We Have Heard the Word of God* (London, 1623), sig. B4r; B2r.

28. M. G. Gifford, *A Sermon on the Parable of the Sower* (London, 1582), sig. A8v.

29. Ibid., B5r, emphasis mine.

30. Harrison, dedicatory epistle.

31. All sermons on the parable of the sower prescribe various exercises that parishioners may practice to improve what we might call their aural fertility. Though preachers vary in their recommendations, they generally agree that good listening involves first preparing oneself to receive the Word, like one prepares the soil before planting. Egerton explains that the ears will work more effectively if the body and mind have been cleansed. Among the conditions he cites for achieving an "obedient heart and eare" (sig. B5r) are avoiding "surfetting and drunkennesse, and disorder in Dyet" (sig. B6v) and keeping one's mind free of "prejudice" by not reading too much on one's own (sig. B7v). Once the ears are ready to receive the Word, the listener must be careful to attend to the entirety of the sermon and ideally should continue to discuss the sermon after leaving church.

32. Although critics disagree about whether salvation is secular or spiritual, what role patience plays in this process, how the story of renewal is structured, and how female characters affect male transformation, there is significant consensus that the male heroes of the late plays learn personal and political skills as they undergo trials of faith in family, God, society, and self. In addition to Bieman, see, for example, John Arthos, "Pericles, Prince of Tyre: A Study in the Dramatic Use of Romantic Narrative," *Shakespeare Quarterly* 4, no. 3 (1953): 257–70; Charles Frey, "'O Sacred, Shadowy, Cold, and Constant Queen': Shakespeare's Imperiled and Chastening Daughters of Romance," in *The Woman's Part: Feminist Criticism of Shakespeare*, ed. Carolyn Ruth Swift Lenz, Gayle Greene, and Carol Thomas Neely (Urbana: University of Illinois Press, 1980), 295–313; Constance Jordan, *Shakespeare's Monarchies: Ruler and Subject in the Romances* (Ithaca: Cornell University Press, 1997); Patricia K. Meszaros, "*Pericles*: Shakespeare's Divine Musical Comedy," in *Shakespeare and the Arts: A Collection of Essays from the Ohio Shakespeare Conference, 1981, Wright State University, Dayton, Ohio*, ed. Cecile Williamson Cary and Henry S. Limouze (Washington, D.C.: University Press of America, 1982), 3–20; Douglas Peterson, *Time, Tide and Tempest: A Study of Shakespeare's Romances* (San Marino, Calif.: Huntington Library, 1972).

33. Whereas Shakespeare's tragedies meditate more heavily on the dangers of aurality—and, thus, not coincidentally, are the focus of Gross's study and Pollard's chapter on poisonous language—the late plays are more concerned with the role of aurality in positive transformations of self.

34. Peggy Muñoz Simonds, *Myth, Emblem, and Music in Shakespeare's* Cymbeline: *An Iconographic Reconstruction* (Newark: University of Delaware Press, 1992). Simonds includes Innogen in this argument; as I shall suggest in the next section, how-

ever, Innogen's auditory experiences differ in significant ways from those of her father and husband.

35. Maurice Hunt, *Shakespeare's Romance of the Word* (Lewisburg, Pa.: Bucknell University Press, 1990), 21, 23. This focus on muteness as a sign of men's impotence recurs in scholarship on the late plays. See, for instance, Martin Orkin, *Local Shakespeares: Proximations and Power* (London: Routledge, 2005).

36. Preface to Egerton, sig. A8r.

37. Citations of *Pericles* follow Suzanne Gossett, ed., *Pericles*, The Arden Shakespeare, 3d series (London: Arden Shakespeare, 2004). I deviate here from my usual practice of citing the Norton (based on the Oxford) edition of the play because of its highly interventionist textual emendations. For a useful critique of the Norton version, see Gossett's introduction, which also provides a thorough overview of the complicated editorial history of the play.

38. Gifford, sig. A8r. Of course, unlike many of the auditors to whom Gifford preaches, Leontes' verbal reactions, the voice of a king, carry significant weight, enabling him to throw the entire "sermon" off-course as well.

39. Ibid., sig. A4v.

40. Ibid., sig. A7r.

41. Campbell Scott and Eric Simonson, *Hamlet*, 178 min. (Hallmark Entertainment, 2000). Scott's Hamlet is physically assaulted through the ears by the Ghost's message; when the Ghost departs, blood pours out from Hamlet's ears, as he doubles over in pain.

42. Many critics have examined the late plays' emphasis on childbearing and fertility, and the implications for male rulers. On childbirth as a form of work, see Maurice Hunt, *Shakespeare's Labored Art: Stir, Work, and the Late Plays*, Studies in Shakespeare (New York: Peter Lang, 1995); on breeding and renewal, see Peterson; on the generativity of political dynasties, see Jordan; on healthy fertility versus incest in *Pericles*, see W. B. Thorne, "Pericles and the 'Incest-Fertility' Opposition," *Shakespeare Quarterly* 22, no. 1 (1971): 43–56; on maternity and the gendering of storytelling, see Helen Hackett, "'Gracious Be the Issue': Maternity and Narrative in Shakespeare's Late Plays," in Richards and Knowles, eds., *Shakespeare's Late Plays*, 25–39; on birth and narrative structure, see Helen Wilcox, "Gender and Genre in Shakespeare's Tragicomedies," in *Reclamations of Shakespeare*, ed. A. J. Hoenselaars, Studies in Literature (Amsterdam and Atlanta: Rodopi, 1994), 129–38.

43. Among the most influential proponents of this view is Northrop Frye, *The Secular Scripture: A Study of the Structure of Romance* (Cambridge, Mass.: Harvard University Press, 1976). See also F. D. Hoeniger, ed., *Pericles*, The Arden Shakespeare, 2d series (London: Methuen, 1963).

44. F. Elizabeth Hart, "'Great Is Diana' of Shakespeare's Ephesus," *SEL* 43, no. 2 (2003): 347–74. See also Gossett, 114–15.

45. This offers clear evidence of the problem inherent in Stanley Cavell's division between masculine, active knowledge and feminine, passive intuition. Such gendered binaries of epistemology are blurred constantly in the late plays, where male characters achieve states of mental and emotional stability by learning to balance an intu-

itive aural openness with an aggressive pursuit of the word. Stanley Cavell, *Disowning Knowledge in Six Plays of Shakespeare* (Cambridge: Cambridge University Press, 1987).

46. See, for example, Hunt; Fawkner; and Palfrey.

47. Doreen Delvecchio and Antony Hammond, eds., *Pericles, Prince of Tyre*, The New Cambridge Shakespeare (Cambridge: Cambridge University Press, 1998). Q2's "defended," however, is a better choice than Q1's "defend." As Suzanne Gossett has pointed out to me, although Delvecchio and Hammond claim "defend" can be used as a past participle, their source, Abbot, does not give an example of a simple verb being used in this way. There is also disagreement among editors over whether the quarto's "parts" should be substituted with "ports," which plays on the early modern understanding of ears as gates of entry into the body and soul. A number of editors have found "parts" to be too vague. According to F. D. Hoeniger, ed., *Pericles*, it is an insufficient match for the military force conveyed by "battery." Of course, if Q2's "defended" is left to stand, an option Hoeniger does not consider, this would lend even more powerful military overtones to the image.

48. Richard Brathwaite, *Essaies Upon the Five Senses* (London, 1620), 9.

49. Ibid.

50. Cited in Smith, *Acoustic World*, 101.

51. Thomas Tomkis, *Lingua: Or the Combat of the* Tongue, *and the Five Senses for Superiority* (London, 1607), sig. A3r.

52. Ibid., sig. A3v. In *Lingua* the gendering of speech as female and hearing as male produces fictional and ideological confusion. For when Lingua claims that Auditus has "beene chaind unto my tongue, / . . . ravisht with my words" (sig. A4r), she challenges not only Microcosm's political structure but its gender order as well. Given the relationship I have been discussing between hearing and the receptive, reproductive body, it is interesting that Auditus's concerns about his superiority over Lingua are expressed in terms of his anxieties about his male role in reproduction. Auditus tells Lingua that without the "use of hearing," her organs of speech produce nothing but "Tunes without sense, words inarticulate." "Words," he continues mischievously, "are thy Children, but of my begetting" (sig. A4r).

53. Most editors agree that Pericles performs some physical action here, even though the quarto includes no stage direction. Such violence would be in keeping with the other late plays, where male heroes unknowingly physically abuse their disguised loved ones—e.g., Posthumous strikes Innogen when she is disguised as Fidele.

54. *Pericles'* description of Marina as inducing starvation the more she offers food recalls characterizations of Cleopatra as a woman who "makes hungry / Where most she satisfies" (*Antony and Cleopatra* 2.2.242–43). Of course, when Cleopatra is hungry for news concerning Antony in 1.5, she seems to have more in common with Pericles than Marina; rather than waiting patiently for the messenger to divulge Antony's message—which "sticks" in the messenger's heart—she boldly declares "Mine ear must pluck it thence" (1.5.41).

55. On music in *Pericles* and specifically whether the audience is made privy to Pericles' aural perspective or to the perspective of the others onstage, see Meszaros. As

she and others have noted, Lysimachus's confirmation that he, too, hears the music ("Music, my lord? I hear—" [5.1.220]) does not necessarily indicate his ability to hear the spheres but may rather represent an attempt to humor Pericles—Lysimachus's claim to hear the music follows his comment to the others regarding Pericles, "It is not good to cross him, Give him way" (5.1.219).

56. C. L. Barber and Richard P. Wheeler, *The Whole Journey: Shakespeare's Power of Development* (Berkeley and Los Angeles, Calif.: University of California Press, 1986), 327.

57. *Oxford English Dictionary*, s.v. "nip," 1.

58. Gifford, sig. B4v, emphasis mine; sig. B6r.

59. Ibid., sig. C2r.

60. Delvecchio and Hammond, note to 5.1.190.

61. When at the end of the play, Pericles marries his daughter off to the governor of Mitteline, one of the very men who tried to procure her sexual services while she was enslaved in the brothel, the connections between the regeneration of a line and Marina's physical body are further established. The marriage arrangement, according to Margaret Healy, may throw into question the ultimate success of Pericles' personal and political recovery. Situating the play within medico-political discourses about sexually transmitted diseases, Healy argues that when Pericles marries his daughter off to the potentially pox-stricken Lysimachus, he places his dynasty in jeopardy once again. Margaret Healy, "*Pericles* and the Pox," in *Shakespeare's Late Plays: New Readings*, ed. Jennifer Richards and James Knowles (Edinburgh: Edinburgh University Press, 1999), 92–107.

62. Barber argues that Pericles' "special relationship to femininity" is evinced by his "avoidance of all aggressive self-assertions" and his use of maternal metaphors (316). On the ways heroes of the late plays unapologetically adopt traits usually assigned to female characters, such as vulnerability, passivity, and emotionality, see Marianne Novy, "Shakespeare's Female Characters as Actors and Audience," in Lenz, Greene, and Neely, eds., *Woman's Part*, 256–70. For more recent discussions of the feminine in these late plays, see, for example, Wilcox, who notes the theme of maternity and argues that the structure of the genre mimics birthing; Hackett, who argues that representations of maternity in the plays shed light on the role of women as generators of narrative; and Fawkner, who argues it is the "noncompetitive atmosphere" (34) of the plays—including their emphasis on emotional states such as pity—that characterizes the plays as feminine.

63. A number of critics have emphasized the eloquence of female characters in the late plays. On Hermione, see Enterline, *Rhetoric of the Body*, esp. chap. 5; M. Lindsay Kaplan and Katherine Eggert, "'Good Queen, My Lord, Good Queen': Sexual Slander and the Trials of Female Authority in *The Winter's Tale*," *Renaissance Drama* 25 (1994): 89–118; Carol Thomas Neely, "*The Winter's Tale*: The Triumph of Speech," *SEL: Studies in English Literature, 1500–1900* 15 (1975): 321–38. On Paulina, see Carolyn Asp, "Shakespeare's Paulina and the *Consolatio* Tradition," *Shakespeare Studies* 11 (1978): 145–58; Patricia Southard Gourlay, "'O My Most Sacred Lady': Female Metaphor in *The Winter's Tale*," *English Literary Renaissance* 5, no. 3 (1975): 375–95; and Wayne. And on Marina's speeches in the brothel, see Stephen Dickey, "Language and Role in *Per-*

icles," English Literary Renaissance 16, no. 3 (1986): 550–66; Lorraine Helms, "The Saint in the Brothel: Or, Eloquence Rewarded," *Shakespeare Quarterly* 41, no. 3 (1990): 319–32. And on all three figures, see Ewbank. Helms's compelling reading of the brothel scenes is suggestive of the complications that accompany the assumption that female eloquence is inherently empowering.

64. Palfrey, 196.

65. Ibid., 211.

66. Indeed, Marina, Paulina, and Innogen showcase impressive rhetorical skills, often convincing male authorities to follow seemingly irrational courses of action. Innogen, disguised as a page, convinces the king to demand that Giacomo tell them about the ring he wears; Paulina, merely the handmaid to the king's dead wife, persuades Leontes not to remarry; and Marina, known only as a poor maid, compels Pericles to speak the first words he has uttered in months.

67. Some of the most interesting work on gender and the late plays has come from studies of their construction of masculinity and what this means for the plays' male protagonists. Critics have suggested that the heroes of these plays become more successful leaders when they adopt traditionally feminine traits, like admitting fault, listening to counsel, and choosing diplomacy over violence. For instance, Smith, *Shakespeare and Masculinity*, discusses the change in forms of masculinity as a function of the advanced age of the actors enacting the roles of the plays' protagonists. Robin Headlam Wells notes in these plays a shift in models of masculinity, from the martial Hercules seen in the histories and tragedies to the pacifist Orpheus embodied by Prospero. Robin Headlam Wells, *Shakespeare on Masculinity* (Cambridge: Cambridge University Press, 2000). I concur that the plays' valuation of feminine attributes leads to more positive portrayals of men.

68. Maus, 182–209.

69. Harrison, 15.

70. Braithwaite, 26–27.

71. Stephano Guazzo, *The Civile Conversation*, ed. Charles Whibley, trans. George Pettie [1581], 2 vols., The Tudor Translations (New York: Alfred A. Knopf, 1925), 51–52.

72. Lucius Annaeus Seneca, *The Workes of Lucius Annæus Seneca, Both Morrall and Naturall* (London, 1614), 218.

73. Richard Younge, *The Victory of Patience, and Benefit of Affliction, with How to Husband It So, That the Weakest Christian (with Blessing from above) May Bee Able to Support Himselfe in His Most Miserable Exigents* (London, 1636), 120.

74. Green, 463. Elizabeth Cary, *The Tragedy of Mariam the Fair Queen of Jewry*, ed. Barry Weller and Margaret W. Ferguson (Berkeley and Los Angeles: University of California Press, 1994), 3.3.183.

75. Cary, 3.1.27–28. See Green, 464.

76. Stephen Gosson, *The School of Abuse* (London, 1579), sig. F4r-v.

77. William Prynne, *Histrio-Mastix: The Players Scourge; or, the Actor's Tragedie* (London, 1633), 921.

78. John Weever, *Ancient Funerall Monuments within the United Monarchie of Great Britaine, Ireland, and the Islands Adjacent with the Dissolved Monasteries Therein Contained* (London, 1631), 75. Interestingly the story takes a bad turn only when the hus-

band realizes what is happening and threatens to sue the Abbot for his impropriety. The Abbot takes the "poor husband" to ecclesiastical court and sues him for defamation.

79. Philip Massinger, *The Bond-Man: An Antient Storie* (London, 1624), sig. F2v.

80. Ibid., sig. D3v.

81. For a discussion of chaste ears in *Comus*, see Jean E. Graham, "Virgin Ears: Silence, Deafness, and Chastity in Milton's *Masque*," *Milton Studies* 36 (1998): 1–17. Though Graham's essay focuses for the most part on the Lady's silence, it offers an interesting argument about the "duplicitous" (14) nature of the Lady's deafness: she claims not to hear, but proves she understands perfectly, Comus's meaning.

82. See, for example, Dickey; Helms; and Bieman.

83. It is worth noting that Marina stops her ears directly after the Bawd intimates that Marina's life as a prostitute will involve miscegenation: she will "taste gentlemen of all fashions . . . [and] shall have the difference of all complexions" (4.2.72–74). Thus, at stake in Marina's aural defensiveness is not only her chaste femininity but (as in the case of Miranda in *The Tempest*) the racial identity of her heirs.

84. We might observe that for male characters, even the less heroic ones, beneficial self-protection is not figured in aural terms. An interesting comparison case is *Pericles*, where Antiochus's protection from harmful words is figured in visual terms. Pericles lets it be known that he has deciphered Antiochus's incestuous relationship with his daughter but won't divulge it publicly, knowing that the news will merely harm his own life (his "breath [will be] gone"), and not Antiochus's: "For vice repeated is like the wandering wind / Blows dust in others' eyes to spread itself; / And yet the end of all is bought thus dear: / The breath is gone, and the sore eyes see clear. / To stop the air would hurt them" (1.1.97–101)

85. Gossett, 118.

86. Mary Zimmerman, dir., *Pericles*, performed at the Goodman Theatre, Chicago, January 7, 2006. This production was first staged in Washington, D.C., November 2004–January 2005.

87. This image is picked up again later in the play when Arviragus assures his father that the British forces will be too distracted during the battle to notice the brothers' presence: "It is not likely / That when they hear their Roman horses neigh, / Behold their quartered files, have both their eyes / And ears so cloyed importantly as now, / That they will waste their time upon our note" (4.4.16–20).

88. Richard III employs a similar strategy before trying to woo Elizabeth. He convinces her mother Queen Elizabeth to "prepare" the young Elizabeth's ears so that she will be receptive to Richard's wooing: "to thy daughter go. / Make bold her bashful years with your experience. / Prepare her ears to hear a wooer's tale (*Richard III* 4.4.273.38–40).

89. Taylor, 34.

90. Ibid.

91. Ibid., 36.

92. As Valerie Wayne has pointed out to me, Innogen seems to recognize here a common motif of misogynist discourse of the period, whereby women are blamed for inciting male lust. If so, then Innogen's aural defensiveness might be read as a de-

flection not only of Giacomo's seductive speech but also of the force of the misogynist accusation he articulates.

93. It is worth pausing to observe Cloten's comical invocation of the term "eunuch" here. Although Cloten's bawdy rhetoric throughout the serenade scene aims to link oral/aural penetration with sexual mastery, his reference to eunuchs undermines this association. Eunuchs are renown for their potent singing voices while equally famous for their sexual impotence, particularly their inability to produce offspring.

94. Wilkinson, sig. A6r.

95. Taylor, 44.

96. Butler, *Excitable Speech*, 19; 15.

97. Ibid., 19.

98. Ibid., 26.

99. Ibid., 2.

100. Ibid., 15.

101. As Lois McNay notes, although Bourdieu's approach to embodied subjectivity has exerted less influence on feminist thought than have the approaches of Foucault and Lacan, his ideas are more generative for theorizing the relationship between female subjectivity and agency. Foucault and Lacan offer "negative paradigms of subjectivity" which, as they tend to produce overly determinist accounts of identity formation, do not sufficiently theorize the ways individuals interact with and shape political and social structures. When such accounts do make room for agency, they tend to confine it to the realm of the symbolic or understand it to work primarily at a prereflexive and, in the case of more materialist approaches, libidinal level. Since many feminist critics have offered eloquent critiques of Foucault and Lacan on precisely these grounds, in the interests of efficiency, I will only briefly summarize these critiques as they are described in Lois McNay, *Gender and Agency: Reconfiguring the Subject in Feminist and Social Theory* (Cambridge: Polity Press, 2000). In the case of Lacan, feminists have struggled with his "uni-directional account of subject formation as the introjection of the repressive law of the symbolic" (8), an account that tends to discount or underemphasize historical and cultural variability and reify the terms of women's subordination through the notion of a phallocentric order. Moreover, insofar as Lacan locates transformative potential in the unconscious, he is unable to ascribe agency to wider material practices and thus "a more substantive account of agency beyond the individualist terms of a libidinal politics is foreclosed" (8). Foucault's earlier work, insofar as it views individuals as powerfully inscribed by disciplinary regimes, also forecloses agency, as many critics have noted. And while his later work on the "care of the self" aims at a more useful notion of individual self-fashioning, it lacks sufficiently detailed elaboration of this idea and can ultimately be accused of offering a "solipsistic outlook of an aesthetics of existence" (9). McNay ultimately argues that a more generative model of agency emerges from theorists who focus more fully on social transformation in their accounts of the emergency of subjectivity. For the study of embodment, she argues persuasively for the usefulness of Bourdieu, whose ideas prove similarly fruitful for my interest in theorizing hearing as an agentive practice.

102. Pierre Bourdieu, *Outline of a Theory of Practice* (Cambridge: Cambridge Uni-

versity Press, 1977). My explanation of Bourdieu's philosophy of agency is greatly indebted to McNay's account.

103. For a critical analysis of Bourdieu's concept of *habitus* as it pertains to the performance of speech acts, see Butler, *Excitable Speech*, chap. 4. Butler argues that in the process of providing a social instead of formal account of the performative forces of language, Bourdieu assumes social positions to be static, rather than themselves constructed *by* performativity. "By claiming that performative utterances are only effective when they are spoken by those who are (already) in a position of social power to exercise words as deeds, Bourdieu inadvertently forecloses the possibility of an agency that emerges from the margins" (156).

104. Taylor, 23.

105. Younge, 119–20.

106. Prynne, 984.

107. Richard Brathwaite, *The Penitent Pilgrim* (London, 1641), 296.

108. I. B., *The Psalme of Mercy: Or, A Meditation Upon the 51. Psalme, by a True Penitent* (London, 1625), 140–41.

109. Robert Greene, *The Repentance of Robert Greene Maister of Artes. Wherein by Himselfe is Laid Open His Loose Life, with the Manner of His Death* (London, 1592), sig. C2v.

110. Robert Greene, *The Second Part of Conny-Catching* (London, 1591), 3.

111. Donne, *Fifty Sermons*, 234.

112. John Downe, *Certaine Treatises . . . Published at the Instance of His Friends* (Oxford, 1633), 10–11.

113. Hadrian Dorrell, *Willobie His Avisa. Or the True Picture of a Modest Maid, and of a Chast and Constant Wife* (London, 1594), 8.

114. Downe, 7; 8.

115. Ibid., 2.

116. Plutarch, *The Philosophie, Commonlie Called, the Morals* (London, 1603), 52.

117. Downe, 2.

118. Ibid., 10.

119. Ibid., 16.

120. Crockett, *The Play of Paradox*.

121. David Sundelson, "'So Rare a Wonder'd Father': Prospero's *Tempest*," in *Representing Shakespeare: New Psychoanalytic Essays*, ed. Murray M. Schwartz and Coppélia Kahn (Baltimore: Johns Hopkins University Press, 1980), 36. Another influential reading of Miranda as powerless under Prospero's patriarchal control is Ann Thompson, "'Miranda, Where's Your Sister?': Reading Shakespeare's *The Tempest*," in *Feminist Criticism: Theory and Practice*, ed. Susan Sellers, Linda Hutcheon, and Paul Perron (Toronto: University of Toronto Press, 1991), 45–55.

122. David Lindley, ed., *The Tempest*, The New Cambridge Shakespeare (Cambridge: Cambridge University Press, 2002), introduction 73; 72. A key exception is James, whom I discuss below.

123. Stephen Orgel, ed., *The Tempest*, The Oxford Shakespeare (Oxford: Clarendon Press, 1987), 16–18.

124. Discussion of the Miranda role in this production can be found in Herbert R.

Coursen, *The Tempest: A Guide to the Play*, Greenwood Guides to Shakespeare (Westport, Conn.: Greenwood Press, 2000), 166.

125. Much earlier scholarship on audience response emphasizes the extent to which audience response is directed or, in Jean Howard's phrase, "orchestrated" by Shakespeare's scripts or by actors of the plays. Jean E. Howard, *Shakespeare's Art of Orchestration: Stage Technique and Audience Response* (Urbana: University of Illinois Press, 1984). For instance, Ralph Berry writes that Shakespeare's crowd-pleasers, like *Richard III*, work because Shakespeare deploys strategies for "controlling an audience[,] . . . welding an audience into a fascinated and delighted unity." Ralph Berry, *Shakespeare and the Awareness of the Audience* (London: Macmillan, 1985), 16. See also Phyllis Rackin, "The Role of the Audience in Shakespeare's *Richard II*," *Shakespeare Quarterly* 36, no. 3 (1985): 262–81.

126. Cited in Gurr, *Playgoing*, 222.

127. Ibid., 216.

128. Rebhorn, *Emperor of Men's Minds*, 149. Exemplifying this rhetorical tradition are the comments of Vives regarding the purpose of rhetoric. According to Vives, one of the main purposes of rhetoric is not "delectare" ("delight") but rather "detenere" ("detain," "occupy") because listeners are seized ("capiuntur") by things that are delightful. Wayne Rebhorn, "'The Emperour of Men's Minds': The Renaissance Trickster as *Homo Rhetoricus*," in *Creative Imitation: New Essays on Renaissance Literature In Honor of Thomas M. Greene*, ed. David Quint et al., *Medieval and Renaissance Texts and Studies* (Binghamton, NY: Center for Medieval and Early Renaissance Studies, 1992), 51.

129. Thomas Heywood, *An Apology for Actors* (London, 1612), sig. G1v; G2v.

130. Prynne, 444.

131. My overview of audience types is greatly indebted to Dympna Callaghan's chapter "What Is an Audience?" in *Shakespeare Without Women*, the implications of which I discuss below.

132. Ibid., 162.

133. Howard, *Shakespeare's Art*, 6. Howard's later work places a greater emphasis on audience members' agency, though this is primarily visual, as women were "spectators, subjects who looked." See *Stage and Social Struggle*, 79.

134. Crockett, 58–59; 70.

135. The centrality of aural sensory perception to playgoing in this still significantly oral-based society is only reinforced in the language used to describe early modern theatergoing: whereas in modern English people go to "see" a play, in early modern English, they went to "hear" one. See Gurr, *Playgoing*, esp. 86–98.

136. I am grateful to P. A. Skantze for informing me about this production. For more on the correspondence between Miranda and the audience, see Barbara A. Mowat, *The Dramaturgy of Shakespeare's Romances* (Athens: University of Georgia Press, 1976), 80–82.

137. Shakespeare's plays often evoke a correlation between the aural experience of characters and that of playhouse audiences. The challenge at the beginning of *2 Henry IV*—"Open your ears; for which of you will stop / The vent of hearing when loud Rumour speaks?" (Induction, 1–2)—is directed not only toward the characters in the

play who cannot resist hearing and spreading rumors about Hotspur's victory; it is spoken for the benefit of the audience, an attempt to seize the attention of a distracted and perhaps rowdy theater crowd. See Smith, *Acoustic World*, 271–77, on Shakespeare's use of prologues and other devices for "establishing the auditory field of a play within the first few moments" (276).

138. Retelling the prehistory of a play is never easy, but Prospero's methods are particularly flat compared to some of Shakespeare's other narrators. The captain in *Twelfth Night* manages to tell the saga of the sunken ship and the loss of Sebastian's life in ten brief but rich lines. *Romeo and Juliet* conveys its backstory through a compact, well-crafted sonnet. In *Pericles* the backstory is given to us by our very own bard in the person of Gower, and *Cymbeline* offers essential information through a dialogue between two gentlemen. Prospero's narration is a tedious monologue, lacking many of the aesthetic features that encourage hearers' attentions in other plays.

139. Some prior scholarship on audience has offered related observations. Meredith Skura, for instance, convincingly outlines the degree to which early modern actors, like their modern counterparts, could be energized by the perceived hostilities of an audience and concomitant anxieties about pleasing them through the performance. An "adversarial relationship" between actor and audience is part of what "generates the electricity of live performance." In a sense, audience members contribute to the success of the theatrical experience through their resistance to the charm of actors. Meredith Anne Skura, *Shakespeare the Actor and the Purposes of Playing* (Chicago: University of Chicago Press, 1993), 16; 17. The power of audience members is elaborated in different, but related, terms in Yachnin, *Stage-Wrights*, which argues that as commercial playing companies became less reliant on aristocratic patrons, they were relatively powerless to influence the political arena and more responsive to the demands of their paying audiences.

140. Meszaros, 14; Bieman, 35; Fawkner; David Richman, *Laughter, Pain, and Wonder: Shakespeare's Comedies and the Audience in the Theater* (Newark: University of Deleware Press, 1990).

141. On controlling audience reactions, see Marco Mincoff, *Things Supernatural and Causeless: Shakespearean Romance* (rpt., Newark: University of Delaware Press, 1992). On the ways these plays engage audiences, see Richard Paul Knowles, "'The More Delay'd, Delighted': Theophanies in the Last Plays," *Shakespeare Studies* 15 (1982): 269–80; Richard Paul Knowles, "'Wishes Fall Out as They're Will'd': Artist, Audience, and *Pericles*'s Gower," *English Studies in Canada* 9, no. 1 (1983): 14–24. Engagement is a psychological term that can be used to describe an audience member's identification with a fictional character or world, an identification that can become so strong that playgoers momentarily forget they are in a theater and believe the events on stage to be real-world happenings. For an introduction to engagement in Shakespeare, see Maynard Mack, "Engagement and Detachment in Shakespeare's Plays," in *Essays on Shakespeare and Elizabethan Drama in Honor of Hardin Craig*, ed. Richard Hosley (Columbia: University of Missouri Press, 1962), 275–96. According to some critics, engagement is central to the pleasures of theatergoing. Gary Taylor distinguishes the "ordinary playgoer"—one who is seeing the play for the first time and is willing to "submit to the collective will" of the playhouse—from the "abnormal"

playgoer, who brings to the theater an a priori investment in the play (from either reading the play-text or viewing other performances). The latter will be denied "the real pleasure stimulated by the performance." Gary Taylor, *To Analyze Delight: A Hedonistic Criticism of Shakespeare* (Newark: University of Delaware Press, 1985), 9. Thomas Cartelli argues that pleasure is "the prevailing aim of Elizabethan playgoing and that engagement, not resistance, is the primary medium through which playgoers experience pleasure." It is when theatergoers identify with the characters, set aside their critical faculties, and allow the theater to resonate with their deepest fantasies and desires that, Cartelli argues, they experience the delights of a play. Thomas Cartelli, *Marlowe, Shakespeare, and the Economy of Theatrical Experience* (Philadelphia: University of Pennsylvania Press, 1991), xiv. The argument that engagement is necessary for pleasure can be accompanied by several problematic claims: first, that involvement with the stage action happens at a deep, emotional, and *thus* irrational or uncritical level; second, that audience members, who, at this deep level are fundamentally the same, find the same experiences pleasurable; third, that the act of critique and a feeling of distance from the stage action are inherently displeasurable experiences. For a summary of some of the challenges that face audience response criticism, see James Hirsh, "Editor's Comment: Morgann, Greenblatt, and Audience Response," *Studies in the Literary Imagination* 26, no. 1 (1993): 1–6. For an able, more recent effort to complicate some of these assumptions, see Jeremy Lopez, *Theatrical Convention and Audience Response in Early Modern Drama* (Cambridge: Cambridge University Press, 2003), which argues that early modern plays encourage and cultivate the audience's awareness of theatrical devices; the experience of self-consciousness is, in fact, a key pleaure of playgoing.

142. Bieman, 7.

143. Fawkner, 17–18.

144. The role of Gower has become the catalyst for a debate over whether engagement or detachment is the primary form of audience response in *Pericles*. According to some critics, Gower's extradramatic address destroys dramatic illusion, provoking audience's detachment (Peterson). Other critics argue that Gower stimulates the audience's involvement in the play (Knowles). On detachment in *Pericles*, see also Mowat, *Dramaturgy*, chap. 2. On detachment in the late plays, see Richman, esp. 111; Mythili Kaul, "*Pericles*: Shakespeare's Parable for the Theatre," *Forum for Modern Language Studies* 28, no. 2 (1992): 97–104.

145. This is the case in Mowat's *The Dramaturgy*, wherein she argues that "each of the last plays . . . [is] characterized by sporadic, carefully controlled audience engagement and by a world simultaneously frightening, awesome, grotesque, and lyrically beautiful" (31). A similar argument can be found in Kwang Soon Cho, "Shakespeare's Control of Audience Response: Dramatic Techniques in *Pericles*," *The Journal of English Language and Literature* 36, no. 4 (1990): 729–48.

146. If the late plays suggest that successful theater requires a continuing negotiation and balance of powers, then Prospero's epilogue to *The Tempest*—wherein he designates authority to his audience—is not quite the redemptive act that some critics have argued it to be. When Prospero admits he needs the audience's help and approval, "your good hands," he seems to recognize finally the agency of audiences and

to accept that the receivers of art exercise important powers in the theater. Yet Prospero's embrace of the audience's point of view does not differ fundamentally from his earlier retreat from interaction with audiences and his assertion of a position of theatrical superiority, for the "renunciation" speech still maintains a model of monologic theatrical power. When he claims in the epilogue that he is subject to the audience's will, he does not reconstruct the power dynamics of fictional world and theatrical space that have dominated the play thus far. He merely places the audience in the position that he imagines *himself* as heretofore occupying. It is telling that Prospero describes the audience's hold over him as a "spell," not so different from his previously held "spirits to enforce, art to enchant" (14), and he envisions the theater audience as capable of determining the outcome of the show. That little has changed is evident in the final line of the epilogue concerning the audience's capacity to direct Prospero's destiny: "And my ending is despair / Unless I be relieved by prayer, / Which pierces so, that it assaults / Mercy itself" (15–18). Here Mercy is imagined to have ears that can be pierced and assaulted by the audience's prayers; Mercy is rendered as a passive auditor with no choice but to grant these pleas. Moreover, although Prospero may elevate the theater audience to a position of power, he does not represent that power as *auditory* in nature: the audience would need to assume the role of sorcerer and great *orator* in order to exercise their command over the play's outcome. Prospero thus reiterates the problematic theatrical economy he has tried to sustain throughout the play, merely substituting the play's audience for himself and the vulnerable, weak ears of Mercy for what he represents as the easily manipulated ears of his on- and offstage audience.

147. Rebhorn, *Emperor of Men's Minds*, 74.

Chapter 4

1. John Webster, *The Duchess of Malfi and Other Plays*, ed. René Weis, The World's Classics (Oxford: Oxford University Press, 1996), 5.3.35–38. Subsequent citations appear in my text.

2. Lee T. Pearcy, *The Mediated Muse: English Translations of Ovid, 1560–1700* (Hamden, Conn.: Archon Books, 1984), 62.

3. I cite the modern reprinting of the 1632 edition, George Sandys, *Ovid's Metamorphosis: Englished, Mythologized, and Represented in Figures*, ed. Karl K. Hulley and Stanley T. Vandersall (Lincoln: University of Nebraska Press, 1970), 8. Subsequent citations appear in my text. In the case of Sandys's poetic translation, found on pp. 136–41 of this edition, I cite by book and line number.

4. Latin citations, noted by book and line number, are taken from Ovid, *The Metamorphoses*, trans. Frank Justus Miller, 3d ed., revised by G. P. Goold, vol. 1 of 2, Loeb Classical Library (Cambridge, Mass.: Harvard University Press, 1977). For my translations of the Latin, I have consulted and modified Miller. I am grateful to Joanna Alexander for her early help with Ovid's Latin.

5. Jonathan Goldberg, *Voice Terminal Echo: Postmodernism and English Renaissance*

Texts (New York: Methuen, 1986), esp. 12. For other incisive readings of "Narcissus and Echo" that resonate with my own approach but focus more specifically on how the poem reflects on language and subjectivity, see Enterline, *Rhetoric of the Body*, esp. chap. 2; Claire Nouvet, "An Impossible Response: The Disaster of Narcissus," *Yale French Studies* 79 (1991): 95–109; and Gayatri Spivak, "Echo," *New Literary History* 24 (1993): 17–43. See also, Joseph Loewenstein, *Responsive Readings: Versions of Echo in Pastoral, Epic, and the Jonsonian Masque* (New Haven, Conn.: Yale University Press, 1984), esp. chap. 1, which I discuss further below.

6. Sandys was not the first Ovid translator or the first seventeenth-century writer to recognize the pun on "aye." Arthur Golding had chosen a similar translation in his 1565 edition, and Ben Jonson performed the same move in *Cynthia's Revels*. Regardless of whether Sandys was the originator of the pun, his use of it certainly characterizes Echo in a compelling manner. Other translators found creative English translations that do not include the aye/I pun. Sandys's contemporary Henry Reynolds translates this moment, "Heare I not one? quoth he; One, sayes the mayde: / Framing a troth from the last word he sayd," in Henry Reynolds, *Mythomystes Wherein a Short Survay Is Taken of the Nature and Value of True Poesy and Depth of the Ancients Above Our Moderne Poets. To Which Is Annexed the Tale of Narcissus Briefly Mythologized* (London, 1632), 91. Thomas Howell slightly less elegantly writes that Narcissus "Dyd saye is anye here to whome, she answereth her a none." Thomas Howell, *The Fable of Ovid Treting of Narcissus, Tra[n]slated out of Latin into Englysh Mytre, with a Moral There Unto, Very Pleasante to Rede* (London, 1560), sig. A3r.

7. The differences between the project of the translation and the project of the commentary have gone unnoticed in criticism on Sandys. Even Pearcy, one of the few critics to address Sandys's ideological positioning in a book that is admirably attuned to translation theory, does not consider the differences between the translation and the commentary. Pearcy sets up the two parts as equal, and he draws from both for evidence of Sandys's ideas.

8. Judith de Luce, "'O for a Thousand Tongues to Sing': A Footnote on Metamorphosis, Silence, and Power," in *Woman's Power, Man's Game: Essays on Classical Antiquity in Honor of Joy K. King*, ed. Mary DeForest (Wauconda, Ill.: Bolchazy-Carducci, 1993), 305–21.

9. Kaja Silverman, *The Acoustic Mirror: The Female Voice in Psychoanalysis and Cinema*, Theories of Representation and Difference (Bloomington: Indiana University Press, 1988), esp. 49; 164–65. On the role of sound-image synchronization in Hollywood films, see also Mary Ann Doane, "The Voice in the Cinema: The Articulation of Body and Space," *Yale French Studies* 60 (1980): 33–50. Doane argues that "[t]echnical advances in sound recording . . . are aimed at . . . concealing the work of the apparatus" (35).

10. Silverman, 164.

11. Aristotle, in Barnes, ed., Book II, 420a, 28–33.

12. William Gearing, *A Bridle for the Tongue: Or a Treatise of Ten Sins of the Tongue. Cursing, Swearing, Slandering, Scoffing, Filthy-Speaking, Flattering, Censuring, Murmuring, Lying and Boasting* (London, 1663), sig. A3r.

13. Dowland, 6.

14. Robinson, 11.

15. Loewenstein, 54. Loewenstein offers a wealth of information about, and richly developed readings of, representations of Echo in the period. For more on literary representations of Echo, see John Hollander, *The Figure of Echo: A Mode of Allusion in Milton and After* (Berkeley: University of California Press, 1981).

16. There have been some attempts to historicize translations of the *Metamorphoses*. Some studies match particular Ovid translations with the early modern authors who draw on Ovid. See Robert H. Ray, "Marvell's 'To His Coy Mistress' and Sandys's Translation of Ovid's *Metamorphoses*," *Review of English Studies: A Quarterly Journal of English Literature and the English Language* 44, no. 175 (1993): 386–88, Anthony Brian Taylor, "George Sandys and Arthur Golding," *Notes and Queries* 33, no. 3 (1986): 387–91, Anthony Brian Taylor, "Shakespeare and Golding: Viola's Interview with Olivia and Echo and Narcissus," *English Language Notes* 15 (1977): 103–6. The primary purpose of these studies, however, is to shed light on non-Ovidian texts, not to explore the historical context of translations of Ovid. More thorough historical work has been done by those interested in contextualizing translators within a history of ideas. For instance, Pearcy's tightly theorized chapters on Sandys's translation deal with Sandys's use of Bacon and general relation to Neoplatonic ideas. The approach that most closely models the kind of historical scholarship on the translated Ovid that I advocate is Raphael Lyne, "Golding's Englished *Metamorphoses*," *Translation and Literature* 5, no. 2 (1996): 183–200. Lyne situates the translator Arthur Golding within his English Renaissance context, suggesting that Golding's "language of heightened Englishness" may be evidence of his "wish to promote his national culture" (183). My approach differs from Lyne's and Pearcy's in that I focus on how early modern social structures—specifically, early modern gender systems—influenced translations of Ovid.

17. Deborah Rubin, *Ovid's Metamorphoses Englished: George Sandys as Translator and Mythographer* (London: Garland, 1985), 21.

18. Loewenstein, 48.

19. Arthur Golding, *The Fyrst Fower Bookes of P. Ovidius Nasos Worke, Intitled Metamorphosis, Translated Oute of Latin into Englishe Meter* (London, 1565), Book III., sig. B2r, emphasis mine.

20. Howell, A2v, emphasis mine.

21. Golding maintains the sense of "forte" in his translation, beginning the line, "By chance," (III. sig. B2v); Howell also introduces this moment with "By chaunce" (sig. A3r). In Reynolds's less literal translation, Narcissus calls out to his friends because he hears a "noise among the bushes greene / That *unawares* her [Echo's] foote did (tripping) make" (91, emphasis mine). Echo's mishap, her unplanned misstep, thus serves as the catalyst for Narcissus's initiated discourse.

22. *Oxford English Dictionary*, s.v. "relate," 2.

23. I am referring here to Jonson's *Cynthia's Revels*, 1.2, in which Mercury calls for Echo and she appears onstage, played by a visible actor. In Jonson's play, Echo does more than just repeat the ends of others' speeches—she speaks about forty independent lines.

24. Sandys completed his translation of the first five books of Ovid's *Metamor-*

phoses while settled in Virginia and published them in 1621 when he returned to England, making this the first printed work known to be written in the colonized New World. The first edition of this five-book translation has not been found, but a copy of the second edition is owned by the Folger Library (STC 18963.5). Sandys made very few changes to his translation as it moved from one edition to the next. For more publishing history and differences between editions, see Fredson Bowers and Richard Beale Davis, *George Sandys: A Biographical Catalogue of Printed Editions in England to 1700* (New York: New York Public Library, 1950); and James G. McManaway, "The First Five Bookes of *Ovids Metamorphosis*, 1621, Englished by Master George Sandys," *Papers of the Bibliographical Society of the University of Virginia* 1 (1848–49): 71–82.

25. For a helpful index of the names and places mentioned in Sandys's commentary, see Christopher Grose, *Ovid's Metamorphoses: An Index to the 1632 Commentary of George Sandys* (Malibu, Calif.: Undena Publications, 1981).

26. On the echoic trope in Petrarch and the Renaissance lyric, see Dubrow, *Echoes of Desire*; Enterline, *Rhetoric of the Body*; Hollander; and Loewenstein.

27. Sandys is not the originator of this comparison of echoes to a rebounding ball. Aristotle, for example, writes in a similar vein: "An echo occurs, when, a mass of air having been unified, bounded, and prevented from dissipation by the containing walls of a vessel, the air rebounds from this mass of air like a ball from a wall." In Barnes, ed., Book II, 419b, 25–27.

28. Sir Francis Bacon, *De Sapientia Veterum, Entitled the Wisdome of the Ancients* (London, 1619). The influence of Baconian thought on Sandys's *Metamorphosis* is discussed at length by Pearcy. See also Grace Eva Hunter, "The Influence of Frances Bacon on the Commentary of Ovid's *Metamorphoses* by George Sandys" (Ph.D. dissertation, Iowa State University, 1940).

29. Bacon's conclusions here diverge significantly from the ones he articulates elsewhere in *Sylva Sylvarum* regarding sound moving in "arched lines" that cannot be tracked or controlled. See my discussion of Bacon in Chapter 2. The contradictory understandings of sound that I discuss in Chapter 2 are manifested even in the same *text*, let alone the same writer.

30. Bacon, *De Sapientia*, 37.

31. Loewenstein's remarks on Bacon's views of Echo are worth quoting in full: "Echo no longer appears as the uncanny discursiveness *of* the world; instead, Echo figures the conformity of discourse *to* the world. Echo no longer opposes human voice, no longer mimics our voice, for her voice has become ours" (24).

32. This version of the Pan-Echo relationship appears in Longus, *Daphnis and Chloe*, trans. George Thornley (London: Heinemann, 1916), III.23.

33. Reynolds, 110.

34. Rubin, esp. 156–58.

35. Scientific descriptions of the voice are not inherently limiting, of course. We have seen in Chapter 2, for instance, that atomist explanations for acoustics resemble some of Shakespeare's models of effective vocal agency. Sandys, however, clearly uses these scientific discourses for a different purpose; Bacon can be used in the commentary to undermine Echo's vocal agency only because Sandys's translation sets Echo up *to be* undermined.

36. See, for example, Enterline, *Tears of Narcissus*, as well as Enterline, *The Rhetoric of the Body*; Deborah S. Greenhut, *Feminine Rhetorical Culture: Tudor Adaptations of Ovid's Heroides* (New York: Peter Lang, 1988); Elizabeth D. Harvey, *Ventriloquized Voices: Feminist Theory and English Renaissance Texts* (New York: Routledge, 1992).

37. Harvey, 122–23.

38. Greenhut, 22–23.

39. In addition to Harvey and Greenhut, see Ann Rosalind Jones, *The Currency of Eros: Women's Love Lyric in Europe, 1540–1620* (Bloomington: Indiana University Press, 1990); and de Luce. Amy Lawrence similarly posits Ovid's Echo as a victim of "a patriarchal system that wants to keep women silent." In Lawrence's study of the female voice in cinema, Echo—her "voice . . . continually taken from her"—is a symbol of cinema's subordination of sound to image. See Amy Lawrence, *Echo and Narcissus: Women's Voices in Classical Hollywood Cinema* (Berkeley and Los Angeles: University of California Press, 1991), esp. 7. An exception is Enterline in *Rhetoric of the Body*.

40. Of course, neither Harvey nor Greenhut is specifically interested in the Echo figure of Ovid's *Metamorphoses*. By singling out their readings of echoic voice, I intend only to demonstrate that oversight of echoic vocal power can occur even among feminist critics who are familiar with Ovid and with his subversive representations of female speech.

41. Harvey, 120.

42. Greenhut, 11–12. For a more recent example of critical underestimations of Echo, see Judith Deitch's reading of Echo in Spenser's "Ephithalamion." Deitch argues that "[s]ince in Ovid's myth Echo only passively re-sounds other voices," Spenser invokes echo to signify "failed poetic descendance." Judith Deitch, "The Girl He Left Behind: Ovidian *Imitatio* and the Body of Echo in Spenser's 'Epithalamion,'" in *Ovid and the Renaissance Body*, ed. Goran V. Stanivukovic (Toronto: University of Toronto Press, 2001), esp. 224.

Epilogue

1. The claim that Kenilworth's festivities were designed as an elaborate marriage proposal has been discussed by many critics and especially usefully in Ilana Nash, "'A Subject without Subjection': Robert Dudley, Earl of Leicester, and *The Princely Pleasures at Kenelworth Castle*," *Comitatus* 25 (1994): 81–102. The claim that Dudley was using Kenilworth to promote his militant Protestant agenda is advanced persuasively in Susan Frye, *Elizabeth I: The Competition for Representation* (New York: Oxford University Press, 1993), esp. chap. 2.

2. My thanks to Bruce Smith for pointing this out to me and encouraging me to consider the significance of the Kenilworth entertainments to my arguments about voice.

3. George Gascoigne, "A Briefe Rehearsall, or Rather a True Copie of as Much as Was Presented before Her Majesti[e] at Kenelworth During Her Last Aboade There,"

in *The Glasse of Governmement, The Princely Pleasures at Kenelworth Castle, The Steele Glas and Other Poems and Prose Works*, ed. John W. Cunliffe (New York: Greenwood Press, 1969), 91–131, esp. 96–97. Subsequent citations of this text will appear in the body of my text.

4. Joseph Loewenstein notes the degree to which the relationship between Echo and her interlocuter in Gascoigne's text differs significantly from that depicted in the echo-lyrics that had been written by Gascoigne's Continental predecessors. In their lyrics, "the voice of Echo measures not only the speaker's ignorance but his power-lessness as well." In Gascoigne, though, "the relation between the Savage Man and his interlocutor is one of pure and mutual docility" (73).

5. Nash, 97.

6. For an extended discussion of Dudley's courtship of Elizabeth, see Susan Doran, *Monarchy and Matrimony: The Courtships of Elizabeth I* (New York: Routledge, 1996), esp. chap. 3.

7. Frye, *Elizabeth I*, 58.

8. See Smith's discussion of Kenilworth's various sounds in *Acoustic World*, esp. 32–37.

9. All citations follow F. J. Furnivall, ed., *Robert Laneham's Letter: Describing a Part of the Entertainment Unto Queen Elizabeth at the Castle of Kenilworth in 1575* (London: Chatto and Windus Duffield, 1907).

10. This case has been made persuasively in David Scott, "William Patten and the Authorship of 'Robert Laneham's Letter' (1575)," *English Literary Renaissance 7* (1977): 297–306.

11. Frye, *Elizabeth I*, 64.

12. Ibid., 65.

13. *Laneham's Letter*, 15.

14. Ibid.

15. Bruce R. Smith, "Landscape with Figures: The Three Realms of Queen Elizabeth's Country-House Revels," *Renaissance Drama* 8 (1977): esp. 62–63.

Bibliography

Adelman, Janet. *Suffocating Mothers: Fantasies of Maternal Origin in Shakespeare's Plays*, Hamlet *to* The Tempest. New York: Routledge, 1992.

Agrippa, Henry Cornelius. *Three Books of Occult Philosophy.* London, 1651.

Alarcon, Norma. "The Theoretical Subject(s) of This Bridge Called My Back and Anglo-American Feminism." In *Making Face, Making Soul: Haciendo Caras*, edited by Gloria Anzaldua, 356–69. San Francisco: aunt lute, 1990.

Andersen, Jennifer, and Elizabeth Sauer, eds. *Books and Readers in Early Modern England: Material Studies.* Material Texts. Philadelphia: University of Pennsylvania Press, 2002.

Anderson, Judith H. *Words That Matter: Linguistic Perception in Renaissance English.* Stanford, Calif.: Stanford University Press, 1996.

Arthos, John. "Pericles, Prince of Tyre: A Study in the Dramatic Use of Romantic Narrative." *Shakespeare Quarterly* 4, no. 3 (1953): 257–70.

Asp, Carolyn. "Shakespeare's Paulina and the *Consolatio* Tradition." *Shakespeare Studies* 11 (1978): 145–58.

Austern, Linda Phyllis. *Music in Children's Drama of the Later Renaissance.* Philadelphia: Gordon and Breach, 1992.

———. "'No Women Are Indeed': The Boy Actor as Vocal Seductress in Late Sixteenth- and Early Seventeenth-Century English Drama." In *Embodied Voices: Representing Female Vocality in Western Culture*, edited by Leslie C. Dunn and Nancy A. Jones, 83–102. Cambridge: Cambridge University Press, 1994.

Austin, J. L. *How to Do Things with Words.* Edited by J. O. Urmson and Marina Sbisà. 2d ed. Cambridge, Mass.: Harvard University Press, 1975.

Babbit, Frank Cole, trans. *Plutarch's Moralia.* Vol. 1. London: Heinemann, 1927.

Bach, Rebecca Ann. "Tennis Balls: *Henry V* and Testicular Masculinity; or, According to the OED, Shakespeare Doesn't Have Any Balls." *Renaissance Drama* 30 (1999–2001): 3–23.

Bacon, Sir Francis. *De Sapientia Veterum, Entitled the Wisdome of the Ancients.* London, 1619.

———. *The Naturall and Experimentall History of Winds.* London, 1653.

———. *Sylva Sylvarum: Or a Naturall Historie.* London, 1626.

Bailey, Cyril, ed. *Epicurus: The Extant Remains.* Hildesheim: Georg Olms Verlag, 1926.

Bamber, Linda. *Comic Women, Tragic Men: A Study of Gender and Genre in Shakespeare.* Stanford, Calif.: Stanford University Press, 1982.

Barber, C. L., and Richard P. Wheeler. *The Whole Journey: Shakespeare's Power of Development.* Berkeley and Los Angeles: University of California Press, 1986.

Barker, William, ed. *Positions Concerning the Training Up of Young Children.* Toronto: University of Toronto Press, 1994.

Barnes, Jonathan, ed. *The Complete Works of Aristotle: The Revised Oxford Translation.* Vol. 1. Bollingen Series. Princeton, N.J.: Princeton University Press, 1984.

Bartels, Emily C. "Strategies of Submission: Desdemona, the Duchess, and the Assertion of Desire." *SEL* 36 (1996): 417–33.

Barthes, Roland. "The Grain of the Voice." In *Image, Music, Text.* Translated by Stephen Heath, 179–89. New York: Hill and Wang, 1977.

Beaumont, Francis. *The Knight of the Burning Pestle.* Edited by John Doebler. Regents Renaissance Drama. Lincoln: University of Nebraska Press, 1967.

Beaurline, L. A., ed. *King John.* New Cambridge Shakespeare. Cambridge: Cambridge University Press, 1990.

Ben-Amos, Ilana Krausman. *Adolescence and Youth in Early Modern England.* New Haven, Conn.: Yale University Press, 1994.

Berry, Cicely. *The Actor and His Text.* New York: Scribner, 1988.

Berry, Ralph. *Shakespeare and the Awareness of the Audience.* London: Macmillan, 1985.

Bevington, David, Lars Engle, Katherine Eisaman Maus, and Eric Rasmussen, eds. *English Renaissance Drama: A Norton Anthology.* New York: W. W. Norton, 2002.

Bieman, Elizabeth. *William Shakespeare: The Romances.* Twayne's English Authors Series. Boston: Twayne Publishers, 1990.

Blanpied, John W. *Time and Artist in Shakespeare's English Histories.* Newark: University of Delaware Press, 1983.

Bloom, Gina. "'Thy Voice Squeaks': Listening for Masculinity on the Early Modern Stage." *Renaissance Drama* 29 (1998): 39–71.

Boose, Lynda E. "Scolding Brides and Bridling Scolds: Taming the Woman's Unruly Member." *Shakespeare Quarterly* 42, no. 2 (1991): 179–213.

Bourdieu, Pierre. *Outline of a Theory of Practice.* Cambridge: Cambridge University Press, 1977.

Boureau, Alain, and Roger Chartier. *The Cultural Uses of Print in Early Modern France.* Translated by Lydia G. Cochrane. Princeton, N.J.: Princeton University Press, 1989.

Bowers, Fredson, and Richard Beale Davis. *George Sandys: A Biographical Catalogue of Printed Editions in England to 1700.* New York: New York Public Library, 1950.

Brathwaite, Richard. *Essaies Upon the Five Senses.* London, 1620.

———. *The Penitent Pilgrim.* London, 1641.

Braunmuller, A. R., ed. *The Life and Death of King John.* Oxford Shakespeare. Oxford: Clarendon, 1989.

Breitenberg, Mark. *Anxious Masculinity in Early Modern England.* Cambridge: Cambridge University Press, 1996.

Brumwick, Ann. *Booke of Receipts.* Wellcome Western Manuscripts 160. C. 1625–1700.

Bruster, Douglas. *Drama and Market in the Age of Shakespeare.* Cambridge: Cambridge University Press, 1992.

———. *Shakespeare and the Question of Culture: Early Modern Literature and the Cultural Turn.* Early Modern Cultural Studies. New York: Palgrave, 2003.

Buhler, Stephen M. "No Spectre, No Sceptre: The Agon of Materialist Thought in Shakespeare's *Julius Caesar.*" *English Literary Renaissance* 26, no. 2 (1996): 313–32.

Burckhardt, Sigurd. "*King John*: The Ordering of This Present Time." *ELH* 33, no. 2 (1966): 133–53.

Burnyeat, M. F. "How Much Happens When Aristotle Sees Red and Hears Middle C? Remarks on *De Anima* 2. 7–8." In *Essays on Aristotle's* De Anima, edited by Martha C. Nussbaum and Amélie Oksenberg Rorty, 421–34. Oxford: Clarendon, 1995.

Butler, Charles. *The English Grammar, or the Institution of Letters, Syllables, and Words in the English Tongue.* London, 1633.

———. *The Principles of Musick, in Singing and Setting: With the Two-Fold Use Therof, (Ecclesiasticall and Civil).* London, 1636.

Butler, Judith. *Excitable Speech: A Politics of the Performative.* New York: Routledge, 1997.

———. *Gender Trouble: Feminism and the Subversion of Identity.* New York: Routledge, 1990.

Bynum, Terrel Ward. "A New Look at Aristotle's Theory of Perception." In *Aristotle's De Anima in Focus*, edited by Michael Durrant, 90–109. New York: Routledge, 1993.

Callaghan, Dympna. "The Castrator's Song: Female Impersonation on the Early Modern Stage." *Journal of Medieval and Early Modern Studies* 26, no. 2 (1996): 321–53.

———. *Shakespeare Without Women: Representing Gender and Race on the Renaissance Stage.* Accents on Shakespeare. New York: Routledge, 2000.

Callender, Christine, and Deborah Cameron. "Responsive Listening as Part of Religious Rhetoric: The Case of Black Pentecostal Preaching." In *Reception and Response: Hearer Creativity and the Analysis of Spoken and Written Texts*, edited by Graham McGregor and R. S. White, 160–78. New York: Routledge, 1990.

Candido, Joseph. "'Women and Fools Break Off Your Conference': Pope's Degradations and the Form of *King John*." In *Shakespeare's English Histories: A Quest for Form and Genre*, edited by John W. Velz, 91–110. Binghamton, N.Y.: Medieval and Renaissance Texts and Studies, 1996.

———, ed. *King John, Shakespeare: The Critical Tradition.* London: Athlone Press, 1996.

Cartelli, Thomas. *Marlowe, Shakespeare, and the Economy of Theatrical Experience.* Philadelphia: University of Pennsylvania Press, 1991.

Cary, Elizabeth. *The Tragedy of Mariam the Fair Queen of Jewry.* Edited by Barry Weller and Margaret W. Ferguson. Berkeley and Los Angeles: University of California Press, 1994.

Castiglione, Baldesar. *The Book of the Courtier.* Translated by Thomas Hoby. The Tudor Translations. London: David Nutt, 1900.

Cavell, Stanley. *Disowning Knowledge in Six Plays of Shakespeare.* Cambridge: Cambridge University Press, 1987.

Chambers, E. K. *The Elizabethan Stage.* 4 vols. Vol. 2. Oxford: Clarendon, 1923.

Charleton, Walter. *Physiologia Epicuro-Gassendo-Charltoniana: Or a Fabrick of Science Natural Upon the Hypothesis of Atoms.* London, 1654.

Charney, Maurice, and Hanna Charney. "The Language of Madwomen in Shakespeare and His Fellow Dramatists." *Signs* 3 (1977): 451–60.

Chartier, Roger. *Forms and Meanings: Texts, Performances, and Audiences from Codex to Computer.* New Cultural Studies. Philadelphia: University of Pennsylvania Press, 1995.

————. *The Order of Books: Readers, Authors and Libraries in Europe between the Four-teenth and Eighteenth Centuries.* Translated by Lydia G. Cochrane. Cambridge: Polity Press, 1994.

Cho, Kwang Soon. "Shakespeare's Control of Audience Response: Dramatic Techniques in *Pericles.*" *The Journal of English Language and Literature* 36, no. 4 (1990): 729–48.

Cixous, Hélène. "The Laugh of the Medusa." *Signs: Journal of Women in Culture and So-ciety* 1, no. 4 (1976): 875–93.

Clucas, Stephen. "The Atomism of the Cavendish Circle: A Reappraisal." *Seventeenth Century* 9, no. 2 (1994): 247–73.

Cohen, S. Marc. "The Credibility of Aristotle's Philosophy of Mind." In *Aristotle Today: Essays on Aristotle's Idea of Science,* edited by Mohan Matthen, 103–26. Edmonton, Alberta, Canada: Academic Printing and Publishing, 1987.

Coleman, Joyce. *Public Reading and the Reading Public in Late Medieval England and France.* Cambridge: Cambridge University Press, 1996.

Colley, John Scott. *John Marston's Theatrical Drama.* Jacobean Drama Studies. Salzburg: Salzburg Studies in English Literature, 1974.

Coursen, Herbert R. *The Tempest: A Guide to the Play.* Greenwood Guides to Shake-speare. Westport, Conn.: Greenwood Press, 2000.

Cousin, Geraldine. *Shakespeare in Performance: King John.* Manchester: Manchester University Press, 1994.

Crane, Mary Thomas. "What Was Performance?" *Criticism* 43, no. 2 (2001): 169–87.

Crick, Julia, and Alexandra Walsham, eds. *The Uses of Script and Print, 1300–1700.* Cam-bridge: Cambridge University Press, 2004.

Crockett, Bryan. *The Play of Paradox: Stage and Sermon in Renaissance England.* Philadelphia: University of Pennsylvania Press, 1995.

Crooke, Helkiah. *Mikrokosmographia: A Description of the Body of Man.* London, 1615.

Crothall, Lucia. "Antonio." *Plays and Players.* December 1979 (cited October 2, 2005); available from http://members.iconn.net/~ab234/Plays/Antonio/ANPlays_Play-ers.html.

Cuffe, Henrie. *The Differences of the Ages of Mans Life.* London, 1607.

Cummings, Peter. "Hearing in *Hamlet*: Poisoned Ears and the Psychopathology of Flawed Audition." *Shakespeare Yearbook* 1 (1990): 81–92.

Curren-Aquino, Deborah T. "Toward a Star That Danced: Woman as Survivor in Shake-speare's Early Comedies." *Selected Papers from the West Virginia Shakespeare and Renaissance Association* 11 (1986): 50–61.

————, ed. *King John: New Perspectives.* Newark: University of Delaware Press, 1989.

de Grazia, Margreta, Maureen Quilligan, and Peter Stallybrass, eds. *Subject and Object in Renaissance Culture.* Cambridge Studies in Renaissance Literature and Culture. Cambridge: Cambridge University Press, 1996.

Deitch, Judith. "The Girl He Left Behind: Ovidian *Imitatio* and the Body of Echo in Spenser's 'Epithalamion.'" In *Ovid and the Renaissance Body,* edited by Goran V. Stanivukovic, 224–38. Toronto: University of Toronto Press, 2001.

Dekker, Thomas. *The Honest Whore with, the Humours of the Patient Man, and the Long-ing Wife.* London, 1604.

————. *The Shoemaker's Holiday.* Edited by Anthony Parr. New York: W. W. Norton, 1997.

de Luce, Judith. "'O for a Thousand Tongues to Sing': A Footnote on Metamorphosis, Silence, and Power." In *Woman's Power, Man's Game: Essays on Classical Antiquity in Honor of Joy K. King,* edited by Mary DeForest, 305–21. Wauconda, Ill.: Bolchazy-Carducci, 1993.

Delvecchio, Doreen, and Antony Hammond, eds. *Pericles, Prince of Tyre.* The New Cambridge Shakespeare. Cambridge: Cambridge University Press, 1998.

DeMollen, Richard L. "Richard Mulcaster and the Elizabethan Theatre." *Theatre Survey* 13, no. 1 (1972): 28–41.

Derrida, Jacques. "Signature Event Context." *Glyph: Johns Hopkins Textual Studies* 1 (1977): 172–97.

————. *Speech and Phenomena and Other Essays on Husserl's Theory of Signs.* Translated by David B. Allison. Evanston, Ill.: Northwestern University Press, 1973.

Des Chene, Dennis. *Life's Form: Late Aristotelian Conceptions of the Soul.* Ithaca, N.Y.: Cornell University Press, 2000.

Desmet, Christy. "Speaking Sensibly: Feminine Rhetoric in *Measure for Measure* and *All's Well That Ends Well.*" *Renaissance Papers 1986* (1987): 43–51.

Dessen, Alan C. *Titus Andronicus.* Shakespeare in Performance. Manchester: Manchester University Press, 1989.

Detmer-Goebel, Emily. "The Need for Lavinia's Voice: *Titus Andronicus* and the Telling of Rape." *Shakespeare Studies* 29 (2001): 75–92.

Dickey, Stephen. "Language and Role in *Pericles.*" *English Literary Renaissance* 16, no. 3 (1986): 550–66.

Diehl, Huston. *Staging Reform, Reforming the Stage: Protestantism and Popular Theater in Early Modern England.* Ithaca, N.Y.: Cornell University Press, 1997.

Digby, Kenelm. *Two Treatises in the One of Which the Nature of Bodies, in the Other, the Nature of Mans Soule; Is Looked Into: In Way of Discovery, of the Immortality of Reasonable Soules.* Paris, 1644.

Doane, Mary Ann. "The Voice in the Cinema: The Articulation of Body and Space." *Yale French Studies* 60 (1980): 33–50.

Dolan, Frances E. "'Gentleman, I Have One Thing More to Say': Women on Scaffolds in England, 1563–1680." *Modern Philology* 92, no. 2 (1994): 157–78.

Dolman, John, trans. *Those Fyve Questions, Which Marke Tullye Cicero, Disputed in His Manor of Tusculanum: Written Afterwardes by Him, in as Manye Bookes, to His Frende, and Familiar Brutus, in the Latine Tounge. And Nowe, Oute of the Same Translated, & Englished.* London, 1561.

Donawerth, Jane. *Shakespeare and the Sixteenth-Century Study of Language.* Urbana: University of Illinois Press, 1984.

Donne, John. *Fifty Sermons. The Second Volume.* London, 1627.

————. *The Sermons of John Donne.* Edited by Evelyn M. Simpson and George R. Potter. Vol. 6. Berkeley and Los Angeles: University of California Press, 1962.

Donovan, Kathleen. *Feminist Readings of Native American Literature: Coming to Voice.* Tucson: University of Arizona Press, 1998.

Doran, Susan. *Monarchy and Matrimony: The Courtships of Elizabeth I.* New York: Routledge, 1996.

Dorrell, Hadrian. *Willobie His Avisa. Or the True Picture of a Modest Maid, and of a Chast and Constant Wife.* London, 1594.

Dowland, John, trans. *Andreas Ornithoparcus His Micrologus, or Introduction: Containing the Art of Singing.* London, 1609.

Downe, John. *Certaine Treatises . . . Published at the Instance of His Friends.* Oxford, 1633.

Dubrow, Heather. *Echoes of Desire: English Petrarchism and Its Counterdiscourses.* Ithaca, N.Y.: Cornell University Press, 1995.

———. " 'The Tip of His Seducing Tongue': Authorizers in *Henry V,* 'A Lover's Complaint,' and *Othello.*" In *Suffering Ecstasy: Essays on Shakespeare's "A Lover's Complaint,"* edited by Shirley Sharon-Zisser. Aldershot, Hampshire: Ashgate, forthcoming.

Dugan, Holly E. "The Ephemeral History of Perfume: Scent and Sense in Early Modern England." Ph.D. dissertation, University of Michigan, 2005.

Dunn, Leslie. "Ophelia's Songs in *Hamlet*: Music, Madness, and the Feminine." In *Embodied Voices: Representing Female Vocality in Western Culture,* edited by Leslie C. Dunn and Nancy Jones, 50–64. Cambridge: Cambridge University Press, 1994.

Dunn, Leslie C., and Nancy A. Jones, eds. *Embodied Voices: Representing Female Vocality in Western Culture.* Cambridge: Cambridge University Press, 1994.

Dusinberre, Juliet. "*King John* and Embarrassing Women." *Shakespeare Survey* 42 (1990): 37–52.

Eaton, Sara. "A Woman of Letters: Lavinia in *Titus Andronicus.*" In *Shakespearean Tragedy and Gender,* edited by Shirley Nelson Garner and Madelon Sprengnether, 54–74. Bloomington: Indiana University Press, 1996.

Egerton, Stephen. *The Boring of the Eare, Contayning a Plaine and Profitable Discourse by Way of Dialogue, Concerning 1. Our Preparation Before Hearing. 2. Our Demeanour in Hearing. 3. Our Exercise After We Have Heard the Word of God.* London, 1623.

Elsky, Martin. *Authorizing Words: Speech, Writing, and Print in the English Renaissance.* Ithaca, N.Y.: Cornell University Press, 1989.

Enterline, Lynn. *The Rhetoric of the Body from Ovid to Shakespeare.* Cambridge Studies in Renaissance Literature and Culture. Cambridge: Cambridge University Press, 2000.

———. *The Tears of Narcissus: Melancholia and Masculinity in Early Modern Writing.* Stanford, Calif.: Stanford University Press, 1995.

Evans, G. Blakemore, ed. *The Riverside Shakespeare.* 2d ed. Boston: Houghton Mifflin Company, 1997.

Ewbank, Inga-Stina. "Shakespeare's Portrayal of Women: A 1970's View." In *Shakespeare: Pattern of Excelling Nature,* edited by David Bevington and Jay L. Halio, 222–29. Newark: University of Delaware Press, 1978.

Fawkner, H. W. *Shakespeare's Miracle Plays:* Pericles, Cymbeline, *and* The Winter's Tale. Rutherford, N.J.: Farleigh Dickinson University Press, 1992.

Felman, Shoshana. *The Literary Speech Act: Don Juan with J. L. Austin, or Seduction in Two Languages.* Translated by Catherine Porter. Ithaca, N.Y.: Cornell University Press, 1983.

Fineman, Joel. "The Turn of the Shrew." In *Shakespeare and the Question of Theory*, edited by Patricia Parker and Geoffrey Hartman, 138–59. New York: Methuen, 1985.

Finnegan, Ruth H. *Literacy and Orality: Studies in the Technology of Communication.* Oxford: Basil Blackwell, 1988.

Finney, Gretchen. "Medical Theories of Vocal Exercise and Health." *Bulletin of the History of Medicine* 40, no. 5 (1966): 395–406.

Fisher, Will. *Materializing Gender in Early Modern Literature and Culture.* Cambridge Studies in Renaissance Literature and Culture. Cambridge: Cambridge University Press, 2006.

———. "The Renaissance Beard: Masculinity in Early Modern England." *Renaissance Quarterly* 54, no. 1 (2001): 155–87.

Fitzgeffrey, Henry. *Satyres: And Satyricall Epigrams. With Certaine Observations at Black-Fryers.* London, 1617.

Fleming, Juliet. *Graffiti and the Writing Arts of Early Modern England.* Material Texts. Philadelphia: University of Pennsylvania Press, 2001.

Folkerth, Wes. *The Sound of Shakespeare.* Accents on Shakespeare. New York: Routledge, 2002.

Fox-Good, Jacquelyn. "Other Voices: The Sweet, Dangerous Air(s) of Shakespeare's *Tempest*." *Shakespeare Studies* 24 (1996): 241–74.

Frangenberg, Thomas. "*Auditus Visu Prestantior*: Comparisons of Hearing and Vision in Charles De Bovelles's *Liber De Sensibus*." In *The Second Sense: Studies in Hearing and Musical Judgement from Antiquity to the Seventeenth Century*, edited by Charles Burnett, Michael Fend and Penelope Gouk, 71–89. London: Warburg Institute, 1991.

Franko, Mark, and Annette Richards, eds. *Acting on the Past: Historical Performance Across the Disciplines.* Hanover, N.H.: Wesleyan University Press, 2000.

French, Sean. "Rickman's Worth." *GQ*. September 1991 (cited October 25, 2005); available from http://www.alan-rickman.com/articles/worth1.html.

Freudenthal, Gad. *Aristotle's Theory of Material Substance: Heat and Pneuma, Form and Soul.* Oxford: Clarendon, 1995.

Frey, Charles H. "Man's Rage/Woman's Grief: Engaging Death in *Titus Andronicus*." In *Re-Visions of Shakespeare: Essays in Honor of Robert Ornstein*, edited by Evelyn Gajowski, 66–88. Newark: University of Delaware Press, 2004.

———. "'O Sacred, Shadowy, Cold, and Constant Queen': Shakespeare's Imperiled Chastening Daughters of Romance." In *The Woman's Part: Feminist Criticism of Shakespeare*, edited by Carolyn Ruth Swift Lenz, Gayle Greene, and Carol Thomas Neely, 295–313. Urbana: University of Illinois Press, 1980.

Frye, Northrop. *The Secular Scripture: A Study of the Structure of Romance.* Cambridge, Mass.: Harvard University Press, 1976.

Frye, Susan. *Elizabeth I: The Competition for Representation.* New York: Oxford University Press, 1993.

Fumerton, Patricia. *Cultural Aesthetics: Renaissance Literature and the Practice of Social Ornament.* Chicago: University of Chicago Press, 1991.

Fumerton, Patricia, and Simon Hunt, eds. *Renaissance Culture and the Everyday.* Philadelphia: University of Pennsylvania Press, 1999.

Furnivall, F. J., ed. *Robert Laneham's Letter: Describing a Part of the Entertainment Unto Queen Elizabeth at the Castle of Kenilworth in 1575.* London: Chatto and Windus Duffield and Company, 1907.

Gair, W. Reavley, ed. *Antonio and Mellida.* The Revels Plays. Manchester: Manchester University Press, 1991.

Gamage, William. *Linsi-Woolsie: Or Two Centuries of Epigrammes.* London, 1621.

Gardiner, Judith Kegan. "Theorizing Age with Gender: Bly's Boys, Feminism, and Maturity Masculinity." In *Masculinity Studies and Feminist Theory: New Directions*, edited by Judith Kegan Gardiner, 90–118. New York: Columbia University Press, 2002.

Gascoigne, George. "A Briefe Rehearsall, or Rather a True Copie of as Much as Was Presented before Her Majesti[e] at Kenelworth During Her Last Aboade There." In *The Glasse of Governmement, The Princely Pleasures at Kenelworth Castle, The Steele Glas and Other Poems and Prose Works*, edited by John W. Cunliffe, 91–131. New York: Greenwood Press, 1969.

Gearing, William. *A Bridle for the Tongue: Or a Treatise of Ten Sins of the Tongue. Cursing, Swearing, Slandering, Scoffing, Filthy-Speaking, Flattering, Censuring, Murmuring, Lying and Boasting.* London, 1663.

Gerbier, Sir Balthazar. *The Art of Well Speaking.* London, 1650.

Gieskes, Edward. "'He Is but a Bastard to the Time': Status and Service in *The Troublesome Raigne of John* and Shakespeare's *King John*." *ELH* 65, no. 4 (1998): 779–98.

Gifford, M. G. *A Sermon on the Parable of the Sower.* London, 1582.

Gilligan, Carol. *In a Different Voice.* Cambridge, Mass.: Harvard University Press, 1982.

Goldberg, Jonathan. "Shakespearean Inscriptions: The Voicing of Power." In *Shakespeare and the Question of Theory*, edited by Patricia Parker and Geoffrey Hartman, 116–37. New York: Methuen, 1985.

———. *Voice Terminal Echo: Postmodernism and English Renaissance Texts.* New York: Methuen, 1986.

———. *Writing Matter: From the Hands of the English Renaissance.* Stanford, Calif.: Stanford University Press, 1990.

Golding, Arthur. *The Fyrst Fouer Bookes of Press. Ovidius Nasos Worke, Intitled Metamorphosis, Translated Oute of Latin into Englishe Meter.* London, 1565.

Gossett, Suzanne, ed. *Pericles.* The Arden Shakespeare. Third Series. London: Arden Shakespeare, 2004.

Gosson, Stephen. *The School of Abuse.* London, 1579.

Gourlay, Patricia Southard. "'O My Most Sacred Lady': Female Metaphor in *The Winter's Tale*." *English Literary Renaissance* 5, no. 3 (1975): 375–95.

Graham, Jean E. "Virgin Ears: Silence, Deafness, and Chastity in Milton's *Masque*." *Milton Studies* 36 (1998): 1–17.

Green, Reina. "'Ears Prejudicate' in *Mariam* and *Duchess of Malfi*." *SEL* 43, no. 2 (2003): 459–74.

Greenblatt, Stephen, ed. *The Norton Shakespeare.* 2d ed. New York: W. W. Norton, 1997.

Greene, Robert. *The Repentance of Robert Greene Maister of Artes. Wherein by Himselfe Is Laid Open His Loose Life, with the Manner of His Death.* London, 1592.

———. *The Second Part of Conny-Catching.* London, 1591.

Greenhut, Deborah S. *Feminine Rhetorical Culture: Tudor Adaptations of Ovid's Heroides.* New York: Peter Lang, 1988.

Grennan, Eamon. "Shakespeare's Satirical History: A Reading of *King John.*" *Shakespeare Studies* 11 (1978): 21–38.

Grose, Christopher. *Ovid's Metamorphoses: An Index to the 1632 Commentary of George Sandys.* Malibu, Calif.: Undena Publications, 1981.

Gross, Kenneth. *Shakespeare's Noise.* Chicago: University of Chicago Press, 2001.

Guazzo, Stephano. *The Civile Conversation.* Translated by George Pettie [1581]. Edited by Charles Whibley. 2 vols. The Tudor Translations. New York: Alfred A. Knopf, 1925.

Gurr, Andrew. *Playgoing in Shakespeare's London.* 2d ed. Cambridge: Cambridge University Press, 1996.

———. *The Shakespearean Stage, 1574–1642.* Cambridge: Cambridge University Press, 1970.

Hackett, Helen. "'Gracious Be the Issue': Maternity and Narrative in Shakespeare's Late Plays." In *Shakespeare's Late Plays: New Readings,* edited by Jennifer Richards and James Knowles, 25–39. Edinburgh: Edinburgh University Press, 1999.

Halberstam, Judith. *Female Masculinity.* Durham, N.C.: Duke University Press, 1998.

Harris, Jonathan Gil. "Atomic Shakespeare." *Shakespeare Studies* 30 (2002): 47–51.

———. *Foreign Bodies and the Body Politic: Discourses of Social Pathology in Early Modern England.* Cambridge Studies in Renaissance Literature and Culture. Cambridge: Cambridge University Press, 1998.

Harris, Jonathan Gil, and Natasha Korda, eds. *Staged Properties in Early Modern English Drama.* Cambridge: Cambridge University Press, 2002.

Harrison, William. *The Difference of Hearers. Or an Exposition of the Parable of the Sower.* London, 1614.

Hart, F. Elizabeth. "'Great Is Diana' of Shakespeare's Ephesus." *SEL* 43, no. 2 (2003): 347–74.

Harvey, Elizabeth D. *Ventriloquized Voices: Feminist Theory and English Renaissance Texts.* New York: Routledge, 1992.

Healy, Margaret. "*Pericles* and the Pox." In *Shakespeare's Late Plays: New Readings,* edited by Jennifer Richards and James Knowles, 92–107. Edinburgh: Edinburgh University Press, 1999.

Hedrick, Donald. "Male Surplus Value." *Renaissance Drama* 31 (2002): 85–124.

Helms, Lorraine. "The Saint in the Brothel: Or, Eloquence Rewarded." *Shakespeare Quarterly* 41, no. 3 (1990): 319–32.

Henderson, Katherine Usher, and Barbara F. McManus. *Half Humankind: Contexts and Texts of the Controversy About Women in England, 1540–1640.* Urbana: University of Illinois Press, 1985.

Herrick, Robert. *Hesperides, or the Works Both Human & Divine.* London, 1648.

Heywood, Thomas. *An Apology for Actors.* London, 1612.

———. *The Fair Maid of the West. Or, a Girle Worth Gold.* London, 1631.

———. *The Second Part of, If You Know Not Me, You Know No Bodie.* London, 1606.

Hirsh, James. "Editor's Comment: Morgann, Greenblatt, and Audience Response." *Studies in the Literary Imagination* 26, no. 1 (1993): 1–6.

Hobson, Christopher Z. "Bastard Speech: The Rhetoric of 'Commodity' in *King John.*" *Shakespeare Yearbook* 2 (1991): 95–114.

Hoeniger, F. D., ed. *Pericles.* The Arden Shakespeare. 2d series. London: Methuen, 1963.

Hoffman, Michael, dir. *William Shakespeare's A Midsummer Night's Dream.* Fox Searchlight Pictures, 1999.

Hollander, John. *The Figure of Echo: A Mode of Allusion in Milton and After.* Berkeley: University of California Press, 1981.

The Holy Bible Containing the Old Testament, and the New: Newly Translated out of the Original Tongues: And with the Former Translations Diligently Compared and Revised, by His Maiesties Speciall Commandement. London, 1613.

Howard, Jean E. *Shakespeare's Art of Orchestration: Stage Technique and Audience Response.* Urbana: University of Illinois Press, 1984.

———. *The Stage and Social Struggle in Early Modern England.* New York: Routledge, 1994.

Howell, Thomas. *The Fable of Ovid Treting of Narcissus, Tra[n]slated out of Latin into Englysh Mytre, with a Moral There Unto, Very Pleasante to Rede.* London, 1560.

Hunt, Maurice. "Antimetabolic *King John.*" *Style* 34, no. 3 (2000): 380–401.

———. *Shakespeare's Labored Art: Stir, Work, and the Late Plays.* Studies in Shakespeare. New York: Peter Lang, 1995.

———. *Shakespeare's Romance of the Word.* Lewisburg, Pa.: Bucknell University Press, 1990.

Hunter, Grace Eva. "The Influence of Frances Bacon on the Commentary of Ovid's *Metamorphoses* by George Sandys." Ph.D. dissertation, Iowa State University, 1940.

I. B. *The Psalme of Mercy: Or, a Meditation Upon the 51. Psalme, by a True Penitent.* London, 1625.

Ingram, William. "What Kind of Future for the Theatrical Past: Or, What Will Count as Theater History in the Next Millennium?" *Shakespeare Quarterly* 48, no. 2 (1997): 215–25.

Irigaray, Luce. *This Sex Which Is Not One.* Translated by Catherine Porter. Ithaca, N.Y.: Cornell University Press, 1985.

Iyengar, Sujata. "Shakespeare in HeteroLove." *Literature/Film Quarterly* 29, no. 2 (2001): 122–27.

James, Heather. "Dido's Ear: Tragedy and the Politics of Response." *Shakespeare Quarterly* 52, no. 3 (2001): 360–82.

Jones, Ann Rosalind. *The Currency of Eros: Women's Love Lyric in Europe, 1540–1620.* Bloomington: Indiana University Press, 1990.

Jonson, Ben. *The Complete Plays of Ben Jonson.* Edited by G. A. Wilkes. Vol. 2. Oxford: Clarendon, 1981.

———. *Poetaster.* Edited by Tom Cain. The Revels Plays. Manchester: Manchester University Press, 1995.

Jordan, Constance. *Shakespeare's Monarchies: Ruler and Subject in the Romances.* Ithaca, N.Y.: Cornell University Press, 1997.

Kahn, Coppélia. *Roman Shakespeare: Warriors, Wounds, and Women.* New York: Routledge, 1997.

Kaplan, M. Lindsay. *The Culture of Slander in Early Modern England.* Cambridge: Cambridge University Press, 1997.

Kaplan, M. Lindsay, and Katherine Eggert. "'Good Queen, My Lord, Good Queen': Sexual Slander and the Trials of Female Authority in *The Winter's Tale*." *Renaissance Drama* 25 (1994): 89–118.

Kargon, Robert Hugh. *Atomism in England from Hariot to Newton*. Oxford: Clarendon, 1966.

Kastan, David Scott. *Shakespeare After Theory*. New York: Routledge, 1999.

———. "'To Set a Form Upon That Indigest': Shakespeare's Fictions of History." *Comparative Drama* 17, no. 1 (1983): 1–16.

Kaul, Mythili. "*Pericles*: Shakespeare's Parable for the Theatre." *Forum for Modern Language Studies* 28, no. 2 (1992): 97–104.

Kehler, Dorothea. "'So Jest with Heaven': Deity in *King John*." In *King John: New Perspectives*, edited by Deborah T. Curren-Aquino, 99–113. Newark: University of Delaware Press, 1989.

Knowles, Richard Paul. "'The More Delay'd, Delighted': Theophanies in the Last Plays." *Shakespeare Studies* 15 (1982): 269–80.

———. "'Wishes Fall Out as They're Will'd': Artist, Audience, and *Pericles*'s Gower." *English Studies in Canada* 9, no. 1 (1983): 14–24.

Korda, Natasha. *Shakespeare's Domestic Economies: Gender and Property in Early Modern England*. Philadelphia: University of Pennsylvania Press, 2002.

Kuriyama, Shigehisa. *The Expressiveness of the Body and the Divergence of Greek and Chinese Medicine*. New York: Zone Books, 1999.

Lahr, John. "Evil Elegance." *Lear's Magazine*. 1992 (cited October 25, 2005); available from http://www.alan-rickman.com/articles/evil_elegance.html.

Lamb, Mary Ellen. "The Countess of Pembroke and the Art of Dying." In *Women in the Middle Ages and the Renaissance: Literary and Historical Perspectives*, edited by Mary Beth Rose, 207–26. Syracuse, N.Y.: Syracuse University Press, 1986.

Laqueur, Thomas. *Making Sex: Body and Gender from the Greeks to Freud*. Cambridge, Mass.: Harvard University Press, 1990.

Lawrence, Amy. *Echo and Narcissus: Women's Voices in Classical Hollywood Cinema*. Berkeley and Los Angeles: University of California Press, 1991.

Leggatt, Alexander. *English Drama: Shakespeare to the Restoration, 1590–1660*. Literature in English Series. London: Longman, 1988.

Lemnius, Levinus. *The Secret Miracles of Nature*. London, 1658.

———. *The Touchstone of Complexions Generallye Appliable, Expedient and Profitable for All Such, As Be Desirous & Carefull of Their Bodylye Health*. London, 1576.

Levine, Nina S. *Women's Matters: Politics, Gender, and Nation in Shakespeare's Early History Plays*. Newark: University of Delaware Press, 1998.

Lindley, David, ed. *The Tempest*. The New Cambridge Shakespeare. Cambridge: Cambridge University Press, 2002.

Linklater, Kristin. *Freeing Shakespeare's Voice: The Actor's Guide to Talking the Text*. New York: Theatre Communications Group, 1992.

Loewenstein, Joseph. *Responsive Readings: Versions of Echo in Pastoral, Epic, and the Jonsonian Masque*. New Haven, Conn.: Yale University Press, 1984.

Longus. *Daphnis and Chloe*. Translated by George Thornley. London: Heinemann, 1916.

Lopez, Jeremy. *Theatrical Convention and Audience Response in Early Modern Drama.* Cambridge: Cambridge University Press, 2003.

Love, Harold. *Scribal Publication in Seventeenth-Century England.* Oxford: Clarendon, 1993.

Luckyj, Christina. *"A Moving Rhetoricke": Gender and Silence in Early Modern England.* Manchester: Manchester University Press, 2002.

Lugones, Maria C., and Elizabeth Spelman. "Have We Got a Theory for You! Feminist Theory, Cultural Imperialism and the Demand for 'the Woman's Voice.'" *Women's Studies International Forum* 6 (1983): 573–81.

Lüthy, Christoph, John E. Murdoch, and William R. Newman., eds. *Late Medieval and Early Modern Corpuscular Matter Theories.* Leiden: Brill, 2001.

Lyne, Raphael. "Golding's Englished *Metamorphoses.*" *Translation and Literature* 5, no. 2 (1996): 183–200.

Mack, Maynard. "Engagement and Detachment in Shakespeare's Plays." In *Essays on Shakespeare and Elizabethan Drama in Honor of Hardin Craig*, edited by Richard Hosley, 275–96. Columbia: University of Missouri Press, 1962.

Mackenzie, Suzie. "Angel with Horns." *The Guardian.* January 3, 1998 (cited October 25, 2005); available from http://www.alan-rickman.com/articles/angel.html.

Madden, John, dir. *Shakespeare in Love.* Miramax Films, 1998.

Magnusson, Lynne. *Shakespeare and Social Dialogue: Dramatic Language and Elizabeth Letters.* Cambridge: Cambridge University Press, 1999.

Manheim, Michael. "The Four Voices of the Bastard." In *King John: New Perspectives*, edited by Deborah T. Curren-Aquino, 126–35. Newark: University of Delaware Press, 1989.

Manzo, Silvia A. "Francis Bacon and Atomism: A Reappraisal." In *Late Medieval and Early Modern Corpuscular Matter Theories*, edited by Christoph Lüthy, John E. Murdoch, and William R. Newman, 209–43. Leiden: Brill, 2001.

Marotti, Arthur F. *Manuscript, Print, and the English Renaissance Lyric.* Ithaca, N.Y.: Cornell University Press, 1995.

Marotti, Arthur F., and Michael D. Bristol, eds. *Print, Manuscript, and Performance: The Changing Relations of the Media in Early Modern England.* Columbus: Ohio State University Press, 2000.

Marshall, Cynthia. "Wound-Man: *Coriolanus*, Gender, and the Theatrical Construction of Interiority." In *Feminist Readings of Early Modern Culture: Emerging Subjects*, edited by Valerie Traub, M. Lindsay Kaplan, and Dympna Callaghan, 93–118. Cambridge: Cambridge University Press, 1996.

Marston, John. *The Malcontent and Other Plays.* Edited by Keith Sturgess. The World's Classics. Oxford: Oxford University Press, 1997.

Massinger, Philip. *The Bond-Man: An Antient Storie.* London, 1624.

Masten, Jeffrey. *Textual Intercourse: Collaboration, Authorship, and Sexualities in Renaissance Drama.* Cambridge Studies in Renaissance Literature and Culture. Cambridge: Cambridge University Press, 1997.

Masten, Jeffrey, Peter Stallybrass, and Nancy Vickers. *Language Machines: Technologies of Literary and Cultural Production.* New York: Routledge, 1997.

Maus, Katharine Eisaman. *Inwardness and Theater in the English Renaissance.* Chicago: University of Chicago Press, 1995.

May, James E. "Imagery of Disorderly Motion in *King John*: A Thematic Gloss." *Essays in Literature* 10, no. 1 (1983): 17–28.

Mazzio, Carla. "Sins of the Tongue." In *The Body in Parts: Fantasies of Corporeality in Early Modern Europe*, edited by David Hillman and Carla Mazzio, 53–79. New York: Routledge, 1997.

———. "Staging the Vernacular: Language and Nation in Thomas Kyd's *The Spanish Tragedy*." *SEL* 38, no. 2 (1998): 207–32.

McClary, Susan. *Feminine Endings: Music, Gender, and Sexuality.* Minneapolis: University of Minnesota Press, 1991.

McGuire, Philip C. *Speechless Dialect: Shakespeare's Open Silences.* Berkeley and Los Angeles: University of California Press, 1985.

McKewin, Carole. "Counsels of Gall and Grace: Intimate Conversations between Women in Shakespeare's Plays." In *The Woman's Part: Feminist Criticism of Shakespeare*, edited by Carolyn Ruth Swift Lenz, Gayle Green, and Carol Thomas Neely, 117–32. Urbana: University of Illinois Press, 1980.

McManaway, James G. "The First Five Bookes of *Ovids Metamorphosis*, 1621, Englished by Master George Sandys." *Papers of the Bibliographical Society of the University of Virginia* 1 (1848–49): 71–82.

McNay, Lois. *Gender and Agency: Reconfiguring the Subject in Feminist and Social Theory.* Cambridge: Polity Press, 2000.

Meszaros, Patricia K. "*Pericles*: Shakespeare's Divine Musical Comedy." In *Shakespeare and the Arts: A Collection of Essays from the Ohio Shakespeare Conference, 1981, Wright State University, Dayton, Ohio*, edited by Cecile Williamson Cary and Henry S. Limouze, 3–20. Washington, D.C.: University Press of America, 1982.

Middleton, Thomas, and William Rowley. *The Changeling.* Edited by Matthew W. Black. Philadelphia: University of Pennsylvania Press, 1966.

Mincoff, Marco. *Things Supernatural and Causeless: Shakespearean Romance.* Reprint, Newark: University of Delaware Press, 1992.

Moulton, Ian Frederick. "'A Monster Great Deformed': The Unruly Masculinity of *Richard III*." *Shakespeare Quarterly* 47, no. 3 (1996): 251–68.

Mowat, Barbara A. *The Dramaturgy of Shakespeare's Romances.* Athens: University of Georgia Press, 1976.

———. "'What's in a Name?' Tragicomedy, Romance, or Late Comedy." In *A Companion to Shakespeare's Works*, edited by Richard Dutton and Jean E. Howard, 129–49. Malden, Mass.: Blackwell, 2003.

Mulcaster, Richard. *Positions Wherin Those Primitive Circumstances Be Examined, Which Are Necessarie for the Training up of Children, Either for Skill in Their Booke, or Health in Their Bodie.* London, 1581.

Mullaney, Steven. *The Place of the Stage: License, Play, and Power in Renaissance England.* Chicago: University of Chicago Press, 1988.

Munro, Lucy. *Children of the Queen's Revels: A Jacobean Theatre Repertory.* Cambridge: Cambridge University Press, 2005.

Nash, Ilana. "'A Subject without Subjection': Robert Dudley, Earl of Leicester, and *The Princely Pleasures at Kenelworth Castle.*" Comitatus 25 (1994): 81–102.

National Organization for Women. "Statement of Purpose." In *Feminist Theory: A Reader*, edited by Wendy Kolmar and Frances Bartkowski, 169–71. Mountain View, Calif.: Mayfield Publishing Company, 1966.

Neely, Carol Thomas. "*The Winter's Tale*: The Triumph of Speech." *SEL* 15 (1975): 321–38.

Norvell, Betty G. "The Dramatic Portrait of Margaret in Shakespeare's Henry VI Plays." *Bulletin of the West Virginia Association of College English Teachers* 8 (1983): 38–44.

Nouvet, Claire. "An Impossible Response: The Disaster of Narcissus." *Yale French Studies* 79 (1991): 95–109.

Novy, Marianne. "Shakespeare's Female Characters as Actors and Audience." In *The Woman's Part: Feminist Criticism of Shakespeare*, edited by Carolyn Ruth Swift Lenz, Gayle Greene and Carole Thomas Neely, 256–70. Urbana: University of Illinois Press, 1980.

O'Connell, Michael. *The Idolatrous Eye: Iconoclasm and Theater in Early-Modern England.* Oxford: Oxford University Press, 2000.

Ong, Walter. *Orality and Literacy: The Technologizing of the Word.* London: Methuen, 1982.

Orgel, Stephen. *Impersonations: The Performance of Gender in Shakespeare's England.* Cambridge: Cambridge University Press, 1996.

———, ed. *The Tempest.* The Oxford Shakespeare. Oxford: Clarendon, 1987.

Orkin, Martin. *Local Shakespeares: Proximations and Power.* New York: Routledge, 2005.

Orlin, Lena Cowen, ed. *Material London, ca. 1600.* Philadelphia: University of Pennsylvania Press, 2000.

Ovid. *The Metamorphoses.* Translated by Frank Justus Miller. 3d ed. revised by G. P. Goold. Vol. 1 of 2. Loeb Classical Library. Cambridge, Mass.: Harvard University Press, 1977.

Oxford English Dictionary. 2d ed. Oxford: Oxford University Press, 1989.

Palfrey, Simon. *Late Shakespeare: A New World of Words.* Oxford English Monographs. Oxford: Clarendon, 1997.

Parker, Andrew, and Eve Kosofsky Sedgwick, eds. *Performativity and Performance.* New York: Routledge, 1995.

Parker, Patricia. *Literary Fat Ladies: Rhetoric, Gender, Property.* London: Methuen, 1987.

———. "On the Tongue: Cross Gendering, Effeminacy, and the Art of Words." *Style* 23, no. 3 (1989): 445–65.

———. *Shakespeare from the Margins: Language, Culture, Context.* Chicago: University of Chicago Press, 1996.

Paster, Gail Kern. *The Body Embarrassed: Drama and the Disciplines of Shame in Early Modern England.* Ithaca, N.Y.: Cornell University Press, 1993.

———. *Humoring the Body: Emotions and the Shakespearean Stage.* Chicago: University of Chicago Press, 2004.

Pearcy, Lee T. *The Mediated Muse: English Translations of Ovid, 1560–1700.* Hamden, Conn.: Archon Books, 1984.

Peterson, Douglas. *Time, Tide and Tempest: A Study of Shakespeare's Romances.* San Marino, Calif.: Huntington Library, 1972.

Phelan, Peggy. "Performing Talking Cures: Artaud's Voice." In *Language Machines: Technologies of Literary and Cultural Production,* edited by Jeffrey Masten, Peter Stallybrass, and Nancy J. Vickers, 233–51. New York: Routledge, 1997.

Playford, John. *A Brief Introduction to the Skill of Musick: For Song and Viol.* London, 1658.

Plutarch. *The Philosophie, Commonlie Called, the Morals.* London, 1603.

Pollard, Tanya. *Drugs and Theater in Early Modern England.* Oxford: Oxford University Press, 2005.

Porter, Joseph A. "Fraternal Pragmatics: Speech Acts of John and the Bastard." In *King John: New Perspectives,* edited by Deborah T. Curren-Aquino, 136–43. Newark: University of Delaware Press, 1989.

Prynne, William. *Histrio-Mastix: The Players Scourge; or, the Actor's Tragedie.* London, 1633.

Rabelais, François. *The Histories of Gargantua and Pantagruel.* Translated by J. M. Cohen. New York: Penguin Books, 1985.

Rackin, Phyllis. "Patriarchal History and Female Subversion in *King John.*" In *King John: New Perspectives,* edited by Deborah T. Curren-Aquino, 76–90. Newark: University of Delaware Press, 1989.

———. "The Role of the Audience in Shakespeare's *Richard II.*" *Shakespeare Quarterly* 36, no. 3 (1985): 262–81.

———. *Stages of History: Shakespeare's English Chronicles.* Ithaca, N.Y.: Cornell University Press, 1990.

Ray, Robert H. "Marvell's 'To His Coy Mistress' and Sandys's Translation of Ovid's *Metamorphoses.*" *Review of English Studies: A Quarterly Journal of English Literature and the English Language* 44, no. 175 (1993): 386–88.

Ray, Sid. "'Rape, I Fear, Was Root of Thy Annoy': The Politics of Consent in *Titus Andronicus.*" *Shakespeare Quarterly* 49, no. 1 (1998): 22–39.

Rea, Steve. "Free Spirit." *Knight-Ridder News Service.* June 5, 1991 (cited October 25, 2005); available from http://www.alan-rickman.com/articles/spirit.html.

Read, Alexander. *The Manuall of the Anatomy or, Dissection of the Body of Man.* London, 1642.

Rebhorn, Wayne A. *The Emperor of Men's Minds: Literature and the Renaissance Discourse of Rhetoric.* Rhetoric & Society. Ithaca, N.Y.: Cornell University Press, 1995.

———. "'The Emperour of Men's Minds': The Renaissance Trickster as *Homo Rhetoricus.*" In *Creative Imitation: New Essays on Renaissance Literature in Honor of Thomas M. Greene,* edited by David Quint, Margaret W. Ferguson, G. W. Pigman III, and Wayne A. Rebhorn, 31–65. Medieval and Renaissance Texts and Studies. Binghamton, N.Y.: Center for Medieval and Early Renaissance Studies, 1992.

Rees, Graham. "Bacon's Speculative Philosophy." In *The Cambridge Companion to Bacon,* edited by Markku Peltonen, 121–45. Cambridge: Cambridge University Press, 1996.

———. *The Oxford Francis Bacon: Philosophical Studies c. 1611–c. 1619.* Vol. 6. Oxford: Clarendon, 1996.

Reynolds, Henry. *Mythomystes Wherein a Short Survay Is Taken of the Nature and Value of True Poesy and Depth of the Ancients Above Our Moderne Poets. To Which Is Annexed the Tale of Narcissus Briefly Mythologized.* London, 1632.

Richards, Jennifer, and James Knowles, eds. *Shakespeare's Late Plays: New Readings.* Edinburgh: Edinburgh University Press, 1999.

Richman, David. *Laughter, Pain, and Wonder: Shakespeare's Comedies and the Audience in the Theater.* Newark: University of Deleware Press, 1990.

Robinson, Robert. *The Art of Pronunciation.* London, 1617.

Rodenburg, Patsy. *The Right to Speak: Working with the Voice.* London: Methuen, 1992.

Rossi, Paolo. *Francis Bacon: From Magic to Science.* Chicago: University of Chicago Press, 1968.

Rowe, Katherine. *Dead Hands: Fictions of Agency, Renaissance to Modern.* Stanford, Calif.: Stanford University Press, 1999.

Rubin, Deborah. *Ovid's Metamorphoses Englished: George Sandys as Translator and Mythographer.* London: Garland, 1985.

Sandys, George. *Ovid's Metamorphosis: Englished, Mythologized, and Represented in Figures.* Edited by Karl K. Hulley and Stanley T. Vandersall. Lincoln: University of Nebraska Press, 1970.

Schalkwyk, David. *Literature and the Touch of the Real.* Newark: University of Delaware Press, 2004.

———. *Speech and Performance in Shakespeare's Sonnets and Plays.* Cambridge: Cambridge University Press, 2002.

Schoenfeldt, Michael C. *Bodies and Selves in Early Modern England: Physiology and Inwardness in Spenser, Shakespeare, Herbert, and Milton.* Cambridge Studies in Renaissance Literature and Culture. Cambridge: Cambridge University Press, 1999.

———. "'Give Sorrow Words': Emotional Loss and the Emergence of Personality in Early Modern England." In *Dead Lovers: Erotic Bonds and the Study of Premodern Europe,* edited by Basil Dufallo and Peggy McCracken. Ann Arbor: University of Michigan Press, forthcoming.

Scott, Campbell, and Eric Simonson, dirs. *Hamlet.* Hallmark Entertainment, 2000.

Scott, David. "William Patten and the Authorship of 'Robert Laneham's Letter' (1575)." *English Literary Renaissance* 7 (1977): 297–306.

Scribner, Sylvia, and Michael Cole. *The Psychology of Literacy.* Cambridge: Cambridge University Press, 1981.

Sedgwick, Eve Kosofsky. "'Gosh, Boy George, You Must Be Awfully Secure in Your Masculinity!'" In *Constructing Masculinity,* edited by Maurice Berger, Brian Wallis, and Simon Watson, 11–20. New York: Routledge, 1995.

Seneca, Lucius Annaeus. *The Workes of Lucius Annæus Seneca, Both Morrall and Naturall.* London, 1614.

Shapiro, Michael. *Children of the Revels: The Boy Companies of Shakespeare's Time and Their Plays.* New York: Columbia University Press, 1977.

Sheridan, Sybil. *Hear Our Voice: Women in the British Rabbinate.* Studies in Comparative Religion. Columbia: University of South Carolina Press, 1998.

Shirley, James. *Changes: or, Love in a Maze.* London, 1632.

Sibscota, George. *The Deaf and Dumb Man's Discourse. Or a Treatise Concerning Those That Are Born Deaf and Dumb, Containing a Discovery of Their Knowledge or Understanding; as Also the Method They Use, to Manifest the Sentiments of Their Mind.*

Together with an Additional Tract of the Reason and Speech of Inanimate Creatures. London, 1670.

Silverman, Kaja. *The Acoustic Mirror: The Female Voice in Psychoanalysis and Cinema. Theories of Representation and Difference.* Bloomington: Indiana University Press, 1988.

Simonds, Peggy Muñoz. *Myth, Emblem, and Music in Shakespeare's* Cymbeline: *An Iconographic Reconstruction.* Newark: University of Delaware Press, 1992.

Skantze, P. A. *Stillness in Motion in the Seventeenth-Century Theatre.* Routledge Studies in Renaissance Literature and Culture. New York: Routledge, 2003.

Skura, Meredith Anne. *Shakespeare the Actor and the Purposes of Playing.* Chicago: University of Chicago Press, 1993.

Smallwood, R. L., ed. *King John.* New Penguin Shakespeare. Harmondsworth: Penguin Books, 1974.

Smith, Bruce R. *The Acoustic World of Early Modern England: Attending to the O-Factor.* Chicago: University of Chicago Press, 1999.

———. "Landscape with Figures: The Three Realms of Queen Elizabeth's Country-House Revels." *Renaissance Drama* 8 (1977): 57–115.

———. *Shakespeare and Masculinity.* Oxford Shakespeare Topics. Oxford: Oxford University Press, 2000.

Snider, Alvin. "Atoms and Seeds: Aphra Behn's Lucretius." *Clio* 33, no. 1 (2003): 1–24.

Snow, Edward. "Language and Sexual Difference in *Romeo and Juliet.*" In *Shakespeare's "Rough Magic": Renaissance Essays in Honor of C. L. Barber,* edited by Peter Erickson and Coppélia Kahn, 168–92. Newark: University of Delaware Press, 1985.

Sofer, Andrew. *The Stage Life of Props.* Ann Arbor: University of Michigan Press, 2003.

Sorabji, Richard. "Body and Soul in Aristotle." In *Aristotle's* De Anima *in Focus,* edited by Michael Durrant, 162–96. New York: Routledge, 1993.

Spear, Gary. "Shakespeare's 'Manly' Parts: Masculinity and Effeminacy in *Troilus and Cressida.*" *Shakespeare Quarterly* 44, no. 4 (1993): 409–22.

Spivak, Gayatri. "Echo." *New Literary History* 24 (1993): 17–43.

Sprengnether, Madelon. "Annihilating Intimacy in *Coriolanus.*" In *Women in the Middle Ages and the Renaissance: Literary and Historical Perspectives,* edited by Mary Beth Rose, 89–111. Syracuse, N.Y.: Syracuse University Press, 1986.

Stallybrass, Peter. "Patriarchal Territories: The Body Enclosed." In *Rewriting the Renaissance: The Discourses of Sexual Difference in Early Modern Europe,* edited by Margaret Ferguson, Maureen Quilligan, and Nancy Vickers, 123–42. Chicago: University of Chicago Press, 1986.

Stallybrass, Peter, and Ann Rosalind Jones. *Renaissance Clothes and the Materials of Memory.* Cambridge Studies in Renaissance Literature and Culture. Cambridge: Cambridge University Press, 2000.

Stead, Christopher. "Pneuma." *Routledge.* 1998 (cited August 11, 2005); available from http://www.rep.routledge.com.proxy.lib.uiowa.edu/article/A092.

Street, Brian V. *Literacy in Theory and Practice.* Cambridge: Cambridge University Press, 1984.

Sundelson, David. "'So Rare a Wonder'd Father': Prospero's *Tempest.*" In *Representing Shakespeare: New Psychoanalytic Essays,* edited by Murray M. Schwartz and Coppélia Kahn, 33–53. Baltimore: Johns Hopkins University Press, 1980.

Taylor, Anthony Brian. "George Sandys and Arthur Golding." *Notes and Queries* 33, no. 3 (1986): 387–91.

———. "Shakespeare and Golding: Viola's Interview with Olivia and Echo and Narcissus." *English Language Notes* 15 (1977): 103–6.

Taylor, Gary. *To Analyze Delight: A Hedonistic Criticism of Shakespeare.* Newark: University of Delaware Press, 1985.

Taylor, Thomas. *The Parable of the Sower and of the Seed. Among Other Things Largely Discoursing of a Good Hart Describing It by Very Many Signes of It.* London, 1634.

Thompson, Ann. "'Miranda, Where's Your Sister?': Reading Shakespeare's *The Tempest.*" In *Feminist Criticism: Theory and Practice,* edited by Susan Sellers, Linda Hutcheon, and Paul Perron, 45–55. Toronto: University of Toronto Press, 1991.

Thorne, W. B. "*Pericles* and the 'Incest-Fertility' Opposition." *Shakespeare Quarterly* 22, no. 1 (1971): 43–56.

Tilley, Morris Palmer. *A Dictionary of the Proverbs in England in the Sixteenth and Seventeenth Centuries.* Ann Arbor: University of Michigan Press, 1950.

Tomkis, Thomas. *Lingua: Or the Combat of the Tongue, and the Five Senses for Superiority.* London, 1607.

Traub, Valerie. "The Sonnets: Sequence, Sexuality, and Shakespeare's Two Loves." In *A Companion to Shakespeare's Works,* edited by Richard Dutton and Jean E. Howard, 275–301. Malden, Mass.: Blackwell, 2003.

Tribble, Evelyn B. *Margins and Marginality: The Printed Page in Early Modern England.* Charlottesville: University Press of Virginia, 1993.

Turner, Henry S. "Nashe's Red Herring: Epistemologies of the Commodity in *Lenten Stuffe* (1599)." *ELH* 68, no. 3 (2001): 529–61.

Vaughan, Virginia Mason. "Between Tetralogies: *King John* as Transition." *Shakespeare Quarterly* 35, no. 4 (1984): 407–20.

———. "*King John*: A Study in Subversion and Containment." In *King John: New Perspectives,* edited by Deborah T. Curren-Aquino, 62–75. Newark: University of Delaware Press, 1989.

Venner, Tobias. *Via Recta Ad Vitam Longam: Or, a Plain Philosophicall Demonstration of the Nature, Faculties, and Effects of All Such Things as by Way of Nourishments Make for the Preservation of Health. . . .* London, 1628.

Vesling, Johann. *Anatomy of the Body of Man.* London, 1653.

Walkington, Thomas. *The Optick Glasse of Humors, or the Touchstone of a Golden Temperature, or the Philosophers Stone to Make a Golden Temper.* London, 1607.

Wall, Wendy. *The Imprint of Gender: Authorship and Publication in the English Renaissance.* Ithaca, N.Y.: Cornell University Press, 1993.

Wayne, Valerie. "Refashioning the Shrew." *Shakespeare Studies* 17 (1985): 159–87.

Webster, John. *The Duchess of Malfi and Other Plays.* Edited by René Weis. The World's Classics. Oxford: Oxford University Press, 1996.

Weever, John. *Ancient Funerall Monuments within the United Monarchie of Great Britaine, Ireland, and the Islands Adjacent with the Dissolved Monasteries Therein Contained.* London, 1631.

Weimann, Robert. "Mingling Vice and 'Worthiness' in *King John.*" *Shakespeare Studies* 27 (1999): 109–33.

Weiss, Adrian. "A Pill to Purge Parody: Marston's Manipulation of the Paul's Environment in the Antonio Plays." In *The Theatrical Space,* edited by James Redmond. Themes in Drama. 81–97. Cambridge: Cambridge University Press, 1987.

Weiss, Theodore. *The Breath of Clowns and Kings: Shakespeare's Early Comedies and Histories.* New York: Atheneum, 1971.

Wells, Robin Headlam. *Shakespeare on Masculinity.* Cambridge: Cambridge University Press, 2000.

Wharton, T. F. *The Critical Fall and Rise of John Marston.* Columbia, S.C.: Camden House, 1994.

Wilcox, Helen. "Gender and Genre in Shakespeare's Tragicomedies." In *Reclamations of Shakespeare,* edited by A. J. Hoenselaars, 129–38. Studies in Literature. Amsterdam: Rodopi, 1994.

Wilkinson, Robert. *A Jewell for the Eare.* London, 1605.

Williams, Stanley T., ed. *The Life and Death of King John.* The Yale Shakespeare. New Haven, Conn.: Yale University Press, 1927.

Wilson, Eric. "Plagues, Fairs, and Street Cries: Sounding Out Society and Space in Early Modern England." *Modern Language Studies* 25, no. 3 (1995): 1–42.

Wixson, Douglas C. " 'Calm Words Folded up in Smoke': Propaganda and Spectator Response in Shakespeare's *King John.*" *Shakespeare Studies* 14 (1981): 111–27.

Worthen, W. B. *Shakespeare and the Authority of Performance.* Cambridge: Cambridge University Press, 1997.

Woudhuysen, H. R. *Sir Philip Sidney and the Circulation of Manuscripts, 1558–1640.* Oxford: Clarendon, 1996.

Wright, Thomas. *The Passions of the Minde in Generall.* Edited by Thomas O. Sloan. Urbana: University of Illinois Press, 1971.

Yachnin, Paul. *Stage-Wrights: Shakespeare, Jonson, Middleton, and the Making of Theatrical Value.* Philadelphia: University of Pennsylvania Press, 1997.

Younge, Richard. *The Victory of Patience, and Benefit of Affliction, with How to Husband It So, That the Weakest Christian (with Blessing from above) May Bee Able to Support Himselfe in His Most Miserable Exigents.* London, 1636.

Zimmerman, Mary, dir. *Pericles.* Performed at the Goodman Theatre, Chicago, January 7, 2006.

Zimmerman, Susan. "Marginal Man: The Representation of Horror in Renaissance Tragedy." In *Discontinuities: New Essays on Renaissance Literature and Criticism,* edited by Viviana Comensoli and Paul Stevens, 159–78. Theory/Culture. Toronto: University of Toronto Press, 1998.

Index

acoustics: Aristotelian theory of, 73–74, 82, 97–98; early modern theories of, 73–77, 82–83, 96–99, 114; experiments in, 76–79, 177–78; in theater, 77. *See also* sound; voice, transmission of

"active audition," defined, 111–14. *See also* hearing, and agency

actors: relationship to audience, 157–58, 237 n.137, 238 n.139; use of voice by, 4, 69. *See also* boy actors; children's acting companies

adolescence and youth, 39–59, 209 n.59

age and aging, boyhood to manhood, 37–48, 63, 206 n.18, 209 nn.58–59. *See also* boy actors, voice changes during puberty

agency: feminist theories of, 12–14; linguistic, 1, 13, 142–43; relation to voice, 5–6, 14; and subjectivity in Bourdieu, Foucault, and Lacan, 235 n.101. *See also* hearing, and agency; vocal agency, female

Agrippa (von Nettesheim), Heinrich Cornelius, 81

air, 2–4, 7, 30, 66–67, 69, 73–76, 81–85, 97–99, 103–4

Alciati, Andrea, 157–58

All's Well That Ends Well (Shakespeare), 121

Amazons, 51, 56–58

Anatomy of the Body of Man (Vesling, trans. Culpeper), 33, 36

Ancient Funerall Monuments (Weever), 134

Anderson, Judith H., 2–3

anima, 81, 215 n.17

antitheatricality, 152–53

Antonio and Mellida (Marston), 9, 17, 28–29, 211 nn.77–78, 212 nn.81–82; male voices in, 50–59; metatheatricality in, 50, 56–57, 59, 64–65, 67; modern production of, 59–60, 212 n.92

Antonio's Revenge (Marston), 26; male voices in, 55–56

Antony and Cleopatra (Shakespeare), 39, 231 n.54

An Apology for Actors (Heywood), 153

Aristotle: and early modern acoustic theory, 73–75, 81–83, 96–98; on voice, 167, 170, 173

The Art of Pronunciation (Robinson), 30, 33, 66, 167

The Art of Well Speaking (Gerbier), 83–84

As You Like It (Shakespeare), 44

atomism, 96–99, 114, 221 n.82, 222 nn. 93, 96, 243 n.35

audience: agency of, 152, 155; correspondence with onstage characters, 152, 154–59, 237 n.147; receptivity of, 153–58; response, 4, 8, 18, 49, 58, 152–58, 227 n.6, 237 n.125, 239 n.146. *See also* engagement and detachment

aural defensiveness, 116; constructive, 127–28, 133–51, 158–59, 234 n.92

aural vulnerability: constructive, 116, 122, 142–51, 157–59; female, 132–42, 153–54, 183; male, 116, 125–32, 140–42; in Shakespeare's late plays, 156–58

Ausonius, 179–80

Austin, J. L., 13, 108

Bach, Rebecca Ann, 24

Bacon, Francis, 7, 66, 73–75, 77–78, 82–83, 89–90, 96–99. See also *The Naturall and Experimental History of Winds*; *Principles and Origins*; *De Sapientia Veterum*; *Sylva Sylvarum*

Barber, C. L., 129

Barthes, Roland, 3–4

Beaumont, Francis, 87–88

Beaurline, L. A., 95

Bieman, Elizabeth, 156

boast, as type of speech, 70–71, 86, 100, 107

bodies, uncontrollable, 10–11, 24–26, 85. *See also* humoral physiology

The Bond-Man (Massinger), 134–35

The Boring of the Eare (Egerton), 118

Bourdieu, Pierre, 143–44, 151, 235 n.101, 236 n.103

Acknowledgments

Many institutions and individuals provided support while I was researching and writing this book, and I am pleased to acknowledge their important contributions.

When I began working on this project, I received generous support from the University of Michigan and a number of colleagues and friends there. My most significant debt is to Valerie Traub, who helped shape the project in inestimable ways and has continued to be my most trusted reader. It is because of her intelligence, generosity, and unflagging support that I became an early modernist and have remained a sane academic. I also thank Bill Ingram, Carla Mazzio, Michael Schoenfeldt, and especially Linda Gregerson for helping me develop my ideas and find a home in early modern studies; P. A. Skantze for encouraging me to think creatively about performance and for being an inspiring example and a kindred spirit; Anne Herrmann, Nadine Hubbs, and Yopie Prins for their unique engagements with my theories of voice; and Elise Frasier, Theresa Braunchneider, Melanie Boyd, and the members of my writing group—Tom Guglielmo, Amanda Lewis, Jonathan Metzl, and Parna Sengupta—for crucial feedback on my work as well as for friendship.

I am grateful to the faculty, staff, and students at other institutions that employed and encouraged me while I was writing. At Lawrence University, my chair, Tim Spurgin, did whatever he could to make sure I found time for my scholarship; it is in no small part because of him that I did. Faith Barrett, Alexis Boylan, Karen Hoffmann, Catherine Hollis, and Monica Rico offered thoughtful comments and much-appreciated camaraderie. I was granted additional time to write during my year at the University of

Wisconsin's Institute for Research in the Humanities. One of the perks of this residency was my close contact with UW's English department, which welcomed me warmly. In particular, I thank Heather Dubrow and Henry Turner for their astute insights on several chapters. Finally, my colleagues and students in the English department at the University of Iowa have provided a stimulating environment in which to write and have made it easy for me to finish the book even while starting a new job. My thanks to my research assistant Judith Coleman for checking references; to Huston Diehl, Miriam Gilbert, Doug Trevor, and my supportive department chair, Jon Wilcox, who have facilitated my transition in countless ways; to Judith Pascoe and Daniel Gross for intimating that I stop revising; and to Alvin Snider for reading and rereading several chapters. His comments were more useful than he realizes.

I received sound advice from several other colleagues who read drafts of these chapters at various stages in their development. I am especially indebted to Bruce Smith, who read the entire manuscript and, from the start, has been a major source of wisdom and encouragement. For valuable suggestions, I also thank Tom Cartelli, Suzanne Gossett, Gil Harris, Heather James, Tanya Pollard, and Valerie Wayne. Finally, I am grateful to Jeff Masten for so strongly supporting this project and my professional development.

Earlier versions of some of the chapters in this book have appeared in print. I thank the presses involved for permitting me to reprint sections from these essays and the editors of these volumes for useful feedback and for understanding so well the aims of my project: "Words Made of Breath: Gender and Vocal Agency in *King John*," *Shakespeare Studies* 33 (2005): 125–55 (issue edited by Susan Zimmerman); "Localizing Disembodied Voice in Sandys's Translation of 'Narcissus and Echo,'" in *Ovid and the Renaissance Body*, edited by Goran Stanivukovic (University of Toronto Press, 2002), pp. 129–54; "'Thy Voice Squeaks': Listening for Masculinity on the Early Modern Stage," *Renaissance Drama* 29 (1998): 39–72 (issue edited by Jeffrey Masten and Wendy Wall, published by Northwestern University Press). Versions of these chapters were also presented before various groups and meetings, including the Group for Early Modern Cultural Studies, the Modern Language Association, Performance Studies International, Early Modern Studies: Inhabiting the Body/Inhabiting the World, as well as the University of Wisconsin-Milwaukee early modern reading group and the University of Wisconsin-Madison early modern colloquium. I acknowledge, above all, the

Shakespeare Association of America, at whose collegial conferences I shared the bulk of this work. My thanks to the individuals who made it possible for me to present at all of these venues, including Leslie Dunn, Mary Floyd-Wilson, Skiles Howard, David Loewenstein, Mark Netzloff, P. A. Skantze, Bruce Smith, and Garrett Sullivan.

Archival work for this project was completed at the British Library, the Wellcome Institute, the Newberry Library, the Folger Shakespeare Library, and especially the Huntington Library, which granted me a short-term fellowship. My thanks to the staff at these libraries as well as to David Suchet, who, during my stay in London, shared with me his insights into the voice as the actor's instrument.

Additionally, I thank the many individuals at the University of Pennsylvania Press who helped shepherd this project along smoothly, especially Jerry Singerman and Erica Ginsburg. I also thank Peter Stallybrass for his generative contribution to the field of material studies and for welcoming me into this series. I would especially like to acknowledge the press's readers, whose perceptive comments on matters large and small made this a much better book.

Last but not least, I have been sustained by devoted family and friends. In addition to friends already mentioned above, I thank Susanna Ryan, Kim Bird, Libby Otto, and especially Brandon Fogel, for many great conversations over the years; and Tooey and Ann Miller for generously letting us turn Pucker Huddle into a writing retreat—indeed, it was. I am deeply grateful to my siblings, Karen Porat, Ronette Throne, and Joel Bloom, who have encouraged and promoted me relentlessly, regardless of whether they could understand what I was writing. I dedicate this book to my parents, Bernice Bloom and Louis Bloom, who celebrated my love of performance and my interest in books at an early age and have done so ever since; and to my partner, Flagg Miller, whose intellectual vigor, adventurous spirit, and boundless attention have kept me centered and also laughing all the way to the finish line. I thank him, above all, for encouraging me to move from the trees to the forest.